Casper Rader

His children and Grandchildren

Johan Casper Rötter 1732-1812

By James Lee Rader   Nov 2006

Second Version

Copyright © 2007 James L Rader

Printed by   www.lulu.com

James L. Rader
2633 Gilbert Way
Rancho Cordova, CA 95670-3513

Introduction to the Second Version

This work continues, it is my hobby and like most hobbies we spend too much time and too much money! This volume incorporates several thousands of dollars of research of Wayne Conduff, a professional land researcher in Greene county Tennessee. Wayne's work answers the question where did they live in early Greene county?

A researcher can now use this work to determine answers to questions like; What Church or Cemetery was close to them, what did they experience in terms of lifestyle. You will see that Casper Rotter's sons actually settled on Lick Creek near present day Mohawk (or Paynes as it was called at an earlier time). You will also see how their children and grand children spread out. This work will also cause you to rediscover the problems of too many Johns, Williams, etc.

I am also adding the yearly tax records for all Rader families in Greene county for most years before the war. A list of all of the Rader deeds before the war (we plotted the major ones but there are many more to do). Extractions of the 1830 through 1860 US census. At this point I have just begun to try to reconcile those records and future versions of this work will include modified family histories as we use those tools to correct earlier work. **I have NOT reconciled the genealogy to the data included ! Can you ? There are too many Williams, Johns, etc!**

I invite you to join in with the research! Can you provide detailed analysis of Casper's descendants anywhere on the planet ! Do you have pictures of their homes, maps of where they lived, Family bibles, diaries or anything which will help us tell their stories. Please help any way you can, editors are most welcome as are fact checkers. <g>

Published copies

This version is the first one to be available in either grayscale paperback or Full Color Hard back. Both versions should be available as you read this at
http://www.lulu.com/content/369372 "Casper Rader 1732-1812 Wythe county, Virginia SECOND Version by James L Rader". I estimate the paperback at $20 and the color hardback at $100

Introduction to the work

There are many competing goals and hopes involved in the production of these books. I say these books because I am currently producing the Rader information for various audiences; Color Coffee table type book, black & white Genealogy type book and DVD-ROM multimedia computer format.

One challenge to this work is that it will never be "done". They are still making Raders and the Raders of the past "Didn't want us to know". The naming conventions used in families further compound the problems. If you will take a moment and visit my web site at http://www.rader.org/wythe.htm you will see a table of hundreds of Primary records which contain people thought to be in Wythe county 1790-1810. Can you figure out which record belongs to which of the families (Phillip, Coonrod, Casper, Steven), I can't!

Another problem is the actual original documents that you have are not available to me! You have pictures, letters, bibles and other memorability. Your family keepsakes contain answers to questions about our ancestors.

All three works are works in progress as you can see by my titling them "The first attempt", "the second attempt" and the file at www.rootsweb.com entitled "the third attempt". I intend to continue limited run publishing and version/edition numbers to allow you to know where we are. The on-demand publishers have increased our quality and cut our costs.

The prices of these works will change as the costs change. A check of my web site at http://www.rader.org/photobook.htm will allow you to know what is going on. The current content of that web page is included below.

Thank you for joining in on our project of telling our ancestors stories. I am in the phone book (listed), on the internet at www.rader.org , email at jim@rader.org.

Thank you – James L Rader 916-366-6833

Acknowledgements

There are so many who came before me who collected much of this information that I don't know where to start. I have been collecting this information for 20 years and some of the noteworthy pioneers are:

Busch, Elane Easterly	Gay, Parker	Rader, Herbert Clayton
Cannon, Cecile Rhodes	Kegley, Mary	Rader, Margaret
Canselor, Ralph	Longino, Frances Rader	Tharpe, Dorothy N.
Carter, Arline Spivey	Rader, Dr. William	
Fedderman, Miles	Rader, Herbert	

Of particular value to this volume is the work of:

Thomas Rader, North Port, Florida over 1,000 photos of stones

Wayne Conduff, Mosheim Tennessee all of the land plats and another 100 photos of the land and stones

Margaret "Sister" Rader of Dulaney Tennessee who would introduce me by "saying he is going to write a book" and I would reply "who me?"

Ralph Canselor who shared hundreds of Pages of research he had done over his lifetime.

Also by James Lee Rader at WWW.RADER.ORG

The Ancestors and Descendants of Henry Rader (1829-1864) December 1991 (99 pages)

First attempt to collect ALL OF THE Rader, Raeder, Reader, Röder, Roeder, Rötter families in America; Compiled by James L. Rader, September 1992 (483 pages)

Second attempt to collect ALL OF THE Rader, Raeder, Reader, Röder, Roeder, Rötter families in America; Compiled by James L. Rader, August 1995 (1,072 pages)

Rader Ramblings Newsletter (33 issues – 1991 – 2000)

Margaret Rader's – Dulaney, Greene County, TN CD-ROM (produced 1999 with photos narration and movies provided by Margaret "Sister" Rader

Coffee table Photograph book "Evelyn Lanore Stevenson & Thomas Glenn Rader; Ancestors and lives of the Raders (20 pages 16"x11" with DVD of all pictures and DVD with Legacy program and Dec 2005 version of All Raders data base; printed by www.MyPublisher.com

Casper Rader 1732-1812 photobook (softbound, color, 15 pages www.viovio.com You can copy the pictures to your computer or order a paperback book for around $20

go to www.rader.org and click on the link

Casper Rader 1732-1812 Wythe county, his children and grandchildren

Table of Contents

Introduction to the Second Version 1
PUBLISHED COPIES 1

Introduction to the work 2
Also by James Lee Rader at WWW.RADER.ORG 5

Casper's Y-DNA 4
The map of the prehistoric migration path of Casper Rader's ancestors 4

FTDNATiP™ Report Family Tree DNA Time Predictor* 5

If you run a Y-DNA test and match these values you are also related to Casper Rader 7
TIME LINE OF CASPER'S LIFE 8

Descendants of Casper Rader Sr 14
FIRST GENERATION 14
The original handwritten ships list 18
Land in 1765 Bethel Twp, Lancaster co, PA (later to become Lebanon county) 22
Map of Land in Bethel Township: 16 Aug 1765 23
Nicholas Scull map 1759 25
W Scull map 1770 26
Photos of the Land in East Pennsboro Township 27
Photos of the Cove 31
Home build with stone (1770s) by the Crockets before Casper moved into the area. 31
The Flohr House 35
Tombstone = Alt Death: 16 Jul 1811, Wytheville, Wythe County, Virginia. 39
The actual will written in pencil 40
Children from this marriage were 47
TENNESSEE FARMING, TENNESSEE FARMERS ANTEBELLUM AGRICULTURE 50
PREFACE. 51
CLARKSVILLE, HOME OF MY CHILDHOOD. 51
EARLY METHODS, MANNERS, AND CUSTOMS. 52
OLD TIME WORKINGS. 52
HOUSE RAISINGS, ETC. 52
THE CORN HUSKING. 53
THE QUILTING BEE. 53

Table of Contents

HARVESTING AND THRESHING.	54
MILLS.	56
SALT.	57
EARLY ROADS.	58
THE OLD-TIME WAGON.	58
THE OLD-TIME STAGE COACH.	59
A Toast to the Old Stage Coach.	59
THE OLD-TIME TAVERN, OR ORDINARY.	60
RAILROADS.	61
A YEAR WITH NO SUMMER (1816).	62
Travels to the westward of the Allegany mountains in Greene county Tennessee	63
Presbyterian ministers	66
Methodist	66
The Reshaping of Everyday life 1790-1840	68
The Tennessee Yeomen, 1840-1860	68
The Agricultural Sections of Tennessee - 8 geological divisions	69
The Improvement in farm Implements	74
Silk production	74
Slaves	74
RADER LAND RECORDS IN GREENE COUNTY TENNESSEE	75
DESCENDANTS OF CASPER RADER SR AS THEY SHOULD APPEAR IN THE 1830 TN CENSUS	82
UNITED STATES CENSUS RECORDS	85
1830 Raders in Greene County	85
1840 Raders in Greene County	85
1850 Raders in Greene County	86
SECOND GENERATION (CHILDREN)	89
Casper's kids in Greene County, Tennessee	89
Map showing original Rader boys in Lick Creek	90
Tax records Greene County 1809-1835	90
Conrad Stayed In Wythe County Virginia	91
Henry moved to Greene county Tennessee	93
Map of Henry's 100 acres on Lick Creek Purchased 1810	97
Map of 246 Acres Henry bought on Lick Creek 1810	98
John moved to Greene county Tennessee	105
Map of Rader land in Lick Creek	106
Map of Bulls Gap land John bought in 1812	108
Map of Land Jacob bought 1820 near Fairview church	113
William died early in Wythe county Virginia	120

Table of Contents

Jacob moved to Greene county Tennessee 122
Map of Jacob owned land in 1805 in Greene County, Tennessee. 123
Casper moved to Sevier county Tennessee 131
Map of Phillip owned land on 26 Sep 1804 in Lick Creek Valley, ... 136
Peter moved to Greene county Tennessee but died in Sullivan County, Tennessee 142
Mary stayed in Wythe county Virginia 144
Catherine stayed in Wythe county Virginia 151
Daniel lost a farm in Madison Co., AL then moved to De Soto Co., Mississippi 153

THIRD GENERATION (GRANDCHILDREN) 156
Map of the Rader family land on Lick Creek 156
They dominated the northern Mohawk area in the third generation 156
Tax records Greene County 1840 - 1862 156

RADERS IN THE 1860 GREENE COUNTY AGRICULTURAL CENSUS 160
Map of Williams first 100 acre parcel #33 is the first purcase and in 1848 his residence (1821) 179
Raders Gap plot #3573 191
Map of Land in Rader's Gap purchased by Casper Rader 1828 192
Map of Land Henry owned in Lick Creek 1853 202
Map of land Andrew owned on 14 Feb 1835 in Lick Creek Valley near Bible Chapel 206
Map of land Andrew owned on 2 Nov 1839 in Bright Hope, ... 207
Swan Pond Creek 207
Map of land Andrew owned on 15 Feb 1848 in Little Chuckey, Greene Co, TN. 208
Site of Rader Mill parcel #302] 208
Site of Rader Mill parcel #302] 209
Swan Pond Creek Parcel #1546] 210
Map of Dulaney Rader's Land 211
Wheeler Road parcel #30049] 214
Map of land Andrew owned in Days Gap parcel #30049 – 384 214
Map of Land John owned land on 16 Feb 1839 in Rader gap, ... 221
Map of land William owned on 15 Mar 1829 in Lick Creek Valley 242
Tom White Holler 093] 255
Map of land Peter R Rader owned on 13 Mar 1845 in Greeneville, ... 259
Caption: Cap David Rader] 286

Source Citations 336

Name Index 340

Casper's Y-DNA

Learn about the use of DNA for your Genealogy
http://www.familytreedna.com/dna101.html

The map of the prehistoric migration path of Casper Rader's ancestors

A LANDMARK STUDY OF THE HUMAN JOURNEY

Who was **your** first ancestor? New DNA studies say that all humans descended from an African ancestor who lived only 60,000 years ago. Uncover the specific paths that led from him to you—the ultimate human history, as written in our genes.

INTERACTIVE ATLAS OF THE HUMAN JOURNEY

EXPLORE THE ATLAS ▶

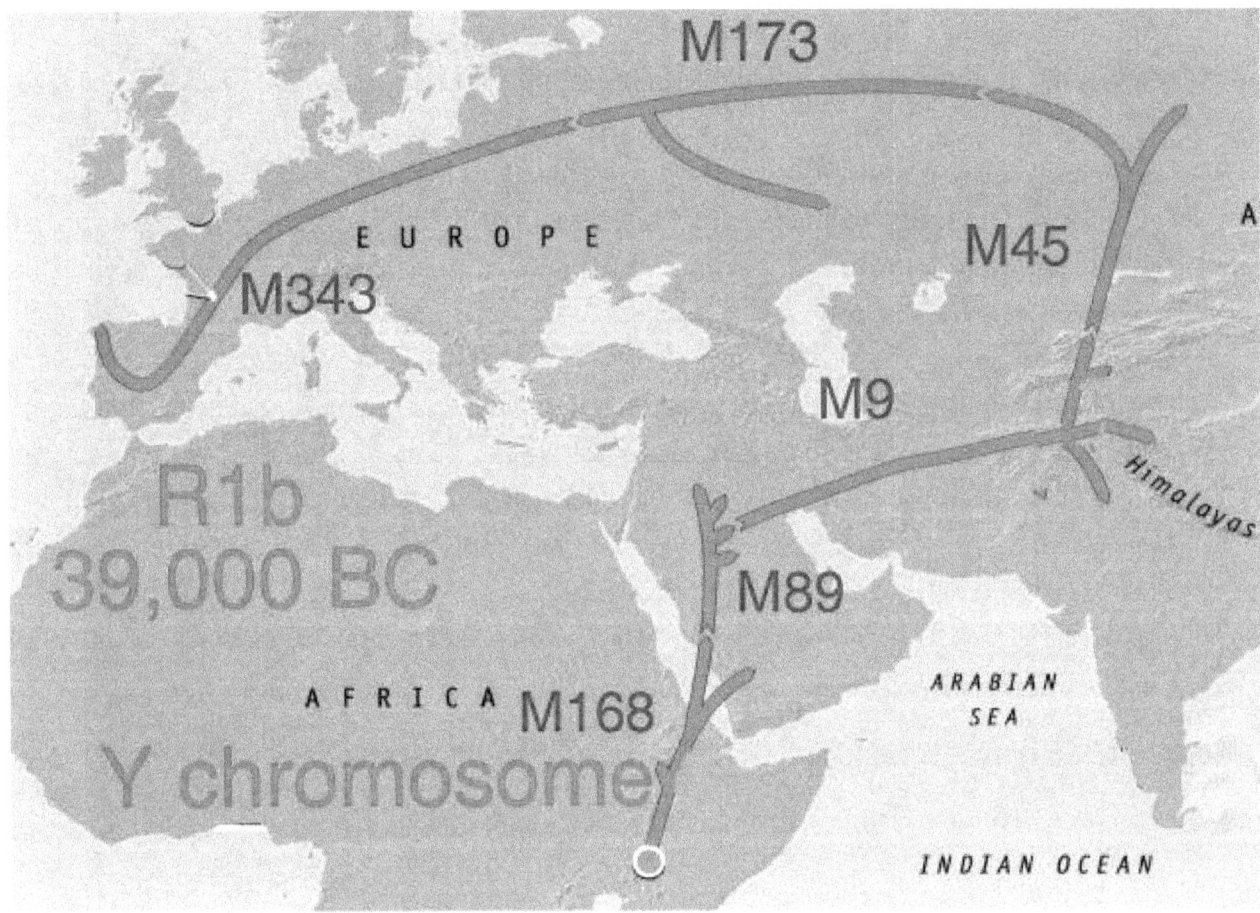

Our line is the R1b. the three of us match exactly all the way out to 37 markers. You share a common ancestor 7-9 generations ago, depending on who you count back from. The test is supporting that connection, especially since a match at 37 markers means there is a 90% chance you share a common ancestor within 5 generations, 95% within 7 generations.

37/37 Your perfect match means you share a common male ancestor with a person who shares your surname (or variant). Your relatedness is extremely close with the common ancestor predicted, 50% of the time, in 5 generations or less and with a 90% probability within 16 generations. Very few people achieve this close level of a match. All confidence levels are well within the time frame that surnames were adopted in Western Europe.

FTDNATiP™ Report Family Tree DNA Time Predictor*

In comparing 37 markers, the probability that the three Raders shared a common ancestor within the last...					
4 generations is	8 generations is	12 generations is	16 generations is	20 generations is	24 generations is
83.49%	97.28%	99.55%	99.93%	99.99%	100%

The above numbers are based exclusively on the comparison of their Y-DNA results, which show no mismatches.

- The FTDNATiP™ results are based on the mutation rate study presented during the 1st International Conference on Genetic Genealogy, on Oct. 30, 2004. The above probabilities take into consideration the mutation rates for each individual marker being compared.

If you would like to be tested and join this study

1. go to Jim Rader's web site at http://www.rader.org/dna/indexM.htm and click on join the study

2. —Or Call Jim Rader at 916-366-6833

3. Or call

> Family Tree DNA - Genealogy by Genetics, Ltd.
> World Headquarters
> 1919 North Loop West, Suite 110
> Houston, Texas 77008, USA
> Phone: (713) 868-1438

Descendants of Casper Rader Sr

```
                        Casper Rader Sr
                        (1732-After 1812)
                     Regina 'Rachel' Gerhardt
                           (1746-1816)
                       Married 21 May 1763
                                |
        ------------------------------------------------------
        |                       |                       |
   Phillip Rader Sr.       Daniel Rader          Heinrich 'Henry' Rader Sr
   (1782-1853)             (Abt 1782-1827)       (1768-1851)
   Catherine E Siddon      Elizabeth Davis       Catherine Etter
   (1796-1826)             (1789-1849)           (Abt 1772-Abt 1847)
   Married 30 Jan 1812     Married Abt 1804      Married 14 Dec 1790
        |                       |                       |
   Philip Rader Jr.        Samuel Emerey Rader   * William W. Rader
   (1824-1899)             (1805-1895)           (1798-1880)
   Margaret Stradley       Elizabeth Franks      Barbara Hauff
   (1827-1907)             (1821-1903)           (1803-1883)
   Married 18 Dec 1846     Married 11 Jul 1854   Married 17 May 1821
        |                       |                       |
   William Nelson Rader    Newton Jasper Rader   * Henry L. Rader
   (1852-1918)             (1862-1938)           (1829-1864)
   Nancy Jane Hine         Mary Ellen Pearson    Mary Ann 'Pollyan' Bowers
   (1855-1931)             (1863-1948)           (1831-1895)
   Married 30 Jan 1873     Married 13 Dec 1882   Married 3 Oct 1850
        |                       |                       |
   Russell Leo Rader       * Oscar Earl Rader    * Reuben H. Rader
   (1891-1969)             (1907-1983)           (1856-1932)
   Hazel Devona Tullis     Ellen Morgan          Martha Frances Hughes
   (1890-1985)             (1909-    )           (1863-1923)
   Married 28 Jan 1911     Married 5 Jul 1925    Married 4 Nov 1886
        |                       |                       |
   Alton Clyde Rader       * Earl Francis Rader  * Guy Hughes Rader
   (1923-       )                                (1887-1959)
                                                 Nona Malabe Duff
                                                 (1887-1962)
                                                 Married 15 Sep 1907
                                                         |
                                                 * Thomas Glenn Rader
                                                   (1910-1965)
                                                 Evelyn Lanore Stevenson
                                                   (1911-1971)
                                                 Married 14 Jul 1936
                                                         |
                                                   * James Lee Rader
                                                     (1942-    )
```

If you run a Y-DNA test and match these values you are also related to Casper Rader

Locus	DYS#	Alleles
1	393	13
2	390	24
3	19*	14
4	391	11
5	385a	11
6	385b	14
7	426	12
8	388	12
9	439	12
10	389-1	13
11	392	13
12	389-2	29
13	458	17
14	459a	9
15	459b	9
16	455	11
17	454	11
18	447	25
19	437	15
20	448	19
21	449	30
22	464a**	15
23	464b**	15
24	464c**	17
25	464d**	18
26	460	11
27	GATA H4	11
28	YCA II a	19
29	YCA II b	23
30	456	16
31	607	15
32	576	16
33	570	17
34	CDY a	34
35	CDY b	37
36	442	13
37	438	12

* Also known as DYS 394
** On 5/19/2003, these values were adjusted down by 1 point because of a change in Lab nomenclature.

Time line of Casper's Life

Chronology Report

Name: Casper Rader Sr

AKA: *a* 1508997/*a*, Casper (Roeter) Rader, Casper (Roeter) Rader Sr., Johan Casper Rader, Gasper Reeder, Gasper Rider, Gasper Ritter, Casper Roeder, Johann Cassber Rotter, Gasper Ruder, Gasper Ryder

Life Range: 25 Jan 1732 - After 18 May 1812

1683	~city of Philadelphia was laid ou:	1683 - The city of Philadelphia was laid out by William Penn.
1685	~Deed of Philadelphia to William Penn:	1685 - Date of the Deed of Philadelphia to William Penn.
1705	~John Harris, Sr. built Log House establishing Harrisburg:	
1732 Jan 25	Birth:	Europe.
1736	~Delaware River land sale:	Iroquois Indians paid for lands upon the Delaware river, south of the Blue Mountains.
1737	~Walking Purchase of 1737:	League of Amity, Walking Purchase of 1737.
1742	~Iriquois ordered Delaware Indians removed:	Council of Iriquois ordered Delaware Indians removed.
1744	~Treaty at Lancaster:	Iroquois sell lands westward "to the setting sun".
1746	Spouse:	**Regina 'Rachel' Gerhardt** (1746-1816). Born in Annville, Lebanon, , Lancaster, Pennsylvania, USA. Died on 31 Oct 1816 in Wytheville, Wythe County, Virginia.
1754	~Poster of the New Theatre in Water Street, Philadelphia.:	1754 - Date of a Poster of the New Theatre in Water Street, Philadelphia.
1754	~French and Indian War:	The French and Indian War (1754-1763)--.
1754 Jun	~Fort Henry, was situated in Bethel township.:	Fort Henry, was situated in Bethel township, what was, and still is, commonly known as Hollow," about three miles north of the village of Millersburg, fifty yards to the east the "Old Shamokin Road," which leads over mountain. The spot was elevated, to enable the guard to look out some distance in every direction. There is no particular mention of this fort in Colonial records, and this omission induces the belief that it was a fort erected by the people of that vicinity for their protection. It was

Chronology Report

Name:	Casper Rader Sr

		sometimes called "Dietrich Six's," doubtless because it stood on the land of Dietrich Six. The records mention several times that the people fled to Dietrich Six's, but the place was not indicated as a military post. The field where it was situated has been under cultivation for many years, and not a single mark remains to indicate where it stood. It was erected some time before June, 1754. In the beginning of June, 1757, the Governor visited Fort Henry, having been escorted thither by sixty substantial freeholders of the county on horseback, completely armed. They presented a very dutiful address to his honor, in which they expressed the warmest loyalty to the King and the greatest zeal and alacrity to serve His Majesty in defense of their country'.
1754 Jul 3	~Washington march on Fort Duquesne:	1754 July 3 English troops under Colonel George Washington march on Fort Duquesne: French victory.
1755	~entire PA frontier was in "great Horror and Confusion":	
1755	~Delaware War:	
1757 Aug 9	~French take Fort William Henry:	August 9 1757 French take Fort William Henry.
1758	~fury of the first Indian outbreak over:	
1762 Aug	~piece conference in Lancaster, PA:	
1763	~Pontiac's war:	
1763	~settlers from Pennsylvania flee their homes:	Fort Niagara, one of the most critical western forts, was not assaulted, but on September 14, 1763 at least 300 Senecas, Ottawas, and Ojibwas attacked a supply train along the (A city in western New York State at the falls of the Niagara river; tourist attraction and honeymoon resort) Niagara Falls portage. Two companies sent from Fort Niagara to rescue the supply train were

Chronology Report

1683	1725	1769	1812	1858	Name:	Casper Rader Sr	
							also defeated. Seventy-two soldiers and wagoners were killed in these actions, which Anglo-Americans called the "Devil's Hole Massacre."
							At this point, major combat in Pontiac's War was effectively over. Although the Indians had won many small victories in 1763, they were short of ammunition by the end of the year, and the large forts remained in British hands. About 450 British soldiers had been killed in the fighting; total Indian losses are unknown. Approximately 4,000 white settlers from Pennsylvania and Virginia had been compelled to flee their homes. The number of white settlers killed has often been given as 2,000, although Gregory Dowd writes that this figure "cannot be taken seriously" because the estimate was a "wild guess" made by (Click link for more info and facts about George Croghan) George Croghan while in faraway London. Historian Daniel Richter characterizes the Indian offensive of 1763 as a campaign of (The mass expulsion and killing of one ethic or religious group in an area by another ethnic or religious group in that area) ethnic cleansing. Before the British military could effectively seize the initiative in the war, an angry group of Pennsylvanians responded to the violence with an ethnic cleansing campaign of their own.
		▶			1763 May 12	Alt Marriage:	Bethel Township, Lancaster County, Pennsylvania.
		▶			1763 May 12	Alt Marriage:	Bethel Township, Lancaster County, Pennsylvania.
		▶			1763 May 21	Marriage:	**Regina 'Rachel' Gerhardt** (1746-1816). In Bethel Township, Lebanon Co., PA.

Chronology Report

Name: Casper Rader Sr

1765	~Congress of American Colonies met in New York.:	1765 - The first Congress of American Colonies met in New York.
1766	Son born (#1):	**Conrad Rader** (1766-1845). Born in Bethel Township, Lancaster County, Pennsylvania. Died on 14 May 1845 in Wythe County, Virginia.
1768	Son born (#2):	**Heinrich 'Henry' Rader Sr** (1768-1851). Born in Bethel Township, Lancaster County, Pennsylvania. Died on 1 Sep 1851 in Greene County, Tennessee.
Abt 1769	Son born (#3):	**John Rader** (Abt 1769-1840). Born in Bethel Township, Lancaster County, Pennsylvania. Died on 3 Feb 1840 in Greene County, Tennessee.
1769	~First permanent settlement in Tennessee area:	The first permanent settlement was established in the Watauga Valley by people from North Carolina and Virginia.
Abt 1770	Son born (#4):	**William Rader** (Abt 1770-1802). Born in East Pennsboro Twp, Cumberland Co., PA. Died in 1802 in Wythe County, Virginia.
1771	Daughter born (#5):	**Catherine M. Rader** (1771-WFT Est 1816). Died WFT Est 1816-1877.
1772	~Watauga Association organized:	In 1772, the British government labeled the settlers in the area as "squatters" and ordered them to leave. The settlers had already made promises with the Native Americans, and would not leave. They organized themselves into the Watauga Association, adopted the laws of Virginia, and established a court. They submitted a petition to place itself under North Carolina government.
Abt 1772	Son born (#6):	**Jacob Rader** (Abt 1772-1822). Born in East Pennsboro Twp, Cumberland Co., PA. Died on 22 Jul 1822 in Greene County, Tennessee.
1774	Son born (#7):	**Casper Rader Jr.** (1774-1830). Born in East

6 Aug 2006

Chronology Report

Name: Casper Rader Sr

		Pennsboro Twp, Cumberland Co., PA. Died in 1830 in Sevier County, Tennessee.
1774	~first Continental Congress met at Philadelphia.:	1774 - The first Continental Congress met at Philadelphia.
1775	~Provincial Congress met at Philadelphia.:	1775 - A Provincial Congress met at Philadelphia.
1776	~Washington District, North Carolina was established:	
1777	~Washington County, North Carolina was established:	Washington County, North Carolina, was established to provide governmental jurisdiction over the Watauga settlements. Its boundaries included all of present-day Tennessee.
1778 Jul 4	Daughter born (#10):	**Anna Marie 'Mary' Rader** (1778-1849). Born in East Pennsboro Twp, Cumberland Co., PA. Died on 19 Dec 1849 in Wythe County, Virginia.
1780 Sep 3	Son born (#9):	**Peter Rader** (1780-1858). Born in East Pennsboro Twp, Cumberland Co., PA. Died on 11 Mar 1858 in Greene County, Tennessee.
1781	Daughter born (#11):	**Catherine Rader** (1781-1844). Born in East Pennsboro Twp, Cumberland Co., PA. Died in 1844 in Wythe County, Virginia.
Abt 1782	Son born (#12):	**Daniel Rader** (Abt 1782-1827). Born in East Pennsboro Twp, Cumberland Co., PA. Died on 27 Oct 1827 in Madison County, Alabama.
1782 Aug 12	Son born (#8):	**Phillip Rader Sr.** (1782-1853). Born in East Pennsboro Twp, Cumberland Co., PA. Died on 2 Nov 1853 in Butler Twp, Montgomery Co Ohio.
1784	~Watauga settlers organized the state of Franklin:	Watauga settlers organized the state of Franklin.
1789	~Area became known as the Southwest Territory:	When North Carolina finally ratified the new Constitution of the United States in 1789, it also ceded its western lands, the Tennessee country, to the Federal Government. This "Cession Act of 1789" designated the area as the Territory of the United States South of the River Ohio.

Chronology Report

Name: Casper Rader Sr

1795	~Territorial Census:	otherwise known as the Southwest Territory. In 1795 a territorial census revealed a sufficient population for statehood.
1796	~Tennessee became a state:	Tennessee became a state.
1802	Death of Child (#4):	**William Rader** (Abt 1770-1802). In Wythe County, Virginia.
After 1812 May 18	Death:	Wytheville, Wythe County, Virginia.
1811 Jul 16	Burial:	St. John's Lutheran, Wytheville, Wythe Co, VA.
	Seal:	

First Generation

We don't know when or where Casper was born, we aren't even sure when he died. His tombstone shows 1811 and the Court Documents show that he signed his will in 1812!

The original handwritten ships logs follow in a few pages and his actual probated will also follows. I have searched for decades for records of Casper and we now have scanned copies of the actual pieces of paper. His will, written in pencil, is in the basement of the Wythe County court house. The ship logs are in the possession of the State of Pennsylvania. Both signatures are on the cover of this book, what do you think his name was? Do you believe, as I do, that both were written by the same person!

The next place we incounter Casper is in what was called Bethel township Lancaster county. That location was later split in two between Labanon and Dauphine counties. The land Casper owned is on that line and intersects with the interstate highway. I have included photographs of the land and maps also

He then moves up to a wonderful place that William Penn called the Land of Lowther, the land Penn reserved for the Indians. The Indians refused to settle on the land so it was sold. Casper paid taxes on that land for two decades, through the Revolutionary War. Check out the photos and maps of that area, The Wallmart in Silver Springs is now on the south side of the land.

His name is spelled; Reader, Rotter, Rider, Ruder, Ryder, Reedar, Reeder, Readers, Rheder, Reedar. One needs to remember that this was a time where educated people spelled phonetically. If you spelled a word consistently one way you were considered stupid/uneducated. A search of the comments of the day include many examples of the attitude of the day. Three quotes which answer the question of why your 18th century ancestor didn't spell his name consistently; "I hope I never meet a man so narrow minded as to spell a word in only one way" - Thomas Jefferson ; "It's a damn poor mind that can only think of one way to spell a word." -Andrew Jackson; "I respect a man who knows how to spell a word more than one way." -- Mark Twain.

It took years to prove that this Casper was our Casper! Finally I came across the deed where he sold the Lowther land which states "I Casper Reader of Wythe County" and "the said Gasper and Rachel"

He spent the rest of his life in Wythe County Virginia.

1. **Casper Rader Sr**, [1,2,3,4,5,6,7,8,9,10,11,12,13,14,15,16], was born in 1732 in Europe, died after 18 May 1812 in Wytheville, Wythe County, Virginia, [16,17,18,19,20,21,22] and was buried on 16 Jul 1811 in St. John's Lutheran, Wytheville, Wythe Co, VA. Other names for Casper were Casper (Roeter) Rader, Casper (Roeter) Rader Sr., [18,19,20,22] Johan Casper Rader, Gasper Reeder, Gasper Rider, Gasper Ritter, Casper Roeder, Johann Cassber Rotter, Gasper Ruder, and Gasper Ryder.

He May have been born in Viernheim Mannheim Baden, Germany !

He arrived in Philadelphia on ship Edinburg 13 August 1750, which sailed from Rotterdam via Portsmouth; we don't know where he boarded

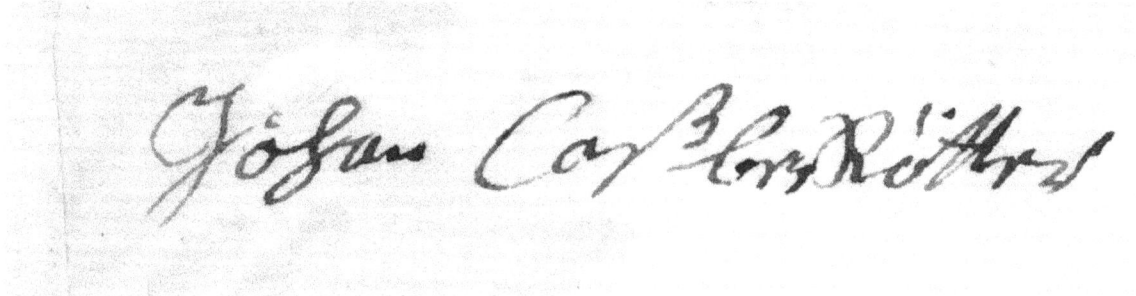

He signed his Oath of allegance on 13 Aug 1750 to Philadelphia, PA. as Johan Casber Rötter found in: the Pennsylvania Archives vault and also Immigration Records: German and Swiss Settlers in America, 1700s-1800s Listed in: Pennsylvania German Pioneers, Vol. I, 1727-1775 Page number: 430

Burial Notes: "In Memory Of Casper Rader Died June 16, 1811 In His 80 Y" Source data also submitted by Sue Murr Ottinger, Rt. 19, Box 326, Lexington, NC. Would appreciate exchange of info and correction of info. pjsharkey@hotmail.com Casper (Roeder) Rader was born in 1732. Headstone reads Casper Rader died June 6, 1811 in his 80th year

General Notes: These two were dead before Casper died in 1812. (Philip 1801) and (Stephen 1809). Casper names a living son Phillip and does not name heirs of Stephen. It would seem that they were not his children ?

Information regarding the Rader family has been taken family interviews with Inez Ladd Powell, dauther of Sarah Elizabeth Rader Ladd, granddaughter of John H. Rader, gr. granddaughter of Samuel Rader, gr. gr. granddaughter of Daniel Rader, and gr. gr. gr. granddaughter of Casper Rader,

On February 17, 1790 Casper's home was located on Reed Creek and the Crab Orchard Fork of Little Walker's Creek in Wythe County, Virginia which was formed from Montgomery County, Virginia in 1789.

Casper and Regina are buried in the St. John's Lutheran Church cemetery.

In the records of Wythe county there is a Phillip Reeder and a Stephen Reeder. Their children consistantly spelled their name Reeder. Casper's name is also spelled Reeder in his will ! These two were dead before Casper died in 1812. (Philip 1801) and (Stephen 1809).

Casper names a living son Phillip and does not name heirs of Stephen. It would seem that they were not his children ?

He was married to Regina 'Rachel' Gerhardt on 21 May 1763 in Bethel Township, Lebanon County, Pa.

Was Deacon at St. John's Lutheran Church in Wytheville in 1798.

Will written 18 May 1812 one year after his tombstone declares he died. There was stonemaker who made many mistakes traveling the shenandoah valley at that time! Casper's Will was probated in Wythe County, Virginia on August 11, 1812 and contains the names of his children and wife.

AND OTHER IMMIGRANTS—1750.

Aug. 13, Nachmittags, 1750. Das Schiff Edinburgh, Capitain James Russel, von Rotterdam über Portsmouth, brachte 314 Passagiere.

Johann Corngibel,*
Johannes Beyer,*
Johannes Beyer jr.,
Michel Hamburgeis,*
J. George Kirshner,*
Valentin Sösttel,
Stoffel Bruning,*
Ludwig Gassler,
Jost Schneider,
Thomas Kegel,*
Thomas Klosse,*
Henrich Kloss,
Andreas Huck,
Jacob Möler,
Georg Schäffer,
Johannes Wien,
Michael Lemer,
Daniel Klein,
Jacob Schäfer,
Johan Fasnacht,*
Johannes Telcher,*
Johannes Delcher,
Jacob Werntz,
David Herbster,*
Jacob Lanish,
Georg Heyle,*
Jacob Loch,
Casper Strohl,
Andreas Ditz,
Philip Conrad Aumüller,
Johann Seybert Gertz,
Johann Henrich Lotz,
Johann Philip Heck,
Casper Bröning,
Joh. Peter Seyfert,
Johan Georg Rabe,
Johan George Flour,*
Johann Georg Müller,
Johan Adam Stein,*
Johan Casper Rötter,
Johann Georg Klein,
Johan Philip Hölsel,
Lorentz Baum,
Christophel Spahr,
Philippus Bücksell,
Johannes Gertz,
Johan Peter Leib,
Johannes Feuerstein,
Hans Georg Renninger,*
Johan Herman Dippel,
Johannes Eulert,
Wendel Renninger,*
Ludwig Pretzman,
Frederick Brinkman,*
Daniel Meerbagh,*
Andreas Spielman,*
Peter Sickenberger,
Valentin Kreischer,
Henrich Pilgram,
Peter Nees,*
Peter Bohre,
Andreas Keanig,*
Carel Keanig,*
Philip Shmith,*
Nicklas Hirt,*
Johannes Kniss,
Christian Haffner,*
Jacob Flug,*
Nicklas Spring,*
Johannes Philips,*
Andreas Bensell,
Jacob Daunneberger,?
Jacob Merckle,
Simon Merckle,
Carl Stedt,
Johannes Mohl,

[Description: Johan Casper Rotter found in:Immigration Records: German and Swiss Settlers in America, 1700s-1800s Listed in: Thirty Thousand Immigrant Names in PA, 1727-76   Page number: 227   He immigrated on 13 Aug 1750 to Philadelphia, PA. Johan Casper Rotter found in: Immigration Records: German and Swiss Settlers in America, 1700s-1800s Listed in: Thirty Thousand Immigrant Names in PA, 1727-76 Page number: 227 . He was 1 of 314 passengers. Is this our Casper ? If not who is he ?

The original handwritten ships list

Johan Philips Jacob Pfoll 75
Johann Georg Hoffner
Peter + Lazurus
George |X| Lees
Hans Michael + Leggy
Diebolt Schubrick

At the Court House at Philadelphia 13 August 1750
Present
Thomas Lawrence Esquire Mayor

The Foreigners whose names are underwritten imported in the Ship Edinburgh Capt. James Russel Master from Rotterdam but last from Portsmouth in England did this day take & subscribe the usual Qualifications

By list 151. 314 whole Freights. 2 dead
           466

Johann + Corngibel   Joh. Peter Seyfert
Johannes X Beyer   Johan Georg Ruber
                            Johan Georg X Flour
J George X Kirchner   Ludwig Kepler
Philip Cornwalff Eric   Jost Snider
william   Thomas + Kegel
Johann Smithmess Garth   Hein us Klosse
Walkin Döttel   Ludwig Flor
Johann Henrich Lott   Andreas Brück
Johann Philipp Lott   Johan Görg Müller
Pofree Bruning   Johan Adam XX Stein
Kaspar Bruning

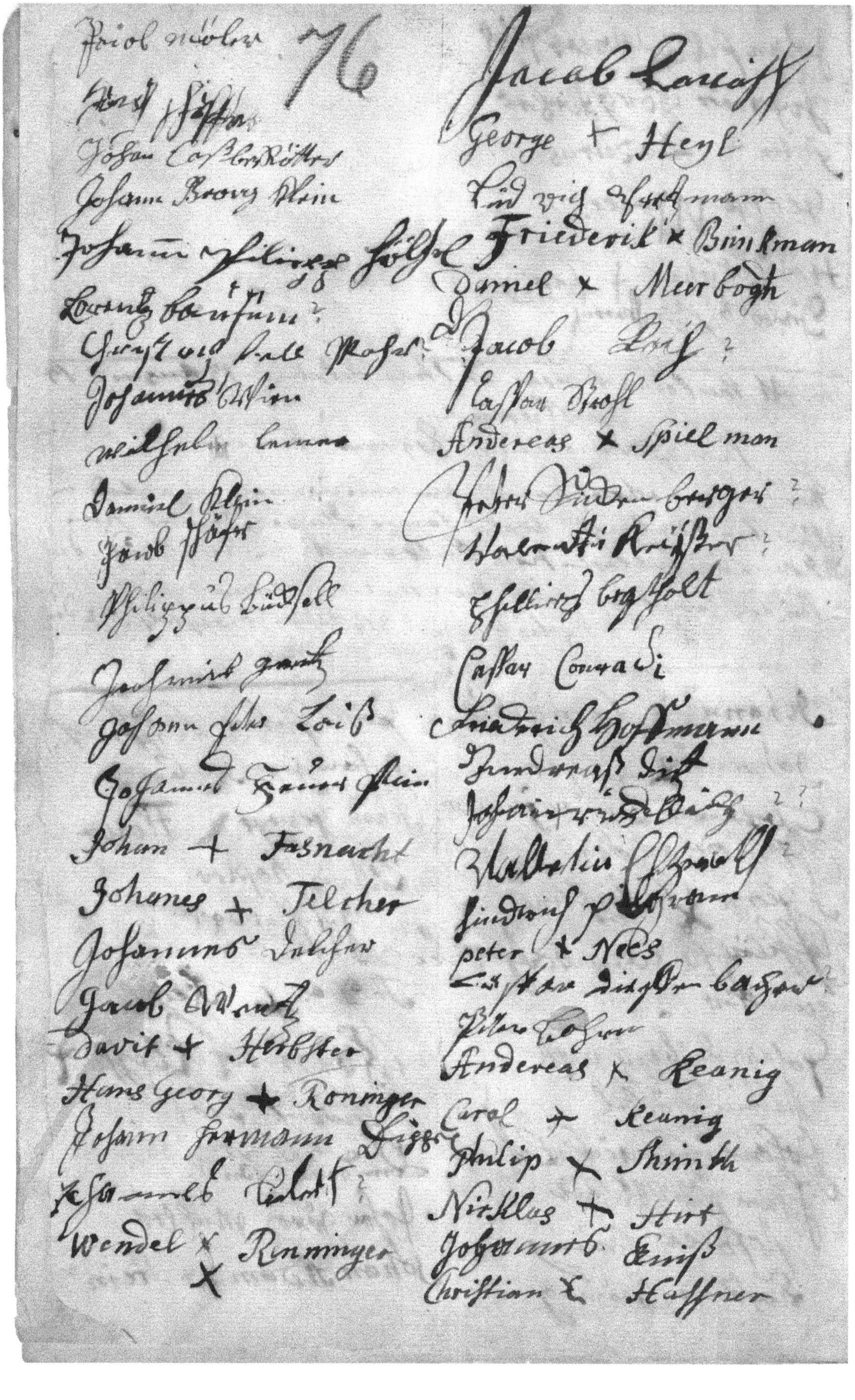

76

Jacob ncöler	Jacob Laucks
[illegible]	George + Heyl
Johan Casper Rötter	Lüdwig [illegible]mann
Johann Beory plein	Friederik x Binkman
Johann Philips Folk	Darnel x Meerbogh
[illegible]	Jacob Leiß?
[illegible]	Caspar [illegible]
Johannes [illegible]	Andereas x Spielman
Wilhelm [illegible]	[illegible] Siedenberger?
Daniel [illegible]	[illegible] Küchler?
Jacob Häfer	[illegible] begholt
Philip[illegible] Siedsell	Caspar Conradi
Jochmid [illegible]	Friedrich Hoffmann
Johann [illegible] Leiß	[illegible]
Johannes [illegible]	[illegible]
Johan + Fasnacht	Valentin [illegible]
Johanes + Telcher	Lüdwig [illegible]
Johannes [illegible]	Peter + Nees
Jacob [illegible]	Caspar Dieffenbacher
David + Herbster	Peter [illegible]
Hans Georg + Roninger	Andereas x Keanig
Johann Hermann Ligg	Carol + Keanig
Johannes [illegible]	Philip + Shmith
Wendel x Renmnyer	Nickllas + Hirt
x	Johannes Leiß
	Christian L Haffner

Michael Matinger

Jacob + Flug	Caspar + Mug
Nicklos N Spring	Johann Georg Dum?
Johannes Wohlflauger	Johannes Haffnar
Johann Jacob Braug	Michel Heinte Vornwald
Simon Peter + Fernantz	Peter x Colles
Johan Ulrich Daumar	Johannes Möller
Henry + Daymer	Crostoffel Möller
Conrod Reuwer ??	Ditrich Nantz
Johann Gottlieb Raby	Conrad Frey Ruff?
Johann Martin Schäffer	Johann Leenham ? Christ
Johann Jörg Hölkes	Johan Adam + Huber
Johanes + Philips	Theobalt Crm?
Johan Christoffel Harpp	Frantz Ciely
Andreas Henfell	Peter x Spengler
Jacob Donnenlang ?	Johanes + Shmit
Samuel Falckmyahr	Peter + Shritt
Jacob Merkle	Severinus + Sheffer
Simon Merkle	Jacob Voll Wal ?
Nicolaus Wahr ?	Georg Laidrich Heilbrunn
Carl Kudt	Johann Laidwich Heilbrun
Johannes Mosl	Christian Dum
Peter + Marcus	Jacob Michael
Conradt Löhm	Jacob Shaffner
Johannes Schmitt	Anthony + Heanz
Johann Philipp Braug?	Jacob + Walter
Godlib + Wejda	Johan Daniel Bübel
	Ludwig Mainner
	Wilhelm Heines
	Christ. Sam. Baufmann
	Johann Ludwig Wittmann

78

Ludwig Boud
Jos. Lendred Drößer ?
Johan Jörg G?
Nicolas Fius
Louß Adam Agnes
Yorg Adam Zobel
Nig gloud Coed
Henry ⊕ Coller
Fillinbs Calbroon
Jacob Z Metziger
Ludwig ffornagel ?
Thomas ⊕ Bough
Johan Adam Vogel
Johan Henry + Sheoman
Johannes Fisher ?
Lendrard Brandner
Henry Sebastian Kreister
Johann Ludwig G Haw ?
Matthias Huß
Nicolaus gerlach
Johannes + Wagner

OATH OF ALLEGIANCE: 10 Apr 1754. PHILADELPHIA, PENNSYLVANIA

Sponsors: 16 Feb 1757, Lincoln County, North Carolina,. Johan Caspar Bolich, son of Johan Adam Bolich and his wife, Christina, was baptized by Rev. Daniel Schumacher February 16, 1757 when 7 weeks old. His sponsor was Caspar Roeder.

Collections of the Genealogical Society of Penna., Baptisms by Rev. Daniel Schumacher (1754-1774)" vol. 279:34. Lincoln County, North Carolina,

Land in 1765 Bethel Twp, Lancaster co, PA (later to become Lebanon county)

Map of Land in
Bethel Township:
16 Aug 1765

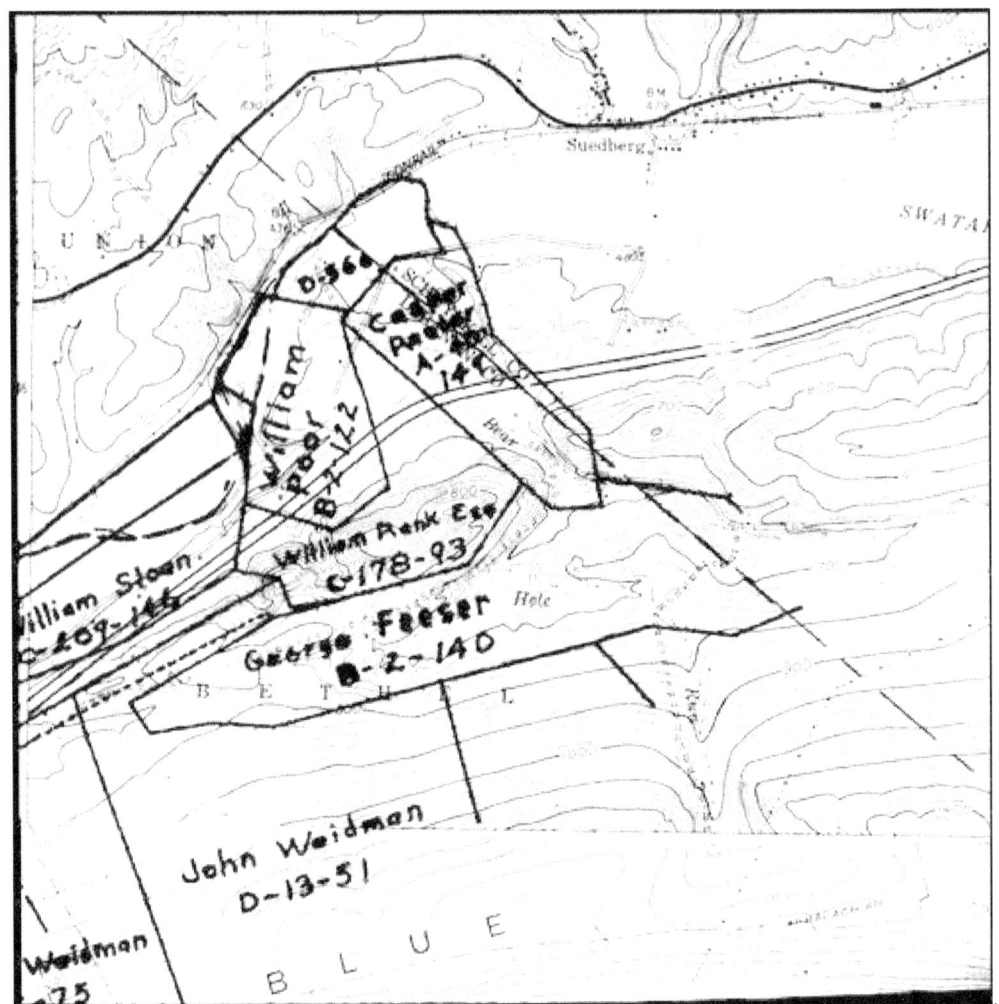

He owned land on 16 Aug 1765 in Bethel Township, Lancaster County, Pennsylvania.[23] In the East Side applications Casper had his land surveyed 8th day of May 1766.

They surveyed 101 acres of land 16 Aug 1765 which was over the blue mountain on Swatara Creek and Trout Creek in Bethel Twp., Lebanon County, Pa. At that time it was Lancaster County, Colony of Pa. The land is currently devided by I-81 and the County line between Schuylkill and Lebanon Counties.

Tax list: 1769, East End of Hanover Twp, Lancaster Co, PA. 1769 John Brunner Collector East End of Hanover collected a tax of 2.6 from Reader, Casper

Nicholas Scull map 1759

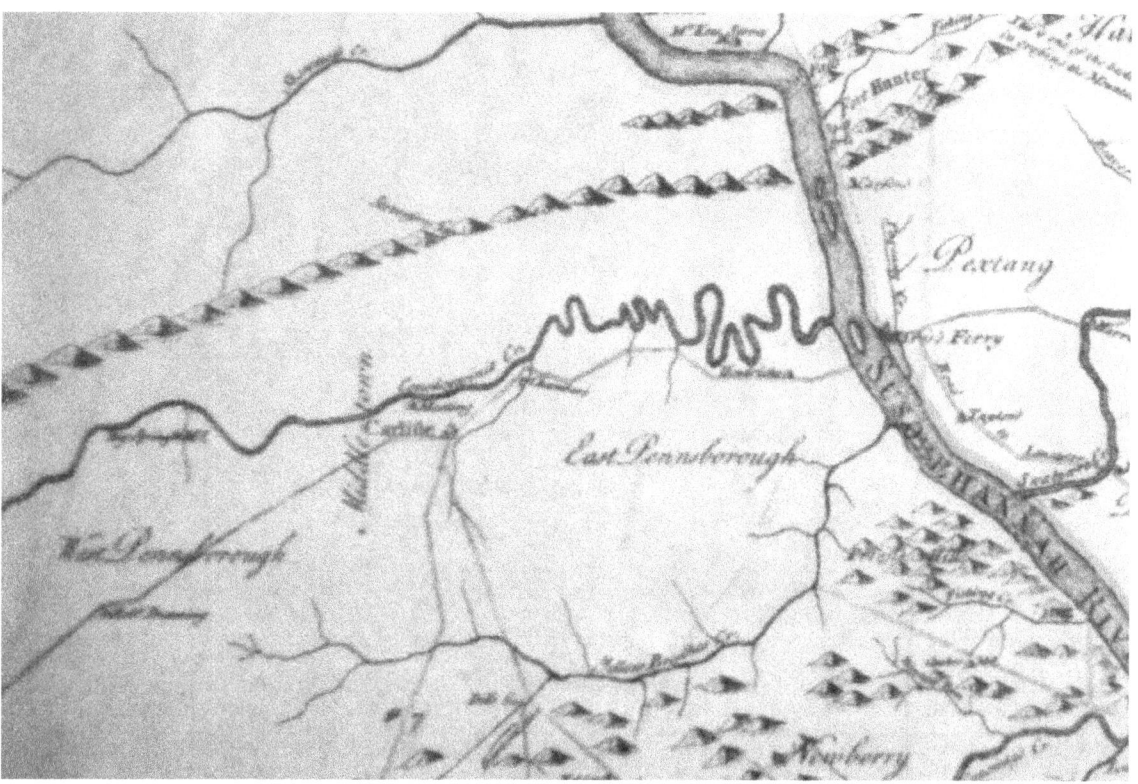

He owned land on 23 May 1770 in East Pennsboro Twp, Cumberland Co., PA.[24] Gasper Reader of East-Pennsborrough township buys 260 acres from Joseph Hinds. This 260 acres is where the current Walmart store is. Cumberland Co deed book (Vol 1, Book P page 156-157)

Before the Revolutionary war they purchased 167 acres of land, 23 May 1770, in East Pennsborough Twp., Cumberland County, Pa. for 70 pounds. On 15 Apr 1791 Gasper Rheder and his wife Rachel sold that land for 477 pounds.

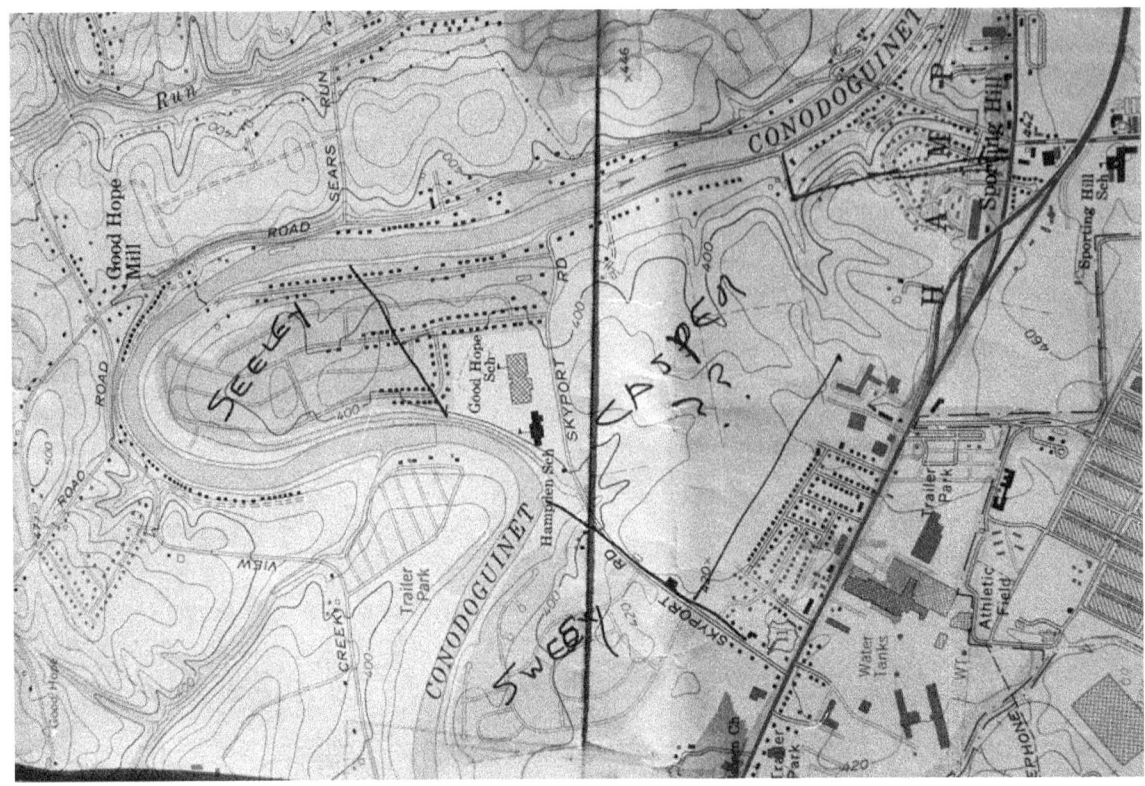

Tax list: 1773, East Pennsboro Twp, Cumberland Co., PA. 1773 Gasper Ruder 2h, 2c, 2s, 150 L, 30c

W Scull map 1770

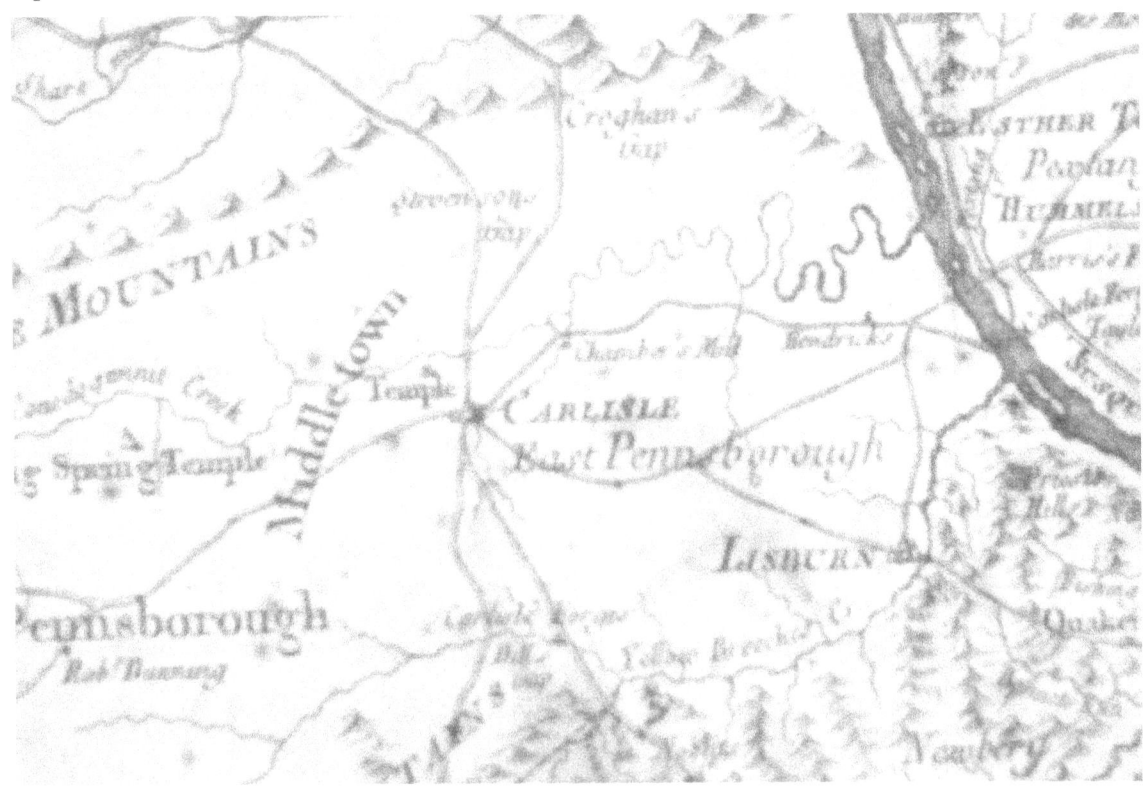

Land purchase: 1 May 1773, East Pennsboro Twp, Cumberland Co., PA. C226-28 Gasper READER, mort. to Joseph HINDS, both of East Pennsborough Twp., _55 (_15 due 1 May 1773, _10 on May 1774-77 annually). 167 a. in East Pennsborough Twp. black oak (cor. Jonas SEELY's tract "Blaak Hool" on its W side), by E side of SEELY's tract "Cave Place" S10W124 white oak S31E112 Spanish oak S42W29 post S22E50½ post, Leonard FISHER S75W162½ post, John BUNNITT N156½ post, Jonas SEELY (TEELY)'s "Blaakhool" N35E to beginning point. North part by propr. location to mortgagee 8 October 1766, surveyed by Col. ARMSTRONG. 23 MAY 1770 Jonathan HOGE, James ROBISON, John HOGE 23 MAY 1770 Jonathan HOGE 22 July 1771 (Exit [writ of] sc[ire] facias to April T. 1796 No. 9)

He had a religion on 18 Dec 1773 in East Pennsboro Twp, Cumberland Co., PA. Register of Marriages and baptisms kept by the REV. TRAUGOTT FREDERICK ILLING Pennsboro Caspar Retter pledged support (0.10.0)

Photos of the Land in East Pennsboro Township

Tax list: 1774, East Pennsboro Twp, Cumberland Co., PA. 1774 Gasper Rider 2h, 2c, 4s, 150 L, 30c

He had a religion on 26 Dec 1774 in East Pennsboro Twp, Cumberland Co., PA. Pennsboro Casper Rotter pledged support (0.10.0) Traugott Frederick Illing who served St. Peters (Lutheran), Middletown, and Caernarvon(Episcopal) in Lancaster county, PA (reference "Register of Marriages and Baptisms kept by the Rev. Traugott Frederick Illing" Harrisburg 1891) He was what was called in those days a German Calvanist, a follower of the Swiss Reformer Zwingli, of which country he was a native. He was pastor to the Lutheran Congregation in German.

Tax list: 1775, East Pennsboro Twp, Cumberland Co., PA. 1775 Gasper Ryder 2h, 2c, 2s, 150 L, 40c

Tax list: 1778, East Pennsboro Twp, Cumberland Co., PA. Gasper Ryder 72 acres, 0 negroes, 2 horses, 2 cattle, Tax 8.12.0 (PArch3-20;35)

Tax list: 1779, East Pennsboro Twp, Cumberland Co., PA. Gasper Reedar 200 acres, 2 horses, 2 cattle, 0 negroes (PArch3-20;150)

Tax list: 1780, East Pennsboro Twp, Cumberland Co., PA. Gaspar Reeder 150 acres, 2 horses, 3 cattle, 0 negroes (PArch3-20;283)

county copy has Casper Roeder 2h, 2c, 150 L

Milit-Beg: 16 Aug 1780, Cumberland County, Pennsylvania.[25] An Acc't of the 5th, 6th, & 7th Classes of the 3D Battalion of Cumberland County Militia called upon to perform a tour of duty by an order of council bearing date YE 1st of August 1780. 1st Company, 6th class (pg 218) Gasper Ritter, Peter Miller, David Hoge, Phillip Gillin, David Walker, Stofel Miers, Hen'y Humbarger (PA Archives fifth series Volume VI Pg 218 -)

Pennsylvania Archives Fifth series volume IV page 218 - An account of the 5th., 6th., and 7th. classes of the 3rd. Battalion of Cumberland County Malatia called upon to perform a tour of duty by an order of council bearing the date of 1 August 1780. 1st. Company, 6th. class (page 218) Gasper Ritter, Peter Miller, David Hoge, Phillip Gillin, David Walker, Stofetl Miers, Henry Humbarger.

23 Aug 1780.[26] The Third Batallion Cumberland County, Saml. Erwin, Col 1780 August, of the 5th, 6th, & 7th Class. pg 224 - 1st Company 6th class Casper Readers, Peter Miller, David Hoge, Phillip Gillin, David Walker, Stofel Miers, Hen'r Humbarger A Henry Humbarger moved to Virginia with Casper

Tax list: 1781, East Pennsboro Twp, Cumberland Co., PA. Gasper Reeder 150 acres, 2 Horses, 3 cattle, 0 negroes (PArch3-20;423)

1781 Stephen Reeder tax 40.0.0 (first and only listing for him?)

Tax list: 1782, East Pennsboro Twp, Cumberland Co., PA. 1782 Caspar Reeder 150 acres, 2 horses, 3 cattle, 0 negroes (PArch3-20;559)

1782 Stephen Reed 442 acres, 2 horses, 3 cattle, 0 negroes (PArch3-20;559)

Tax list: 12 Apr 1787, Montgomery , VA.. They came to the Cove before the 1787 Census which shows Gasper Rheder. He obtained an exemption from paying taxes on his blind horse in 1788 and Gasper Reader purchased 200 acres of land for 250 pounds 1 Aug 1789.

Montgomery County tax 1787

Apr 9 Conrod Rheder Conrod Rheder 1
Apr 12 Gasper Rheder Gasper Rheder 1 9,8
Jun 16 Philip Reedor Philip Reedor 3,5
Steven Reedor Steven Reedor 3,5

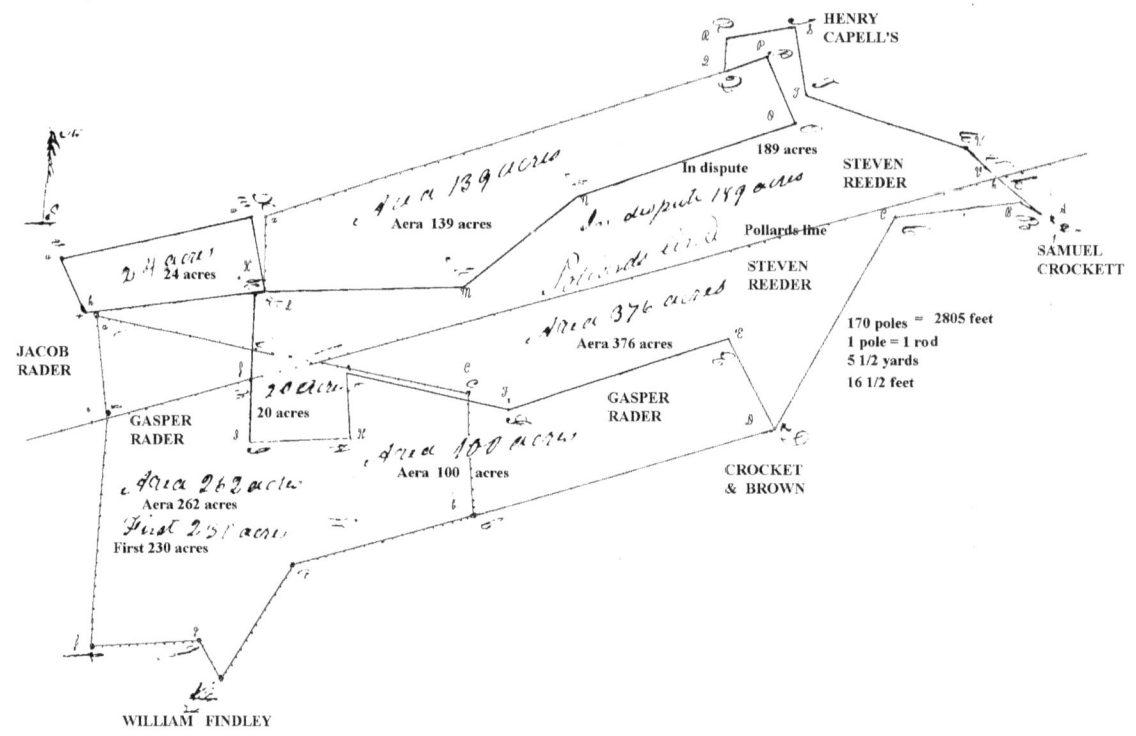

Map of Casper's land in the Cove, Wythe County, VA

Photos of the Cove

Tax list: 9 Aug 1787, Montgomery County, VA. Montgomery County Personal Property Tax 1787 (district of Davd M Gau

Conrad Rheder Conrod Rheder - - - 1

12 Gasper Rheder Gasper Rheder 1 - - 9 8

June 18 Philip Reeder Philip Reeder - - - 3 5

Stephen Reedor Stephen Reedor - - - 3 5

He was involved in a court case on 1 Jul 1788 in Montgomery, VA.. Casper was a plaintiff in a court case Montgomery Co., VA,

Home build with stone (1770s) by the Crockets before Casper moved into the area.

Tax list: 2 Sep 1788, Montgomery, VA.. Montgomery County tax 1788

May 7 Philip Reeder Philip Reeder 1

Jun 28 Conrod Rheder Conrod Rheder -

Sep 2 Gasper Rheder Gasper Rhider & Hen. Reeder 1 10

Gasper Rheder had 1 child 10 horses and paid 9/2. Conrod Rheder paid 6/28

Land purchase: 1789, Cove, Wythe co., VA. 1789 Casper purchased 200 acres in the Cove from Samuel Montgomery.

Tax list: 1789, Montgomery County, VA. Montgomery County tax 1789 "List B" by Netti Schreiner-Yantis

and actual 1789 personal property tax by David McGarock

White Males Slaves Horses

1790 person charged males over 21 16-21 years Feb 17 Reider, Philip Reider, Philip 0 0 1

Rheder, Casper Rheder, Casper 1 0 10

Mar 3 Reider, Stephen Reider, Stephen 0 0 1

1790

Feb 2 Rheder, Conrod Rheder, Conrod 0 0 1

17 Rheder, Henry Rheder, Henry 0 0 1

Casper Rheder with 1 white male between 16 and 21 and 10 horses. Conrod had 1 horse Henry also had 1 horse

Tax list: 17 Sep 1789, Montgomery County, Virginia. Montgomery County Personal Property Tax 1789 David McGasock comm

Sep 17 Philip Rader Philip Rader 1

Casper Rheder Casper Rheder 1 10

Mar 3 Stephen Reeder Stephen Reeder 1

Feb 2 Conrod Rheder Conrod Rheder 1

17 Henry Rheder Henry Rheder 1

Resided: 17 Feb 1790, Wythe County, Virginia. On Casper's home was located on Reed Creek and the Crab Orchard Fork of Little Walker's Creek in Wythe County, Virginia which was formed from Montgomery County, Virginia in 1789.

location of taxpayers - - - - -

Feb 17 (Reed Creek, Crab Orchard Fk. of Little Walkers)

Geroge Davies, Sr., John Hambleton, John Hammelton, Phenuel Henderson, Jonathan Pauley, Casper Rheder, Henry Rheder, Philip Reider, Daniel Robenett, James Robinett, Adam Seek, James Wadell.

March 3 ("In the Cove of Reed Creek) Stephen Reider, Walter Crockett

Tax list: 10 Jun 1790, Montgomery, VA.. Montgomery County Personal Property Tax 1790

(district of John Robinson formerly the upper district of Botetourt Co and now the lower of Montgomery)

June 10 Casper Reed Casper Reed 1 5

June 24 George Reetor 5 5

June 23 John Rector John Rector 5

(district of David McGavrock

Ap 1 Stephen Reider Stephen Reider 1

He owned land on 15 Apr 1791 in East Pennsboro Twp, Cumberland Co., PA. Cumberland Co deed book (Vol 1, Book P page 158-159)

Gasper Rheder and Rachel his wife of the County of Wythe sold the above land to Leonard Fisher for 477 pounds of Pennsylvania money. note the purchase and the sale were recorded at the same time! This deed has his name as follows:

Casper Reader, Gasper Rheder and Rachel his wife of the County of Wythe, Gasper Rhider & Rachel his wife, Casper Reader signed and Rachel Reader made her mark, Casper Ridder and Rechel his wife

He owned land in 1792 in Montgomery, VA.. 1792 Casper Rader had 100 acres surveyed in the Cove, adjoining Walter Crockett (Montgomery County Order Book 1, p. 322; Montgomery County Deed Book B, p 16; Wythe County Survey Book 1, p 35)

Tax list: 8 May 1793, Wythe County, Virginia. Wythe County Personal property Tax 1793

Jas. Davis Land Property roll (3 of 3)
Aple 11 Phillip Reedor 1 2
May 7 Stephen Reedor 1 3
May 8 Conrod Rheador 1 2
Gaspor Reador 2 10
John Rheador 1
Henry Rheador 1 3
Wythe County Land Tax 1793
Casper Reader 200 60 3
Phillip Reador 40 4 4
" 200 y 10
Stephen Reader 122 7 12 4
Conrod Reader 32 y 1 12 3/4

Tax list: 1794, Wythe County, Virginia. Wythe County Land Tax 1794

Casper Reeder 200 60 3
Phillip Reedrr 40 4 4
" 200 y 10 3 1/2
Stephen Reader 122 7 12 4
Conrod Reader 32 y 1 12 3/4

Tax list: 1795, Wythe County, Virginia. Wythe County Land Tax 1795

Casper Rhoder 200 60 3
Phillip Reeder 40 4 4
" 200 y 10
Stephen Reeder 122 7 12 4
Conrod Rheder 32 y 1 12 3/4
1795 Deed Book 1, 320 Henry Rader to Verner Knipp, survey made 1783 for 100 acres Pine Ridge

Wythe County Land Tax 1796
Phillip Reeder 1 20 3/4 3 4
Gasper Rader 100 60 1
" 100 20
Phillip Reador 40 4 4
" 200 y 10

Stephen Reader 122 7 12 4

Tax list: 1797, Wythe County, Virginia. Wythe County Land Tax 1797

> Gasper Rader 100 60 1
> " 100 20
> Phillip Reador 40 4 4
> " 200 y 10
> Stephen Reader 122 7 12 4
> Conrod Reader 32 y 1 12 3/4
> Book B
> Henry Rader 130 15 0/9

Tax list: 1798, Wythe County, Virginia. Wythe County Land Tax 1798

> Gasper Rader 100 60 1
> " 100 20
> Stephen Reader 122 7 12 4
> Conrod Reader 32 y 1 12 3/4
> Book B
> Henry Rader 130 15 0/9

He had a religion on 30 May 1798 in Wytheville, Wythe County, Virginia. deacon of the St. John's Lutheran Church

> The 4th German Congregation to be organized was St. Johns Evangelical Lutheran Church. Casper Rather was one of it's officials. in 1800 he and three of his sons financially supported the building of the St. John's Lutheran Church See "Wythe County Chapters" edited and published by James S. Presgraves

Tax list: 1799, Wythe County, Virginia. Wythe County Land Tax 1799

> Phillip Reeder 1 20 3/4 3 4
> Phillip Reador 40 4 4
> " 200 y 10
> Stephen Reader 122 7 12 4
> Conrod Reader 32 y 1 12 3/4
> Book B
> Henry Rader 70 33 0/9

Tax list: 1800, Wythe County, Virginia. Casper lived northwest of Brush Mountain and had one male over 16 and owned ten horses and one slave.

> Gasper Reader with 1 white male 16-21 and

> a second listing with 2 16-21 and 1 slave and 10 horses

The Flohr House

He had a religion on 11 Oct 1800 in Wytheville, Wythe County, Virginia. he and three of his sons financially supported the building of the St. John's Lutheran Church(See "Wythe County Chapters" edited and published by James S. Presgraves).

List of Subscribers for the building of St. John's church in 1800
Wytheville, Wythe Co., VA
John Räder 1
Jacob Röder 1
Casper Räder Sr. 10
Casper Räder Jr. 2

Daniel Etter donated one acre of land for St. John's congregation. Casper Rader and George Armbruster were the elders.

Tax list: 1801, Wythe County, Virginia. Wythe County Land Tax 1801

Gasper Rader 100 60 1
" 100 20
Phillip Reador 40 4 4
" 200 y 10
Stephen Reader 122 7 12 4
Conrod Reader 32 y 1 12 3/4
John Rader 1 35 55
Jacob Rader (cove) 100 50 50
Book B
William Rader 40 20 8
same 60 40 12

He had an estate probated on 2 Jun 1801 in Wythe County, Virginia. appraisal by Gasper Rader June 2, 1801

Will of Philip Reeder Nov 10, 1801
wife Mary, (sons); Jacob, Joshiah (Daughters); Dianna, Ivana, Pamrla, Mandana
lands adjoining Gasper Rader Dec 15, 1801

Tax list: 1802, Wythe County, Virginia. Wythe County Land Tax 1802

Gasper Rader 100 60 1
" 100 20
Phillip Reader 40 4 4
" 200 y 10
Stephen Reader 122 7 12 4
Conrod Reader 32 y 1 12 3/4
John Rader 1 35 55
Jacob Rader (cove) 100 50 50
Stephen Rader
Casper Rader et al for church
Book B
Henry Reder
William Rader 40 20 8
same 60 40 12
1802 Deed book 3, 182 Henry Reder & Cathrine to Michael Brown, Jr. 110 acres
1802 Deed book 3, 214 Henry Reder to Henry Cassell 33 acres, to Michael Brown 50 acres
June 1802 Deed book 4, 43 Coonrod Rader to Jacob Rader, the body of the deed says Coonrod & Betsey Rader to Peter Rader, 32 acres in Cove and 27 acres in Cove
Inventory of Estate of William Rader Feb 1, 1802

Land warrant: 28 Sep 1802, Wythe Co, TN. GRANTEE Rader, Gasper. grantee. DATE 28 September 1802. NOTE Location: Wythe County. NOTE Description: 230 acres in the Cove adjoining William Finley, Stephen Reeder, and his own land. NOTE Source: Land Office Grants No. 51, 1802-1803, p. 97 (Reel 117).

Tax list: 1803, Wythe County, Virginia. Wythe County Land Tax 1803

>   Gasper Rader 100 60 1
>   " 100 20
>   Phillip Reador 40 4 4
>   " 200 y 10
>   Stephen Reader 122 7 12 4
>   Conrod Reader 32 y 1 12 3/4
>   Jacob Rader (cove) 100 50 50
>   Stephen Rader 14
>   Jacob Rader (cove) 322
>   Casper Rader and others (church)
>   Book B
>   William Rader 40 20 8
>   same 60 40 12
>   Stephen Reeder appraises estate of John Godfried Young Mar 8, 1803
>   1803 deed book 4, 225 John & Mary Rader to Michael Cormany, 300 acres Holston

Tax list: 1804, Wythe County, Virginia. Wythe County Land Tax 1804

>   Gasper Rader 100 60 1
>   " 100 20
>   Phillip Reador 40 4 4
>   " 200 y 10
>   Stephen Reader 122 7 12 4
>   Conrod Reader 32 y 1 12 3/4
>   Jacob Rader (cove) 100 50 50
>   Stephen Rader 14
>   Jacob Rader (cove) 322
>   Casper Rader and others (church)
>   Book B
>   William Rader 40 20 8
>   same 60 40 12

Tax list: 1805, Wythe County, Virginia. Wythe County Land Tax 1805

>   Gasper Rader 100 60 1
>   " 100 20
>   Phillip Reador 40 4 4
>   " 200 y 10
>   Stephen Reader 122 7 12 4
>   Stephen Rader 78
>   Coonrod Rader 32 y 1 12 3/4
>   Jacob Rader (cove) 100 50 50
>   Stephen Rader 14
>   Casper Rader and others (church)
>   Book B

William Rader 40 20 8
same 60 40 12
settlement of estate of William Rader, late Christina Rader, 21 Sep 1805 Cash paid to Casper Rader, Henry Helvy, Henry Stephens, Robert Crockett
St. John's church in Wytheville, Wythe Co., VA
Samuel Röder born Apr 20, 1805 parents Daniel Röder & Elizabeth baptized June 1, 1805 sponsors parents
Joseph Schröder born March 17, 1805 parents Christian Schröder & catharine baptized June 1, sponsors Casper Röder & w. Barbara
Nancy Röder born June 18, 1805 parents Conrad Röder & Elizabeth baptized Aug 25, 1805 sponsor Catharine Lydy
Elizabeth Röder born Aug 26, 1805 parents Philip Röder & Rebecca baptized Nov 3, 1805 sponsors Philip & Wife

Tax list: 1806, Wythe County, Virginia. Wythe County Land Tax 1806

Gasper Rader 100 60 1
" 100 20
Phillip Reador 40 4 4
" 200 y 10
Stephen Reader 122 7 12 4
Stephen Rader 78
Stephen Rader 50
Stephen Rader 14
Coonrod Rader 32 y 1 12 3/4
Jacob Rader (cove) 100 50 50
Casper Rader and others (church)
Feb 1806 Deed book 4, 335 Stephen Reeder relinquished title to land 75,000 taxed etc. etc

Tax list: 1807, Wythe County, Virginia. Wythe County Land Tax 1807

Gasper Rader 100 60 1
" 100 20
Phillip Reador 40 4 4
" 200 y 10
Stephen Reader 122 7 12 4
Stephen Rader 78
" 131
Stephen Rader 14
Coonrod Rader 32 y 1 12 3/4
Jacob Rader (cove) 100 50 50
Casper Rader and others (church)
Book B
William Rader 40 20 8
same 60 40 12
buyer at estate sale for Daniel Johnston - 21 Mar 1807 Stephen Reeder

He appeared on the census in 1810 in Wythe County, Virginia. 1810 Wythe County census

Rader, Conrod males 2 (1-10), 1 (45 up) females 1 (1-10), 1 (10-16), 1 (26-45)
Raider, Casper males 1 (45 up) females 1 (10-16), 1 (45 up)
Reeder, Jacob males 1 (1-10), 1 (16-26) females 2 (1-10), 1 (16-26)

Reeder, Mary males 1 (16-18) females 2 (10-16), 1 (16-26), 1 (26-45)
Reeder, Samuel males 1 (10-16), 3 (16-18) females 2 (16-26)
Ritter, Daniel males 2 (1-10), 1 (26-45) females 1 (1-10), 1 (26-45)
Ritter, Sarah males 2 (16-18), females 2 (1-10), 1 (26-45)

Tax list: 1810, Wythe County, Virginia. Wythe County Land Tax 1810

Gasper Rader 100 60 1
" 100 20
Phillip Reador 40 4 4
" 200 y 10
Stephen Reader 122 7 12 4
Stephen Rader 78
" 167
" 50
Stephen Rader 14
Coonrod Rader 32 y 1 12 3/4

Tax list: 1811, Wythe County, Virginia. Wythe County Land Tax 1811

Gasper Rader 100 60 1
" 100 20
Stephen Reader (heirs) 122 7 12 4
Stephen Rader " 78
" 167
Stephen Rader 50
" 14
Coonrod Rader 32 y 1 12 3/4

Tombstone = Alt Death: 16 Jul 1811, Wytheville, Wythe County, Virginia.

Alt. Buried: 16 Jul 1811, St John's Church, Wytheville, Wythe Co, VA. Stone reads "Casper Rader died July 16, 1811 in his 80th year.   Casper and Regina are buried in the St. John's Lutheran Church cemetery. His will was signed in 1812. There was a stone carver who was known for errors operating in the valley at the time !

The actual will written in pencil

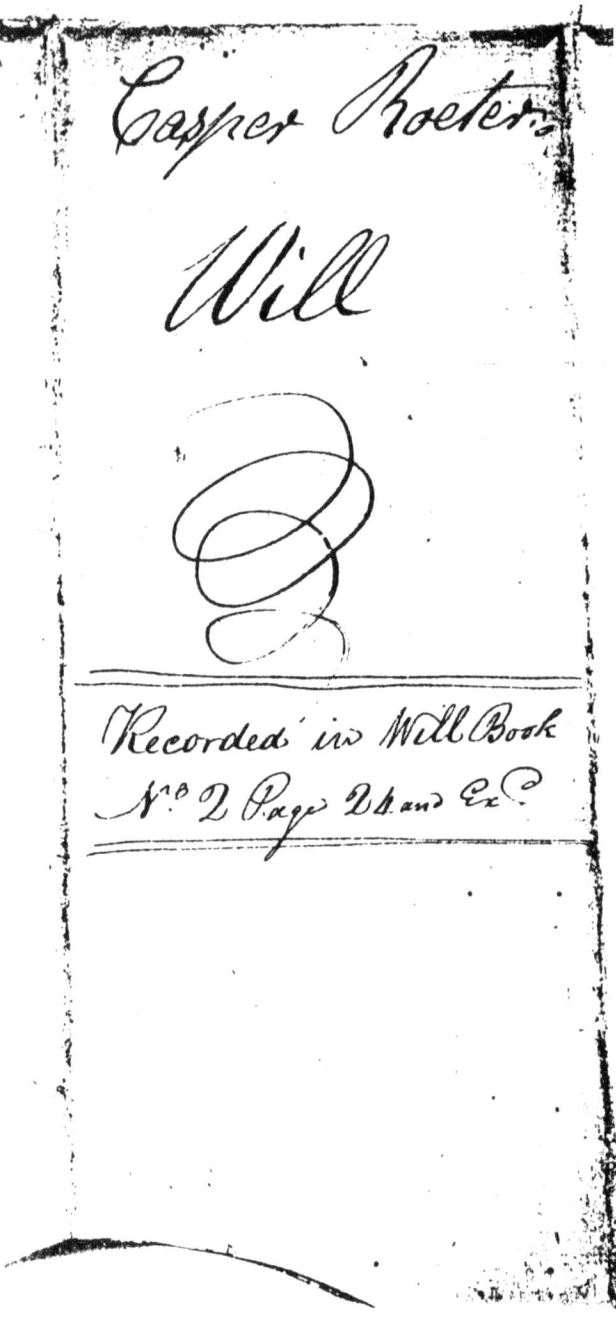

Buried: 1812, St. John Lutheran Cem., Wytheville, VA.[19, 21, 22]

Tax list: 1812, Wythe County, Virginia. Wythe County Land Tax 1812

Stephen Reader (heirs) 122 7 12 4
Stephen Rader " 78
" " 167
Stephen Rader " 50
" " 14
Coonrod Rader 32 y 1 12 3/4
book B
Sam Reeder 135

In the name of God amen. I Casper Roeter of the County of Wythe & State of Virginia being weak in body but of perfect mind & memory & calling to mind the mortality of the body, do make & ordain this my last will & testament in manner following: I recommend my soul to God that gave it & my body to the Earth to be buried in a decent manner: & as touching such wordly estate wherewith it hath pleased God to bless me with in this life: I give & bequeath in the following manner, first I give & bequeath unto my Wife Regina during her Widowhood all my personal estate consisting in one negro woman Jude & all my household & kitchen furniture bed & bedding my Clock & case my Stove & Cupboard & all that is therein: likewise my stock of horses, Cattle, sheep & hogs & all the farming utensils Waggon & Gears, & all the hay & grain now in my posesion. likewise one third of all the hay & grain that my son Peter or his heirs or assigns shall raise on the plantation during her widowhood, which said plantaton, together with all the lands I now posses I have sold unto my son Peter for which he is to pay Five hundred Pounds, which money as it becomes due after my decease is to be equally devided among my heirs together with the Conrad Roeter, Henry Roeter, John Roeter

& the children of my Dec'd Son William Roeter (viz Samuel mary & susan) (shall have their fathers part) Jacob Roeter Casper Roeter mary the wife of Christopher Brown, Peter Roeter, Philip Roeter Daniel Roeter & Catrine wife of Jonathan Leady, with this exception that those that have receiv'd money or property of me in my life time and which stands charg'd against them must pay up out of their legacy said Accounts so charg'd I likewise request that my wife Reginia shall remain in quiet possesion of the house I now live in and of the garden adjoining thereto for & during her widowhood & after her death all the personable property above mentioned & all she may die possess'd of shall be devided equally among my afores'd heirs each receiving an equal share except the children of my dec'd Son William Roeter who shall have one share devided equally among them; & it is my request that my Executors make my son Peter Roeter a Title to the Lands I sold him, & I do hereby appoint George Flohr, Lewis Wohlfart & Jacmus L. Lindenberger to be my Executors of this my last will & testament hereby revoking & disallowing all other wills & testaments ratifying & confirming this & no other to be my last will & testament in whereof I have hereunto set my hand & seal this 18th day of May One Thousand Eight Hundred & Twelve — interlin'd before sign'd

attest: Casper Roeter (Seal)
Leonard ———
Henry + Cassel

At a Court of Quarterly Session held for Wythe County, at the Court House, on Tuesday the 11th day of August 1812. This the Last Will & Testament of Gasper Rader Dec.d was presented in Court and proved by the Oaths of Leonard Umbarger, John Brown & Henry Cassell the Subscribing Witnesses thereto and the same is Ordered to be Recorded. And on the motion of George Flohr Lewis Woolford & John L. Lindenbarger the Executors named in the said Will who entered into Bond with Henry Umbarger Sr William Hay & Nicholas Darter their Securities in the sum of Three thousand Pounds conditioned as the Law directs, and took the Oath required by Law, Probate of the said Will is granted them.

Teste,
Jacob T. Fishback DC

[Caption: back]
He signed a will on 18 May 1812.

He signed a will on 18 May 1812 in Wytheville, Wythe County, Virginia. Casper's Will was probated in Wythe County, Virginia on August 11, 1812 and contains the names of his children and wife. CASPER'S WILL PROBATED 18 MAY 1812 IN WYTHE CO, VA. WILL BOOK #2 PAGE 24 DTD MAY 18 1812 RECORDED AUG 11, 1812

Will of Caper Rooter (Casper Rader) May 18 1812, it was probated August 12, 1812 (his tombstone has died July 16, 1811) I assume he died July 16, 1812

Will of Casper Roeter

In the name of God amen, I Casper Roeter of the county of Wythe & State of Virginia being weak in body but of perfect mind & memory & calling to mind the mortality of the body, do make & ordain this my last will & Testament on manner following:

I recommend my soul to god that gave it & my body to the earth to burried in a decient manner & as touching such wordly estate wherewith it hath pleased god to blefs me with in this life: I give & bequeath in the following manner, FIRST I give and bequeth unto my wife Regina during her Widowhood all my personal estate consisting in one Negro woman (Iude) & all my household & kitchen furnature bed & bedding my clock & Can my stole & cup-board & all. That is therein: likewise my stock of horres Cattle, sheep & hogs & all the farming utensils Waggons & gears & all the hay & grain now in prossefsion: likewise one third of all the hay & grain that my son Peter or his heirs or assigns shall raise on the plantation during her widowhood, wherto said plantation together with all the lands I now posses I have sold unto my son Peter for which he is to pay five hundred pounds, which money as it becomes due after my decease is to be equally divided among my heirs Conrad Roeter, Henry Roeter John Roeter (& the children of my dec son William Roeter (viz Samuel & susan) shall have their fathers part) Jacob Roeter Casper Roeter Mary the wife of Christopher Brown, Peter Roeter Philip Roeter Daniel Roeter % Cathrine wife of Jonathan Leady, with this exception that those that have recv'd money or property of me in my life time and which stands charged against them must pay up out of their legacy said amounts w charged I likewise request that my wife Regina shall remain in quiet posesion of the home I now live in and of the gardens adjoining thereto for & during her widowhood & after her death all the personable property above mentioned & all she may die posses'd of shall be divided equally among my afore Heirs each recieving an equal share except the children of my dead son William Roeter who shall have one share divided equally among them & it is my request that my Executor make my son Peter Roeter a Title to the lands I sold him, & I do herby appoint George Flohr, Lewis Wohlfort & John L.

Sindenburger to be my Executor of this my last will & Testament herby revoking & disallowing all other wills & testaments ratifying & confirming this & no other to be my last & Testament in whereof I shall hereunto set my hand & seal this 18th day of may one thousand eight nhundred and twelve.

Casper Roeter

He had an estate probated on 18 Aug 1812 in Wythe County, Virginia. Among the items owned were the following: a pot rack, a kitchen dresser, fire dogs, tongs and soffle[shovel], a fire plate, buckets, an iron pot and "jugg" pewter dishes, coffeepot and ladle, copper tea "kittle" coffeepot and "earten" dish, a "Duch" oven and skillet, tim bucket and fifteen cups, pewter "bason" 19 spoons, 20 plates, tin dishes, iron wedges, mall and pinchers, a conch shell, a pair of stilliards [steelyards], candlesticks, snuffers, coffee mill, candle mould, corner cupboard and contents, sugar and coffee, sundry brass ladles and flesh fork, sundry German books ,a flat iron and looking glass, a table, knives and forks, a clock, a stove and pipe, a hat, 4 hand towels, 5 table cloths, 2 hanks of thread, a "chist" an old gun, a horse collar, a woman's saddle, a watering pot, a foot adz, baskets, a barrel, handsaw and auger, a barrel with 8 bread baskets, a bag with flour, 4 sheets, a muslin sheet, 8 "toe" sheets, a "bead" spread, flax thread, 2 lbs of flax, 10 yards of linnen, yellow check, striped linsay cloth, some blue cloth, callico curtains, 3 coverlets, broad ax, frying pan, cutting knife, feathers, a pain of glass, several beds and bedsteads, 6 chairs, an old flax wheel and reel, hard soap, sifters, another "chist" bushels of wheat, rye and oats, dried apples, "beecon", cotton wheel and cards, an iron pot, 2 axes, a grindstone, 24 crocks, a churn, hogs lard, 8 chairs, a flax wheel, two cows, 5 sheep, a mare, a horse, a Negro woman and child, hay, a cutting box, a jack screw, corn, and another bed and bedstead

Tax list: 1813, Wythe County, Virginia. Wythe County Land Tax 1813 (book A)

Mar 22 The heirs of Phillip Reeder both sides of Cove creek 365
same Evansham
Gasper Rader Waters of Cove' Creek 100
same " " 100
The Heirs of Stephen Reader Waters of Reed Creek 78
" " " " 50
" " " " 14
" " " " 135
Book B
Gasper Ritter 300 on Reed Creek
William Raders 40 on Walkers creek
" 60 "
Sam Reeder 135 on Reed Creek

Tax list: 1814, Wythe County, Virginia. Wythe County Land Tax 1814 (book A)

Gasper Rader Waters of Cove' Creek 100
same " " 100
The Heirs of Stephen Reader Waters of Reed Creek 89

" " " " 50
" " " " 115
" " " " 167
" " Wythe town 167
Book B
Gasper Ritter 300 on Reed Creek
Sam Reeder 135 on Reed Creek

Tax list: 1815, Wythe County, Virginia. Wythe County Land Tax 1815 (book A)

Gasper Rader Waters of Cove' Creek 100
same " " 100
The heirs of Phillip Reeder both sides of Cove creek 365
same Evansham
Jacob Rader Cove Creek 134
Book B
Wm Raders Estab 40 on Walkers Creek
same 60 "
Sam Reeder 135 on Reed Creek

Casper married **Regina 'Rachel' Gerhardt**,[16, 18, 19, 20, 22] daughter of **John Conrad Gerhardt** and **Regina Gerhard**, on 21 May 1763 in Bethel Township, Lebanon Co., PA.[16, 17, 18, 19, 22, 27, 28] Regina was born in 1746 in Annville Lebanon, , Lancaster, Pennsylvania, USA,[16, 17] died on 31 Oct 1816 in Wytheville, Wythe County, Virginia[16, 17, 18, 19, 20, 21, 22, 29] at age 70, and was buried on 31 Oct 1816 in St. John's, Lutheran, Wytheville, Wythe Co, VA.[19, 21, 22] Other names for Regina were @I508999@, Regina Rachael Gerhardt, and Regina [Rachel] Gerhart.

Marriage Notes: "Early Lutheran Baptisms and Marriages in Southeastern Pennsylvania", by Genealogical Publishing Company, 1988.1. "Early Lutheran Baptisms and Marriages in Southeastern Pennsylvania", by Genealogical Publishing Company, 1988.

Casper and Regina were married in the Bethel Township of Berks County, Pennsylvania by the Reverend John Casper Stover(See "Early Lutheran Baptisms and Marriages in Southern Pennsylvania" by the Genealogical Publishing Company of Baltimore for the records of John Casper Stover from 1730 to 1779). The same record states that Casper Rader and Regina Gerhardt sponsored a child born to George and Magdalena Sedelmeyer in Bethel on March 17, 1762. Berks County was formed in 1752 from Lancaster, Philadelphia and Chester Counties.

Noted events in their marriage were:

Seal: MARRIED BY REV. JOHN CASPER STOVER

Alt Marriage: 12 May 1763, Bethel Township, Lancaster County, Pennsylvania.

Burial Notes: stone reads "Rachel Rader consort of Casper Rader Died Oct. 31, 1816 in her 70th year"

General Notes: In December 1817 commissioners were appointed to settle with John L. Lindenberger, executor of the estates of Casper Rader, Philip Armbrister and Daniel Green (Kegley vol IV, p 197)

Facts about this person:

Burial St. John's Lutheran Church, Wytheville, Wythe County, Virginia

The exact location of Regina's birth is not known. She may have been born in Germany, or in Pennsylvania.

Lutheran

Housewife

"In Her 70Th Year"

Married by Rev. John Casper Stoever

"Early Lutheran Baptisms and Marriages in Southeastern Pennsylvania", by Genealogical Publishing Company, 1988.1. "Early Lutheran Baptisms and Marriages in Southeastern Pennsylvania", by Genealogical Publishing Company, 1988.

Alt Birth: 1746, Germany Or Pennsylvania.[18, 19, 20, 22]

Children from this marriage were:

+ 2 M i. **Conrad Rader**[1, 2, 3, 5, 6, 7, 8, 10, 11, 12, 13, 14, 15, 16, 18] was born in 1766 in Bethel Township, Lancaster County, Pennsylvania[16, 17, 30] and died on 14 May 1845 in Wythe County, Virginia[16, 17] at age 79.

Conrad married **Elizabeth Ory**[16, 18] (b. 11 Jun 1772, d. 6 May 1848) on 3 Jul 1788 in Montgomery County, Virginia.[16, 17, 18, 31]

+ 3 M ii. **Heinrich 'Henry' Rader Sr**[1, 2, 3, 5, 6, 7, 8, 10, 11, 12, 13, 14, 15, 16] was born in 1768 in Bethel Township, Lancaster County, Pennsylvania,[17, 20] died on 1 Sep 1851 in Greene County, Tennessee[17] at age 83, and was buried in Time, Pike Co, IL.

Heinrich married **Catherine Etter**[18] (b. Abt 1772, d. Abt 1847) on 14 Dec 1790 in Wytheville, Wythe County, Virginia.[16, 17, 18, 28]

Heinrich next married **Catherine Propts** on 11 Feb 1813 in VA.

+ 4 M iii. **John Rader**[1, 2, 3, 4, 5, 6, 7, 8, 10, 11, 12, 13, 14, 15, 16, 18] was born about 1769 in Bethel Township, Lancaster County, Pennsylvania[16, 17] and died on 3 Feb 1840 in Greene County, Tennessee[17] about age 71.

John married **Mary Etter**[18] (b. 1776, d. 6 Mar 1848) on 17 Dec 1793 in Wythe County, Virginia.[17, 18, 32]

+ 5 M iv. **William Rader**[1, 2, 3, 5, 6, 7, 8, 10, 11, 12, 13, 14, 15, 16, 18] was born about 1770 in East Pennsboro Twp, Cumberland Co., PA[16, 17, 18] and died in 1802 in Wythe County, Virginia[17, 18] about age 32.

William married **Christina 'Diney' Helvey Or Alvery** (b. 1770, d. Apr 1815) on 14 Dec 1790 in Wytheville, Wythe County, Virginia.[17, 18]

William next married **Christina Helvy** on 12 Jan 1796 in Wytheville, Wythe County, Virginia.

William next married **Tiney Alvery** on 12 Jan 1796 in , Wythe, Virginia.

+ 6 M v. **Jacob Rader**[1, 2, 3, 4, 5, 6, 7, 8, 10, 11, 12, 13, 14, 15, 16, 18] was born about 1772 in East Pennsboro Twp, Cumberland Co., PA[4, 16, 17, 18] and died on 22 Jul 1822 in Greene County, Tennessee[17] about age 50.

Jacob married **Elizabeth Woods Been Hedrick** (b. 1771, d. 1860) on 25 Jan 1806 in Wythe County, Virginia.[17, 18]

+ 7 M vi. **Casper Rader Jr.**[1, 2, 3, 5, 6, 7, 8, 10, 11, 12, 13, 14, 15, 16, 18] was born in 1774 in East Pennsboro Twp, Cumberland Co., PA,[16, 17, 18] died in 1830 in Sevier County, Tennessee[17, 18] at age 56, and was buried in Fox Cemetery, Sevier County, Tennessee.

Casper married **Barbara Armbrister**[16, 18] (b. Abt 1775, d. 8 Mar 1845) in 1802 in Wythe County, Virginia.[16, 17, 18]

Casper next married **Mary Ann Milliron** (b. 6 Apr 1840, d. 24 Apr 1933) WFT Est 1854-1887.

+ 8 M vii. **Phillip Rader Sr.**[1, 2, 3, 5, 6, 7, 8, 10, 11, 12, 13, 14, 15, 16, 18, 33, 34] was born on 12 Aug 1782 in East Pennsboro Twp, Cumberland Co., PA,[34, 35] died on 2 Nov 1853 in Butler Twp, Montgomery Co Ohio[17, 18] at age 71, and was buried in Sugar Grove cem, Butler Twp, Montgomery Co Ohio.

Phillip married **Margaret Rebecca Cress** (d. Bef 1813) in 1803 in Unk.[17, 18]

Phillip next married **Catherine Elizabeth Siddon** (b. 1796, d. 1826) on 30 Jan 1812 in Montgomery Ohio.[34]

Phillip next married **Catherine Sheets**[34] (d. 10 Aug 1852) ..approx 1827 in Ohio.[34]

+ 9 M viii. **Peter Rader**[1, 2, 3, 5, 6, 8, 10, 11, 12, 13, 14, 15, 16, 18] was born on 3 Sep 1780 in East Pennsboro Twp, Cumberland Co., PA,[16, 17, 18] died on 11 Mar 1858 in Greene County, Tennessee[17, 18] at age 77, and was buried in Blountville Cemetery, Sullivan County, Tennessee.

Peter married **Tarkis (Dorcas) Dorcas**[18] (b. 1783, d. 10 Jul 1868) in 1812 in Wythe County, Virginia.[17, 18]

+ 10 F ix. **Anna Marie 'Mary' Rader**[1, 2, 3, 5, 6, 7, 8, 10, 11, 12, 13, 14, 15, 16, 18] was born on 4 Jul 1778 in East Pennsboro Twp, Cumberland Co., PA,[16, 17, 18, 19, 22] died on 19 Dec 1849 in Wythe County, Virginia[17, 18, 19, 22] at age 71, and was buried in 1849 in St. John Cemetery, Wytheville, Wythe Co., VA.[19, 22]

Anna married **Christopher A. 'Stophel' Brown Jr**[18, 19, 22] (b. 7 Nov 1774, d. 20 Sep 1850) about 1800 in Wythe County, Virginia.[17, 18, 19, 22]

+ 11 F x. **Catherine Rader**[1, 2, 3, 5, 6, 7, 8, 9, 10, 11, 12, 13, 14, 15, 16, 18] was born in 1781 in East Pennsboro Twp, Cumberland Co., PA[17] and died in 1844 in Wythe County, Virginia[17, 18] at age 63.

Catherine married **Jonathan Leady**[18] (b. 1779, d. 1852) before 18 Jun 1805 in Wythe County, Virginia.[17, 36]

+ 12 M xi. **Daniel Rader**[1, 2, 3, 5, 6, 7, 8, 10, 11, 12, 13, 14, 15, 16, 18, 37, 38] was born about 1782 in East Pennsboro Twp, Cumberland Co., PA[16, 17, 18, 38] and died on 27 Oct 1827 in Madison County, Alabama[17, 38] about age 45.

Daniel married **Elizabeth Davis**[38] (b. 1789, d. May 1849) about 1804 in Wythe County, Virginia.[17, 18, 38]

Tennessee Farming, Tennessee Farmers Antebellum Agriculture

> The following 20 pages contain very informative exerpts from old sources. They have educated me about the life and times of the Raders of Greene county. Some are from diaries of visitors in the late 1700 s some are well footnoted non fiction works. All are currently available and I encourage you to seek them out and read the complete work. The books are available in the used book market, places like www.alibris.com , www.amazon.com , I include the web addresses of those online

in the Upper South by Donald L. Winters

Page 19

The other alternative open to settlers without the means or the inclination to purchase land was to become a squatter. Many availed themselves of the opportunity to move onto unoccupied land, private or public, and take up farming. The owners rarely complained about such intrusions; mant private owners, in fact, encouraged the practice because it brought improvements, and thereby enhanced value, to their property. If the owner put up his land for sale later, as was usually the case, he customarily offered the squatter the privilege of first refusal. - - - -

After obtaining a farm site, settlers had to turn quickly to the tasks of construction of the family dwelling and putting in the first crop. A crude log cabin, erected in a week to ten days – less with the help from the neighbors—usually provided the first house. Typically, a single, square room, measuring fifteen to twenty feet on a side, it was made from round logs, notched at both ends and with the bark removed. If the family was fortunate enough to have help from neighbors, the builders sometimes hewed two sides of the timbers flat and squared the logs to achieve a better fit.

The reshaping of Everyday life 1790-1840 by Jack Larkin

Page 108

"families built log houses and lived in them for two generations or more"

Last of the Pioneers: Or Old Times in East Tenn.; Being the Life and Reminiscences of Pharaoh Jackson Chesney (Aged 120 Years): Electronic Edition. Chesney, Pharaoh Jackson, b. 1781? Webster, J.C. (John Coram), b. 1861. 130 p. Knoxville, Tenn. S. B. Newman & Co., Printers & Bookbinders 1902. http://docsouth.unc.edu/neh/webster/webster.html © This work is the property of the University of North Carolina at Chapel Hill. It may be used freely by individuals for research, teaching and personal use as long as this statement of availability is included in the text.

PREFACE.

Dwelling alone, in a cabin of the most primitive description, on the summit of Copper ridge, five miles south of Maynardville, Union county, Tennessee, is unquestionably, one of the most remarkable men in the state of Tennessee, if not in the entire United States. He is remarkable not only on account of the great age to which he has attained, but equally so on account of the wonderful preservation of his bodily and mental powers.

CLARKSVILLE, HOME OF MY CHILDHOOD.

I was born and reared in the town of Clarksville, Mecklenburg county, in Old Virginia, and this is why I always speak of Clarksville as my childhood home. This beautiful town, built on a lovely strip of level bottom land, was at first laid out on the south side of the river, just below where the Roanoke and Dan come together. Old Master Jackson had a large plantation and a magnificent home just below town, but almost joining it. Old Master Johnathan Jackson did a great deal of business in town, while young master, Corbin Jackson, was a stock dealer, and often took me on his buying trips to assist him in bringing back the stock he would buy. It was on one of these long trips buying up droves of cattle and sheep, that he came down into Tennessee, as far down as **Surgoinsville, Hawkins county**, that he became so favorably impressed with East Tennessee, that he was determined to one day make his home somewhere along Clinch mountain, in the beautiful valley.

In addition to this being a land of plenty to eat, and of peace and prosperity, there was, also, plenty of amusements of all kinds to keep up a fellow's spirits. No use of dying of the "blues" on a plantation of darkeys. These were generally allowed liberty to go where they pleased on the plantation, and, just so a man did a good day's work, and the feeding and wood-chopping besides, he was allowed to enjoy himself in any reasonable way, so no harm or damage was done.

EARLY METHODS, MANNERS, AND CUSTOMS.

OLD TIME WORKINGS.

The most distinguishing feature or characteristic of early pioneer days was the many social gatherings of neighbors for mutual assistance in the performance of labor too heavy for a single individual. The land was grown over with heavy timber and it all had to be cleared and fenced. One man could not manage the heavy logs alone, and so the neighbors would be informed that on a certain day they were to meet at this man's "new ground," and participate in a log-rolling and rail-splitting. Accordingly they all came with their axes and mauls. Some would be put to chopping down the trees, some to chopping off the cuts, some to splitting rails, and some to rolling together into large heaps such logs as would not split into rails. The boys would also come to pile, in large heaps, the brush and small limbs.

HOUSE RAISINGS, ETC.

These men were strong and hardy, and the amount of work that was done at one of these "workings" would astonish people of the present day. It was a favorite occasion for the showing off of strength and general physical manhood, and many and severe were the tests to which the aspirants for honor were subjected. While there was generally plenty of home-made liquor on hand, and of which, each one usually partook quite freely, it was not the modern kind that takes the reason from the mind, and puts the devil into the heart. The utmost good humor prevailed, and, the funnier they became, the friendlier they were.

Or, it may have been a settler's cabin to be built; for, when a new family came into the neighborhood, the neighbors would all join in, and build them a house. This usually required two "workings." The first day they would go to the woods and get the logs ready. Some would chop down the trees; some would measure and cut off the logs; some would "scutch" the logs; and others would come along with a broadaxe, and hew two sides of the logs flat. The next day these logs would be hauled or dragged to the place where the cabin was to be built, and the "house-raising," would take place.

Four men would be selected to "carry up the corners," which consisted in notching and fitting the logs so that they would be close together, while the others would bring up the logs. This would continue until what we would consider a very low, one-story pen would be built. Then the end logs would be gradually shortened, and sloped, and the long poles to support the roof would be laid up instead of side logs. After these poles were all up, long, thin clap-boards would be put on, and heavy weight-poles would be used to hold them down, as there were no nails. In the meantime, some of the men had been splitting out logs into pieces four or five inches thick, for the floor. These were called puncheons, and were fitted in for the floor, making it as tight as possible. This much of the work usually constituted the day's work, leaving, for the man who was to occupy the house, the job of building a stick-and-mud chimney, to chink and daub the cracks, and to lay the hearth of flat stones. When the house was completed, the owner usually gave an old-fashioned party in honor of the friends whose kindness had furnished him a home.

The door of the primitive log cabin extended from the first log at the bottom to the top one, and was closed with a shutter made of puncheons similar to the floor, except they were thinner. These pieces were fastened together by wooden pins, and the door was hung with wooden hinges. The fireplace occupied the greater amount of the space of one end. When this was piled full of wood and set on fire, and a large pine knot thrown on, the room was sufficiently heated and lighted. These cabins were usually built near a good spring of water, and, in most cases, in the middle of the clearing, so that the approach of a bear, a wolf, or an Indian could be seen.

THE CORN HUSKING.

In the late fall, when the corn was ripe, and gathered in, there would be at each settler's cabin, another gathering of neighbors, this time, to help husk out the corn. This social function was a regular, annual feature, and was looked forward to with much interest. Much fun was, in some way or other, injected into the occasion. It was a custom rarely omitted to have a jug of corn juice placed in the center of the corn heap, and the crowd was divided into two equal divisions, and placed on opposite sides, and the race was to see which side would be the first to reach the jug. Other contests were to impose a fine of a gallon of "the article" on the one husking the fewest number of red ears.

THE QUILTING BEE.

Frequently, also, at the same time, the farmer's wife would embrace this occasion to have the ladies, young and old, of the neighborhood come and assist her in quilting a quilt. When the two affairs came off on the same day, the night would be most surely devoted to games, plays and dancing. In those days, everybody was invited, and everybody expected to come or render a good excuse at the first opportunity. If there happened to be some one in the neighborhood who was not deemed worthy to be invited, he construed it to mean that his permanent absence from that community would fill a long-felt want. It was also expected of a person having a "working," that he would, for the time at least, lay aside any little petty differences, or prejudice, that might exist between himself and a neighbor, and invite him along with the others. So, to a great extent, these gatherings were directly instrumental in wiping out old grudges and renewals of friendship. But as the people became more prosperous, they became more independent, and began drifting apart. Prosperity seems to breed selfishness, and degrades the social standard of the people. Later, I have seen the chasm between the people widened by differences in political and religious opinions to such an extent as to almost wipe out all reverence for the good old customs of the good old times of long ago. Schools and churches may increase, education and religion may become more widely diffused, but the world will never again witness the generosity, the hospitality, the unadulterated community of common interest, and common welfare, as that exhibited in the relations of pioneers to each other. The log cabin and the pioneer can never again be factors of our civilization. It is doubtful if history could ever repeat itself to the extent of their reproduction. There is no longer a westward march toward civilization, no longer a frontier. Alas! for the good old days of our grandparents. In those days a life seemed to count for much. All the power and influence of an individual seemed directed toward a worthy end, and left an impression, recognized and felt by every one. Now a life seems to be swallowed up and forgotten in the rushing, mighty whirl of these days of steam and electricity.

The plain, simple food, and the plain, simple dress, and the freedom from the worry and excitement induced by the fierce competition and rivalry, and the greed of fame and fortune, resulted in good health and long life to the people; and hence, with an undisturbed mind and body, and a full measure of days, they were enabled to more fully fulfil the great object of their existence on earth. The excesses and indulgences of modern times were the rarest exceptions. Though lacking much that we are disposed to call advantages, still what they accomplished must be considered something wonderful.

HARVESTING AND THRESHING.

The amount of wheat and oats raised in the early days of our country was very small compared with the present. But if the people were under the necessity of using the same methods of cutting their wheat, and cleaning out the grain, as were used fifty years ago, very little would be raised now.

In those days, the grain was cut with a reap-hook. This was done by the person taking hold of as much of the straws as he could hold in his left hand, then using the reap-hook with his right hand, with a quick stroke, cut off the straws, and place them in bunches to be tied in bundles. The bundles were placed in shocks until thoroughly dry, then they were taken to the threshing-floor of the barn, and the heads all placed toward the center, and the butts outward. The grain was then beaten out with a hickory flail. Some used horses to tramp out the grain. The grain and chaff was then gathered up and poured into a fan mill and cleaned. This was a slow, laborious process, and it required so much time and labor that very little wheat was grown. Oats were fed in the sheaf, and only enough were threshed for seed. In time, the cradle was invented, and with this a good hand would cut from two to four acres a day. About the time the cradle came into use, some yankees invented a threshing machine. The first machine did not separate the grain from the chaff, and the fan mill was used the same as before. In a year or two, a machine was brought out that threshed and separated the grain. This machine marks the era of the wheat field. Wheat was no longer raised in patches, but fields were sown with it, as well as with oats. The reap-hook and the wooden flail were laid aside, and the darkeys had an easier time.

The meadows then consisted of a narrow level strip of land along the branch or creek. The grass was cut with an old Dutch scythe, that was sharpened on an iron stake driven into a stump or block, and beaten out with a hammer. This required to be done very frequently, and but little could be cut in a day. But as better blades were made with which to cut the grass, larger spaces were put in meadow, and more hay was raised. Later on, came the mowing machine, which did more to revolutionize farming than any one invention. The farmer then realized that any good land, no difference whether it was bottom land or not, would produce hay. Then he began to rest his land from corn by growing grass on it. Hay proved to be a great fattening food for stock, and was so much cheaper than corn that its use was very much increased. This resulted in the farmer keeping his cattle on the farm and fattening them on grass, and was the means of making far better times for him. The land was fresh and fertile, and produced abundant crops of corn, but it was not profitable to raise more than was needed for home use, as there was not much market for it. True enough, vast quantities of it was distilled into whiskey, but this article sold for fifty cents a gallon, and many farmers furnished the corn to the distiller and took a share of the product. The woods afforded acorns and chestnuts sufficient to fatten the hogs, and very little corn was fed to them. The great trouble was that there was so much woods that the hogs became wild, and late in the fall, the trouble of capturing and killing them was a tremendous job.

MILLS.

The first saw mills, and indeed the only ones that were in the country until within the last thirty years were the old sash saws. It required a whole day to saw a large log into inch lumber. The machinery was very simple and cumber-some, but the arrangement for feeding and backing the log, was very ingenious for that day and time.

It was, as soon as practicable, the custom to have a saw mill in every community, and though the amount of lumber sawed was small, still it had a wonderful effect on building. The floors were made of planks; the doors were made of it; tables; shelves, and boxes were made of it; and the conveniences of the home were much increased by the use of lumber. Houses could be more easily and quickly built, and were much more tasty and comfortable. It is said that Gov. Blount imported weatherboarding from North Carolina, his former home, with which to encase the huge log mansion built for him in Knoxville.

The little "corn-crackers" were usually built at the same time and operated by the same power as the saw-mill. The mill-stones were of a very rough, inferior character, and the grinding was necessarily slow. The grist was almost invariably left at the mill for several days, the miller usually being able to guess with tolerable accuracy when it could be called for. It is related that a rather witty boy on calling for his meal, was informed that it was just put up for grinding, and that he could wait until it was ground, and take it back with him. He concluded to do so. He stood by and watched the tiny, little stream of meal come out, and, at last, said to the miller, "I could eat this meal as fast as this mill can grind it. "How long could you eat it?" asked the miller. "Until I starved to death," answered the boy. Before these corn mills were built the people were subjected to the greatest inconvenience in order to procure bread. Many, indeed, did much of the time without it. Instead, corn was parched and eaten so, or the corn was pounded into meal, and baked into bread. Adam Meek, who settled about the year 1785, in the valley near Strawberry Plains, obtained his meal for a long time near Greeneville. But the early county records show that among the first acts of the county courts were premits to dam the creeks and erect mills. Knox county court was organized on June 16, 1792, and the records show that on the same day, Wm. Henry obtained leave to build a mill on Roseberry creek. Grainger county court was organized June 13,1796, and at this term of court, permits were issued to Nichols T. Perkins to erect a mill on Chamberlain, now Stiffey creek; to Wm. Thompson, on Buffalo creek; and to Wm. Stone, near the mouth of Richland creek. In the year 1786, a man by the name of Hazlitt built a mill on Beaver creek, near Mr. Meek. After six or seven years this was replaced by a better one built by James Walker. Adam Peck was the first settler on Mossy creek, and built a mill just below the present town in 1788. Some of these old time mills have been entirely destroyed, others have been rebuilt and equipped with modern milling machinery.

Before the settlers could obtain meal parched corn was a staple article of diet. On many of the long expeditions against the Indians the soldiers carred with them bags of parched corn, and slices of dried bear's or deer's flesh.

SALT.

Salt was for a long time a great luxury with the old settlers, and, as you may imagine, was difficult to obtain. People, on their hunting expeditions discovered trails leading or converging to a point, like the spokes of a wheel, and by following these trails, discovered that they lead to "salt licks." These salt licks were places where salt-water oozed from the ground, and to which the deer and buffalo would come to lick the salt. Hence, they were called "salt licks." The people boiled and evaporated this water, and thus obtained their first supplies of salt. The licks were the best places for the hunter to kill these animals. At the same time, other beings would know by instinct or experience, the same thing as the white hunter. The Indian had known, long before the white man, this favorite spot, and he, too, most likely, would be watching beside this same lick, and the white man would have to exercise the greatest caution, or he would receive a bullet that was at first intended by the Indian for a deer. When the Indians learned that the white men were hunting at the lick, they kept almost a continual watch on the trails that led to them, so that it became too dangerous for the settlers to hunt at them. The panther also knew that the deer would come to lick the salt-water and it was not an infrequent sight to see two or three of these ferocious brutes lying stretched on the limbs of as many trees, ready to spring on the unsuspecting animal that chanced to pass within reach. He, too, was a foe to be dreaded by the hunter; for such a mark for a rifle as he would make stretched out his full length on a horizontal limb, would constitute a temptation too strong to be resisted by the hunter. Stange as it may seem, more shots by an experienced hunter would result in wounding than in killing the animal; and then, unless badly crippled, he would make a ferocious assault on the hunter, who considered himself fortunate to escape with his life. If he did not have time to reload his gun, and the beast came on him, he would fight, using his gun barrel and large hunting knife.

EARLY ROADS.

The first roads in the newly settled country were narrow worn lanes, scarce two feet wide, lightly trodden over pine needles and fallen leaves among the tree trunks by the soft moccasined feet of the tawny savages as they silently walked in Indian file through the forests. These paths were soon deepened and worn bare by the heavy hobnailed shoes of the early settlers. Others were formed by the slow tread of domestic cattle, the best of all path-makers, as they wound around the hillsides to pasture or to drinking place. Then a scarcely broader bridle-path for horses, perhaps with blazed trees as guide posts, widened slowly to traveled roads and uneven cart ways. These roads followed and still wind today in the very lines of the footpath and the cattle track. Wet and marshy places were laid with poles cut in ten foot lengths and laid closely across the road. Some of these laid with pine poles served their purpose after a use of fifty years. They were called corduroy roads, and was the first effort at road improvement. The first turnpike in America was made when I was a small boy (1785-86) in Virginia, starting at Alexandria and extending down the Shenandoah Valley. It was at a tavern on this turnpike, while on a cattle drive to Petersburg, with my master, that I saw George Washington. I was a small boy, and did not then know how great a man he really was, but I well remember how he looked.

THE OLD-TIME WAGON.

I saw the first wagon ever used in the part of Virginia where I lived. It was the same kind as was first used everywhere in the new settlements where wagons were used at all. It was called the Conestoga wagon, that being the name of the place in Pennsylvania where they were first made. They were of the same general plan upon which wagons of the present day are made--the difference consisting only in such improvements as have been made to render it less clumsy and more durable. Suitable iron was so scarce that not much of it was used on these old-time wagons. The axles were made of a tough, young pine sapling, which being daily greased with pine tar, became so tough and hard as not to need skeins, and would last for years without them. Very few of them had iron tires; and the first man to bring into the country about Blain's Cross Roads, in 1840, a wagon with tires made of iron, was, I believe, old Buckeye Crawford, who came from North Carolina, about that year, and settled by House Mountain. The hind wheels were much higher than they are now made; and, for a reason I never knew. The beds were very long, and were curved, being higher at each end than the middle. It took a blacksmith six weeks to make and iron one of these beds. They had no locks to these wagons, the convenient brake being an invention of the last forty years. A lock chain with a little fastening device was used, and a wheel was not merely checked in its speed, but locked fast. Consequently the tires would soon be ground into many thin places.

THE OLD-TIME STAGE COACH.

A Toast to the Old Stage Coach.

"Long ago, at the end of the route,
The stage pulled up, and the folks stepped out.
They have all passed under the tavern door--
The youth and his bride, and the gray three-score.
Their eyes were weary with dust and gleam,
The day had gone like an empty dream.
Soft may they slumber, and trouble no more
For their eager journey, its jolt and roar,
In the old coach over the mountain."

The writer finds that Uncle Pharaoh's description of the old-time stage coach in use when he was a boy, in the latter part of the eighteenth century, is almost identical with that given by Thomas Twining, an English writer, who traveled in New England in one of these vehicles in 1795. So, the latter's description is given.

"The vehicle was a long car with four benches. Three of these in the interior held nine passengers. A tenth passenger was seated by the driver on the front bench. A light roof was supported by eight slender pillars, four on each side. Three large leather curtains suspended to the roof, one at each side, and the third behind, were rolled up or lowered at the pleasure of the passengers. There was no place nor space for baggage, each person being expected to stow his things as he could, under his seat or legs. The entrance was in front, over the driver's bench. Of course the three passengers on the back seat were obliged to crawl across all the other benches in order to get to their places. There were no backs to the benches to support and relieve us during a rough and fatiguing journey over a newly and ill-made road."

The vehicle was called a stage coach because the distance between the stations on the route were called stages; and usually a fresh relay of horses was in readiness at each station. The distance between New York and Philadelphia is two hundred and ninety-seven miles, and in 1812, it took six days to make the journey by stage coach. The fare for each passenger was twenty dollars, besides way-expenses of seven dollars more. The expense by wagon was five dollars a hundred weight for persons and property, and the way-expenses were twelve dollars, for it took twenty days. Each station was an inn, or ordinary, and afforded accommodations for the passengers, at a moderate expense. Not only did these afford food and lodging for the traveler, but he could also procure, if he chose to do so--and he usually did--almost any kind of drink which suited his taste. These various drinks were made of home products, and mixed under various names.

THE OLD-TIME TAVERN, OR ORDINARY.

As has been stated, these taverns were located on the stage routes, and were usually a day's journey apart, so that rest could be afforded for the horses, and food and shelter for the traveler. Encouragement and protection were afforded these houses of entertainment by the county courts; and no one was permitted to open and run an establishment of the kind without a license. The prices to be charged for meals and drinks was fixed by law; and, in some places, the number of drinks to each person, were limited, in order to control drunkenness.

Very stringent restrictions were placed on landlords in regard to the keeping of strangers. The names of these were given to the town authorities, who could, if they saw fit, warn such persons to leave at once, as might appear to be of a suspicious character, or whose presence at the place might be considered as dangerous or undesirable. In case action was taken, a record was made of it. Our ancestors were kind and hospitable to the worthy, but sternly intolerant of wrong-doers, or even of those suspected of evil intentions. Landlords were closely watched, and held strictly accountable, under heavy penalties, for the conduct of travelers or other persons frequenting their place. No loud singing, dancing, or other boisterous noises were allowed. Drunkenness was strictly forbidden, and landlords were subject to have their license revoked, and heavy fines imposed, who allowed such conduct. A favorite location for the tavern was at a ferry; and the landlord who was so fortunate as to control the patronage of a tavern and a ferry, held a position truly envied by his less fortunate neighbors, and was sure of a competence not afforded by any other calling of that day.

The better class of old-time taverns always had a parlor. This was used as a sitting room for women travelers, or might be hired for the exclusive use of one wealthy person or family. It was not so jovial a room as the tap-room, where the drinks were dispensed, though in winter, an open fireplace gave to the formal furnishings that look of good cheer and warmth and welcome which is ever present, even in the meanest apartment, when from the great logs the flames shot up glowing and crackling. We are more comfortable now, with our modern ways of house-heating, but our rooms do not look as warm as when we had the old open fireplace.

The tap room was usually the largest room of the tavern. It had universally a great fireplace, a bare, sanded floor, and ample seats and chairs. It often had, also, a rather tall, rude writing desk, at which a traveler might write a letter or sign a contract, and where the landlord made out his bills and kept his books. But the principal feature of this room was the various kinds of drinks made and sold there.

RAILROADS.

No railroads were built in lower Virginia before the time we left there to come to East Tennessee (about 1838), but several short lines of road had been built in the mining regions of Pennsylvania, and were in operation then. I never saw these railroads, but well remember the descriptions given me of them, by persons who had seen them.

The track consisted of pieces of timber with strap iron spiked down on top of them. These spikes would soon come loose, and the ends of the straps would turn up, and were called "snake-heads." These snake-heads were sometimes forced up through the cars, and did great damage. Snake-heads were as common in early railroading as snags were in early steamboating. Scarcely was a trip ever made that some serious accident of some kind did not occur. Few of these mishaps were fatal to life, but they generally resulted in crippling the machinery so that horses or oxen, often both, had to be impressed in order to drag the clumsy locomotive and its load to the nearest station for repairs. The brakes were very poor and would not stop the train. When they came to a station, the engineer opened the safety valve and allowed the steam to escape, two big negroes would seize the end of the train, and hold it, while timbers would be placed across the track in front of the wheels. Both the engineer and the conductor favored a curved track in order that they might look back and see that everything was all right.

A YEAR WITH NO SUMMER (1816).

We call this (1901-2) a long, hard winter, but I remember a winter in Old Virginia, when I was a young man, that far surpassed any winter remembered by the oldest inhabitants. I heard the people here in East Tennessee speak of it after I came here over twenty years afterward. The winter of 1815 had been, as was then usual, a very severe one, and the cold frozen weather extended far into the new year. When time came for gardening in the spring, the fury of winter had not abated in the least. In April, the snow was from four to six feet deep. In May, the surface only had melted, and the ground could not be reached for planting purposes. In June, the snow had melted, but the ground was still frozen hard, and toward the end of the month another snow had fallen, sufficiently for sleighing purposes, and lasted for days.

On the morning of July 4, the water froze in the wells and pitchers of the early settlers, and there was excellent skating in the neighborhood ponds. Snow fell toward noon, and the usual Independence Day exercises were held in an old-time log church, warmed by blazing log fires, and participated in by men, women and children clad in mid-winter clothing.

The spring, when it came in reality, was so short and severe that no vegetation could grow in it. In August, the corn that had struggled against the adverse conditions of climate, went to tassel so early that it was useless for anything except fodder. In the spring of 1817, farmers were obliged to pay unheard-of prices for seed corn raised in 1815. All kinds of breadstuffs went up until flour brought $17.00 a barrel.

The winter following, as well as that preceding this remarkable summer, was likewise one of intense cold. All the streams were frozen over solid, and the usual hauling was done over the ice the same as on the land. The public health, however, was never better, and though the crops were a failure, the old-time settler did not lose spirit, or become discouraged.

There never was such a time before or since for hunting deer. The snow had frozen so that a crust was formed on top that would hold up the weight of the dogs, but the sharp feet of the deer would break through, and they could not escape their pursuers, and so they were nearly all killed. They were never afterward very plentiful except in the mountains. Their flesh, however, was not very good, as they had become poor through starvation, but were hunted and killed for mere sport. Many domestic animals likewise perished from cold and hunger. No, sir, our winters now do not compare with the old-time winters. They have been becoming milder for a hundred years or more.

Travels to the westward of the Allegany mountains in Greene county Tennessee

Author: Michaux, Franpcois Andrbe, 1770-1855.

Title: Travels to the westward of the Allegany mountains : in the states of Ohio, Kentucky, and Tennessee, in the year 1802

/ by F.A. Michaux ; translated from the French.

Publication date: 1805.

http://kdl.kyvl.org

http://kdl.kyvl.org/cgi/t/text/text-idx?c=kyetexts;cc=kyetexts;sid=aef8bf6f366c6ea2b910013294ab1f25;q1=tennessee;idno=b92-160-29919448;view=toc

(Page 89 Chapter XXIV)

Knoxville, the seat of government of the State of Tennessee, is situated on the river Holston, which, at this place, is 150 fathoms in width. The houses, in number about 200, ara, almost all, of wood. - - -

On 17th of September 1802 I took my leave --

I crossed the river Holston at Macby, fifteen miles from Knoxville: here the soil becomes better, and the plantations are nearer together, although still so distant as not to be within sight of each other.

At a short distance from Macby, the road, for the space of a mile or two, runs beside a coppice, very thickly (pg 90) set with trees, the largest clumps being twenty or twenty-five feet across. I had never seen any part of a forest in a similar state; and I made this observation to the inhabitants of the country, who informed me that this spot was formerly part of a barren, or meadow, which had become naturally re-covered with wood within the last twelve or fifteen years, since the custom of setting fire to them, as practised in all the Southern States, had been discontinued. This circumstance seems to prove, that the extensive meadows of Kentucky and Tennessee owe their origin to some conflagration, which had consumed the forests, and that they are preserved in that state by the custom, which still prevails, of setting fire to them annually. When on these occasions chance preserves any spots of them for a few years from the ravages of the flames, the trees spring up again; but, being extremely close, the fire, which at length catches them, burns them completely, and again reduces them to the state of meadows.

On the first day I stopped in a place where the majority of the inhabitants were Quakers, who had come from fifteen or eighteen years before from Pennsylvania. The one with whom I lodged had a good plantation, and his log-house was divided into two apartments, which is very uncommon in this country. Some very fine apple-trees were planted round the house, which, although raised from seeds, produced fruit of an extraordinary size and excellent quality: this is another proof how well these countries are adapted for the culture of fruit-trees. Here, as in Kentucky, the preference is given to the peach, on account of the brandy made from it. At my host's I met with two families of emigrants, consisting together of ten or twelve persons, who were going to settle in Tennessee. Their torn garments, and the bad plight of their children, who followed barefooted, and in their shirts, were indications of their poverty; a very uncommon occurrence in the United States. The riches of the inhabitants of the Western Country do not, however, consist in money; for I am well convinced that a tenth of them do not possess a single dollar; but each man lives on his own freehold, and derives from it an abundance of every necessary of life; and the money arising from the sale of a horse or a few cows is always more than sufficient to procure him all those secondary articles, which come from the English manufactories.

On the following day I passed near an iron work, situated thirty miles from Knoxville, and stopped a short time to take a (pg 91) specimen of the ore. The iron obtained from it is said to be of excellent quality. At this place the road divides into two branches, both leading to Jonesborough; but, as I was desirous of seeing the banks of the river Nolachuky, celebrated in this country for their fertility, I took that to the right.

Six or seven miles from the iron-work, small rock crystals are found on the road; they are two or three lines in length, and beautifummy transparent. The faces of the pyramids, which terminate the two extremities of the prism, are parallel and equal: they are uncombined, and dissemminated in reddish, slightly argillaceous land. -- In less than ten minutes I could collect forty of them.

On the 21st I arrived at Greenville, which does not contain more than forty houses, built of squared beams, arranged like the trunks of trees of the log-houses. From hence to Jonesborough is twenty-five miles. In the interval the country is rather hilly; the soil is more adapted to the culture of wheat than of maize; and the houses on the road are at a distance of three miles from each other.

Jonesborough, the last town in Tennessee, contains about 150 houses, built of planks, and standing on both sides of the road. The place contains four or five stores, and the merchants who keep them trade with Baltimore and Richmond. Every article of English manufacture is sold very dear here, as well as at Knoxville. A newspaper, in large folio, here once a week. Indeed papers are hitherto the only works which have been printed in those towns or villages lying to the westward of the Alleganies, where printing offices are established.

(pg 94)
Chap. XXVII of East Tennessee, or Holston.—Cultures, &c.

East Tennessee, or Holston, is situated between the highest part of the Alleganys, and Cumberland Mountains: in length, it comprises an extent of nearly a hundred and forty miles; the principal differences between it and West Tennessee are that the (pg 95) lime-stone appears to lie deeper; that the beds of it, which form the mass, inclined to the horizon, are divided at small intervals, by strata of Quartz; and, finally, that the country is watered by a great number of small rivers, descending from the neighbouring mountains, which cross it in all directions. The best land is on their banks.

Maize also forms one of the principal branches of culture here, but it seldom grows to a greater height than seven or eight feet, and thirty bushels per acre is considered a very good crop. The nature of the soil, which is rather stony, seems better adapted to the growth of wheat, rye, and oats, which are, consequently, cultivated more here than in Cumberland. Cotton is not grown in any quantity, on account of the cold, which sets in very early. It may be inferred, from what has been said, that Holston is in every respect inferior in fertility to Cumberland and Kentucky.

To turn the superabundance of their grain to advantage, the inhabitants breed a great number of cattle, which they send a distance of 500 miles to the maritime towns of the central and Southern states. Very few of these animals are lost in their passage, although they have a great number of rivers to cross, and the country is nearly an uninterrupted forest, added to which they are extremely wild, from being accustomed to the woods.

This part of Tennessee began to be inhabited in 1775, and its population has increased so much, that, at this time, the number of its inhabitants is estimated at 70,000, including three or four thousand negro slaves.

Presbyterian ministers

dominated education during the early history of the county. Dr. Samuel Doak, educator and minister of Mount Bethel Church, obtained a charter for a private Presbyterian academy in 1784 which became Washington College in 1795. Doak served as its president until 1818, when he resigned to establish, with his son Samuel Witherspoon Doak, another classical school called Tusculum College. In 1794 Dr. Hezekiah Balch founded Greeneville College, the first college west of the Alleghenies. Tusculum and Greeneville Colleges merged to form the Tusculum College that endures today. The county also is associated with the founding of Methodism in Tennessee as the site of Ebenezer Church, established in 1792 by the Earnest family. An early Quaker meeting took place at New Hope Meeting near Ripley Creek in 1795.

Methodist

Holston Methodism From Its Origin to the Present Time Vol I
by Price, R.N. **Binding:** Hard Cover **Publisher:** Publishing House of the M.E. Church, South **Date Published:** 1904
Description. 'From the introduction of Methodism into the Holston Country to the year 1804'Confirmation on all Domestic Orders!

Preface

The provincial character of the Holston Conference, hemmed in, as it is, on all sides by mountains, weakens the interest of our people in the events of the outside world, ad intensifies their interest in whatever is local.

Short notices of obscure men have been prepared for an Appendix

One hundred year portrait 1775-1875
by Richard Harrison Doughty

Page 111 Methodism in The Greeneville Area

Van Pelt's Chapel. One of the first Methodist societies in Tennessee was organized in the home of Benjamin Van Pelt, and a chapel bearing his name was erected before 1792 (21) This church was built on the north side of Lick Creek, on what is now the road from the mouth of Lick Creek to the village of Mosheim, about four miles north of Warrensburg. (22) Van Pelt's residence was one of Bishop Asbury's favorite stopping places as is recorded in his Journal:

Chapter VI page 135 From 1788 to 1792

One of the first Societies in East Tennessee was organized in the residence of Benjamin Vanpelt, in Greene County, and a Chapel named Vanpelt's chapel was built before the year 1792. This was the fourth Methodist meetinghouse in the Holston Country, and the third in Tennessee, of which we have any account. Possibly it would fall lower on the list if we had the dates of erection of all early meetinghouses in Southwestern Virginia. How long before the erection of Vanpelts' Chapel the Society existed at that place, we know not; but certainly not long. At an early date there was a camp ground at Carter's Station, in the western part of Greene County, and possibly a Society and Chapel.

In 1792 a Society was organized on the south bank of the Nollichucky, a few miles east of Greeneville. This society consisted at that time largely of the families of Henry and Felix Earnest. Soon after the organization of the society a meetinghouse was built and christened Ebenezer. The Society having been organized between July and September, 1792, it is possible that the meetinghouse was built that fall.

Page 192 the Bishop's Journal says

spring 1792

"Saturday 6 – Rode to Greene, and crossed the Grand Island ford of Nollichucky. The lowlands are very rich, the uplands barren. Stopped and fed at Greene Courthouse. Here was brought a corpse to the grave in a covered carriage drawn by four horses. Solemn sight! Be instructed, O my soul! A whisky toper gave me a cheer of success as one of John Wesley's congregation! I came on alone through heavy rains, over bad hills and poor ridges, to Brother Vanpelt's, on Lick Creek. He is a brother to Peter, my old friend, first friend on Staten Island. I was weary, damp, and hungry; but had a comfortable habitation, and kind, loving people, who heard, refreshed, and fed me. We had a large congregation at Brother Vanpelt's Chapel, where I had liberty in speaking. I left the young men to entertain the people a while longer, and returned and read Mr. Westley's sermon on riches.

The Reshaping of Everyday life 1790-1840

Southerners worked a longer growing season and faced a punishing hot summer climate

In the winter, his father felled trees, split raild and built fences

At 11 he was given an old gun to scare the pests away from the fields

At 12 he was able to hold the plough and guide the horse

At 13 he began to split rails and build fences himself

The Tennessee Yeomen, 1840-1860.

(Hardcover) by Blanche Henry Clark **Hardcover:** 200 pages **Publisher:** Octagon Books (June 1971) **Language:** English **ISBN:** 0374916691

Nor was a man's prosperity due to the fact that he owned a slave; he owned a slave merely because he had a bit of surplus cash to invest. (p 8)

Among the small farmers of East Tennessee, as high as 93 per cent were non-slaveowners - - (p 9)

Economic status of more than one half of the non-slaveholders compared very favorably with that of the slaveholders who owned similar amounts of land. (9 10)

Finally a school system, inadequate indeed, was established in 1830. In 1839 the revenue for schools amounted to only 56 cents per pupil. The term lasted four months, and the teacher was paid 16 dollars. It was not until Andrew Johnson was governor, in 1853, that any definite measures for the advancement of education were taken. A school rate of two and one-half cents on each $100 of taxable property and 25 cents on each poll was set (p 15)

The Agricultural Sections of Tennessee - 8 geological divisions

1. Beginning at the eastern boundary of the state is the Unaka region, the mountainous area I which Johnson County is located. It is impossible to bring the land into extensive cultivation because the topography is rugged and the soil is generally poor and thin - - - -   The valleys of East Tennessee form a second geological division. The land, containing limestone, shale, and sandstone, forms many long, rich agricultural valleys, in which the general farm crops can be produced. All of the cereals, wheat in particular, can be grown abundantly in the area. Greene, located in this valley country, is one of the fairly prosperous counties in the state, and world have ranked even higher in early days had markets been more accessible. (p 23)

Landholding and Slaveholding status of heads of families in 1850 and 1860 in Greene county

	1850	1860
Total heads	2,168	2,557
% Slaveholders	9.96	8.80
% non Slaveholders	90.04	91.20
% landless	39.99	35.55
% landowners	60.01	64.45

(Page 28)

Number of Acres of Land Listed in Census of Greene county in 1850 and 1860

	1850	1860
Improved	124,445	150,854
Unimproved	186,560	193.049
Total	311,005	343,903

(page 33)

Size of Acreage owned by Landowning Heads of Families in Greene County in 1850 and 1860

acres	1850	1860
1 – 50	6.92	9.47
51 -100	17.52	19.05
101 – 200	36.20	36.17
201 – 300	16.76	16.63
301 – 400	7.53	5.46
401 – 500	5.00	3.40
501 – 1,000	4.92	3.82
1,001 – 5,000	1.69	1.09
5,001 – over		0.06

(page 35)

Landholding status of Slaveholding and non-Slaveholding heads of families in Greene county,

	1850	1860
Slaveholders		
Total heads	216	225
% landless	6.94	4.00
% landowners	93.06	96.00
Non-slaveholders		
Total heads	1,952	2,332
% landless	43.65	38.59
% landowners	56.35	61.41

(page 43)

Size of Landholdings of of families in Greene county

	Slaveholding heads		Non-Slaveholding	
acres	1850	1860	1850	1860
1 – 50	2.99	.93	7.64	10.75
51 -100	6.97	7.87	19.45	20.74
101 – 200	25.87	27.31	38.09	37.50
201 – 300	15.42	21.30	17.00	15.92
301 – 400	11.44	12.04	6.82	4.47
401 – 500	12.44	9.26	3.64	2.51
501 – 1,000	15.92	13.43	2.91	2.37
1,001 – 5,000	8.96	6.48	.36	.28
5,001 – over				

(page 47 and 48)

Size of Acreage Cultivated

Percentage of	Slaveholding heads		Non-Slaveholding	
acres	1850	1860	1850	1860
1 – 50	2.99	.93	7.64	10.75
51 -100	6.97	7.87	19.45	20.74
101 – 200	25.87	27.31	38.09	37.50
201 – 300	15.42	21.30	17.00	15.92
301 – 400	11.44	12.04	6.82	4.47
401 – 500	12.44	9.26	3.64	2.51
501 – 1,000	15.92	13.43	2.91	2.37
1,001 – 5,000	8.96	6.48	.36	.28
5,001 – over				

(page 57)

Look at page 167 on for Raders in the 1860 Greene county Agricultural census

Comparison of percentage of Slaveholding and nonslaveholding
Heads of families who owned more than 300 acres in Greene county

	1850	1860
Slaveholder	48.76	41.21
Nonslaveholder	13.76	9.70

In a rich valley county, such as Greene, only slightly above 35% were 50 acre farmers, while the larger proportion cultivated as much as 100 or 200 acres. Men in this county often raised marketable crops, rather than confining themselves to subsistence farming as did their neighbors in more mountainous areas.

(Page 54)

In Greene County the majority cultivated 51 to 100 acres (p 56)

Greene exceeded her neighboring counties in land values. The average estimate per acre in 1840 was $3.64 ---The fertile valley lands of Greene County were the basis for the evaluation in that county being greater than others in the area (p 60)

The percentage of non-slaveholders in East Tennessee ranged from 84 to 92 per cent. Land values were not low in this area because there were so many non-slaveholding farmers, but there were so many non-slaveholding farmers because the land was poor. – as the land was often unsuited for production on a marketable scale, especially of crops such as cotton and tobacco, slave labor was not profitable for the section and was not prevalent. (p 61)

In Greene county the land of the slaveholder always exceeded that of the non-slaveholder in value by $125 to $250. This is explicable in 1850 because the Slaveholder always owned more unimproved land. (p 64)

In 1854 State of Tennessee bonds bearing interest at 6 per cent (p 81)

In 1854 – Scanty exhibits as a result of the drouths, bad weather at the time of the Fair and financial panic were all causes of the decline. (p 91)

In the 1830's and continuing until the time of the war, many Tennesseans began to question the wisdom of the – same land-killing procedure which had depleted the soil of the eastern states – practiced in Tennessee and fertile soil had been extravagantly wasted (p 111)

Rather than resort to scientific methods of preservation and restoration of the soil, the farmers had merely cultivated new acres as the old lands had been exhausted. (p 112)

Deep and careful plowing and sub-soiling, which would help its preservation, were urged (p 115)

Suggestions for diversification were very much the same. -- , suggested as the staple products fot Tennessee, corn, oats, wheat, the grasses, and livestock, - - - of great importance in the rotation were clover, turnips, tares, peas, and beans, and other leguminous plants which ut back into the soil the nitrogen exhausted by some crops. (p117)

In 1857 - - - it was fully realized that the area in East Tennessee between the Cumberland and Allegheny mountains was an extensive and valuable wheat growing region. --- after 1850, the completion of the East Tennessee and Georgia Railroad to Knoxville - - opened an outlet to the Atlantic ports (p 118)

East Tennessee also produced much stock. The vast amounts of unimproved land available in the mountain areas made the cost nominal. Often stock was bought for a mere trifle, allowed to graze, and, when fattened, sold at a handsome profit to drovers going to the coast or farther in the South (p 121)

As late as 1859 one correspondent reported that at no period had an equal amount of stock been driven from East Tennessee, and never had the prices been as good (p 127) Nashville "Union and American", January 16, 1859

The Improvement in farm Implements

In frontier days in Tennessee the crudest methods of agriculture were employed all over the state, and in later days these were maintained to some extent in East Tennessee, where the topography of the land and, in some instances, the poverty of the farmers made the use of improved machinery impracticable. At the beginning of the nineteenth century clumsy wooden plows, harrows, sickles, scythes, hoes, and an occasional crude threshing machine were the usual farm implements.

Gradually the prejudice against iron plows, arising out of fear of the metal damaging the soil, was dissipated. (page 130)

Harvesting of grains was done first with the scythe and sickle and later with a cradle. This method was continued in East Tennessee for a considerable period after reapers were used in other sections of the state.

By 1840, threshing machines were used rather extensively in all sections except Eat Tennessee. (page 131)

Silk production

In 1840, -- east Tennessee produced 501 pounds (p 135)

The peak of the silk fad in Tennessee must have been reached 1843

By 1850 the counties in East Tennessee led in the production of silk.

By 1860 the production was down to 71 pounds for the whole state

(p 139)

As wheat became a more marketable crop, some of the counties, especially Greene, had a tremendous increase in production. Corn was also a good crop in the area (p156)

Slaves

It is not the owning of slaves which made him more prosperous. He was able to buy a few slaves because he was a bit more prosperous

Rader land records in Greene County Tennessee

All Rader land Records before the War

	Rader	Date		acres	from		book	page	Parcel	
1	John	1801	22-Sep	200	Thomas Province		24	186		
2	Phillip	1804	26-Sep	290	Thomas Keef	Grantee	7	50	#114	Lick Creek
3	Jacob Rader			22.5	Saymore Catching	Grantee	7	53		not plotted
3	Jacob	1805	14-Nov	188	Danial Slavens	Grantee	7	54	#744	Lick Creek
4	Jacob	1805	14-Oct	22	Danial Slavens	Grantee	7	54	#1339B	Lick Creek
5	Jacob	1805	14-Nov	43	Danial Slavens	Grantee	7	54	#1339A	Lick Creek
6	Phillip			290	Jackson	Vincent	8	180	grantor	
7	Jacob	1808	22-Nov	196	Isaac Walker	Grantee	8	417	#1339C	Lick Creek
8	Henry	1810	9-Jan	140	Andrew McPherron		9	36	#313	Lick Creek
9	Henry	1810	9-Jan	146	Andrew McPherron		9	36	#313B	Lick Creek
10	Henry	1810	11-Aug	100	William McPherron		1B	378	#2398	Lick Creek
9	Henry	1812	24-Jun	100	Tennessee grant		1B	378	Grantee	
10	John	1812	16-Sep	110	Henry Cross		9	438	#1326A	Lick Creek
11	John	1812	16-Sep	50	Henry Cross		9	439	#1326B	Lick Creek
12	Robert Reader			100	Elijah Billingsley		11	183		not plotted
13	John	1817	6-Jan	20	tennessee grant				#13516	Lick Creek
14	John Sr	1819	23-Feb	200	Leady	John	12	37	grantor	
15	Jacob Rader			land	John&Peggy Rader		12	231		not plotted
15	Jacob	1820	22-Mar	50	Andrew Bryan		12	411	#1335A	Lick Creek
16	Jacob			50	Bryan	Andrew	12	411	Grantee	
17	Jacob	1820	22-Mar	119	Andrew Bryan	Grantee	12	412	#342	Lick Creek
18	William	1821		100	Samuel Dunwoody		13	7	#33	Little Chucky
17	Jacob Rader	1820	13-Nov	land	Peter&Elizabeth Rader		13	84		not plotted

Source Citations

#	Name	Year	Date	Acres	From/To		Book	Page	Ref	Location
20	Jacob	1825	14-May	50	Tenn Land Grant				#27123	southside
21	Jacob	1826	24-Jan	50	Tenn Land Grant				#27124	southside
22	Jacob	1826	24-Jan	50	Tenn Land Grant				#26602	southside
23	John	1826	9-Dec	25	tennessee grant				#1002	Lick Creek
21	Casper	1828	27-Oct	30	Jesse Self(dec)		15	117	#3573	Lick Creek
23	Casper	1828	27-Oct	30	Self	J.B., Jesse	15	117	Grantee	
24	William	1829	15-Mar	48	John Love		15	123	#1339D	Lick Creek
25	Casper	1829	1-Nov	175	Isaac Mace		19	48	#15869	Lick Creek
26	Jacob	1830	29-Mar	200	Tenn Land Grant				#27125	southside
25	Jacob Rader and John Brady	1830	19-Jun	300	Tenn Land Grant				#1292	southside
26	William Rader			15	John Love		15	124		not plotted
27	Jacob (est), William			50	Love	John	15	124	Grantee	
28	Peter&Elizabeth Rader			part	Jacob Rader		17	277		not plotted
29	Jesse&Martin Rader			part	Jacob Rader		17	277		not plotted
30	Joseph&William Rader			part	Jacob Rader		17	277		not plotted
31	Jacob Estate			Part	Rader	Elizabeth, Peter	17	277	grantor	
29	Jacob Estate			Part	Cobble	Sally ET VIR	17	277	grantor	
30	Jacob Estate			Part	Willoughby	Eliza ET Vir	17	277	grantor	
31	Jacob Estate			Part	Rader	Jesse, Martin G	17	277	grantor	
32	Jacob Estate			Part	Rader	Joseph, William	17	277	grantor	
33	John	1832	12-Jul	40	tennessee grant				#23491	Lick Creek
34	Andrew	1835	14-Feb	146	Adam Kinser		17	339	#1546	Lick Creek
35	John Sr	1835	6-Nov	TD	Etter	John (TR)	18	62	grantor	
33	William	1836	1-May	10.5	James Patterson		18	167	#17928	Little Chucky
34	William	1837	3-Jul	2	tennessee grant				#21685	Little Chucky
35	John	1839	16-Feb	600	tennessee grant				#25102	Lick Creek

#	Name	Year	Date	Acres	Party 1	Party 2	Vol	Pg	Ref	Location
36										
37	William	1837	30-Sep	100	Henry Feezell		19	67	#1711	Little Chucky
38	John	1838	9-Jan	86	Abraham Peters		19	158	#1335	southside
39	John	1838	9-Jan	61	Abraham Peters		19	158	#13091	southside
37	Elizabeth	1829	5-Oct	22	John Love		19	252	#1339G	Lick Creek
38	Jacob (by shff)			Int	Gillespie	George T Et AL	19	275	grantor	
39	Andrew			145	McDaniel	James	19	328	grantor	
40	Willaim Rader			8 ¾	Alfred Russell		19	362		not plotted
41	John (Sr)			20	Borin	Abraham	20	22	grantor	
42	Andrew	1839	2-Nov	100	Isaac N Magill		20	99	#545	Little Chucky
43	John Jr			TD	Murray	Rubin TR	20	150	grantor	
41	Admins William Et Al			98	Shields	John	20	164	grantor	
42	John Rader			48	John Love		20	238		not plotted
43	Admins William Et Al			82	Bowers	John	20	263	grantor	
44	Joseph	1840	27-Aug	65	Vincent Jackson		20	340	#1358C	Lick Creek
45	Jesse&Martin Rader			86	Jacob Cobble		20	410		not plotted
46	William	1841	31-Mar	106	Alfred Russell		20	438	#1339E	Lick Creek
47	William Rader			2 tracts	Alfred Russell		20	438		not plotted
45	William	1841	5-Apr	21	Alfred Russell (Love)		20	440	#1358d	Little Chucky
46	Andrew Rader			7	Nancy Love		20	513		not plotted
47	William	1841	31-Mar	10	Alfred Russell		20	563	#342	Lick Creek
48	William Rader			land	Peter,Jesse,Martin Rader		20	563		not plotted
49	Jesse, Peter R, Martin G			59	Rader	William	20	563	grantor	
50	Jesse	1833	13-Apr	80	John Love		20	604	#1358C	Lick Creek
51	Joseph	1841	9-Dec	137	Alfred Russell		20	640	#1358a	Lick Creek
49	Jesse	1841	19-Jun	90	Alfred Russell		20	640	#1339F	Lick Creek
50	Henry Rader jr			29	Robert McPherron		20	758		not plotted

Source Citations

#	Name	Year	Date	Acres	Other Party		Vol	Page	Ref	Location
51	William Rader			2 tracts	Martin G Rader		21	34		not plotted
52	Martin G (by Shff)	1843	20-Feb	2 trs	Rader	William	21	34	grantor	
53	Willaim Rader			2 tracts	Martin G Rader		21	74		not plotted
54	Jacob	1843	10-Oct	112	James Woods		21	263	#22119	southside
53	Jesse Rader			51	John Willoughby		21	280		not plotted
54	William Rader			35	John Willoughby		21	281		not plotted
55	William	1844	21-Aug	310	Adam Proffit		21	348	#1272	Little Chucky
56	John Rader			150	John Love		21	502		not plotted
57	William Rader			25	Henry Feezel		21	707		not plotted
58	Eli	1862		49.5	John Welty		22	190		southside
59	William (of henry)	1846	27-Oct	250	John Nelson (geo T Gilispie		22	219	#1913	Little Chucky
57	William Rader			250	John G Nelson		22	219		not plotted
58	Jesse	1846	2-Nov	105	Henderson Lady		22	235	#1339C	Lick Creek
59	Peter R	1845	13-Mar	7.5	John Rhea (dec)		22	393	#1018	Little Chucky
60	Peter R Rader			1	John Rhea		22	395		not plotted
61	Andrew	1848	15-Feb	325	George Andes		23	108	#302	Little Chucky
62	Andrew	1847	22-Feb	107	Shields	John	23	124	grantor	
63	Jacob & Lorina	1848	21-Feb	168	Tenn Land Grant				#26161	southside
64	Henry			INT	Mace	Jackson	23	128	grantor	
61	Jacob (Et UX Et Al			40	Nease	Henry	23	287	grantor	
62	Jacob (Et UX Et Al			25	Nease	Jacob	23	288	grantor	
63	Valentine S	1849	26-Jan	172	David H. Good		23	309	#1358	Little Chucky
64	Catherine	1849	8-Jun	120	Abraham Peters heirs		23	442	#9103	southside
65	Catherina (Et Al			159	Peters	Jacob	23	443	grantor	
66	Catherina (Et Al			130	Chuck	John Freshour	23	598	grantor	
67	James M, Samuel ET AL ET UX			3 trs	Black	Christopher	23	601	grantor	
65	John Rader			200	Thomas Province		24	186		not

66	Joseph			TD		Jackson	Thomas TR	24	213	grantor	plotted
67	Joseph			137		Crosby	Lemuel	24	222	grantor	
68	Joseph			76		Crosby	Lemuel	24	223	grantor	
69	Joseph			137		Yoe	Benjamine	24	253	grantor	
70	Joseph			TD		Crosby	Lemuel Jr	24	268	grantor	
71	William Rader			76		Joseph Rader		24	372		not plotted
69	Joseph			76		Rader	William	24	372	grantor	
70	Andrew			INT		Henry	Robert	24	399	grantor	
71	Hiram Rader			2 tracts		John Freshour(est)		24	517		not plotted
72	Cathrine Rader			2 tracts		John Freshour(est)		24	517		not plotted
73	Elizabeth Rader			2 tracts		John Freshour(est)		24	517		not plotted
74	Barbara Rader			2 tracts		John Freshour(est)		24	517		not plotted
75	John Rader			2 tracts		John Freshour(est)		24	517		not plotted
73	Mary Rader			2 tracts		John Freshour(est)		24	517		not plotted
74	Michail Rader			2 tracts		John Freshour(est)		24	517		not plotted
75	Jacob Rader			2 tracts		John Freshour(est)		24	517		not plotted
76	Margert Rader			2 tracts		John Freshour(est)		24	517		not plotted
77	Peter Rader			2 tracts		John Freshour(est)		24	517		not plotted
78	Coleen Rader			2 tracts		John Freshour(est)		24	517		not plotted
79	Abraham	1851	1-Oct	50		Wm Conway Maloney		25	22	#25376	southside
77	Joseph	1850	28-Nov	65		Jackson	V L	25	38	grantor	
78	John A Rader			140		William Day		25	67		not plotted
79	Abraham			50		Renner	John Sr.	25	85	grantor	
80	Henry Sr (est)			132		Black	Joseph	25	470	grantor	
81	William			9		Susong	Alexander	25	635	grantor	
82	Henry	1853	23-Aug	55		Samuel L Jenkins		26	182	#18103A	Lick Creek
83	Henry	1853	23-Aug	36.5		Samuel L Jenkins		26	194	#18103	Lick Creek
81	Jacob Rader			12 ½		John McKay		26	346		not plotted
82	Martin	1852	9-Sep	96		Alfred Russell		26	425	#1339	Lick Creek

Source Citations

#	Name	Year	Date	Acres	Other Party (last)	Other Party (first)	Vol	Page	Ref	Location
83	Peter	1841	3-Aug	25	Alfred Russell		26	492	#1359C	Lick Creek
84	Peter R Rader			2tracts	Alfred Russell		26	492		not plotted
85	Henry	1854	28-Dec	91.5	Black	Christopher	27	14	grantor	
86	John			150	Jackson	Thomas	27	38	grantor	
87	Reuben M.			8.5	Drake	William W	27	167	grantor	
85	Henry			137	Black	Christopher	27	172	grantor	
86	Valentine S Rader			20	Alfred Russell		27	418		not plotted
87	Andrew	1855	dec	41.25	Samuel Donwoody (dec)		27	453	#33	Little Chucky
88	Jesse	1855	24-Dec	54	Thomas P Morgan		27	469	#1359F	Lick Creek
89	Andrew Rader			3	Andrew Andes		27	499		not plotted
90	Andrew Rader			134	Alfred Russell		27	599		not plotted
91	Reuben Rader			2tracts	Thomas Self		28	61		not plotted
89	Reuben Rader			9 ½	William W Drake		28	189		not plotted
90	Reuben M (Et Ux)	1856	29-Oct	int	Hunter	James M	28	249	grantor	
91	James M.			8	Hale	John	28	389	grantor	
92	I.N. Rader			50 ½	William Blair		28	528		not plotted
93	Reuben M			Lot	McCollough	Alexander	28	545	grantor	
94	Reuben Rader			43 ¾	Joseph Worley		28	652		not plotted
95	Reuben Rader			50	Joseph Worley		28	653		not plotted
93	Henry	1858	4-Jan	159.5	Martin Welty		29	71	#1245	Little Chucky
94	William			R of W	E. tenn & Va RR		29	160	grantor	
95	Peter R			7.5	Rhea	Mary Sr.	29	375	grantor	
96	jesse			R of W	E. tenn & Va RR		29	410	grantor	
97	Peter R			R of W	E. tenn & Va RR		29	413	grantor	
98	William			R of W	E. tenn & Va RR		29	420	grantor	
99	Andrew G			102	Guthries	James, Lewis	29	477	grantor	
97	Andrew Rader			1	Jacob Baughard		29	479		not plotted
98	Andrew Rader			6 ½	Isaac Bible		29	480		not plotted
99	Andrew G Rader			13 ¼	Andrew Moore		29	494		not plotted
100	Jesse			105	Walace	Riley	29	523	grantor	

#	Name	Year	Date	Acres	Other Party	First	Bk	Pg	Ref	Location
101	Jesse			54	Pinkston	Francis	29	583	grantor	
102	Willaim Sr.			10	Reed	John	29	632	grantor	
103	Peter	1860		50	Riley Wallace		30	79	#1359B	Lick Creek
101	Peter R Rader			50	Riley Wallace		30	80		not plotted
102	Andrew Rader			Interest	Hannah Smith		30	280		not plotted
103	Andrew Rader			20	Jacob Woolaver		30	286		not plotted
104	Andrew Rader			Interest	Katharine,Phebe Smith		30	395		not plotted
105	Eli	1860	18-Feb	63.75	Alfred Gable		30	588	#1335	southside
106	Reuben M Rader			land	Andrew G Rader		30	637		not plotted
107	Andrew	1860		384	tennessee grant		30	779	#30049	Little Chucky
105	Jane P (britton)	1858	4-Nov	135	Danial Britton (dec)		31	28	#31	Little Chucky
106	Rebecca (britton)	1858	4-Nov	397	Danial Britton (dec)		31	28	#1549	Little Chucky
107	Jesse	1860	18-Jun	77	Franklin Pinkston		31	28	#1359E	Lick Creek
108	John	1861	11-Jun	72	Joseph Basinger & Catherine Ricker		31	507	#1358	Little Chucky
109	John Rader			72 ½	Joseph Basinger		31	507		not plotted
110	Andrew Rader			37	Israel G Smith		31	554		not plotted
111	Reuben M Rader			land	Thomas Jackson		31	554		not plotted
109	Peter R Rader			37	Stephen Courtney		32	487		not plotted
110	John A Rader			94	Andrew G Rader		32	544		not plotted
111	John N	1862	9-Feb	96	Anderson W Walker		33	2	#856	southside
112	J..N.Rader			91	A.W. Walker		33	2		not plotted
113	John	1858	5-Oct	56.75	William Matthew		33	377	#19037	Little Chucky
114	William Rader			325	Andrew Rader		33	563		not plotted
115	William Rader			134	Andrew Rader		33	563		not plotted
113	William Rader			3	Andrew Rader		33	563		not plotted
114	Danial Rader			8	William Rader(etux)		34	162		not plotted
115	J.N.Rader			interest	A.W.Walmer		34	189		not

116	William Rader	13	#26692	Tn Land Grant		not plotted
117	William Rader	5	#25710	Tn Land Grant		not plotted
118	Andrew Rader	2	#29393	Tn Land Grant		not plotted
119	William			Evans	James	grantor
120	John (Et Al by C&M)			Lee	Caroline, James	grantor

Descendants of Casper Rader Sr as they should appear in the 1830 TN Census

----

| 192 | 2 | Henry | Reader | 1 2 | 1 | ‖ | 1 1 1 |

Two slave children under 10 and 1 female slave age 10-24

m62 |--2-Heinrich 'Henry' Rader Sr b. 1768, PA, d. 1 Sep 1851, Greene County, Tennessee

m22 | |--3-Daniel Rader   b. 1808, TN, d. 25 Jul 1854, Greene County, Tennessee

m20 | |--3-Henry Thomas Rader Jr. b. 1810, TN, d. 3 Jul 1860, , , Cooke, Tennessee

m18 | |--3-Andrew W. S Rader   b. 1812, TN, d. 10 Sep 1889, Timber Ridge, Greene Co, TN

f58 | +Catherine Etter   b. Abt 1772, PA, d. Abt 1847, Greene County, Tennessee

f27 | |--3-Rachel Rader   b. Abt 1803, VA, d. 1855, Williamson Co, IL

f14 | |--3-Catherine M. Rader   b. 1816, TN, d. Bef 1859, Greene County, Tennessee

f11 | |--3-Issabella Rader   b. 1819, TN, d. 1 Sep 1879

| 188 | 9 | John | Reader | 1 1 1 | 1 | ‖ | 2 1 1 |

M61 |--2-John Rader b. Abt 1769, PA, d. 3 Feb 1840, Greene County, Tennessee

M20 | |--3-Samuel Rader   b. Abt 1810, TN, d. Bef 1850, , , Greene, Tennessee

M   age 15-20

| M | age 10-15 |
| M | age 5-10 |

F54 | +Mary Etter b. 1776, VA, d. 6 Mar 1848,   Greene County, Tennessee

F22 | |--3-Sophia Rader   b. 1808, VA, d. 13 Feb 1868, Coles Co. Illinois

F17 | |--3-Isabella 'Ibbie' Rader   b. 1813, TN, d. Feb 1884, Hawkins County, Tennessee

F11 | |--3-Lucinda Rader   b. 1819, TN, d. 3 Aug 1893, Tennessee

F10 | |--3-Emaline Rader   b. 1820, VA

| 192 | 10 | Elizabeth | Reader | 1 1 | ‖ | 1 |

d|--2-Jacob Rader   b. Abt 1772, PA, d. 22 Jul 1822, Greene County, Tennessee

m19 | |--3-Martin George Rader   b. 1811, TN, d. Bef 1850, Capt. Mcpherons, Greene Co, TN

m11 | |--3-Peter R. Rader   b. 1819, TN, d.16 May 1877, Bulls Gap, Greene County, Tennessee

f59 | +Elizabeth Woods Been Hedrick b. 1771, VA, d. 1860, Greene County, Tennessee

| 193 | 4 | John | Reader | 2 3 | 1 | ‖ | 1 |

m37 | |henrys--3-John Rader   b. 1793, VA, d. 8 Nov 1839, Caney Branch, Greene County, Tennessee

M35 | | johns --3-John Rader Jr.   b. 1795, VA, d. After 1860, Greene County, Tennessee

| 192 | 8 | Jesse | Reader | 1 | ‖ 1 1 | 1 |

m26 | | jacobs --3-Jesse Rader   b. 1804, VA, d. 1890, Greene County, Tennessee

| 188 | 18 | Casper | Reader | 1 | 1 | ‖1 | 1 |

m29 | | henrys --3-Casper J. Rader Jr.   b. 1801, TN, d. 6 Oct 1883, Brizil, Clay Co, IN, Or MO

| 192 | 4 | Joseph | Reader | 1 | 1 | ‖ | 1 |

m29 | | jacobs --3-Joseph Rader   b. Abt 1801, VA d. , Clay County, Illinois

| 192 | 3 | William | Reader | 1 | 1 | 1 | ‖ 1 | 1 |

m31 | |jacobs--3-William Rader   b. 1799, VA, d. 25 Nov 1877, Mohawk, Greene Co, TN

m32 | | henrys --3-William W. Rader   b. 1798, VA, d. 16 Apr 1880, Greene County, Tennessee

M25 | | johns --3-William Rader   b. Abt 1805, TN

f18 | | jacobs --3-Susannah Rader   b. Abt 1812, TN, d. 1892

f22 | | jacobs --3-Elizabeth 'Eliza' Rader   b. 1808, VA d. 27 Dec 1893, Greene County, Tennessee

f24 | | jacobs --3-Sarah 'Sally' Rader   b. 1806, VA d. Bef 1860, Midway, Greene Co., TN

F24 | | johns --3-Mary Rader   b. 1806, VA d. Bef | | 1847

F29 | | johns --3-Sarah 'Sally' A. Rader   b. 1801, VA, d. 18 Aug 1886, McMINN COUNTY, TENNESSEE

F31 | |johns--3-Elizabeth Rader   b. 1799, VA, d. 13 Sep 1871, Mohawk, Greene Co, TN

F33 | |johns--3-Catherine "Caty" Rader b. Abt 1797, VA

f35 | |henrys--3-Elizabeth 'Betsey' Rader b. 1795, VA, d. 29 Sep 1866, Warrensburg, Greene Co, TN

f36 | |henrys--3-Mary Rader   b. Abt 1794, VA, d. 6 Mar 1848, Greene County, Tennessee

In Virginia ??

d|--2-William Rader b. Abt 1770, PA, d. 1802, Wythe County, Virginia

d| +Christina 'Diney' Helvey Or Alvery b. 1770, VA, d. Apr 1815

f30 | |--3-Mary Ann Rader   b. 1800, VA

f30| |--3-Susan "Susannah" Rader b. 1800, VA

f28 | |--3-Samuel Rader   b. 1802, VA

| +Christina Helvy [83944]
| +Tiney Alvery [94690]

United states census records

I include the Census records so that you can try to resolve the questions remaining

1830 Raders in Greene County

PAGE NO	LINE NO	LAST_NAME	FIRST_NAME	FWM0_5	FWM5_10	FWM10_15	FWM15_20	FWM20_30	FWM30_40	FWM40_50	FWM50_60	FWM60_70	FWF0_5	FWF5_10	FWF10_15	FWF15_20	FWF20_30	FWF30_40	FWF40_50	FWF50_60
161	14	Jacob	Reader	2	2	2			1									1		
188	9	John	Reader		1	1	1				1				2	1	1			1
188	18	Casper	Reader	1				1					1				1			
191	18	Max	Rudder	1	1				1				2	1	1			1		
192	2	Henry	Reader					1	2			1			1	1	1			1
192	3	William	Reader	1	1				1					1			1			
192	4	Joseph	Reader	1				1									1			
192	8	Jesse	Reader					1					1	1			1			
192	10	Elizabeth	Reader			1	1												1	
193	4	John	Reader	2	3				1								1			
207	last	Henry	Ritter		2				1				1	1	1		1			
209	4	Danl	Ritter			1	2	2				1		1		1	1			1

1840 Raders in Greene County

LINE_NO	LAST_NAME	FWM0_5	FWM5_10	FWM10_15	FWM15_20	FWM20_30	FWM30_40	FWM40_50	FWM50_60	FWM60_70	FWM70_80	FWF0_5	FWF5_10	FWF10_15	FWF15_20	FWF20_30	FWF30_40	FWF40_50	FWF50_60	FWF60_70	FWF70_80	TOTAL
11	Andrew	1				1						1	1				1					5
5	John				1			1						1						1		4
10	Casper	1	1	1			1					2	1			1						8
b-5	Hanah	1	1	2	1	1						1		1		1		1				10
b	Catherine		2	2	2	1													1	1		9

	Name													Total
16	Henry	1		1				1			1	2		6
18	Martin G	1		1				2	1			1		6
20	Peter				1								1	2
26	Jesse		1		1			1		1		1		5
1	Joseph		2	1		1			2		1	1		8
3	Wm	2	1	1	1	1				1		1		8
25	Henry			1			1		1		1			4
23	Wm				1					1				2
29	Wm	1	2	2	1		1		1	1	1			10

1850 Raders in Greene County

Given Name	Age	Birth	Sex	Race	Birth Place	County	Locality	M432-Roll	Page
AB	24	1826	M	W	TN	COCKE	11-DIST	874	399
ISAAC	3	1847	M	W	TN	COCKE	11-DIST	874	399
MALINDA	24	1826	F	W	TN	COCKE	11-DIST	874	399
SAML J	1	1849	M	W	TN	COCKE	11-DIST	874	399
ELIZABETH	30	1820	F	W	TN	COCKE	11-DIST	874	401
MARTIN L	5	1845	M	W	TN	COCKE	11-DIST	874	401
DANL	21	1829	M	W	TN	COCKE	11-DIST	874	401
JOHN A	3	1847	M	W	TN	COCKE	11-DIST	874	401
BOHEMIA	27	1823	F	W	TN	COCKE	11-DIST	874	401
HANNAH	0	1850	F	W	TN	COCKE	11-DIST	874	401
POLLY A	3	1847	F	W	TN	COCKE	11-DIST	874	401
SAML	26	1824	M	W	TN	COCKE	11-DIST	874	401
GEORGE E	1	1849	M	W	TN	COCKE	11-DIST	874	401
JAMES M	31	1819	M	W	TN	COCKE	11-DIST	874	401
ARANIUS	1	1849	M	W	TN	COCKE	11-DIST	874	403
MARY MAG	29	1821	F	W	TN	COCKE	11-DIST	874	403
ADAM F	1	1849	M	W	TN	COCKE	11-DIST	874	403
DARIUS	0	1850	M	W	TN	COCKE	11-DIST	874	403
JOS	27	1823	M	W	TN	COCKE	11-DIST	874	403
ISAAC F	8	1842	M	W	TN	COCKE	11-DIST	874	403
CHRISTINA	3	1847	F	W	TN	COCKE	11-DIST	874	403
SARAH C	5	1845	F	W	TN	COCKE	11-DIST	874	403
ELI	30	1820	M	W	TN	COCKE	11-DIST	874	403
LYDIA	6	1844	F	W	TN	COCKE	11-DIST	874	403
SALINA	4	1846	F	W	TN	COCKE	11-DIST	874	403
BARBARY	27	1823	F	W	TN	COCKE	11-DIST	874	403
ANNA M	25	1825	F	W	TN	GREENE	9-DIVN	880	245
ANDREW J	27	1823	M	W	TN	GREENE	9-DIVN	880	245
MALINDA A	1	1849	F	W	TN	GREENE	9-DIVN	880	245

MARGARET	4	1846	F	W	TN	GREENE	10 sub	880	306
JAMES	0	1850	M	W	TN	GREENE	10 sub	880	306
JOSEPH	19	1831	M	W	TN	GREENE	10 sub	880	306
MARTIN	15	1835	M	W	TN	GREENE	10 sub	880	306
WILLIAM	52	1798	M	W	VA	GREENE	10 sub	880	306
BARBARY	47	1803	F	W	VA	GREENE	10 sub	880	306
ANDREW	22	1828	M	W	TN	GREENE	10 sub	880	306
MADISON	8	1842	M	W	TN	GREENE	10 sub	880	306
HENRY	21	1829	M	W	TN	GREENE	10 sub	880	306
REBECCA	16	1834	F	W	TN	GREENE	10 sub	880	306
CASPER	12	1838	M	W	TN	GREENE	10 sub	880	306
ANDREW	38	1812	M	W	TN	GREENE	10 sub	880	317
LIDIA	38	1812	F	W	TN	GREENE	10 sub	880	317
SARAH	15	1835	F	W	TN	GREENE	10 sub	880	317
GEORGE	5	1845	M	W	TN	GREENE	10 sub	880	317
BARBARY	13	1837	F	W	TN	GREENE	10 sub	880	317
MARTHA	1	1849	F	W	TN	GREENE	10 sub	880	317
MARY	7	1843	F	W	TN	GREENE	10 sub	880	317
CAROLINE	9	1841	F	W	TN	GREENE	10 sub	880	317
WILLIAM	11	1839	M	W	TN	GREENE	10 sub	880	317
VALENTINE S	28	1822	M	W	TN	GREENE	10 sub	880	319
FRANKLIN	5	1845	M	W	TN	GREENE	10 sub	880	319
LOUISA	26	1824	F	W	TN	GREENE	10 sub	880	319
HARRIET	3	1847	F	W	TN	GREENE	10 sub	880	319
NANCY	13	1837	F	W	TN	GREENE	10 sub	880	319
LEWIS	3	1847	M	W	TN	GREENE	10 sub	880	323
JAMES	16	1834	M	W	TN	GREENE	10 sub	880	323
DELILA	38	1812	F	W	TN	GREENE	10 sub	880	323
MALVINA	11	1839	F	W	TN	GREENE	10 sub	880	323
MARY	0	1850	F	W	TN	GREENE	10 sub	880	323
WILLIAM	8	1842	M	W	TN	GREENE	10 sub	880	323
ELIZA	14	1836	F	W	TN	GREENE	10 sub	880	323
CAROLINE	6	1844	F	W	TN	GREENE	10 sub	880	323
RITHY	28	1822	F	M	NC	GREENE	10 sub	880	325
HENRY	82	1768	M	W	PA	GREENE	10 sub	880	325
DAWSON	1	1849	M	W	TN	GREENE	10 sub	880	335
ALEXANDER	21	1829	M	W	TN	GREENE	10 sub	880	335
TENNESSEE	45	1805	F	W	TN	GREENE	10 sub	880	335
JESSE	46	1804	M	W	VA	GREENE	10 sub	880	335
NANCY	3	1847	F	W	TN	GREENE	10 sub	880	335
JESSEE	21	1829	M	W	TN	GREENE	10 sub	880	335
MELVINA	15	1835	F	W	TN	GREENE	10 sub	880	335
WILLIAM	51	1799	M	W	VA	GREENE	10 sub	880	335
GEORGE	5	1845	M	W	TN	GREENE	10 sub	880	335
PETER R	28	1822	M	W	TN	GREENE	10 sub	880	335
ELIZABETH	40	1810	F	W	TN	GREENE	10 sub	880	335
ELIZA	1	1849	F	W	TN	GREENE	10 sub	880	335

LEWIS	13	1837	M	W	TN	GREENE	10 sub	880	335
ELIZABETH	51	1799	F	W	VA	GREENE	10 sub	880	335
MARY	20	1830	F	W	TN	GREENE	10 sub	880	335
LEMUEL	18	1832	M	W	TN	GREENE	10 sub	880	335
MARTHA	10	1840	F	W	TN	GREENE	10 sub	880	335
KIZIAH	26	1824	F	W	TN	GREENE	10 sub	880	335
EMILY	5	1845	F	W	TN	GREENE	10 sub	880	335
JOHN	16	1834	M	W	TN	GREENE	10 sub	880	335
JOSEPH	49	1801	M	W	VA	GREENE	10 sub	880	335
ELIZABETH	76	1774	F	W	VA	GREENE	10 sub	880	335
CORNELIUS	15	1835	M	W	TN	GREENE	10 sub	880	335
ELBERT	19	1831	M	W	TN	GREENE	10 sub	880	336
ELIZABETH	6	1844	F	W	TN	GREENE	10 sub	880	336
ANDREW	5	1845	M	W	TN	GREENE	10 sub	880	336
LAWSON	7	1843	M	W	TN	GREENE	10 sub	880	336
JACOB	7	1843	M	W	TN	GREENE	10 sub	880	336
MARY	42	1808	F	W	NC	GREENE	10 sub	880	336
MARY	36	1814	F	W	TN	GREENE	10 sub	880	336
MARY	14	1836	F	W	TN	GREENE	10 sub	880	336
MARY	6	1844	F	W	TN	GREENE	10 sub	880	336
LETTICE	1	1849	F	W	TN	GREENE	10 sub	880	336
OLENA	9	1841	F	W	TN	GREENE	10 sub	880	336
PENELOPE	9	1841	F	W	TN	GREENE	10 sub	880	336
SYNTHA	27	1823	F	W	TN	GREENE	10 sub	880	336
RUBEN	28	1822	M	W	TN	GREENE	10 sub	880	336
JOHN	3	1847	M	W	TN	GREENE	10 sub	880	336
TENNESSEE	5	1845	F	W	TN	GREENE	10 sub	880	336
JESSE	34	1816	M	W	TN	GREENE	10 sub	880	336
JAMES	16	1834	M	W	TN	GREENE	10 sub	880	336
JAMES	14	1836	M	W	TN	GREENE	10 sub	880	336
REBECCA	12	1838	F	W	TN	GREENE	10 sub	880	336
MARTHA	10	1840	F	W	TN	HANCOCK	32 sub	881	4
CYNTHA	5	1845	F	W	TN	HANCOCK	32 sub	881	4
ELIZABETH	7	1843	F	W	TN	HANCOCK	32 sub	881	4
MARY	5	1845	F	W	TN	HANCOCK	32 sub	881	8
ELIZABETH	43	1807	F	W	VA	HANCOCK	32 sub	881	8
MANDA	7	1843	F	W	TN	HANCOCK	32 sub	881	8
DAVID	35	1815	M	W	NC	HANCOCK	32 sub	881	8
NANCY	0	1850	F	W	TN	HANCOCK	32 sub	881	8
JULIA	9	1841	F	W	TN	HANCOCK	32 sub	881	8
ELENDER	3	1847	F	W	NC	HANCOCK	32 sub	881	13
DANIEL	27	1823	M	W	NC	HANCOCK	32 sub	881	13
NICA	30	1820	F	W	NC	HANCOCK	32 sub	881	13
MARY	1	1849	F	W	TN	HANCOCK	32 sub	881	13
CATHARIN	16	1834	F	W	NC	HANCOCK	32 sub	881	18
MATILDA	15	1835	F	W	NC	HANCOCK	32 sub	881	18
SARAH	18	1832	F	W	NC	HANCOCK	32 sub	881	18
MARY	60	1790	F	W	NC	HANCOCK	32 sub	881	18

JOSEPH	58	1792	M	W	NC	HANCOCK	32 sub	881	18
MANLY	3	1847	M	W	TN	HANCOCK	32 sub	881	18
NANCY	23	1827	F	W	TN	HAWKINS	14-DIST	882	426
JOHN	22	1828	M	W	TN	HAWKINS	14-DIST	882	426
NANCY	1	1849	F	W	TN	MONROE	17-DIST	891	106
JOHN	13	1837	M	W	TN	MONROE	17-DIST	891	106
ANGALINE	7	1843	F	W	TN	MONROE	17-DIST	891	106
MADISON	12	1838	M	W	TN	MONROE	17-DIST	891	106
CAROLINE	9	1841	F	W	TN	MONROE	17-DIST	891	106
LUCY	30	1820	F	W	TN	MONROE	17-DIST	891	106
DAVID	50	1800	M	W	NC	MONROE	17-DIST	891	106
ADELIA A	4	1846	F	W	TN	SULLIVAN	1-DIVN	897	17
ELIZABETH	22	1828	F	W	TN	SULLIVAN	1-DIVN	897	17
LANDON H	2	1848	M	W	TN	SULLIVAN	1-DIVN	897	17
CALVIN	34	1816	M	W	TN	SULLIVAN	1-DIVN	897	17
PETER	69	1781	M	W	TN	SULLIVAN	1-DIVN	897	28
DORCAS	67	1783	F	W	NC	SULLIVAN	1-DIVN	897	29
MARGARET	8	1842	F	W	TN	SULLIVAN	1-DIVN	897	113
ELLEN	0	1850	F	W	TN	SULLIVAN	1-DIVN	897	113
MARTHA	14	1836	F	W	TN	SULLIVAN	1-DIVN	897	113
JAS P	36	1814	M	W	TN	SULLIVAN	1-DIVN	897	113
ADOLPHUS	6	1844	M	W	TN	SULLIVAN	1-DIVN	897	113
INDIANA	3	1847	F	W	TN	SULLIVAN	1-DIVN	897	113
ELIZABETH	40	1810	F	W	TN	SULLIVAN	1-DIVN	897	113
ANGELINA	27	1823	F	W	OH	WASHINGTON	4 sub east	898	118
E D	32	1818	M	W	TN	WASHINGTON	4 sub east	898	118
DORCUS L	2	1848	F	W	TN	WASHINGTON	4 sub east	898	118
JAMES P	5	1845	M	W	TN	WASHINGTON	4 sub east	898	118

Second Generation (Children)

Casper's kids in Greene County, Tennessee

The sons of Johan Casper Rotter (Rader) moved from Wythe county Virginia to The Lick creek valley near present day Mohawk. When they first moved there Mohawk was known as "Payne" or was it something else ?.

The 1809 tax records for Captain Kirks district shows that John Reader owns 200 acres in W.L.C. and that there is 1 white poll, his brother Henry has 105 acres on the Wasters of L.C. and also has one white poll, and finally brother Jacob has 496 acres on Waters L.C. and one poll. Phillip does not appear in the tax records ever so he must have gone to Ohio before 1810

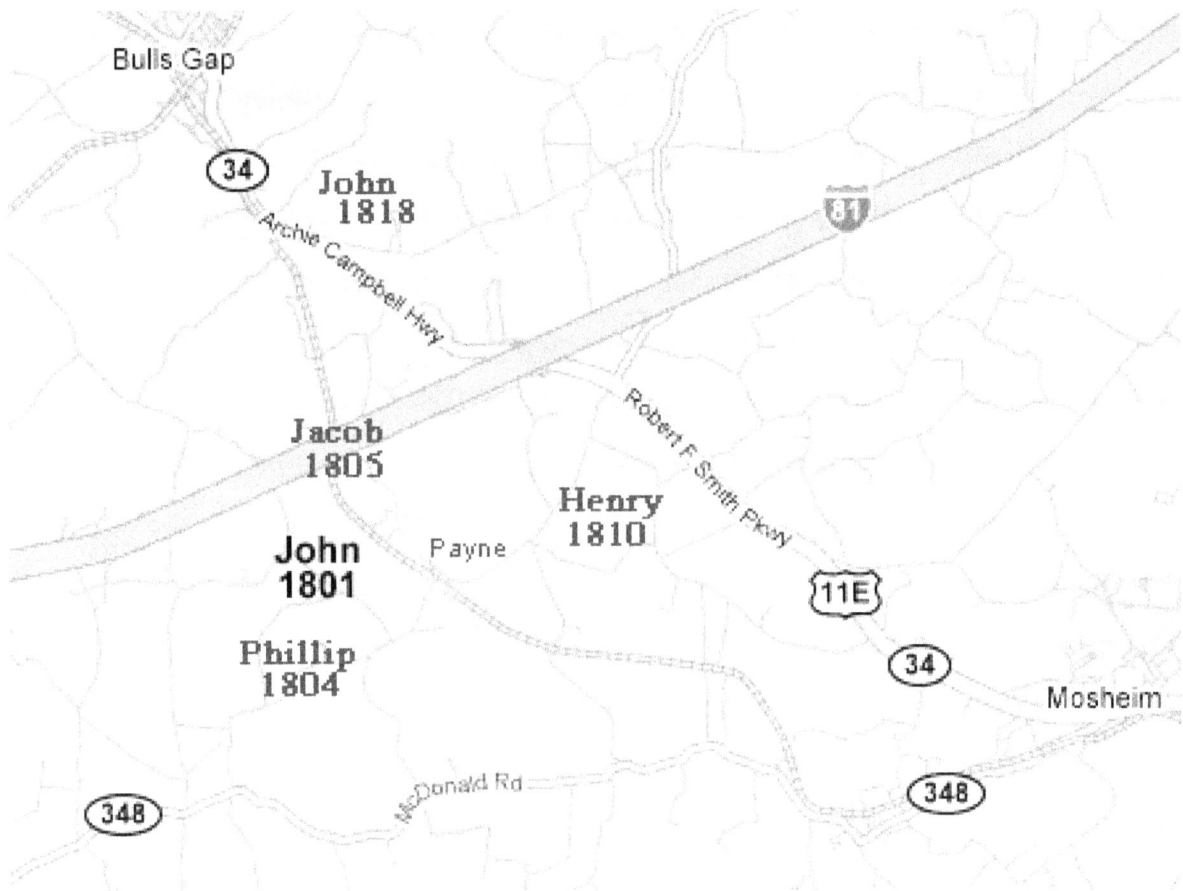

Map showing original Rader boys in Lick Creek

Tax records Greene County 1809-1835

Half of the second generation went to Tennessee, Daniel ended up in Mississippi, the rest stayed in Virginia The following tax table shows the Rader boys in Greene County Tennessee. For the first 10 years they all stayed in the Lick Creek area near present day exit 23 of highway 81

	1809	1810	1811	1812	1813	1814	1815	1816
Captain Kirk								
John	200	200	200	360	390	445	390	390
Henry	105	240	240	240	240	240	240	240
Jacob	496	496	496	496	473	475	475	475
John jr							-1	-1
Captain John Kilgore								
Peter					100	-1		
Captain M.W. Bresler								
Elisabeth								100

	1828	1829	1830	1831	1832	1833	1834	1835
Captain Laughner's								
William	little chucky		100	100		100	100	100
Captain Parson's								
Jacob	225	125			-1			
Captain Mc Pheron's								Captair
Casper	-1	30	30	56	30	30	30	30
Jacob Dr.	659	659						
Henry	240	240	240	240	240	240	240	240
Daniel		1 pole	1 pole	1 pole	1 pole	1 pole		
John Sr.	160	160	106	76	76	129	210	129
William		1 pole	124	124	124	124	124	124
Jesse		1 pole	137.5	137.5	180	180	261	200
Joseph		1 pole	170	76	76	76	76	76
John Jr.	50 school	1 pole	50	50	50	1 pole	1 pole	1 pole
Elizabeth			172	172	172	172	172	172
Martin			120.5	120	120	163	161.5	161.5
Henry Jr				1 pole	1 pole	1 pole	1 pole	
Andrew							1 pole	1 pole
Samuel							1 pole	1 pole
Captain Heasles								
William							33.5	37.5

As the Grandchildren moved out on their own we have more people in the Genealogy than there are in the tax records. The 1830 US Census does not end the confusion as it lists less people than expected. Some either died or moved away

Conrad Stayed In Wythe County Virginia

2. Conrad Rader[1, 2, 3, 5, 6, 7, 8, 10, 11, 12, 13, 14, 15, 16, 18] (*Casper Sr*[1]) was born in 1766 in Bethel Township, Lancaster County, Pennsylvania[16, 17, 30] and died on 14 May 1845 in Wythe County, Virginia[16, 17] at age 79. Death Notes: Conrad Rader died May 14, 1845 aged 79 years (family bible of Nancy O. Rader his daughter who married James Siggle

> The St. John's Lutheran Church record of Wytheville, Virginia recorded the birth of Conrad and Elizabeth's daughter Nancy Rader

> Conrad Rader died May 14, 1845 aged 79 years

(family bible of Nancy O. Rader his daughter who married James Siggle 1822) Bought land in Wythe Co., Virginia on 11 Feb 1794 and sold land on 30 Aug 1822.

Noted events in his life were:

Alt Birth: 1764, Lancaster, Pennsylvania.[17]

Alt Birth: Abt 1766, Lancaster Co. PA..

He owned land on 2 Feb 1790 in Wythe County, Virginia. Conrad was living in in the vicinity of New River around Reed Creek and Mack Creek (See "Montgomery County, Virginia - Circa 1790" by Netti Schreiner-Yantis).

He owned land on 11 Feb 1794 in Wythe County, Virginia. Bought land on and sold land on 30 Aug 1822

Tax list: 23 Apr 1800, Wythe County, Virginia. Conrad was still living and had one male over 16 years of age in his household and owned one horse and no slaves.

He owned land on 18 Jun 1805 in Wythe County, Virginia.

He appeared on the census in 1810 in Wythe County, Virginia. CENSUS PAGE 852 of the 1810 Virginia Census. He and his family did not move to Green County.

He appeared on the census in 1810 in Wythe County, Virginia.

Census 2: 1820. WYTHE COUNTY, VIRGINIA CENSUS PAGE 221

He owned land on 30 Aug 1822 in Wythe County, Virginia.

Alt Death: 1827.[18]

Conrad married **Elizabeth Ory**,[16, 18] daughter of **Calvin Ory** and **Unknown**, on 3 Jul 1788 in Montgomery County, Virginia.[16, 17, 18, 31] Elizabeth was born on 11 Jun 1772 in Montgomery Co. VA.[16, 17, 18, 39] and died on 6 May 1848 in Wythe County, Virginia[16, 17, 18] at age 75. Other names for Elizabeth were Elizabeth Dury, and Elizabeth Fry.

Marriage Notes: The record of the marriage of Conrad to Elizabeth Fry can be found in "A Brief of Wills and Marriages in Montgomery and Fincastle Counties, Virginia, 1733-1831" compiled by Anne Lowry Worrell. "Know all mem by these presents that we Cunrod Reeder + Danl Etter of the County of Montgomery + State of Virginia are held + primty Bound to the Governour for the Time being in the Just + full sum of fifty pounds current money to the payment of which we bind ourselves our + each of us, our Heirs + firmty by these presents sealed with our seals + dated this 3 rd day of July 1788.

The condition of the above obligation is such that whereas the above Bound Conrod Reeder hath this day obt. a License for his Marriage to Elizabeth Ory of s. County now of there shall be no lawful cause to obstruct this marriage then the above obligation to be void use to remain in foreshi Syned Sealed &

Deliv. in the presence of Wm. Trigy Conrad Reeder (mark) Danl O. Etter (mark) Sir

Please to assce Marriage license for Coonrod Rader and my Daughter Elizabeth for I am willing your Calvin Ory June 3, 1788

General Notes: Elizabeth Rader died May 6, 1848 aged 75 years, 10 months + 25 days. There is considreable discussion of her maiden name, James C. Spraker writes the forrowing: Ms Worrell's compilation of marriages has a number of mistakes, including the name "Fry" used instead of "Ory". One source misread the name as "Pry", no doubt because of the rarity of the Ory name in this part of Virginia. Mrs Worrell, it appears, misinterpreted that first mispelling as a variant of the german "Pf" sound, thus erroneously rendering the name as "Fry". As you can see, this error is a mistake in the second degree, a mispelling from an already mispelled secondary source. Since Calvin Ory himself signed his letter it would be absurd to believe that he did not know how to spell his own name

Children from this marriage were:

+ 13 F i. **Catherine Rader** was born about 1789 in Wythe County, Virginia.[16]

    Catherine married **Jacob T Fishback** (b. 1765) on 19 Jun 1815 in Wythe County, Virginia.

+ 14 M ii. **Conrad Rader** was born about 1790.

+ 15 M iii. **James Rader** was born in 1801.

    James married **Nancy L.** (b. 1816).

+ 16 F iv. **Nancy O. Rader**[16] was born on 18 Jun 1805 in Wytheville, Wythe County, Virginia,[17,32] died on 6 Sep 1885 in Wytheville, Wythe County, Virginia[16,17,40] at age 80, and was buried in St. Peters', Lutheran Cem.[40]

    Nancy married **James Seagle**[16] (b. 14 Oct 1801, d. 16 Jan 1883) on 22 Oct 1822 in Wytheville, Wythe County, Virginia.[16,40]

+ 17 F v. **Judith Ora Rader**[41] was born on 11 May 1811 in Wythe County, Virginia and died on 28 Jun 1887 in Wythe County, Virginia at age 76.

    Judith married **Absolom Fisher** (b. 27 Jan 1808, d. 3 Jun 1887) on 23 May 1833 in Wythe County, Virginia.

+ 18 F vi. **Rebecca Rader**[5,13,18] was born about 1811 in Wythe County, Virginia[17,18] and died about 1860 in Senatobia, Mississippi[17,18] about age 49.

    Rebecca married **Alfred Bryam** (b. 1808) on 5 May 1831 in Madison County, AL.

Henry moved to Greene county Tennessee

3. Heinrich 'Henry' Rader Sr[1,2,3,5,6,7,8,10,11,12,13,14,15,16] (*Casper Sr*[1]) was born in 1768 in Bethel Township, Lancaster County, Pennsylvania,[17,20] died on 1 Sep 1851 in Greene County, Tennessee[17] at age 83, and was buried in Time, Pike Co, IL.

    Death Notes: Heinrich died September 1, 1851 in Greene Co, TN, at 83 years of age. His body was interred in Timber Ridge, Greene Co, TN

General Notes: References:

    1. Greene County, Tennessee deed book volumn 2, page 13 dated Novembe r 15, 1843.

    2. Greene County, Tennessee deed book 25, page 470 dated October 16, 1852.

3. Greene County, Tennessee Settlements volumn June 1855 to December 1869, page 167 and 168, dated 11/30/1859.

4. Wythe County, Virginia Deed Book No. 2, page 277 dated 1798. Also f ound in "1800 Tax Lists & Abstracts of Deeds, 1796-1800, of Wythe Coun ty, Virginia", by Netti Schreiner-Yan

tis, 1971.

5. Greene County, Tennessee deed book number 7, pages 50 and 54 respectively.

6. Greene County, Tennesee Tax List.

7. Greene County, Tennessee Inventory of Estates, Vol. 1843-1854, pag e 484-487.

8. Greene County, Tennessee County Court Minutes, Vol. 1849-1854, pag e 174, dated 9/1/1851.

9. Greene county, Tennessee County Court Minutes, Vol. 1849-1854, pag e 188 and 265, dated 10/6/1851 and 4/5/1852 respectively.

Farmer

Henry was in GREENE COUNTY, TENNESSEE as early as 1804 and possibly sooner. On September 26, 1804 Henry witnessed the land deed of his brother Phillip Rader and on November 14, 1805 he witnessed the

land deed of his brother Jacob Rader(GREENE COUNTY, TENNESSEE deed book number 7, pages 50 and 54 respectively).

Noted events in his life were:

Alt Birth: 1766, Lancaster, Pennsylvania.

Alt Birth: Abt 1 Jan 1768, Lancaster Co. PA.[42]

Tax list: 1788, Montgomery County, Virginia.

Resided: 17 Feb 1790, Wythe County, Virginia. Henry was living on Reed Creek and the Crab Orchard Fork of Little Walker's Creek. At this time he owned one horse and had no male s in his household over 16 years of age.

He owned land on 12 Sep 1795 in Wythe Co, TN. Wythe County Deed Book 1 - Henrey Reder and Caty sold to Varner Knipp, 100 acres Reed Creek, branch of New River, on the north side of Pine Ridge between the land of Jacob Plessley [Blessing] and Jacob Pruner.

He owned land in Jul 1796 in Wythe County, Virginia. Henry and Catherine Etter Rader - Land Grants at Richmond, VA (Virginia State Library Card File:) Grant 34 - p. 402 Rader, Henry * JUL 1796 Montgomery Co., VA. 33 acres on Crockett's Branch, waters of Cove Cr., a branch of Reed Creek. Grant 49 - p. 58 Rader, Henry

He owned land on 11 Jun 1798 in Wythe County, Virginia. In Henry Rider and his wife Catherine sold 20 acres of land to John Erwin located on a branch of Reed Creek called Dry Run located in Wythe County, Virginia

. Apparently HENRY and CATHERINE started planning the move to Tennessee when in 1798 Henry and his wife Catherine sold 20 acres of land to John Erwin located on a branch of Reed Creek in Wythe County, Virginia(Wythe county Deed Book No. 2, page 277 dated 1798) HENRY and JOHN, JACOB, and PHILLIP, plus PETER

ETTER and JOHN ETTER were making land purchases in Greene County from 1798 to 1804 when HENRY and CATHERINE actually made the move.

Tax list: 1800, Wythe County, Virginia. Henry was listed in the tax list with one male over 16 and owned three horses and no slaves.

He owned land on 16 Apr 1801 in Wythe County, Virginia. (2 grants) 1. 50 acres on waters of Reed Creek adjoining Jacob Darter and his own land. 2. 55 acres on Reed Creek adj. Erwin, Guillion, Plessey and extending

Grant 49 - p. 58 Rader, Henry 16 APR 1801 WYTHE COUNTY, VIRGINIA

He owned land in 1802 in Wythe County, Virginia. They sold three pieces of property (DB 3, p. 325, p. 214, 125)

He had a religion in 1804 in Greene County, Tennessee. HENRY and CATHERINE were early if not original members of the Sinking Springs Lutheran Church. Their family page is number 7 in the church register, where five baptisms of their children are listed. They may have changed to another church as they do not appear in the communion lists after those early years.

[Caption: Idell Road parcel #313]

[Caption: 650 north Mohawk]

He owned land on 26 Sep 1804 in Greene County, Tennessee. Henry was in Greene County, Tennessee as early as 1804 and possibly sooner. On September 26, 1804 Henry witnessed the land deed of his brother Phillip Rader and on November 14, 1805 he witnessed the land deed of his brother Jacob Rader(Greene County, Tennessee deed book number 7, pages 50 and 54 respectively). They settled on Lick Creek in the western part of Greene County.

He owned land on 14 Nov 1805 in Greene County, Tennessee. he witnessed the land deed of his brother Jacob Rader

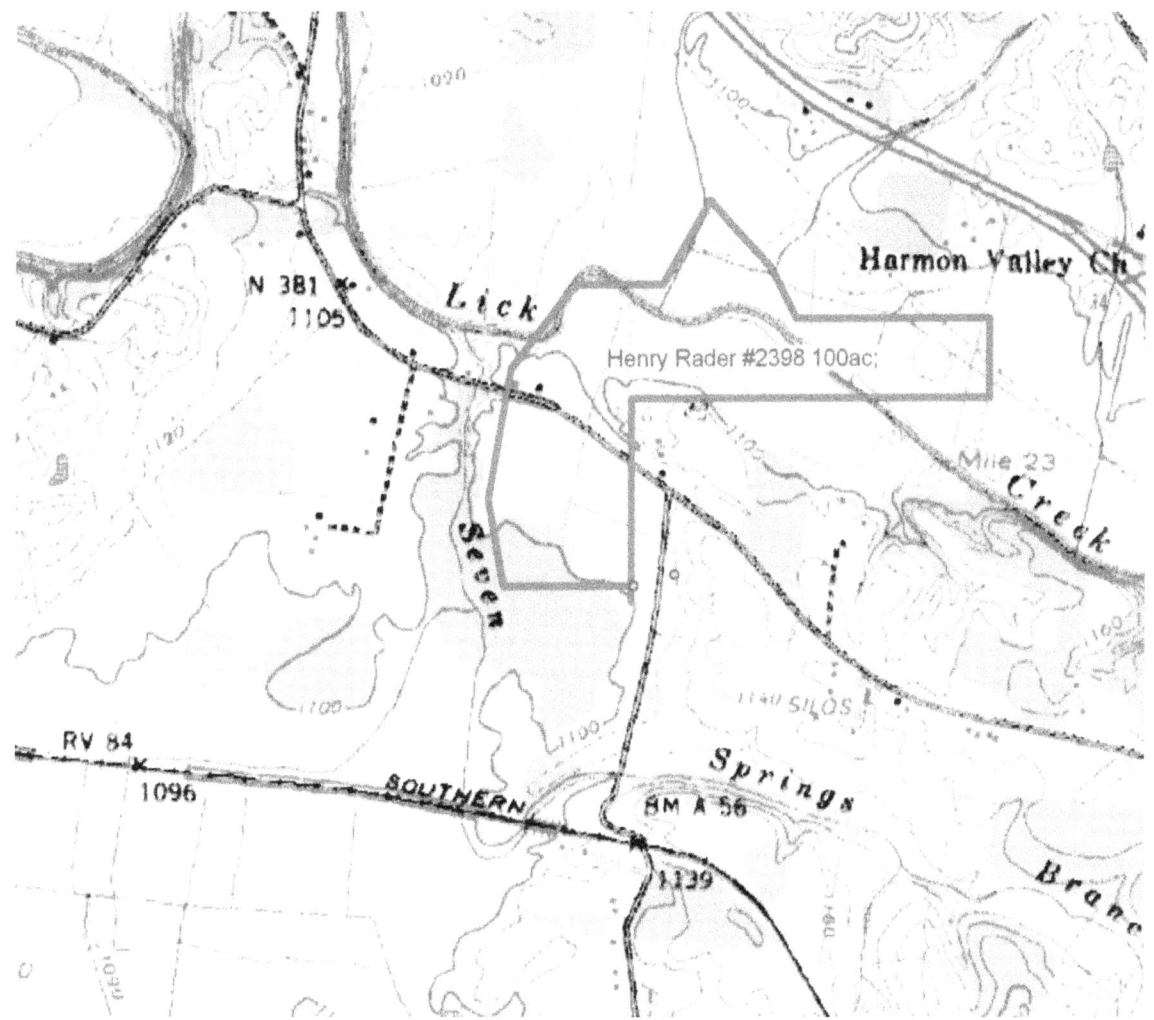

Map of Henry's 100 acres on Lick Creek Purchased 1810

[Description: #2398 purchased recorded Greene county Deed book 1B page 378 11 Aug 1810

(3 Jun 1808)]

He owned land in 1809 in Greene County, Tennessee. In 1809 Henry was living in Captain Joseph Kirk's district in Greene County, Tennessee and owned 105 acres of land.

He purchased land adjoining JACOB RADER and JOHN ETTER on the north side of Lick Creek. He sold 105 acres to same JOHN ETTER in 1809 and moved less than a half of a mile West near the are called Payne (it is now called Mohawk), where he was a highly successful farmer.

From 1810 through 1815 he was living in the same district and owned 240 acres of land.

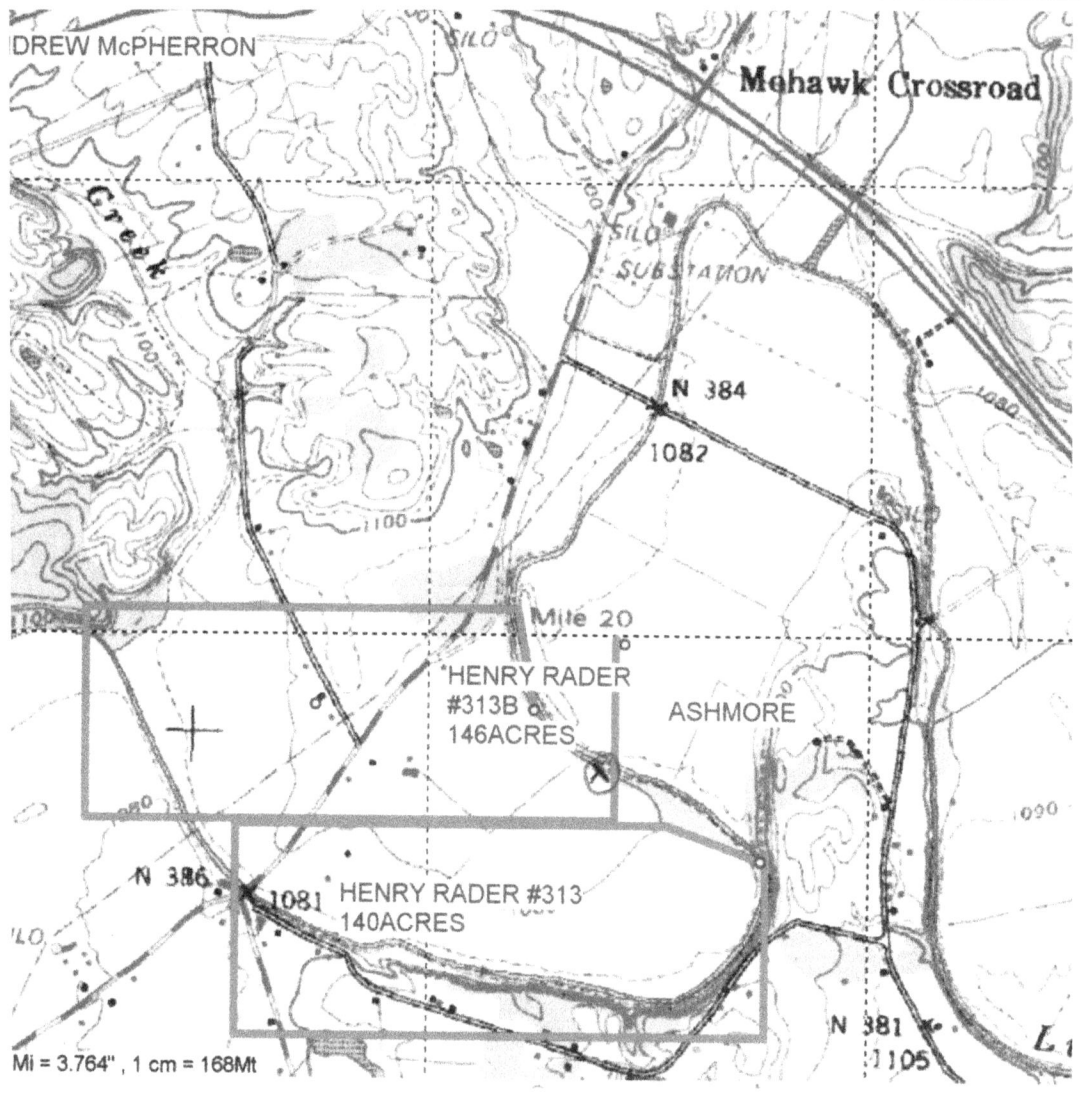

Map of 246 Acres Henry bought on Lick Creek 1810

He owned land in 1810 in Greene County, Tennessee. From 1810 through 1815 he was living in the same district and owned 240 acres of land. He purchased 3 parcels and sold #2398 right away to Etter.

He purchased two from Henry Cross #1326A and #1326B 9 Jan 1810.

He owned land on 9 Jan 1810 in Mohawk, Greene County, Tennessee. Greene county Deed book 9 page 36 Andrew McPherron sold 140 acres to Henry #313, and also #313b 146 Acres

He owned land in 1811 in Lick Creek Valley, Greene County Tennessee.

He owned land in 1812 in Lick Creek Valley, Greene County Tennessee.

[Caption: first tract he bought]

He owned land in 1810 in Lick Creek Valley, Greene County Tennessee.

He owned land in 1813 in Lick Creek Valley, Greene County Tennessee. Henry settled on the Lick Creek 240 acres before 1810. He paid taxes on both pieces of land through 1835 or later. He paid taves on 132 acres from 1840 through 1851 with 2 salves.

He owned land on 15 Dec 1815 in Wythe County, Virginia. They sold three pieces of property in Wythe County in 1802 (DB 3, p. 325, p. 214, 125) and made a final sale 15 DEC 1815 which was probably his share of his father's estate. (DB 6, 373)

He appeared on the census in 1830 in Greene County, Tennessee. All of the Reader/Rader families in the Greene Co. TN 1830 Federal Census

> READER, CASPAR, 188 --- 10001 - 10001
> READER, ELIZABETH, 192 --- 0011 - 0000001
> READER, HENRY, 192 --- 000120001 - 00111001 3 slaves
> READER, JACOB, 161 --- 222001 - 000001
> READER, JESSE, 192 --- 00001 - 11001
> READER, JOHN, 188 --- 01110001 - 00211001
> READER, JOHN, 193 --- 230001 - 000001
> READER, JOSEPH, 192 --- 10001 - 00001
> READER, WILLIAM, 186 --- 210001 - 01001
> READER, WILLIAM, 192 --- 110001 - 010001
>
> RITTER, DANIEL, 209 --- 001220001 - 01011001
> RITTER, HENRY, 207 --- 020001 - 111001
>
> RUDDER, ALEX, 191 --- 110001 - 211001

He owned land in 1840 in Greene County, Tennessee. In 1840 and 1847 Henry was living in district number 6 in Greene County, Tennessee and owned 132 acres of land.

Henry had sold one of his slaves named Jane to his son Andrew Rader (Greene County, Tennessee deed book volume 2, page 13 dated November 15, 1843).

He owned property on 15 Nov 1843 in Greene County, Tennessee. Henry had sold one of his slaves named Jane to his son Andrew Rader (GREENE COUNTY, TENNESSEE deed book volume 2, page 13 dated).

He signed a will on 21 Dec 1846 in Greene County, Tennessee.[18, 28] Henry wrote his Will December 21, 1846

Henry Rader wrote his will December 21, 1846; it was probated September 1, 1851. $2400 It reads as follows:

I, Henry Rader, do make and publish this my last will and testament hereby revoking and making void all other wills by me at any time made. First--I direct that my funeral expenses and all my debts be paid as soon after my death as possible out of any money that I may die possessed of or may first come into the hands of my executor. Secondly--That my beloved wife, CATHARINE, remain on the premises including the dwelling house where I now live during her natural life and that she shall have the use of my lands that I may die possessed of, and that my slaves, namely, Alfred, Mariah and Ellis remain with my beloved wife on the plantation to help to support her during her natural life, and that my personal property also remain with her for her use during her life, except so much thereof as will be sufficient to defray my funeral expenses and debts as above stated. Thirdly--That as soon as possible after the death of my wife, CATHERINE, I direct that my slaves, namely, Alfred, Mariah and Ellis be set free. Fourthly--That all the personal property belonging to my estate after the death of my wife to be sold on a twelve month credit and also the lands that I may die possessed of on a twelve month credit or two years as my executor may think best for the best interest of my heirs. Fifthly--That an equal distribution be made of my estate among all my lawful heirs without distinction, taking into view what small part some of them have received, except my son HENRY RADER I direct that he shall have one dollar out of my estate to his share and no more. The balance that will be coming to my daughter, MARY LAUCHNER to be equally divided among her lawful heirs born of her own body, except her son, DANIEL LAUCHNER, I direct that he shall not have anything. Sixthly--A schedule or memorandum of the amount of what some of my heirs has received out of their part. My daughter, MARY LAUCHNER has received $123.25 My son, JOHN RADER has received 62.00 My daughter, ELIZABETH BOWERS has received 132.80 My daughter, RACHEL BASINGER has received $110.00 My son, CASPER RADER, has received 38.00 My daughter, CATHERINE SMITH has received 93.00 My daughter, ISABELLA has received 95.00 Seventhly, It is my desire that this my last will and testament be carried into effect and Lastly--I do hereby nominate and appoint my son, WILLIAM RADER, my executor. In witness whereof I do to this my will set my hand this 21st day of December 1846. Attest: 21st day of December 1846 WILLIAM RADER Valentine S. Rader

and was probated in Greene County, Tennessee September 1, 1851

The Will mentioned wife Catherine, sons: Henry, John, Casper, Daniel, William; daughters: Elizabeth Bowers, Rachel Basinger, Catherine Smith, Isabella Smith, and Mary Lauchner. Son William was executor, witnessed by William Rader, Valentine S. Rader and Bondsman William Rader of Jacob. The Will also directed that Henry's slaves were to be set free after his death. William Rader, son of Henry, apparently renounced his executorship of the Will of Henry but reconsidered and accepted that position 9/1/1851 with Andrew Rader and William Rader of Jacob his security

He owned property in 1850. VALUE $800.00

1850 Census: 11 Oct 1850, Greene County, Tennessee. Henry Rader 82 M none 800 born Pennsylvania

   kithy 28 F born N Carolina
   Henry Rader son 40 m farmer 1400
   Anna 35 F
   Powel 6 M
   Granville 3 m

Alt Death: 1 Sep 1851, Greene County, Tennessee.[28] Henry wrote his Will December 21, 1846

and was probated in Greene County, Tennessee September 1, 1851

The Will mentioned wife Catherine, sons: Henry, John, Casper, Daniel, William; daughters: Elizabeth Bowers, Rachel Basinger, Catherine Smith, Isabella Smith, and

Mary Lauchner. Son William was executor, witnessed by William Rader, Valentine S. Rader and Bondsman William Rader of Jacob. The Will also directed that Henry's slaves were to be set free after his death. William Rader, son of Henry, apparently renounced his executorship of the Will of Henry but reconsidered and accepted that position 9/1/1851 with Andrew Rader and William Rader of Jacob his security

He had an estate probated on 25 Sep 1851 in , , Greene, Tennessee.[20] Henry's real estate property was sold at auction, as directed by his Will, on September 25, 1851 [2]. The personal property of Henry was sold at public auction and the results recorded December 1, 1851 [7]. Henry's Will indicated that his heirs were to share equally from the p roceeds of his personal estate as directed by his Will. Henry's Will indicated that his daughter Mary Laughner had already received $123.25 (her son Daniel was not to receive anything according to the Will), son John had already received $62.00, daughter Elizabeth Bowers had reseived $132.80, daughter Rachel Baysinger had received $110.00, son Casper had received $38.00, daughter Catherine Smith had received $93.00, daughter Isabella Smith had received $95.00, son Henry to receive only $1.00. This meant that each of these heirs would have their proceeds reduced by these amounts. As shown by the Inventory of Henry's Estate, the amont from the sale was $1316.95 [7] which was divided among the heirs as indicated in the settlement document [3]. Henry had 11 children but son Henry was to receive only $1.00 which amounted to each of the other children of Henry receiving aproximately $181.70. Using this as a guide, Mary Laughner's heirs can be identified as those receiving $6.38 per person (excluding Daniel) and John Rader heirs can be identified as those receiving $11.57 per person. Henry's slaves Alfred and his wife Mariah and their children Ellis an d Martha Ann were set free April 5, 1852 as directed by Henry's Will and were allowed to remain ion the State of Tennessee for a period of three years. Security was provided by William H. Glasscock, George Jackson, Henry Rader, Martram V. Glasscock and Leland Davis [9]

He owned property on 5 Apr 1852 in Greene County, Tennessee. Henry's slaves Alfred and his wife Mariah and their children Ellis an d Martha Ann were set free April 5, 1852 as directed by Henry's Will a nd were allowed to remain ion the State of Tennessee for a period of t hree years. Security was provided by William H. Glasscock, George Jack son, Henry Rader, Martram V. Glasscock and Leland Davis [9].

He had an estate probated on 5 Dec 1859 in Greene County, Tennessee. Henry's property was sold at auction, as directed by his Will, on September 25, 1851(Greene County, Tennessee deed book 25, page 470 dated October 16, 1852). Henry's estate was divided among his heirs on December 5, 1859(Greene County, Tennessee Settlements volume June 1855 to December 1869, page 167). In this settlement each heir mentioned in Henry's Will received an equal share of approximately 181 dollars except those specifically exempted by the Will. Henry did not mention his sons Daniel and Andrew Rader in his Will but each received an equal heirs share in the settlement. The settlement also listed Henry's grandchildren by his deceased daughters Mary Rader Laughner and Catherine Rader Smith.

Heinrich married **Catherine Etter**,[18] daughter of **Daniel Etter** and **Mary Magdalen Rein**, on 14 Dec 1790 in Wytheville, Wythe County, Virginia.[16, 17, 18, 28] Catherine was born about 1772 in Lebanon, PA,[16, 17, 18, 20, 42] died about 1847 in Greene County, Tennessee[16, 17, 18, 20, 28]

about age 75, and was buried in Timber Ridge Presbyterian Church Cemetery, Greene County, Tennessee. Other names for Catherine were Catherine Etter, and [16] Catherine Propts.

Marriage Notes: Married by John Stanger, Minister of the Gospel.. "Annals of Southwest Virginia, 1769-1800", by Lewis Preston Summers, part 2 of Vol. 1.2. "Wythe County Marriages, 1790-1850", by John Vogt and T. William Kethley, Jr.1. "Annals of Southwest Virginia, 1769-1800", by Lewis Preston Summers, part 2 of Vol. 1.2. "Wythe County Marriages, 1790-1850", by John Vogt and T. William Kethley, Jr.

The record of the marriage of Henry and Etter,Catherine is recorded in the "Annals of Southwest Virginia 1769-1800" by Lewis Preston Summers, part two of volume one. They were married by John Stanger, minister of the gospel.

Noted events in their marriage were:

Seal: REV. JOHN STANGER

Alt Marriage: 14 Dec 1790, , Rev John Stanger, Wythe, Virginia.

Alt Marriage: 11 Feb 1813, Virginia.

General Notes: He married Catherine Etter. Catherine was born circa 1772 in Lebanon, PA. Catherine was the daughter of Daniel Etter and Mary Magdalen Rein (Disputed). Catherine died circa 1847 in Greene Co, TN. Her body was interred Timber Ridge Presbyterian Church Cemetery, Green Co. TN.

Noted events in her life were:

Alt Birth: Abt 1772, Lebanon County, Pennsylvania.

She appeared on the census in 1840. GREENE COUNTY, TENNESSEE PAGE 77

Children from this marriage were:

+ 19 M i. **John Rader**[1, 2, 3, 6, 8, 10, 11, 12, 14, 15, 16, 43] was born on 11 Sep 1793 in Wytheville, Wythe County, Virginia,[16] died on 8 Nov 1839 in Caney Branch, Greene County, Tennessee[16] at age 46, and was buried in Old St. James, Lutheran.

John married **Hannah Scott**[16] (b. 10 Feb 1795, d. 24 Jul 1871) on 25 Aug 1814 in Greene County, Tennessee.[16]

+ 20 F ii. **Mary Rader**[1, 2, 3, 6, 8, 10, 11, 12, 14, 15] was born about 1794 in Wythe County, Virginia and died on 6 Mar 1848 in Greene County, Tennessee about age 54.

Mary married **John Lauchner** (b. 1790, d. 1849) on 8 Feb 1816 in James Guthrie Jp, Greene Co, TN.[44]

+ 21 F iii. **Elizabeth 'Betsey' Rader**[1, 2, 3, 6, 8, 10, 11, 12, 14, 15, 20] was born on 15 Apr 1795 in Wythe County, Virginia,[20] died on 29 Sep 1866 in Warrensburg, Greene Co, TN at age 71, and was buried in Sinking Springs, Lutheran, Greene Co, TN.

Elizabeth married **Jonas Bowers**[20, 45] (b. 31 Aug 1796, d. 21 Dec 1838) on 20 Aug 1818 in Jos. E. Bell, M.G., Greene Co, TN.

Source Citations

+ 22 M iv. **William W. Rader**[1, 2, 3, 6, 8, 10, 11, 12, 14, 15] was born on 15 Jun 1798 in Wythe County, Virginia,[46] died on 16 Apr 1880 in Greene County, Tennessee at age 81, and was buried in , Timber Ridge Cem, Greene, Tennessee.

  William married **Barbara Hauff** (b. 19 May 1803, d. 24 Apr 1883) on 17 May 1821 in Rev Phil. Henkel, Greene Co, TN.[44]

+ 23 M v. **Casper J. Rader Jr.**[1, 2, 3, 6, 8, 10, 11, 12, 14, 15] was born on 19 Apr 1801 in Greene County, Tennessee, died on 6 Oct 1883 in Brizil, Clay Co, IN, Or MO[47] at age 82, and was buried in 1883 in Mc Cullough, Washington Twp, Potnam Co, IN.

  Casper married **Anny Brown** (b. 1805, d. Abt 1833) on 29 Nov 1828 in M.G. Wilson, Jp, Greene Co, TN.[44]

  Casper next married **Anna Mary Mace** (b. 15 Oct 1816, d. 22 Nov 1883) on 31 Jul 1834 in , Jesse W Haile, Ld, Greene, Tennessee.[44]

+ 24 F vi. **Rachel Rader**[1, 2, 3, 6, 8, 10, 11, 12, 14, 15] was born about 1803 in Wythe County, Virginia, died in 1855 in Williamson Co, IL about age 52, and was buried in , Frank Campbell F, Williamson, Illinois.

  Rachel married **Michael Basinger Jr.** (b. 24 Aug 1806, d. 29 Jul 1855) on 30 Dec 1823 in Rev Phil Henkel, Greene Co, TN.

+ 25 M vii. **Daniel Rader**[1, 2, 3, 6, 8, 10, 11, 12, 14, 15] was born on 9 Jan 1808 in Greene County, Tennessee and died on 25 Jul 1854 in Greene County, Tennessee at age 46.

  Daniel married **Nancy Mathews** (b. 14 Sep 1808, d. 23 Oct 1894) on 13 Oct 1830 in Greene County, Tennessee.

+ 26 M viii. **Henry Thomas Rader Jr.**[1, 2, 3, 6, 8, 10, 11, 12, 14, 15] was born on 28 May 1810 in , , Greene, Tennessee and died on 3 Jul 1860 in , , Cooke, Tennessee at age 50.

  Henry married **Anny Brown** (b. 1805, d. Abt 1833).

  Henry next married **Anna Mary Mace** (b. 15 Oct 1816, d. 22 Nov 1883) on 21 Jul 1836 in , Rev G. Easterly, Greene, Tennessee.[44]

+ 27 M ix. **Andrew W. S Rader**[1, 2, 3, 6, 8, 10, 11, 12, 14, 15] was born on 23 Nov 1812 in Greene County, Tennessee,[28, 48] died on 10 Sep 1889 in Timber Ridge, Greene Co, TN at age 76, and was buried in Timber Ridge, Greene Co, TN.[21]

  Andrew married **Lydia Andes** (b. 16 May 1813, d. 18 Jun 1880) on 1 Apr 1834 in Greene County, Tennessee.[28]

  Andrew next married **Elizabeth Gammon** (b. 19 Dec 1824, d. 6 Nov 1892) on 20 Jan 1881.

  Andrew next married **Lillie Kinser** (b. 1813).

+ 28 F x. **Catherine M. Rader**[1, 2, 3, 6, 8, 10, 11, 12, 14, 15] was born on 19 Jan 1816 in Sinking Springs, Greene County, Tennessee and died before 1859 in Greene County, Tennessee.

Catherine married **John F. Washington Smith** (b. 1813, d. 1896) on 24 Mar 1836 in , Rev G. Easterly, Greene, Tennessee.

+ 29 F xi. **Issabella Rader**[1, 2, 3, 6, 8, 10, 11, 12, 14, 15] was born on 24 Jun 1819 in Greene County, Tennessee and died on 1 Sep 1879 at age 60.

Issabella married **Isaac Smith** (b. 8 Mar 1823) on 9 Sep 1845 by William Rader, Jp, Greene Co, TN.

+ 30 M xii. **Johannes Pieter Richard Rader**[1, 2, 3, 6, 8, 10, 11, 12, 14, 15] was born on 2 Jun 1820 in , , Greene, Tennessee and died on 2 Jun 1820 in Greene County, Tennessee.

Heinrich next married **Catherine Propts** on 11 Feb 1813 in VA.

Marriage Notes: THis does not seem to be correct because his first wife lived until 1847

General Notes: Henry could have remarried to a lady named Kithy, born in North Carolina in 1822. She was listed in his household in the 1850 census.

John moved to Greene county Tennessee

4. John Rader[1, 2, 3, 4, 5, 6, 7, 8, 10, 11, 12, 13, 14, 15, 16, 18] (*Casper Sr*[1]) was born about 1769 in Bethel Township, Lancaster County, Pennsylvania[16, 17] and died on 3 Feb 1840 in Greene County, Tennessee[17] about age 71.

Death Notes: John Rader died intestate in Greene County, Tennessee in August of 1840. Leland Davis was appointed by county court to act as administrator of his estate. The court also appointed William Willoughby, Thomas Jackson and Vincent Jackson as commissioners to set aside a portion of the estate left by John Rader to be used by his widow Mary Rader(Greene County, Tennessee County Court volumn January 1839 to December 1843,pages 159 and 167, dated September 7, 1840 and October 5, 1840 respectively) The personal estate of John Rader was sold at public auction on October 2 and 3 of 1840. The sale of individual items and those who purchased them is recorded in the Greene County, Tennessee Inventory of Estates, volumn 1828 to 1854, page 574, dated October 5, 1841. Some of the items purchased were: scythe and cradle - $2.00, broad axe - $2.12, hammer and anvil - $.65, one loom - $2.50, candlestand - $1.91, harrow - $2.51, plow - $3.07, pair of spectacles - $.50, razor and box - $1.01, umbrella - $1.26, windmill - $14.06, big kettle - $3.20, fur hat - $2.12, bed - $5.00, horse - $35.00, cow - $9.56 and books - $.79. His personal estate was sold for a total of $373.13.

Noted events in his life were:

Alt Birth: 1768, Lancaster, Pennsylvania.[17] Alt Birth: 1780.

MARRIAGE # 1: 14 Mar 1797. EVENSHAM, WYTHE COUNTY, VIRGINIA

The record of the marriage of John and Etter, Mary is recorded in the "Annals of Southwest Virginia 1769-1800" by Lewis Preston Summers, part two of volumn one.

He owned land in 1798 in Evansham {Wytheville}, Wythe, Virginia. He purchased lot 46 in Evansham in 1798. It was located on the south side of Main st., nine lots southwest of the Cross Street

He owned land in 1800 in Evansham {Wytheville}, Wythe, Virginia. John and Mary sold land to John W. Doak located in (Wythe county Deed Book No. 2, page 496 dated 1800). Evansham was the original name for Wytheville, Virginia.

He had a religion in 1800 in Wytheville, Virginia. John was listed as a subscriber for the building of the St. John's Lutheran Church in Wytheville, Virginia (See "Wythe Conuty Chapters" edited and published by James S. Presgraves).

Resided: 24 May 1800, Wythe County, Virginia. John was living and had one male in his household over 16 years of age and owned one horse and no slaves.

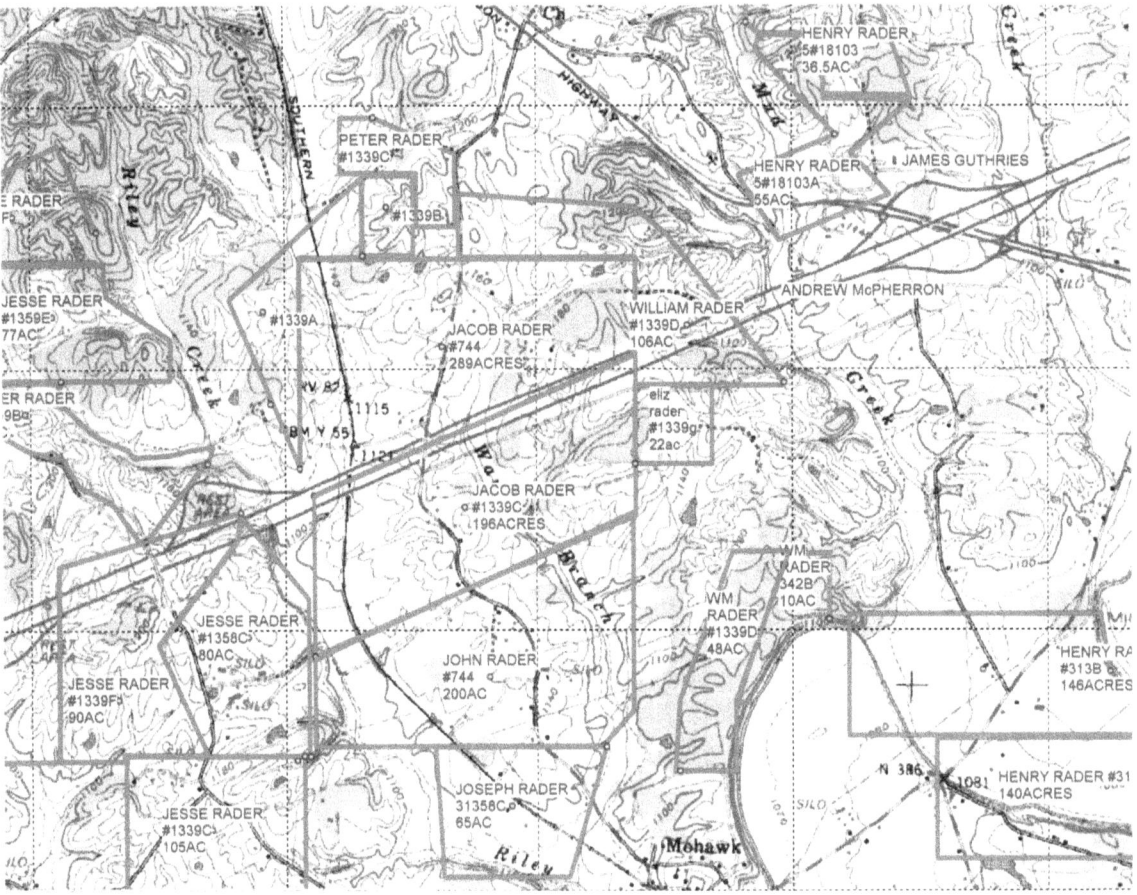

Map of Rader land in Lick Creek

He owned land on 22 Sep 1801 in Greene County, Tennessee. John Rader moved from Wythe County, Virginia to Greene County, Tennessee prior to 1801 according to a land deed for the purchase of 200 acres from Thomas Province located in Greene County (Greene County Deed Book volumn 24, page 186 dated September 22, 1801).

He owned land on 22 Sep 1801 in Greene County, Tennessee. John Rader moved from Wythe County, Virginia to Greene County, Tennessee prior to 1801 according to a land deed for the purchase of 200 acres from Thomas Province located in Greene County(Greene County Deed Book volumn 24, page 186 dated September 22, 1801). This same 200 acres was later sold to John Lady in 1819(Deed Book volumn 1, page 37 dated February 23, 1819).

He owned land on 22 Sep 1801 in Greene County, Tennessee. John Rader moved from Wythe County, Virginia to Greene County, Tennessee prior to 1801 according to a land deed for the purchase of 200 acres from Thomas Province located in Greene County(Greene County Deed Book volumn 24, page 186 dated September 22, 1801). This same 200 acres was later sold to John Lady in 1819(Deed Book volumn 1, page 37 dated February 23, 1819).

He owned land on 31 May 1803. John and wife Mary sold 300 acres of land to Michael Cormany

He owned land on 31 May 1803 in Wythe Co, TN. John and wife Mary sold 300 acres of land to Michael Cormany

On 29 Jul 1807 in Greene County, Tennessee. John Rader was appointed by the Greene County, Tennessee Court of Common Pleas to rear Daniel Etter, son of John and Mary Etter, and to teach him the trade of wagon maker(Page 237).

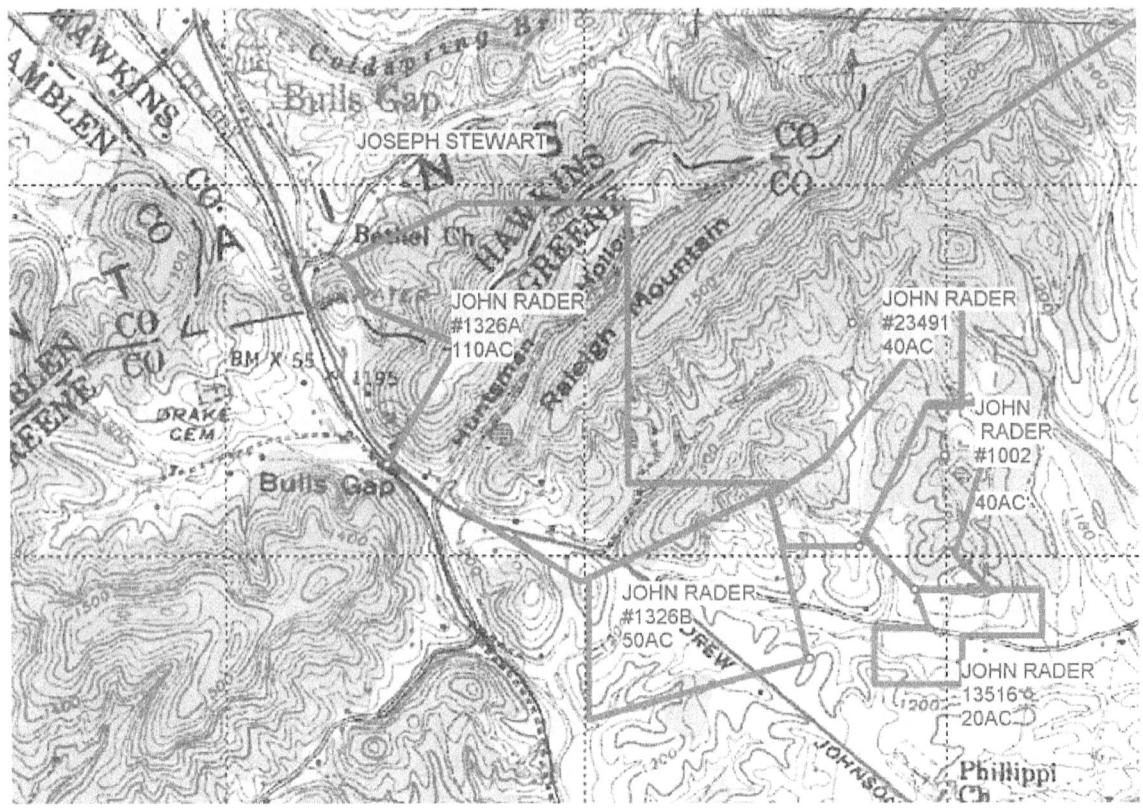

Map of Bulls Gap land John bought in 1812

Description: Deed book #9 page 438 110 acres - page 439 50 acres from Henry Cross (16 Sep 1812)]

He owned land in 1809 in Bulls Gap, Tennessee. From 1809 to 1811 John was living in Captain Joseph Kirk's district on the waters of Lick Creek and owned 200 acres of land. By 1812 he had purchased 160 additional acres in Bulls Gap, Tennessee lying in Greene, Hawkins and Jefferson Counties. By 1829 he had sold the 200 acres and had only the 160 acres at Bulls Gap.

He owned land in 1809 in Lick Creek Valley, Greene County Tennessee. The Greene County tax list indicated he owned 200 acres of land.

From 1809 to 1811 John was living in Captain Joseph Kirk's district on the waters of Lick Creek and owned 200 acres of land.

He was adopted on 15 Nov 1809 in Wythe County, Virginia. Thr court appointed John Rader guardian for Samuel, Anne, and Susanna Rader, orphans of William Rader, deceased, in 1805, and on November 15, 1809, samuel was to be bound out to Christopher Oury to learn the trade of a taylor, and annie was to be bound out to Christopher, son of Christopher Bown. These were his brother William Rader's children, as William had died about 1802

He owned land in 1812 in Lick Creek Valley, Greene County Tennessee. Tax records show 360 acres for both 1812 and 1813

He owned land on 16 Sep 1812 in Lick Creek Valley, Greene County Tennessee.[49] purchased two parcels from Henry Cross By 1812 he had purchased 160 additional acres in Bulls Gap, Tennessee lying in Greene, Hawkins and Jefferson Counties. #1326A and #23491

[Caption: 072]

He owned land on 16 Sep 1812 in Lick Creek Valley, Greene County Tennessee.[49] purchased two parcels from Henry Cross By 1812 he had purchased 160 additional acres in Bulls Gap, Tennessee lying in Greene, Hawkins and Jefferson Counties.

[Caption: John's old Brick house on old 11E]

[Description: #060]

He owned land on 16 Sep 1812 in Lick Creek Valley, Greene County Tennessee.[49] purchased two parcels from Henry Cross By 1812 he had purchased 160 additional acres in Bulls Gap, Tennessee lying in Greene, Hawkins and Jefferson Counties. #1326A and #23491

[Caption: Bulls Gap]

He owned land on 16 Sep 1812 in Lick Creek Valley, Greene County Tennessee.[49] purchased two parcels from Henry Cross By 1812 he had purchased 160 additional acres in Bulls Gap, Tennessee lying in Greene, Hawkins and Jefferson Counties. #1326A and #23491

[Caption: 1326b]   [Description: (16 sep1812)]

He owned land in 1813 in Lick Creek Valley, Greene County Tennessee. tax records show 390 acres

[Caption: 13516]   [Description: Tennessee Land Grant for 20 acres (6 Jan 1817)]

He owned land in 1814 in Lick Creek Valley, Greene County Tennessee. tax records show 445 acres

[Caption: Tennessee land grant 1002][Description: (12 Jul 1832)]

He owned land in 1815 in Lick Creek Valley, Greene County Tennessee. tax records for 1815 and 1816 show 390 acres

He owned land on 6 Jan 1817 in Lick Creek Valley, Greene County Tennessee. Purchased Tennessee Land Grant #13516 containing 20 acres

[Caption: 071]

He owned land on 6 Jan 1817 in Lick Creek Valley, Greene County Tennessee. Purchased Tennessee Land Grant #13516 containing 20 acres

He owned land on 23 Feb 1819 in Greene County, Tennessee. This same 200 acres was later sold to John Lady in 1819 (Deed Book volumn 1, page 37 dated February 23, 1819).

He appeared on the census in 1820. WYTHE COUNTY, VIRGINIA CENSUS PAGE 611

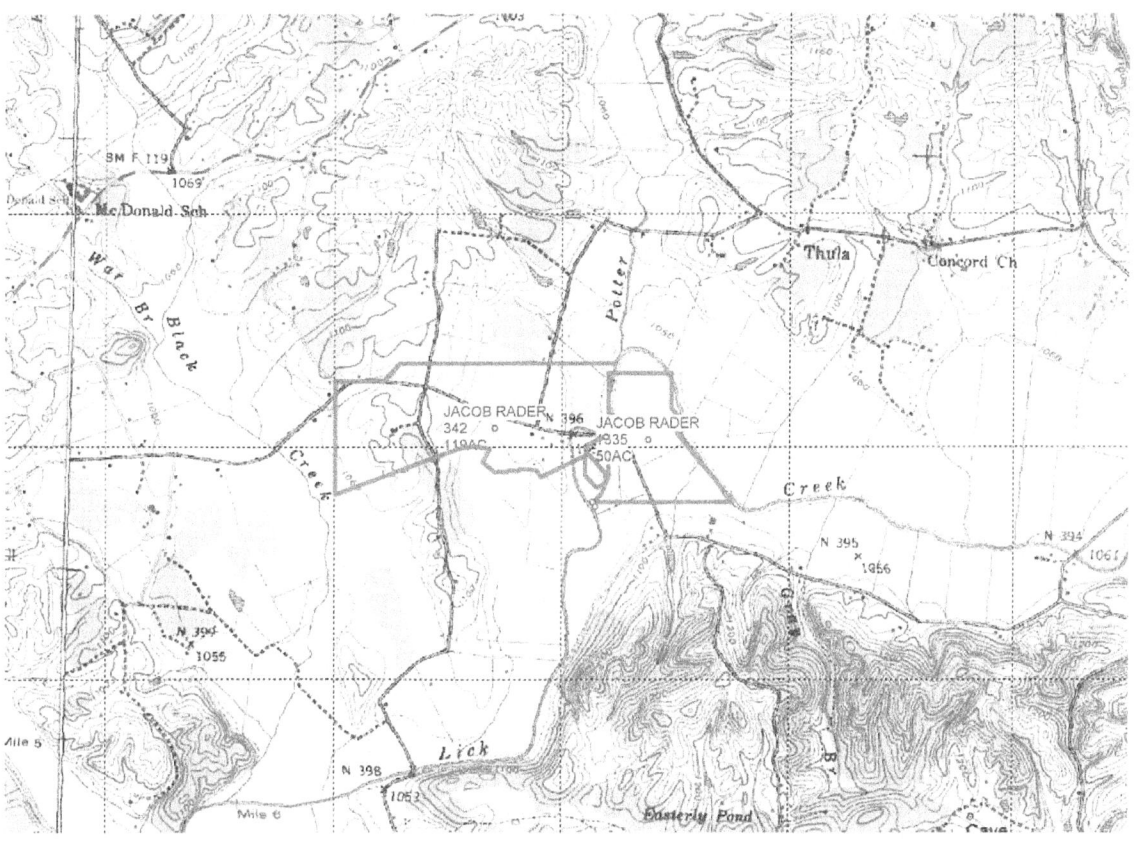

Map of Land Jacob bought 1820 near Fairview church

He owned land on 22 Mar 1820 in Lick Creek Valley, Greene County Tennessee. Purchased two parcels from Andrew Bryan; 50 acres # 1335A and 119 acres #342

He owned land on 12 Mar 1822 in Greene County, Tennessee. John signed a deed of trust to Merryman Payne for the 160 acres he owned lying in Greene, Hawkins and Jefferson Counties to secure a loan of ninety dollars and seventy cents from Deaderick and Sevier of Greeneville, Tennessee.

[Caption: Old Stage Rd & Babbs Mill Rd]

[Description: #059]

He owned land on 9 Dec 1826 in Bulls Gap, Greene County, Tennessee. Tennessee Land Grant #1002 containing 25 acres

He owned land on 9 Dec 1826 in Bulls Gap, Greene County, Tennessee. Tennessee Land Grant #1002 containing 25 acres

He owned land in 1828 in Lick Creek Valley, Greene County Tennessee. tax records show 160 acres for 1828 and 1829 By 1829 he had sold the 200 acres and had only the 160 acres at Bulls Gap.

Census 2: 1830. WYTHE COUNTY, VIRGINIA CENSUS PAGE 351

He owned land in 1830. tax records show 106 acres for 1830

He owned land in 1831 in Lick Creek Valley, Greene County Tennessee. tax records for 1831 and 1832 show 76 acres

He owned land in 1833 in Lick Creek Valley, Greene County Tennessee. tax records for 1833 show 129 acres

He owned land in 1834 in Lick Creek Valley, Greene County Tennessee. tax records show 210 acres for 1834

He owned land in 1835 in Lick Creek Valley, Greene County Tennessee. tax records show 129 acres for 1835

He owned land on 6 Nov 1835 in Lick Creek Valley, Greene County Tennessee. Again on November 6, 1835 John mortaged his property consisting of 50 acres located in Bulls Gap, Tennessee and 31 acres located on War Creek on the waters of Lick Creek. This property was used to secure a loan of $287.63 from Lewis Woolford of Wythe County, Virginia with John Etter acting as trustee for the benefit of Lewis Woolford (Greene County Deed Book volumn 18, page 63 dated November 6, 1835). Both John Rader and Lewis Woolford died before this last debt was repaid and the executors of the estate of Lewis Woolford sued the estate of John Rader to recover the $287.63 (Greene County, Tennessee Chancery Court volumn May 1825 to March 1836, page 481 dated 1842).

John probably mortaged his property in 1835 to defray expenses in a lawsuit filed against him and James Guthrie on November 9, 1835 in Greene County, Tennessee Chancery Court (Chancery Court record dated November 9, 1835, page 279). The case involved the rightful ownership of 90 acres of land John possessed lying in Greene, Hawkins and Jefferson Counties. The case was heard on February 16, 1837 and resulted in John loosing ownership of the property, some of the same property he had mortgaged in 1835.

He owned land on 9 Nov 1835 in Greene County, Tennessee. John mortaged his property consisting of 50 acres located in Bulls Gap, Tennessee and 31 acres located on War Creek on the waters of Lick Creek. This property was used to secure a loan of $287.63 from Lewis Woolford of Wythe County, Virginia with John Etter acting as trustee for the benefit of Lewis Woolford(Greene County Deed Book volumn 18, page 63 dated November 6, 1835).

John probably mortaged his property in 1835 to defray expenses in a lawsuit filed against him and James Guthrie on November 9, 1835 in Greene County, Tennessee Chancery Court(Chancery Court record dated November 9, 1835, page 279). The case involved the rightful ownership of 90 acres of land John possessed lying in Greene, Hawkins and Jefferson Counties. The case was heard on February 16, 1837 and resulted in John loosing ownership of the property, some of the same property he had mortgaged in 1835. A final disposition of the case was filed in the Greene County, Tennessee Deed Book numner 22, page 412 dated March 24, 1847. Also a complete history of the case was filed in Chancery Court dated February 17 1837, page 306 with a final disposition filed in Chancery Court dated September 14, 1837, volumn May 1825 to March 1836, page 315.

Census 3: 1840. GREENE COUNTY, TENNESSEE PAGE 73

He owned land in 1840 in Lick Creek Valley, Greene County Tennessee. tax records show 125 acres for 1835 and zero from then on. In 1840 John was living in district number six and owned three separate pieces of land, one containing 50 acres, another 44 acres and one containing 31 acres.

Alt Death: 3 Feb 1840, Greene County, Tennessee. In 1840 John was living in district number six and owned three separate pieces of land, one containing 50 acres, another 44 acres and one containing 31 acres.

Estate Sale: 3 Oct 1840, , , Greene, Tennessee.[18] John Rader died intestate in Greene County, Tennessee in August of 1840. Leland Davis was appointed by county court to act as administrator of his estate. The court also appointed William Willoughby, Thomas Jackson and Vincent Jackson as commissioners to set aside a portion of the estate left by John Rader to be used by his widow Mary Rader (Greene County, Tennessee County Court volumn January 1839 to December 1843,pages 159 and 167, dated September 7, 1840 and October 5, 1840 respectively)

The personal estate of John Rader was sold at public auction on October 2 and 3 of 1840. The sale of individual items and those who purchased them is recorded in the Greene County, Tennessee Inventory of Estates, volumn 1828 to 1854, page 574, dated October 5, 1841. Some of the items purchased were: scythe and cradle - $2.00, broad axe - $2.12, hammer and anvil - $.65, one loom - $2.50, candlestand - $1.91, harrow - $2.51, plow - $3.07, pair of spectacles - $.50, razor and box - $1.01, umbrella - $1.26, windmill - $14.06, big kettle - $3.20, fur hat - $2.12, bed - $5.00, horse - $35.00, cow - $9.56 and books - $.79. His personal estate was sold for a total of $373.13.

He had an estate probated on 14 Feb 1844 in Greeneville, Greene County, Tennessee. The settlement of John Rader's estate was a legal nightmare and was finally sorted out in Chancery Court in Greeneville, Tennessee on February 14, 1844. The final decree for this case can be found in Chancery Court record volumn June 1841 to June 1848, pages 455 through 457, dated June 1844.

This final decree is valuable since it lists all the children of John and Mary Rader, the husbands of all his daughters and the location of each of his children. As a result of the decree, the remainder of John's land was sold at public auction on June 10, 1844 at the Greeneville Courthouse to William Drake and Anthony B. Keele for $67.75.

Mary Rader, the wife of John Rader, died in 1848 and left a Will dated April 2, 1847. This Will was probated in Greene County, Tennessee on March 6, 1848 which is used as her death date since the exact date is not known.

Mary gave most of her personal estate to her daughters; Sarah and Sophia were not mentioned. The remainder of her estate was sold at public auction on April 3, 1848 and is recorded in the Greene County, Tennessee Inventory of Estates, volumn June 1843 to March 1854, page 320.

After John died Mary lived the remainder of her life with her oldest daughter Elizabeth.

Greene County Tennessee Chancery Court Minutes P. 455

Leland Davis, Adm. & Petitioner vs. Widow & heirs at law of John Rader, Sr. dec'd.

Feb. Term 1843. In August 1840 John Rader, Sr. died intestate owning personal property & 2 tracts of land personal property sale included notes amounting to $373.13. Estate still owes $380.86. Rader owned land near Bulls Gap adjoining Wm. Drake - 48 acres, another tract 35 acres in Hawkins County adjoining Wm Keel.

John Rader died leaving a widow, Mary Rader and the following heirs: John Rader, William and his wife Elizabeth, James Altone & wife Catharine, Andrew Guthrie and his wife Isabel, Samuel, Jesse, and William Rader of Greene County Frederick M. Etter & wife Sarah of Monroe County Tennessee Leander W. Hudson & wife Sophia, residence unknown. Wm. Jenkins and wife Evaline of Hawkins County, William Colyer and wife Lucinda residence unknown. Petitioner wants land sold to pay debts. June Term 1844 - 25 Acre tract sold to Anthony B. Keale $17.25, 40 acre tract to Wm. Drake for $40.50. Applied to debts - deeds of transfer made and & admistrator to pay costs.

He owned land on 24 Mar 1847 in Lick Creek Valley, Greene County Tennessee. A final disposition of the case was filed in the Greene County, Tennessee Deed Book numner 22, page 412 dated March 24, 1847. Also a complete history of the case was filed in Chancery Court dated February 17 1837, page 306 with a final disposition filed in Chancery Court dated September 14, 1837, volume May 1825 to March 1836, page 315.

John married **Mary Etter**,[18] daughter of **Daniel Etter** and **Mary Magdalen Rein**, on 17 Dec 1793 in Wythe County, Virginia.[17, 18, 32] Mary was born in 1776 in Wythe County, Virginia[17, 18] and died on 6 Mar 1848 in Greene County, Tennessee[17, 18] at age 72.

Marriage Notes: LDS film #34254 Wythe county Marriage Register--1790-1905 1793--On the 17th day of Dec Joined together John Reader and Mary Etter by virtue of a license by: J. finley Esqr.

The record of the marriage of John and Etter,Mary is recorded in the "Annals of Southwest Virginia 1769-1800" by Lewis Preston Summers, part two of volumn one. On May 24, 1800 John was living in Wythe County, Virginia and had one male in his household over 16 years of age and owned one horse and no slaves. In 1800 John was listed as a subscriber for the building of the St. John's Lutheran Church in Wytheville, Virginia(See "Wythe Conuty Chapters" edited and published by James S. Presgraves).

John Rader and Mary Etter were married in Wythe County, Virginia on December 17, 1793. See the "Annals of Southwest Virginia" by Summers, page 1377.

Noted events in their marriage were:

Alt Marriage: 17 Dec 1794, , Rev John Stanger, Wythe, Virginia.[18]

    Death Notes: Greene Co. TN Wills

    Will of Mary Rader

I Mary Rader do make and publish this my Last Will and testament, hereby revoking and making void all other wills by me at any time made.

First, I direct that my funeral expences and all my Debts Doctorbills etc. be paid as soon after my Death as possible out of any moneys that I may die possessed of or may first come into the hands of my Executor.

Secondly, I give and bequeath to my daughter Elizabeth Rader, my best bed and firtature consisting of bedstid, under bed, feather bed, two pillows and slips, one sheat three blankets, one nedle worked counter pane. and one nine dimented quilt, also one set of red flowerd earthen plates and my two dishes and also one dutch oven, one biscuit baker and lid, and one small pot and my new dark grounded callico dress, for trouble that she has had in taking care of me.

Thirdly, I give and bequeath to my daughter Lucinda Colyer my Blue mareene cloak.

Fourthly, I give and bequeath to my daughters namely Catharine Altom, Elizabeth Rader, Isabella Guthrie, Lucinda Colyer and Emaline Jenkins, the balance of my wearing cloths to be equally distributed among them and if they cannot agree amongs themselves how to divide them they must leave it to some disinterested person to divide them for them.

Fifthly, that all the balance of the property that I may die possessed of to be sold on at twelve months credit and the proseeds thereof to be equally divided amongst all my lawful heirs if there should be any, after defraying my Funeral Expenses and Debts as heretofore named.

Lastly, I do hereby nomindle and appoint William Rader my son in law my Executor and that he shall not be required to enter into bond with security. In witness whereof I do to this my will set my hand and seal this the second daty of April one Thousand eight hundred and forty seven.

Mary X Rader (her mark)(seal)

Signed sealed and published in our presences and we have subscribed our names hereto in the presence of the testator this the 2nd day of April 1847.

Samuel Crosby

Jesse Rader, Sr.

General Notes: the will of Mary Rader 6 March 1848 $100 To daughter, Elizabeth Rader, bed furniture etc. and 1 set red flower earthen plates. To daughter, Lucinda Colyer, my blue mercer cloak. To daughters, Catharine Altom, Esabella Guthrie, Emaline Jenkins, balance of my wearing cloths. Executor: Son-in-law, William Rader. Will dated: 2 April 1847.
Witnesses: Lemuel Crosby, Jesse Rader Senr. Signed: Mary Rader
(her x)
Facts about this person:

Will April 02, 1847

Green Co. Tn.

!The will of Mary is shown as "probated" 6 March 1848. Only the daughters Elizabeth, Lucinda, Catharine, Esabella, and Emaline are shown. A son-in-law William Rader is the executor. (The Will execution date is 2 April 1847).

Would appreciate exchange of info and correction of info. pjsharkey@hotmail.com

Greene COUNTY TENNESSEE Wills

Will of Mary Rader

I Mary Rader do make and publish this my Last Will and testament, hereby revoking and making void all other wills by me at any time made.

First, I direct that my funeral expences and all my Debts Doctorbills etc. be paid as soon after my Death as possible out of any moneys that I may die possessed of or may first come into the hands of my Executor.

Secondly, I give and bequeath to my daughter Elizabeth Rader, my best bed and firtature consisting of bedstid, under bed, feather bed, two pillows and slips, one sheat three blankets, one nedle worked counter pane. and one nine dimented quilt, also one set of red flowerd earthen plates and my two dishes and also one dutch oven, one biscuit baker and lid, and one small pot and my new dark grounded callico dress, for trouble that she has had in taking care of me.

Thirdly, I give and bequeath to my daughter Lucinda Colyer my Blue mareene cloak.

Fourthly, I give and bequeath to my daughters namely Catharine Altom, Elizabeth Rader, Isabella Guthrie, Lucinda Colyer and Emaline Jenkins, the balance of my wearing cloths to be equally distributed among them and if they cannot agree amongs themselves how to divide them they must leave it to some disinterested person to divide them for them.

Fifthly, that all the balance of the property that I may die possessed of to be sold on at twelve months credit and the proseeds thereof to be equally divided amongst all my lawful heirs if there should be any, after defraying my Funeral Expenses and Debts as heretofore named.

Lastly, I do hereby nomindle and appoint William Rader my son in law my Executor and that he shall not be required to enter into bond with security. In witness whereof I do to this my will set my hand and seal this the second daty of April one Thousand eight hundred and forty seven.

Mary X Rader (her mark)(seal)

Signed sealed and published in our presences and we have subscribed our names hereto in the presence of the testator this the 2nd day of April 1847.

Samuel Crosby

Jesse Rader, Sr.

Noted events in her life were:

Alt Birth: 1776, Pennsylvania.

She appeared on the census in 1840. GREENE COUNTY, TENNESSEE PAGE 73

She had an estate probated on 6 Mar 1848 in Greene County, Tennessee. Mary Rader, the wife of John Rader, died in 1848 and left a Will dated April 2, 1847. This Will was probated in Greene County, Tennessee on March 6, 1848 which is used as her death date since the exact date is not known. Mary gave most of her personal estate to her daughters; Sarah and Sophia were not mentioned. The remainder of her estate was sold at public auction on April 3, 1848 and is recorded in the Greene County, Tennessee Inventory of Estates, volumn June 1843 to March 1854, page 320. After John died Mary lived the remainder of her life with her oldest daughter Elizabeth.

JOHN MARRIED MARY ETTER, DAUGHTER OF DANIEL ETTER AND MARY MAGDALEN REIN (DISPUTED) 18 DEC 1793 IN WYTHE CO, VA BORN 1776 DIED MAR 1848 IN GREEN CO, TN. CHILDREN: JOHN RADER JR., CATHERINE "CATY" RADER, ELIZABETH RADER, SOPHIA RADER SARAH A "SALLY" RADER, WILLIAM RADER, MARY RADER, SAMUEL RADER, ISABELLA "IBBIE" RADER, LUCINDA RADER, EMALINE RADER.

!Believed that he moved to Greene Co. about 1801.

Children from this marriage were:

+ 31 M   i.   **John Rader Jr.**[1, 2, 3, 6, 8, 10, 11, 12, 14, 15] was born in 1795 in Wythe County, Virginia and died after 1860 in Greene County, Tennessee.

John married **Ethelinda M. Smiley** (b. 1796, d. Bef 1860) on 29 Oct 1818 in Greene County, Tennessee.

+ 32 F   ii. **Catherine "Caty" Rader**[1, 2, 3, 6, 8, 10, 11, 12, 14, 15] was born about 1797 in , Wythe, Virginia.

Catherine married **James Altom** (b. Abt 1794) on 7 May 1814 in , , Greene, Tennessee.

+ 33 F   iii. **Elizabeth Rader**[1, 2, 3, 4, 6, 7, 8, 10, 11, 12, 14, 15] was born on 3 May 1799 in Wythe County, Virginia and died on 13 Sep 1871 in Mohawk, Greene Co, TN at age 72.

Elizabeth married **William Rader** (b. 28 Jun 1799, d. 25 Nov 1877) on 23 Nov 1820 in Gap Creek, Greene County Tennessee.[4]

+ 34 F   iv. **Sarah 'Sally' A. Rader**[1, 2, 3, 6, 8, 10, 11, 12, 14, 15] was born on 22 Aug 1801 in Wythe County, Virginia and died on 18 Aug 1886 in McMINN COUNTY, TENNESSEE at age 84.

Sarah married **Fredrick Washington Etter** (b. 15 May 1805, d. 31 Oct 1856) on 29 Nov 1828 in Greene County, Tennessee.

Sarah next married **Valentine Patton** on 7 Apr 1820.

+ 35 M   v.   **William Rader**[1, 2, 3, 6, 8, 10, 11, 12, 14, 15] was born about 1805 in , , Greene, Tennessee.

William married **Peggy Baysinger** (b. Abt 1805) on 26 Jan 1824 in , , Greene, Tennessee.

+ 36 F   vi. **Mary Rader**[1, 2, 3, 6, 8, 10, 11, 12, 14, 15] was born on 27 Feb 1806 in Wythe County, Virginia and died before 1847.

Mary married **Jessie Rader** (b. 1816) before 1844 in , , Greene, Tennessee.

+ 37 F vii. **Sophia Rader**[1, 2, 3, 6, 8, 10, 11, 12, 14, 15] was born on 22 Jul 1808 in Botetourt County, Virginia and died on 13 Feb 1868 in Coles Co. Illinois at age 59.

    Sophia married **Leander M. Hudson** (b. 5 Sep 1809, d. 19 Dec 1879) on 22 Oct 1832 in Greene County, Tennessee.

+ 38 M viii. **Samuel Rader**[1, 2, 3, 6, 8, 10, 11, 12, 14, 15] was born about 1810 in , , Greene, Tennessee and died before 1850 in , , Greene, Tennessee.

    Samuel married **Delilah Kinser** (b. 1812) on 11 Jul 1833 in , , Greene, Tennessee.

+ 39 F ix. **Isabella 'Ibbie' Rader**[1, 2, 3, 6, 8, 10, 11, 12, 14, 15] was born in 1813 in Greene County, Tennessee, died in Feb 1884 in Hawkins County, Tennessee at age 71, and was buried in Cumberland Presbyterian Cemetery, Hawkins County, Tennessee.

    Isabella married **Andrew Guthrie** (b. 18 Dec 1801, d. 3 Aug 1867) on 11 Sep 1832 in Greene County, Tennessee.

+ 40 F x. **Lucinda Rader**[1, 2, 3, 6, 8, 10, 11, 12, 14, 15] was born in 1819 in Greene County, Tennessee, died on 3 Aug 1893 in Tennessee at age 74, and was buried in Phillips Cem, St Clair, TN.

    Lucinda married **William Colyer** (b. 9 Jan 1818, d. 9 Aug 1893) on 14 Jan 1839.[50]

+ 41 F xi. **Emaline Rader**[1, 2, 3, 6, 8, 10, 11, 12, 14, 15] was born in 1820 in Wythe County, Virginia.

    Emaline married **William Jenkins** (b. 1815) on 8 Oct 1840 in John Walker, Jp, Greene Co, TN.

William died early in Wythe county Virginia

5. William Rader[1, 2, 3, 5, 6, 7, 8, 10, 11, 12, 13, 14, 15, 16, 18] (*Casper Sr*[1]) was born about 1770 in East Pennsboro Twp, Cumberland Co., PA [16, 17, 18] and died in 1802 in Wythe County, Virginia [17, 18] about age 32.

General Notes: William Rader was born about 1770 in East Pennsboro, Cumberland COUNTY, PENNSYLVANIA He died in 1802 in Wythe Co, VIRGINIA

The marriage of William and Christina Alvery is recorded in the "Annals of Southwest Virginia 1769 - 1800" by Lewis Preston Summers.

An inventory of the estate of William Rader was taken on February 1, 1802 in Wythe County, Virginia and was settled on September 21, 1805. The Will of his father dated May 18, 1812 indicated that William was deceased and had left the following children: Samuel Rader, Mary Rader and Susan Rader. A footnote in the 1800 Wythe county tax list indicated that William had died in 1802 and that his widow had remarried to Absalom Fickle.

An inventory for the Estate of William Rader (1 Feb 1801) was recorded 13 JUL 1802 (Wythe Co p. 216). Settlement was 21 SEP 1805 (recorded Oct 1805 (p 331) Among the items owened by William Rader were 9 hogs, a horse and mare, 7 cows, 2 yearling heiffers, a "yew" and a lamb, horse gears, cutting "nife" and steel, 17 geese, a "bar Share and Shovel plough" feather beds and furniture, a chest, a wheel and cotten cards, a spinning wheel, 3 small bags, a man's saddle, 3 pots, an oven and a skillet, a dresser and furniture, tinware, a bottle and a "pale" work tools, an ax, a mattock, a hoe, wooden ware, a grindstone, broom, slays and harness.

The following is from "The lost Children of WYTHE COUNTY, VIRGINIA 1790-1878 by Mary B. Kegley 198510 Apr 1805 John Rader guardian of Samuel, Anne and Susanna Rader children of Wm. Rader deceased. John Rader was a taylor in the town of Evansham [Wytheville] 15 Nov 1809 John Rader guardian of Samuel Rader and Anne Rader, orphans of William Rader deceased. Samuel was to be bound out to Christopher Oury to be a tailor and Anne Rader to Christopher Brown, son of Christopher. 12 Apr 1815, Susannah orphan of William Rader, deceased, chose John Repass her guardian, and Anne her sister, chose Christopher Brown, as they were "upwards of age 14"

Noted events in his life were:

Alt Birth: Abt 1772, , , Lancaster, Pennsylvania.

Alt Birth: 1780.

Alt Death: 1801, Wythe County, Virginia.[17]

He had an estate probated on 13 Jul 1802 in Wythe County, Virginia. . An inventory of the estate of William Rader was taken on February 1, 1802 in Wythe County, Virginia and was settled on September 21, 1805. The Will of his father dated May 18, 1812 indicated that William was deceased and had left the following children:.Samuel Rader, Mary Rader and Susan Rader. A footnote in the 1800 Wythe county tax list indicated that William had died in 1802 and that his widow had remarried to Absalom Fickle. An inventory for the Estate of William Rader (1 Feb 1801) was recorded 13 JUL 1802 (Wythe Co p. 216). Settlement was 21 SEP 1805 (recorded Oct 1805 (p 331) Among the items owened by William Rader were 9 hogs, a horse and mare, 7 cows, 2 yearling heiffers, a "yew" and a lamb, horse gears, cutting "nife" and steel, 17 geese, a "bar Share and Shovel plough" feather beds and furniture, a chest, a wheel and cotten cards, a spinning wheel, 3 small bags, a man's saddle, 3 pots, an oven and a skillet, a dresser and furniture, tinware, a bottle and a "pale" work tools, an ax, a mattock, a hoe, wooden ware, a grindstone, broom, slays and harness

William married **Christina 'Diney' Helvey Or Alvery**, daughter of **Henry Helwig Sr.** and **Susannah Gail**, on 14 Dec 1790 in Wytheville, Wythe County, Virginia.[17, 18] Christina was born in 1770 in Wythe County, Virginia[17, 18] and died in Apr 1815[17, 18] at age 45. Other names for Christina were Christina "Diney" Alvery, Tiney Alvery, Tiney Helvey, and[18] Tiney Helvy.

Marriage Notes: The marriage of William and Christina Alvery is recorded in the "Annals of Southwest Virginia 1769-1800" by Lewis Preston Summers

Noted events in their marriage were:

Alt Marriage: 12 Jan 1796, Wythe County, Virginia By Rev. John Stanger.

Noted events in her life were:

Alt Birth: 1772, Virginia.

Children from this marriage were:

+ 42 F i. **Mary Ann Rader** was born in 1800 in Wythe County, Virginia.

Mary married **William Stowers** (b. 27 Nov 1812, d. 25 Jan 1902) in 1834 in Bland, Virginia.[51]

Mary next married **John Cregan** on 19 Jun 1815.

+ 43 F ii. **Susan "Susannah" Rader** was born in 1800 in Wythe County, Virginia.

Susan married **James "Black Jim" Hager Jr.** (b. 1791, d. 15 Oct 1859) on 31 Dec 1822 in Tazewell Co., Virginia.

Susan next married **Nathan Turley** (b. 1797) on 31 Dec 1862 in Kanawha County Virginia.

+ 44 M iii. **Samuel Rader** was born in 1802 in Wythe County, Virginia.

William next married **Christina Helvy** on 12 Jan 1796 in Wytheville, Wythe County, Virginia.

William next married **Tiney Alvery** on 12 Jan 1796 in , Wythe, Virginia.

Jacob moved to Greene county Tennessee

6. Jacob Rader[1, 2, 3, 4, 5, 6, 7, 8, 10, 11, 12, 13, 14, 15, 16, 18] (*Casper Sr*[1]) was born about 1772 in East Pennsboro Twp, Cumberland Co., PA[4, 16, 17, 18] and died on 22 Jul 1822 in Greene County, Tennessee[17] about age 50.

Death Notes: The death date of Jacob is not known but his Will was probated in GREENE COUNTY, TENNESSEE on July 22, 1822. Jacob Reader (Rader) 22 July 1822 $1200 Wife, Elizabeth, to get equal part. Executors: Wife, Elizabeth, John Etter. Written 18 May 1822. Witnesses: Turner Sharpe, James Guthrie. signed : Jacob Rader

General Notes: References:1. "Wythe County Chapters" edited and published by James S. Presgraves.2. Greene County, Tennessee Deed Book 7, page 54, dated 11/14/1805.3. Greene County, Tennessee Deed Book number 17, page 277.4. Greene County, Tennessee Inventory of Estates, pages 354 and 355 and dated 10/18/1834.

Jacob married Elizabeth Woods Been Hedrick in Wythe Co, VIRGINIA, January 25, 1806. Elizabeth was born 1771. Elizabeth died 1860 in Greene Co, TENNESSEE

A will submitted by Cliford R. Canfield for PETER HEDRICK of Wythe county 24th FEB 1832 shows

"- to my daughter Elizabeth who was intermarried with Jacob Reader.. "

Noted events in his life were:

Alt Birth: 1771.

Alt Birth: Abt 1774, , , Lancaster, Pennsylvania.

Alt Birth: 1780.

He had a religion in 1800 in Wytheville, Wythe County, Virginia. In 1800 Jacob was listed as a subscriber for the building of the St. John's Lutheran Church in Wytheville, Virginia(See "Wythe County Chapters" edited and published by James S. Presgraves).

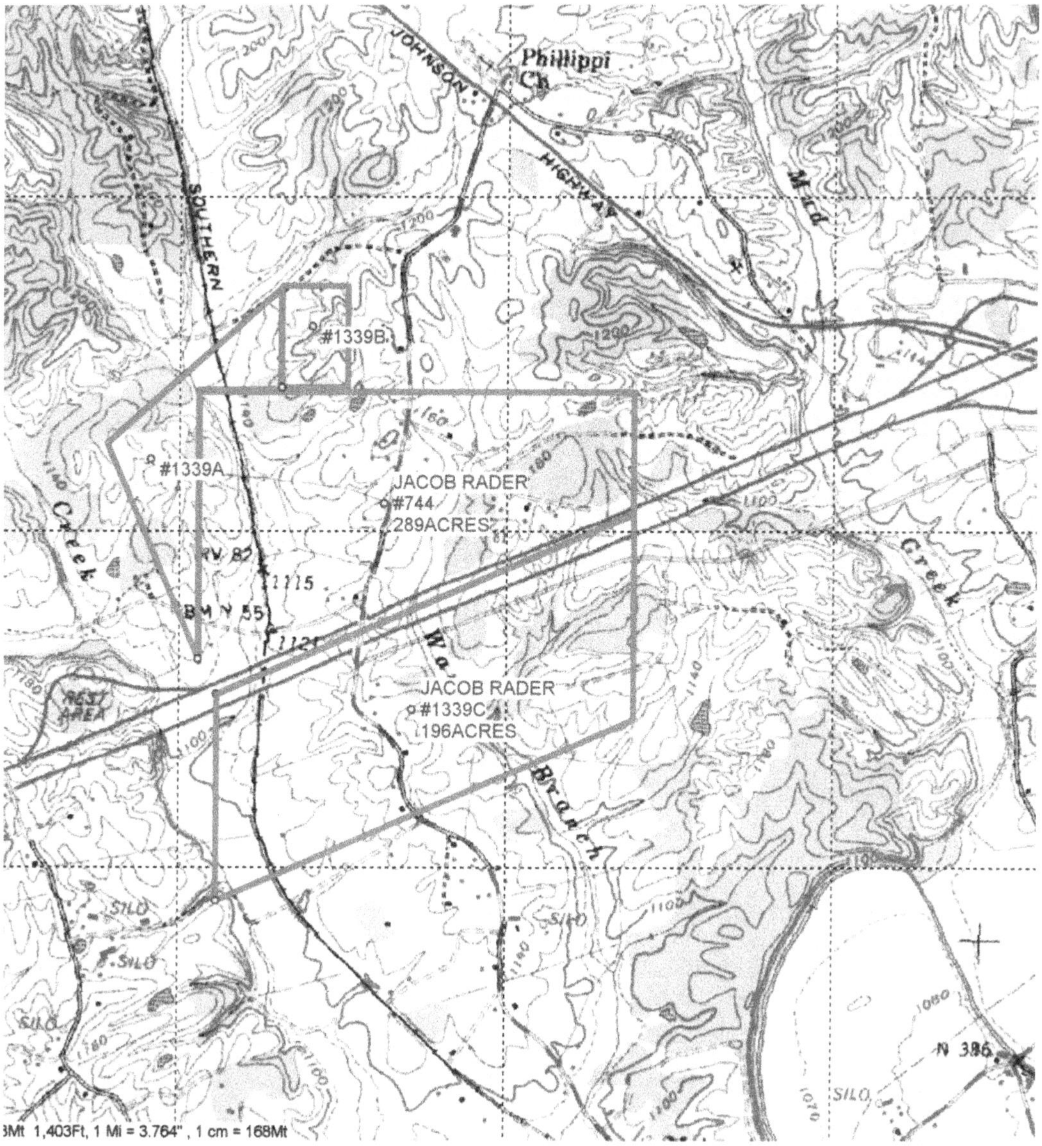

Map of Jacob owned land in 1805 in Greene County, Tennessee.

The Greene County, Tennessee tax lists of 1809 through 1812 indicated Jacob owned a total of 496 acres of land located on Lick Creek in Captain Joseph Kirk's Company.

from Danial Slavens 188 acres 14 Nov 1805, 22 acres 14 Oct 1805, 43 acres 14 Nov 1805 and from Isaac Walker 196 acres 22 nov 1808

He owned land in 1805.

[Caption: The graveyard is in the cluster of trees] [Description: 074] He owned land in 1805.

[Caption: The old Rader house site]

[Description: 004]

He owned land in 1805.

He owned land on 14 Oct 1805 in Lick Creek Valley, Greene County Tennessee. Purchased parcel # 1339B containing 22 acres from Danial Slavens

He owned land on 14 Nov 1805 in Greene County, Tennessee. The following is a brief history of Jacob and Elizabeth Rader who made their way from Wythe County, Virginia sometime after 1806 to Greene County, Tennessee. On November 14, 1805 Jacob purchased 289 acres of land located on the north side of Lick Creek in Greene County, Tennessee and listed his residence as Wythe County, Virginia. They made their home on the rich bottom lands of Lick Creek in the western end of the county near Bulls Gap. On November 14, 1805 Daniel Slavens sold 284 acres of land located on the north side of Lick Creek in Greene County, Tennessee to Jacob Rader of Wythe County, Virginia. This deed was witnessed by his two brothers Henry and Phillip Rader.

He owned land on 14 Nov 1805 in Lick Creek Valley, Greene County Tennessee. purchased parcel #744 containing 188 acres from Danial Slavens

He owned land on 14 Nov 1805 in Lick Creek Valley, Greene County Tennessee. purchased parcel #1339A containing 43 acres from Danial Slavens

He owned land on 22 Nov 1808 in Lick Creek Valley, Greene County Tennessee. purchased parcel #1339c containing 196 acres from Isaac Walker

He appeared on the census in 1810. WYTHE COUNTY, VIRGINIA CENSUS PAGE 850

Tax list: 1812, Greene County, Tennessee. The Greene County tax list of 1812 indicated he owned 496 acres of land.

He owned land in 1816 in Greene County, Tennessee. In 1816 Jacob lived in Captain Thomas Self's Company on Lick Creek and owned 475 acres of land.

He owned land in 1820.

He owned land on 22 Mar 1820 in Lick Creek Valley, Greene County Tennessee. Purchased parcel 1335A containing 50 acres from Andrew Bryan

[Caption: the old Log house sat behind this house]

[Description: 096]

He owned land on 22 Mar 1820 in Lick Creek Valley, Greene County Tennessee. Purchased parcel # 342 containing 119 acres from Andrew Bryan

[Caption: 097]

He owned land on 22 Mar 1820 in Lick Creek Valley, Greene County Tennessee.

He signed a will on 18 May 1822 in Greene County, Tennessee. Wife to get parcel they live on and equal part with children

rest divided equally amongst children girls and boys to draw equal part with no difference to be made

Alt Death: 22 Jul 1822, Greene County, Tennessee.[28]

He had an estate probated on 22 Jul 1822 in Greene County, Tennessee. The death date of Jacob is not known but his Will was probated in Greene County, Tennessee on July 22, 1822. Jacob Reader (Rader) 22 July 1822 $1200 Wife, Elizabeth, to get equal part. Executors: Wife, Elizabeth, John Etter. Written 18 May 1822. Witnesses: Turner Sharpe, James Guthrie. signed : Jacob Rader

He had an estate probated on 22 Jul 1822. GREENE COUNTY, TENNESSEE

Tax list: 1828, Greene County, Tennessee. The 1828 tax list indicated Jacob was deceased and that his estate amounted to 659 acres of land located on Lick Creek in Captain McPherons Company.

Alt Death: Abt 1829, Mohawk, , , Tennessee.[18]

He appeared on the census in 1830 in Lick Creek Valley, Greene County Tennessee. In 1830 Elizabeth was living along Lick Creek and owned 172 acres of land(Tax list).

Tax list: 1830, Lick Creek Valley, Greene County Tennessee. The tax list of 1830 did not contain Jacob but did indicate his widow Elizabeth was living in Captain McPherons Company on Lick Creek and owned 172 acres of land. In 1840 she was living in District number 6 and owned 172 acres of land.

He had an estate probated on 18 Oct 1834 in Greene County, Tennessee. This Will was probated in Greene County, Tennessee on July 22, 1822. On January 30, 1830 the family of Jacob Rader divided the landed estate of their father [3]. This deed was witnessed by James Scott, Jesse Glasscock, William wiscarver and David Mace and is important since it identified the heirs of Jacob Rader: Elizabeth Rader, William Rader, Joseph Rader, Jesse Rader, Jacob Cobble and Sally Cobble, John Willoughby and Eliza Willoughby, Martin G. Rader, and Peter Rader. The deed stated that Elizabeth Rader was widow of Jacob Rader and was living on the estate left by Jacob and that Peter Rader was to inherit the homeplace after his mother Elizabeth died.

The inventory of Jacob Rader's estate was recorded in Greene County, Tennessee on October 18, 1834 [4]. This record indicated that John Etter and Elizabeth Rader were executors of the Will of Jacob Rader and that Joseph Davis and Peter Cobble had been appointed by the Court to settle with the executors. This settlement listed the heirs of Jacob Rader:"William Rader receipt for his full share of his father's estate", "Joseph Rader receipt for his full share of his father's estate", "Jesse Rader receipt for his full share of his father's estate", "Jacob and Sally Cobbles receipt for their full share of the estate of Jacob Rader dec'd", "John willaby and Eliza his wife receipt for their full share of the estate of J. Rader dec'd", "M. G. Rader receipt for his full share of the estate of Jacob Rader dec'd", "Also the receipt of William Rader guardian for P. R. Rader one of the minor heirs of Jacob Rader dec'd"

. The tax list of 1830 did not contain Jacob but did indicate his widow Elizabeth was living in Captain McPherons Company on Lick Creek and owned 172 acres of land. In 1840 she was living in District number 6 and owned 172 acres of land.

On May 18, 1822 Jacob wrote his Will and indicated that all his heirs were to share in his property.

This Will was probated in Greene County, Tennessee on July 22, 1822. On January 30, 1830 the family of Jacob Rader divided the landed estate of their father [3]. This deed was witnessed by James Scott, Jesse Glasscock, William wiscarver and David Mace and is important since it identified the heirs of Jacob Rader:

Elizabeth Rader,
William Rader,
Joseph Rader,
Jesse Rader,
Jacob Cobble and Sally Cobble,
John Willoughby and Eliza Willoughby,
Martin G. Rader,
and Peter Rader.

The deed stated that Elizabeth Rader was widow of Jacob Rader and was living on the estate left by Jacob and that Peter Rader was to inherit the homeplace after his mother Elizabeth died.

The inventory of Jacob Rader's estate was recorded in Greene County, Tennessee on October 18, 1834 [4]. This record indicated that John Etter and Elizabeth Rader were executors of the Will of Jacob Rader and that Joseph Davis and Peter Cobble had been appointed by the Court to settle with the executors.

This settlement listed the heirs of Jacob Rader:"William Rader receipt for his full share of his father's estate", "Joseph Rader receipt for his full share of his father's estate", "Jesse Rader receipt for his full share of his father's estate", "Jacob and Sally Cobbles receipt for their full share of the estate of Jacob Rader dec'd", "John willaby and Eliza his wife receipt for their full share of the estate of J. Rader dec'd", "M. G. Rader receipt for his full share of the estate of Jacob Rader dec'd", "Also the receipt of William Rader guardian for P. R. Rader one of the minor heirs of Jacob Rader dec'd"

The GREENE COUNTY, TENNESSEE tax lists of 1809 through 1812 indicated Jacob owned a total of 496 acres of land located on Lick Creek in Captain Joseph Kirk's Company.

On January 30, 1830 the family of Jacob Rader divided the landed estate of their father and this is recorded in a deed of the same date, deed book number 17, page 277. This record is important since it lists all the children and son in laws of Jacob Rader.

The inventory of Jacob Rader's estate was recorded in the GREENE COUNTY, TENNESSEE Inventory of Estates, pages 354 and 355 and dated October 18, 1834. This record also lists all the children of Jacob Rader.

Elizabeth, the wife of Jacob Rader, died sometime between 1860 and 1870. She was living in GREENE COUNTY, TENNESSEE with her youngest son Peter R. Rader in 1850 and 1860 (Census).

Jacob married **Elizabeth Woods Been Hedrick**, daughter of **Unknown** and **Unknown**, on 25 Jan 1806 in Wythe County, Virginia.[17, 18] Elizabeth was born in 1771 in Black Lick, Rural Retreat, Wythe Co., VA,[4, 17, 18, 52] died in 1860 in Greene County, Tennessee[17, 18, 28] at age 89, and was buried in Mohawk, , , Tennessee. Other names for Elizabeth were Elizabeth Bean, Elizabeth Woods Been Hedrick, and Elizabeth Woods.[18]

Noted events in their marriage were:

Alt Marriage: Abt 1797, , , , Virginia.

> General Notes: A will submitted by Cliford R. Canfield for PETER HEDRICK of Wythe county 24th FEB 1832 shows "-to my daughter Elizabeth who was intermarried with Jacob Reader .."
>
> Elizabeth was living in Greene County, Tennessee with her youngest son Peter R. Rader in 1850 and 1860(Census).

Noted events in her life were:

Tax list: 1830, Greene County, Tennessee. The tax list of 1830 did not contain Jacob but did indicate his widow Elizabeth was living in Captain McPherons Company on Lick

Creek and owned 172 acres of land. In 1840 she was living in District number 6 and owned 172 acres of land.

She had an estate probated on 30 Jan 1830 in Greene County, Tennessee. On January 30, 1830 the family of Jacob Rader divided the landed estate of their father and this is recorded in a deed of the same date, deed book number 17, page 277. This record is important since it lists all the children and son in laws of Jacob Rader. The inventory of Jacob Rader's estate was recorded in the Greene County, Tennessee Inventory of Estates, pages 354 and 355 and dated October 18, 1834. This record also lists all the children of Jacob Rader. Elizabeth, the wife of Jacob Rader, died sometime between 1860 and 1870. She was living in Greene County, Tennessee with her youngest son Peter R. Rader in 1850 and 1860(Census).

She has conflicting death information of Abt 1864 and Mohawk, Greene Co, TN.

Children from this marriage were:

+ 45 M i. **William Rader**[1, 2, 3, 4, 6, 7, 8, 10, 11, 12, 14, 15] was born on 28 Jun 1799 in Wytheville, Wythe County, Virginia and died on 25 Nov 1877 in Mohawk, Greene Co, TN at age 78.

William married **Elizabeth Rader** (b. 3 May 1799, d. 13 Sep 1871) on 23 Nov 1820 in Gap Creek, Greene County Tennessee.[4]

(Duplicate Line. See Person 33)

+ 46 M ii. **John Rader**[4, 7] was born about 1800 in Wythe County, Virginia and died before 1822.

+ 47 M iii. **Joseph Rader**[1, 2, 3, 4, 6, 7, 8, 10, 11, 12, 14, 15] was born about 1801 in , Wythe, Virginia and died in Clay County, Illinois.

Joseph married **Tennessee Tennessee** (b. Abt 1805) about 1825 in Tennessee.[4]

+ 48 M iv. **Jesse Rader**[1, 2, 3, 4, 6, 7, 8, 10, 11, 12, 14, 15] was born in 1804 in VA and died in 1890 in Greene County, Tennessee at age 86.

Jesse married **Catharine (Ketron) Catron** (b. Abt 1823, d. 8 Dec 1896).

Jesse next married **Elizabeth Willoughby** (b. Abt 1810, d. 10 Mar 1875) on 22 Oct 1828 in Greene County, Tennessee.[4]

Jesse next married **Eliza J. 'Hannah' Willoughby** (b. 10 Aug 1854, d. 26 Nov 1938) on 26 Oct 1828.

Jesse next married **Catherine Laughner** (b. 1823, d. 9 Dec 1896) on 14 Oct 1875 in Greene County, Tennessee.

+ 49 F v. **Sarah 'Sally' Rader**[1, 2, 3, 4, 6, 7, 8, 10, 11, 12, 14, 15] was born on 21 Mar 1806 in Wythe County, Virginia[32] and died before 1860 in Midway, Greene Co., TN.

Sarah married **Jacob 'Jake' Cobble** (b. 1798, d. Bef 1860) on 2 Sep 1825 in Greene County, Tennessee.[28]

+ 50 F vi. **Elizabeth 'Eliza' Rader**[1, 2, 3, 4, 6, 7, 8, 10, 11, 12, 14, 15] was born on 15 Jul 1808 in Wytheville, Wythe County, Virginia,[52] died on 27 Dec 1893 in Greene

County, Tennessee[52] at age 85, and was buried in Willoughby Cem, Gap Creek, Greene Co, TN.

Elizabeth married **John M. Willoughby** (b. 12 May 1805, d. 18 Sep 1869) on 23 Apr 1829 in Greene County, Tennessee.[53]

+ 51 M vii. **Jacob Rader**[4, 7] was born about 1809 in Greene County, Tennessee and died before 1822.

+ 52 M viii. **Martin George Rader**[1, 2, 3, 4, 6, 7, 8, 10, 11, 12, 14, 15] was born on 23 Feb 1811 in Mohawk, Greene Co, TN and died before 1850 in Capt. Mcpherons, Greene Co, TN.

Martin married **Mary A. 'Polly' Lady** (b. 10 Dec 1815, d. 11 Dec 1895) on 16 Jul 1833 in Greene County, Tennessee.

+ 53 F ix. **Susannah Rader**[4, 7] was born about 1812 in Greene County, Tennessee and died in 1892 about age 80.

Susannah married **William Etter** (b. 21 Apr 1806, d. 29 Aug 1860) on 19 Sep 1830 in Greene County, Tennessee.[54]

+ 54 M x. **Peter R. Rader**[1, 2, 3, 4, 6, 7, 8, 10, 11, 12, 14, 15] was born on 15 Oct 1819 in Mohawk, Greene Co, TN and died on 16 May 1877 in Bulls Gap, Greene County, Tennessee at age 57.

Peter married **Kegish S. 'Kissiar' Rhea Ray?** (b. Abt 1824, d. 3 Jan 1903) on 31 Dec 1844 in Greene County, Tennessee.

Peter next married **Kezia S. Rhea** (b. 28 Jun 1824, d. 3 Jan 1903) on 31 Dec 1844.

Casper moved to Sevier county Tennessee

7. Casper Rader Jr.[1, 2, 3, 5, 6, 7, 8, 10, 11, 12, 13, 14, 15, 16, 18] (*Casper Sr*[1]) was born in 1774 in East Pennsboro Twp, Cumberland Co., PA,[16, 17, 18] died in 1830 in Sevier County, Tennessee[17, 18] at age 56, and was buried in Fox Cemetery, Sevier County, Tennessee.

Death Notes: The following is exerpted from "In the Shadow of the Smokies:

Casper Rader died 27 Jan 1834 age 5y,5m,19 days Henry Rader died 8-16-1826 Casper Rader died 8-8-(unreadable) Barbary Rader died (unreadable)

Burial

Fox Cemetery, Sevier Co. TN.

Casper , Jr. Rader was born about 1774 in East Pennsboro, Cumberland

COUNTY, PENNSYLVANIA

General Notes: Casper is reported to be buried in Fox Cemetery, Sevier County, TENNESSEE I have been there but the older stones could not be read. It is also reported that Barbara and both children are buried there. There are several members of the Schroder family buried in the Fox Cemetery.

Casper Rader received 117 acres in District E, Block 2 in 1810
Casper Rader received 50 acres in District E, Block 2 in 1825

Daniel Rader received 131 acres in District E, Block 12 in 1810

There is a Casper Rader listed in the 1830 census as being 50-60 years old

Joseph Shrader was born March 17, 1805 in Wythe County, Va. He is buried at Fox Cemetary.

Sevier County Cemeteries

FOX CEMETERYhttp://www.sevierlibrary.org/genealogy/cemeteries/flat/fox.htm

RADER -

Casper Died 27 Jan 1834 5y 5m 19d (slate-badly sunken)
Barbary 8 Mar 1845 8 ___ 1846 Aged __ (slate 60y? 3m 3d)
Henry Died 16 Aug 1826 (slate)
Casper Died 8 Aug _8__ (slate)
Note--All four Rader stones are slate and are fading badly

Noted events in his life were:

Alt Birth: Abt 1776, , , Lancaster, Pennsylvania.

Alt Birth: 1784.

Tax list: 17 Feb 1790, Wythe County, Virginia. Casper was living in the vicinity of Reed Creek and the Crab Orchard

Fork of Little Walker's Creek.

Tax list: 23 Apr 1800, Wytheville, Wythe County, Virginia. Casper was living in Wythe County, Virginia on April 23, 1800 and had one male in his household over 16 years of age and no horses or slaves. In 1800 Casper was listed as a supporter for the building of the St. John's Lutheran Church in Wytheville, Virginia (See "Wythe County Chapters" edited and published by James S. Presgraves). The St. John's Lutheran Church record of Wytheville, Virginia indicated that Casper and Barbara Armbruster Rader sponsored a child born to Christian Schroder in 1805.

He had a religion in 1805 in Wytheville, Wythe County, Virginia. The St. John's Lutheran Church record of Wytheville, Virginia

indicated that Casper and barbara Armbruster Rader sponsored a

child born to Christian Schroder in 1805

He owned land on 23 Nov 1809 in Sevier County, Tennessee. Casper purchased 177 acres of land in Grant #1265 on the waters of flat creek. This propety is connected to a property owned by Daniel Rader.

He appeared on the census in 1810 in Wythe County, Virginia. The Will of George Armbruster written October 30, 1802 and probated in Wythe county November 10, 1802 (Will Book No. 1, page 234) indicated his daughter Barbara had married a Rader.

Note: 13 Mar 1824, Sevier Co, TN. Casper Rader of Sevier Co, TN signs a note for his deceased wife Barbara Armbrister

He owned land on 28 Jun 1825 in Sevier County, Tennessee. Casper purchased 50 acres of land Grant #277

He appeared on the census in 1830 in Sevier Co, TN. LINE 21 PAGE 117

1830 Sevier County, TENNESSEE Census Lists Casper as Head OF Household 1male 50-60 1 female 40-60

Alt Death: 8 Aug 1830, Sevier County, Tennessee.

He appeared on the census in 1840 in Census Of Wife Only.

Casper married **Barbara Armbrister**,[16, 18] daughter of **George Armprister** and **Barbara**, in 1802 in Wythe County, Virginia.[16, 17, 18] Barbara was born about 1775 in George, Virginia,[16, 17, 18] died on 8 Mar 1845 in Sevier County, Tennessee[17, 18] about age 70, and was buried in Fox Cemetery, Sevier County, Tennessee. Other names for Barbara were Barbara Armprister, and Barbary Armprister.

Marriage Notes: The Will of George Armbruster written October 30, 1802

and probated in Wythe county November 10, 1802 (Will Book No.1, page 234) indicated his daughter Barbara had married a Rader. There is no positive evidence, however, that this was Casper.

> General Notes: 1830 CENSUS LISTS CASPER HEAD OF HOUSEHOLD 1 MALE 50-60 1 FEMALE 40-60
>
> 1840 CENSUS LISTS BARBARA HEAD OF HOUSEHOLD 1 FEMALE 50-60 1 FEMALE 70-80

Noted events in her life were:

She appeared on the census in 1830. SEVIER COUNTY, TENNESSEE LINE 21 PAGE 117

Census 1: 1840. SEVIER COUNTY, TENNESSEE

> Rader, Barbary males 0   females 0000000101

Children from this marriage were:

+ 55 M i. **Henry Rader** died on 16 Aug 1826 in Sevier County, Tennessee and was buried in Fox Cemetery, Sevier County, Tennessee.

+ 56 M ii. **Casper Rader** was born on 8 Aug 1829, died on 27 Jun 1834 in Sevier County, Tennessee at age 4, and was buried in Fox Cemetery, Sevier County, Tennessee.

Casper next married **Mary Ann Milliron** WFT Est 1854-1887. Mary was born on 6 Apr 1840 in Armstrong Co., PA and died on 24 Apr 1933 in McCrea's furnace, Wayne Twp, Armstrong Co, PA at age 93.

> General Notes: My great-grandmother, Lovina Rader and her mother, Mary Ann (Milliron) Rader are enumerated twice on the 1860 census: once (12 August 1860), with Henry Rader, the father and husband, in his parents' household, and once [26 June 1860] in Mary Ann's father's family (one county over). Since Lovina was born on 5 May 1860, my theory is that either Mary Ann went home to be with her father and step-mother for the birth of her first child, or she took the baby to visit so her father could see his (first, I think) grandchild, and just happened to be in that household when the census-taker came. As Elissa says, "Every record tells a story." (even if we can't be 100% sure what it is!)
>
> Christine
> Christine Crawford-Oppenheimer
> Hyde Park, NY

8. Phillip Rader Sr. [1, 2, 3, 5, 6, 7, 8, 10, 11, 12, 13, 14, 15, 16, 18, 33, 34] (*Casper Sr*[1]) was born on 12 Aug 1782 in East Pennsboro Twp, Cumberland Co., PA,[34, 35] died on 2 Nov 1853 in Butler Twp, Montgomery Co Ohio[17, 18] at age 71, and was buried in Sugar Grove cem, Butler Twp, Montgomery Co Ohio. Other names for Phillip were Phillip Rader,[55] Phillip Rader, and[55] Phillip Reader.

Birth Notes: Paper by Margaret Elizabeth Morrett Riley

written at DePauw university 1917

Pro-German to Pro-American

A family by the name of Rader, left Germany, for America about the year 1750. During the rough voyage, the father and mother died, and the three sons, Conrad, Jasper and John were bound out according to the custom. They were taken by different families, in this case, and as it happened, never to meet again

One of the boys was taken to Virginia, in the neighborhood of Wythe Courthouse. Nothing is known of his life or family, except that his son Philip Rader was born August 12, 1782. Philip was raised with little education, but he told his children, of having many good times in a place called Bells Knob. He married Miss Cross and in 1803 moved to Ohio, locating somewhere on the Stillwater. We have been told that he had the only four horse team, in the neighborhood. In 1802 or 1803, Philip hauled the Poplar logs for the home where Henry Waymire was born, just after he moved a Hoover family from Cordina.

When the Indian War broke out in 1812, he enlisted at Dayton, Ohio, under General William H. Harrison, for six months. His Colonel's name was brier. At the end of six months, he hired as a teamster, finding his own team, to haul supplies to the soldiers. He was on the Oglaze or Maimee River during the Battle of Tippecanoe. His four children died young, and his wife died about 1814.

Written by M. Elizabeth Morrett, 1917, DePauw University (Source 3)"....Philip Rader was born August 12, 1782. Philip was raised with little education, but told his children of having many good times in a place called Bells Knob. (VA) He married Miss Cross and in 1803 moved to Ohio, locating somewhere on the Stillwater. We have been told that he had the only four horse team in the neighborhood. In 1802 or 1803, Philip hauled the Poplar logs for the home where Henry Waymire was born, just after he moved a Hoover family from Cordina."

Death Notes: Philip Rader, Sr., d. November 2, 1853, at age 72y-2m-21d, and is bur in Sugar Grove cem, Butler Twp, Montgomery Co Ohio (L.D.M. Brien, Montgomery Co Ohio Cem Records, kp. 162). His will, dated October 29, 1853, proven December 12, 1853, and admitted to probate at Dayton, Montgomery Co Ohio, and recorded at Rochester, Fulton Co Ind, April 4, 1854, leaves his estate to "my children": Chnthian Julien; Mary Pearson; Catharine Jenkins; Andrew Rader; Henry Rader; Julien Rader; Bethany Stephens; "the heirs of my dau Henrietta Fentriss"; "the heirs of my dau Eliza Jan Ball"; son, David, dau Barbara Rader; son, Philip Rader

(Jean C. Tombaugh, Fulton Co Ind Wills).

Philip Rader, Sr., d. November 2, 1853, at age 72y-2m-21d, and is bur in Sugar Grove cem, Butler Twp, Montgomery Co Ohio (L.D.M. Brien, Montgomery Co Ohio Cem Records, kp. 162). His will, dated October 29, 1853, proven December 12, 1853, and admitted to probate at Dayton, Montgomery Co Ohio, and recorded at Rochester, Fulton Co Ind, April 4, 1854, leaves his estate to "my children": Chnthian Julien; Mary Pearson; Catharine Jenkins; Andrew Rader; Henry Rader; Julien Rader; Bethany Stephens; "the heirs of my dau Henrietta Fentriss"; "the heirs of my dau Eliza Jan Ball"; son, David, dau Barbara Rader; son, Philip Rader

(Fulton Co, Ind. Abstracts of Wills 1838-1899, Jean C. Tombaugh, Fulton Co Ind Wills).

General Notes: !See note under Henry Rader (Phillip's brother).

HE MARRIED REBECCA ARMBRUSTER DEC 9 1813 WYTHE CO., VA.

This is the part which does not add up: "Their family (Philip Sr) consisted of six children, all of whom are living except one, and of who "Cap" is the second. They died at their old home in Ohio just one year apart, the mother in 1852 and the father in 1853" Oh, page 25

A family history was written by Wilbur Rader, grandson of Philip Rader, Sr. The history was in the possession of Fay Morrett Sterling at the time of her death and was passed on to her husband - thereby lost to future generations of Raders

Alt Birth: 1775.
Alt Birth: 1780, Pennsylvania.
Alt Birth: 26 Mar 1784, East Pennsboro Twp, Cumberland Co., PA.[16,17]
Alt Birth: 26 Nov 1784, Timberville, Rockingham Co., VA.[55]
Alt Birth: 1788.

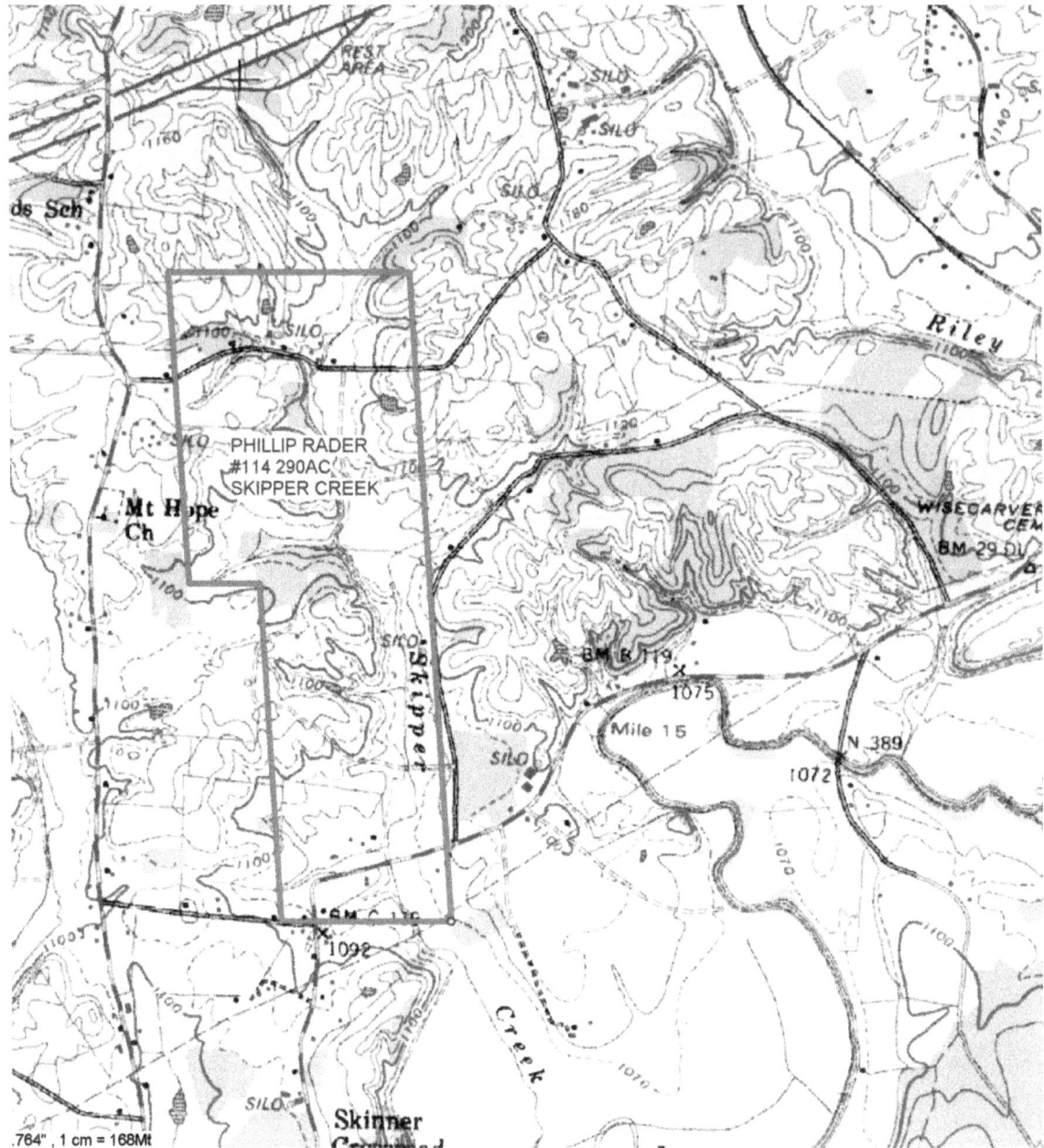

Map of Phillip owned land on 26 Sep 1804 in Lick Creek Valley,

Greene County Tennessee. Greene county Tennessee Deed book 7 page 50

> Phillip purchased 290 acres from Thomas Keef on Skipper Creek

He owned land on 26 Sep 1804 in Lick Creek Vally, Greene County Tennessee. Greene county Tennessee Deed book 7 page 50

> Phillip purchased 290 acres from Thomas Keef on Skipper Creek

He owned land on 14 Nov 1807 in Lick Creek Vally, Greene County Tennessee. Phillip sold to Vinsent Jackson for $200 which he bought for $200

[Caption: Phillip Rader on Skipper creek 094] [Description: parcel #114]

Military: 1812, Dayton, OH. At the breaking out of the Indian War of 1812 he enlisted at Dayton, Ohio, under General William R. Harrison, serving one term of six months. He then found his own team, hired out as a teamster, hauling supplies to the soldiers

He appeared on the census in 1830. BUTLER TOWNSHIP, MONTGOMERY COUNTY, OHIO PAGE 252

Census 1: 1840. BUTLER TOWNSHIP, MONTGOMERY COUNTY, OHIO PAGE 212

Resided: 1845, Akron, Summit County, OH.

He owned property on 1 May 1848. INDIANA LAND GRANT

Census 2: 1850. HENRY TOWNSHIP, FULTON COUNTY, INDIANA PAGE 405 LINE 62

He appeared on the census on 26 Jul 1850 in Henry Township, Fulton County, Indiana. Philip Rader, Sr. 67 M farmer $855 land born Pa.

Catharine	56	F		born Carolina
Andrew	21	M	school teacher	born Ohio
David	20	"	laborer	born Ohio
Henry	15	"		born Ohio
Lisa	17	F		born Ohio
Julian	12	"		born Ohio

Alt Death: 15 Dec 1853, Akron, Fulton County, Indiana.[34]

Phillip married **Margaret Rebecca Cress** in 1803 in Unk.[17, 18] Margaret was born in Wythe County, Virginia[17, 18] and died before 1813 in Dayton, Montgomery County, Ohio.[17, 18] Another name for Margaret was Rebecca.[18]

Marriage Notes: Philip was married three times, his first wife's maiden name was cross. There were four children all dieng very young.

Noted events in their marriage were:

Alt Marriage: 1803, Wythe County, Virginia.[17, 18]

General Notes: "Philip (Jr) mother died in 1826, and one year later his father married Mrs. George

Knox, a widow with six children, namely: Nancy Knox, Sarah (Knox) Hart, Susie (Knox) Pfeutz, John Know, Rebecca Knox and Mary Knox. To this union were born three boys and three girls, making a total of sixteen children and six step-children. The last six were: Andrew, David, Barbara (Rader) Rudy (visited us from PA), Eliza J., Henry C. and Julia (Rader) Sheppard." (Written by M. Elizabeth Morrett, "Pro-German to Pro-American", 1917, DePauw University) No documentation regarding these facts but it is possible that Knox was his 3rd wife and Sheets was his 4th wife.

1. Married to ? Cross in Virginia. Marriage ending about 1814. Died about 1814 in Ohio.

(Info submitted by A. Shepherd)

"Fulton Co Ind history tells that Philip Rader, Sr. was m. (1st) to Miss Cress who died; and that there were four children born who also died (Rader family history says her name was Cross). No marriage record has been located to prove or disprove that statement." (Source 1)

CHILDREN:

4 Children…no names…assumed infant deaths…no info regarding locality of birth or death.

(Info submitted by A. Shepherd)

Will of Jacob Cress - filed for probate 1st Tuesday of May, 1811

Will record book Vol. A, page 35, case 70

Dayton, Ohio courthouse

In the name of God, Amen. Whereas, I, Jacob Cress, being sick of body, but of perfect mind and memory, knowing that it is ordained for all men, once to die, do make this, my last will in testament in the following manner, that is to say,

First:

I give unto my sons, John and Abraham, each, one horse, saddle and bridle. Also, the 1/4 section of land I now live on to be equally divided between said John and Abraham Cress.

My wife: Elizabeth Cress, is to have the 1/3 part of all the produce raised on said land, as long as she may live or remain a widow.

Unto my daughter, Sally Cress, I give a cow and a bed.

The money that is owing to me in Virginia, or elsewhere, I want collected, and the aforesaid land paid up and the balance, if any, I give to my wife, Elizabeth Cress, for her use, if she should need it. Also, all my household and kitchen furniture, as long as she remains a widow or may live. And, after her death, to be equally divided among my five daughters: Elizabeth, Rebeckah, Barbara, Mary, and Sally.

All the farming utensils and jointer tools are to be divided between John and Abraham Cress.

The wagon and hind gear to be sold and the creatures and stock that may be on hand at my death, I also give to my wife in the afore said manner.

The mares that I have given to Philip Rader, he is not to be charged with, as I give to him one and the other he paid for to my satisfaction.

I also appoint my beloved wife, Elizabeth Cress, my executrix, and my son, John Cress, my sole executor of this, my last will and testament.

In witness where of, I have here unto set my hand and seal the 13th Day of May, in the year of our Lord, One thousand, eight and ten.

his
Jacob X Cress
mark
his
Josiah X Lamb
mark
Witnesses: Daniel Hoover - Nicholas Cobel

Will for Probate in Common Pleas Court, Dayton, Ohio. First Tuesday of May, 1811. By the Court,

B. Va n Clive, Clerk

Noted events in her life were:

Alt Death: Abt 1811.

Phillip next married **Catherine Elizabeth Siddon** on 30 Jan 1812 in Montgomery Ohio.[34] Catherine was born in 1796 in North Carolina[34] and died in 1826 in Ohio[34] at age 30. Other names for Catherine were ? Cross, and[34] Elizabeth Siddon.[34]

Marriage Notes: about 1813 Philip married Elizabeth Siddon. To them were born 5 daughters and a son, Synthia Murden, Henrietta Murden, Mary Pearson, Catherine Jinkins, Philip. Christina Stevens (aks Bethany) was born in 1826

Noted events in their marriage were:

None-Ending: Abt 1814, Ohio.

None-Ending: 1826, Ohio.

General Notes: #2. Married to Elizabeth Siddon. Married aft. 1814 in Ohio. Marriage ending 1826. Died 1826

(Info submitted by A. Shepherd)

"There is proof of the (2nd) marriage of Philip Rader to Elizabeth Siddon, January 30, 1812 (L.D.M. Brien, Montgomery Co Ohio Marriages 1803-1851). Elizabeth Rader, wife of Philip, d. 1824, at age 32 years, and is bur in Old Mill Creek cem, Butler Twp, Montgomery Co Ohio (L.D.M. Brien, Montgomery Co Ohio Cem Records, p. 153).

(Source 1)

Noted events in her life were:

She appeared on the census in 1850. HENRY TOWNSHIP, FULTON COUNTY, INDIANA PAGE 405 LINE 62

Census 1: 1870. HENRY TOWNSHIP, FULTON COUNTY, INDIANA PAGE 119 LINE 78

Children from this marriage were:

+ 57 F i. **Synthia Rader**[34] was born on 13 Jan 1812 in Ohio.[34]

Synthia married **Julien Murden**[34] (b. 1818).[34]

+ 58 F ii. **Henrietta Rader**[34] was born on 7 Mar 1818 in Montgomery County, Ohio.[34]

Henrietta married **Joseph Fentres**[34] in 1837.[34]

Henrietta next married **Joseph Fortress** on 22 Sep 1837 in Montgomery County, Ohio.

+ 59 M iii. **Francis J. Rader** was born in 1819 in Ohio.

Francis married **Harriet Palmer**.

+ 60 F iv. **Mary Rader**[34] was born on 3 May 1820 in Ohio[34] and died in 1899 in Miami co, Indiana[34] at age 79.

Mary married **William N. Pearson**[34,34].

+ 61 F v. **Catherine Rader**[34] was born on 4 Feb 1822 in Ohio.[34]

Catherine married **David C. Jenkins**[34] in 1841-Jul 1841.[34]

Catherine next married **David Clarkson Jenkins** (b. 20 Jun 1822, d. 12 Aug 1892) on 4 Jul 1841.

+ 62 F vi. **Hanna J. Rader** was born about 1823 in Montgomery County, Ohio.

Hanna married **Jeremiah Cupp** on 23 Mar 1845 in Montgomery County, Ohio.

+ 63 M vii. **Philip Rader Jr.**[33,34] was born on 7 Jul 1824 in Montgomery County, Ohio,[34] died on 28 Aug 1899 in Akron, Henry Township, Fulton County, Indiana[34] at age 75, and was buried in 1899 in Akron, Henry Township, Fulton County, Indiana.

Philip married **Margaret Stradley**[34] (b. 21 Jun 1827, d. 6 Jan 1907) on 18 Dec 1846 in Akron, Fulton County, Indiana.[34]

+ 64 M viii. **William Rader** was born in 1826 and died on 15 Sep 1895 in Kewanna, Fulton County, Indiana at age 69.

William married **Mary Ann** (b. 1828, d. 17 Aug 1914).

+ 65 F ix. **Christina Bethany Rader**[34] was born in Jul 1826 in Ohio[34] and died on 19 Jan 1904 in Rochester, Fulton County, Indiana[34] at age 77.

Christina married **Jacob Stevens Esq.**[34] (b. 15 May 1824, d. Abt 1886) in Oct 1844.[34]

Phillip next married **Catherine Sheets**[34] ..approx 1827 in Ohio.[34] Catherine was born in North Carolina,[34] died on 10 Aug 1852 in Akron, Fulton County, Indiana, and was buried in Omega Cemetery, Akron, Fulton County, Indiana. Another name for Catherine was Catherine Sheetz.

Marriage Notes: There were 6 children from this marriage, 3 daughters and 3 sons. Andrew Rader, the oldest son lived in Prescott, Wisconsin

She was previously married to George Knox and had 6 childred which were raised with the Rader children

Noted events in her life were:

Alt Death: 1853.[34]

Children from this marriage were:

+ 66 M i. **Andrew Rader**[34] was born on 28 Sep 1828 in Ohio and died in 1900 in Prescott, Pierce County, Wisconsin[34] at age 72.

Andrew married **Louisa Fisher** (b. 29 Jun 1836, d. 13 Nov 1890) on 23 Nov 1854.

Andrew next married **Francis M.** (b. Jul 1854) in 1893.

+ 67 M ii. **David Andrew "Cap" Rader Capt.**[34] was born on 29 Mar 1830 in Montgomery County, Ohio, died on 6 Mar 1908 in Rochester, Fulton co., Indiana[34] at age 77, and was buried in Hoover Cemetery, Fulton County, Indiana.

David married WFT Est 1824-1869.[34]

David married **Rachiel** (b. 1804).

David next married **Delila Dawson** (b. 25 Jan 1839, d. 21 May 1904) on 6 Mar 1864 in Fulton County, Indiana.

+ 68 F iii. **Barbara Rader**[34] was born on 1 Jan 1832[34] and died on 23 Feb 1898 in Pierce Co, WI[34] at age 66.

Barbara married **A. M. Rudy**[34][34].

+ 69 F iv. **Eliza Jane Rader**[34] was born on 11 Aug 1833 in Montgomery County, Ohio,[34] died on 2 Dec 1852 in Fulton County, Indiana[34] at age 19, and was buried in Omega Cemetery, Akron, Fulton County, Indiana.

Eliza married **Aaron Miller Ball** (b. 3 Feb 1827) on 13 Mar 1851 in Fulton County, Indiana.

+ 70 M v. **Henry C. Rader**[34] was born on 25 Jan 1836 in Ohio[34] and died in Colton, CA.[34]

Henry married **Sarah** (b. Oct 1850) about 1887.

+ 71 F vi. **Julia Ann Rader**[34] was born in 1838 in OH[34] and died in Jan 1898 in Iowa[34] at age 60.

Julia married **Oliver Garriott**[34] (d. 1871) WFT Est 1819-1865.[34]

Julia next married **Sheppard**.

Peter moved to Greene county Tennessee but died in Sullivan County, Tennessee

9. Peter Rader[1, 2, 3, 5, 6, 8, 10, 11, 12, 13, 14, 15, 16, 18] (*Casper Sr*[1]) was born on 3 Sep 1780 in East Pennsboro Twp, Cumberland Co., PA,[16, 17, 18] died on 11 Mar 1858 in Greene County, Tennessee[17, 18] at age 77, and was buried in Blountville Cemetery, Sullivan County, Tennessee.

General Notes: On April 23, 1800 Peter Rader was living in Wythe County, Virginia and had one male over 16 years of age in his household and owned one horse and no slaves. The St. John's Lutheran Church record indicates that Peter and was born on October 29, 1812. The Sullivan County, Tennessee census of 1850 listed a Peter and Dorcas Rader with Peter's birth date as 1781 in Pennsylvania and Dorcas's birth date as 1783 in North Carolina. This Peter Rader purchased 50 acres of land in Sullivan County, Tennessee on November 16, 1807 from George Woolford(Sullivan County Deeds volumn 11, page 62 dated November 16, 1807). It is not known if any of these are actually part of Casper Rader's family.

CENSUS 23 APR 1800 IN WYTHE CO, VA OCCUPATION: WHEELWRIGHT, HE MARRIED TARKIS (DORCAS) BORN 1783 IN NC DIED 1820 CHILDREN ELIZA, JAMES J, ELKANAH D, MALINDA, CALVIN M.

Facts about this person:

Burial   March 1858 Blountville Cemetery, Sullivan Co. TN.

Noted events in his life were:

He was employed. WHEELWRIGHT

Alt Birth: 1776, PA.[18]

Alt Birth: 3 Sep 1781, East Pennsboro Twp, Cumberland Co., PA.

He appeared on the census on 23 Apr 1800. WYTHE COUNTY VIRGINIA

He appeared on the census on 23 Apr 1800 in Wythe County, Virginia.

Alt Death: 1820, Greene County, Tennessee.[17]

Census 1: 1840. GREENE COUNTY, TENNESSEE PAGE 76

Census 2: 1850. DISTRICT 1, SULLIVAN COUNTY, TENNESSEE PAGE 28 LINE 247

He appeared on the census in 1850 in Sullivan Co., TN. RADER   PETER   69   M   W   TN   SULLIVAN   1-DIVN   897   28   RADER   DORCAS   67   F   W   NC   SULLIVAN   1-DIVN   897   29

Alt Death: After 1850, Sullivan County, Tennessee.

Alt Death: 11 May 1869, Blountville, Sullivan County, Tennessee.

Peter married **Tarkis (Dorcas) Dorcas**[18] in 1812 in Wythe County, Virginia.[17, 18] Tarkis was born in 1783 in North Carolina,[17, 18] died on 10 Jul 1868 in ?[17, 18] at age 85, and was buried in Blountville Cemetery, Sullivan County, Tennessee.

General Notes: Facts about this person:

Burial Blountville Cemetery, Sullivan Co. TN.

Noted events in her life were:

Alt Death: 1820, ?.[17, 18]

She appeared on the census in 1850. DISTRICT 1, SULLIVAN COUNTY, TENNESSEE PAGE 28 LINE 247

She has conflicting death information of 16 Jul 1869 and Blountville, Sullivan County, Tennessee.

Children from this marriage were:

+ 72 F   i.   **Eliza Rader** was born on 29 Oct 1812 in Blountville, Sullivan County, Tennessee.[32]

+ 73 F   ii.   **Elizabeth Rader** was born in 1812 and died WFT Est 1813-1906 at age 1.

+ 74 M   iii. **James J. Rader** was born in 1814 in Blountville, Sullivan County, Tennessee.

James married **Elizabeth T. T.** (b. 1810).

James next married **Permilia Jane** (b. 1839).

+ 75 M   iv.   **Elkanah D. Rader** was born in 1817 in Blountville, Sullivan County, Tennessee.

Elkanah married **Angelina** (b. 1822).

+ 76 F   v.   **Malinda Rader** was born about 1817 in Blountville, Sullivan County, Tennessee.

Malinda married **James Vaughan Jr.**.

Malinda next married **James Vaughn Jr.**.

+ 77 M   vi.   **Calvin M. Rader** was born on 9 Feb 1818 in Blountville, Sullivan County, Tennessee, died on 24 Apr 1890 in Blountville, Sullivan County, Tennessee at age 72, and was buried in Blountville Cemetery, Sullivan County, Tennessee.

Calvin married **Elizabeth** (b. Abt 1820).

Calvin next married **Elizabeth** (b. 1828).

Calvin next married **Lodemia Caroline Millard** (b. 9 May 1840, d. 4 Oct 1915) on 7 Sep 1876 in Sullivan County, Tennessee.

Mary stayed in Wythe county Virginia

10. Anna Marie 'Mary' Rader [1, 2, 3, 5, 6, 7, 8, 10, 11, 12, 13, 14, 15, 16, 18] (*Casper Sr[1]*) was born on 4 Jul 1778 in East Pennsboro Twp, Cumberland Co., PA, [16, 17, 18, 19, 22] died on 19 Dec 1849 in Wythe County, Virginia [17, 18, 19, 22] at age 71, and was buried in 1849 in St. John Cemetery, Wytheville, Wythe Co., VA. [19, 22] Other names for Anna were Anna Maria "Mary" Rader, Anna Marie (Maria) (Mary)(Roderin) Rader, [19, and 22] Anna Marie (Mary) Rader.

> General Notes: There is confusion as there are 2 Mary Browns in Wythe Co 1. Anna Maria Rader (Jul 1778-Dec 1849) wife of Christopher Brown (Nov 1774-Sep 1850) of Michael 2. Mary Rader (d. May 1822) wife of Christopher Brown of Andrew The will of Michael Brown of Hanover twp., Lancaster Co., PA was written 3-25-1785 and probated 4-27-1785. (Book A pg 1 Dauphin Co., PA)
>
> MARY MARRIED CHRISTOPHER "STOPHEL" BROWN, SON OF MICHAEL BROWN IN HANOVER TWP, LANCASTER CO, PA 1785, CHILDREN DANIEL , SALOME, LYDIA, ROSANNA, JAMES ANDREW.
>
> Facts about this person:
>
> Burial   December 1849
>
> St. Johns Lutheran Cemetery, Wythe Co. VA.
>
> Did she marry a Christopher Brown? See page 52 of book by J. R. Cameron.

Noted events in her life were:

> She appeared on the census in 1810. WYTHE COUNTY, VIRGINIA CENSUS PAGE 822
>
> Census 1: 1820. WYTHE COUNTY, VIRGINIA CENSUS PAGE 207
>
> Alt Death: 10 May 1822, Wythe County, Virginia. [17, 18, 19, 22]
>
> Census 2: 1830. WYTHE COUNTY, VIRGINIA CENSUS PAGE 314
>
> Alt Death: 19 Dec 1849, Wythe County, Virginia.

Alt Death: 19 Dec 1849, Wythe County, Virginia.[17]

Anna married **Christopher A. 'Stophel' Brown Jr**,[18, 19, 22] son of **Michael Brown** and **Unknown**, about 1800 in Wythe County, Virginia.[17, 18, 19, 22] Christopher was born on 7 Nov 1774 in Lancaster Co. PA., died on 20 Sep 1850 in Wythe County, Virginia at age 75, and was buried in 1850 in St. John Cemetery, Wytheville, Wythe Co., VA.[19, 22]

Noted events in their marriage were:

Alt Marriage: , Hanover, Lancaster, Pennsylvania, USA.

General Notes: Hi Jim, (SAMIE MELTON [smmelton@home.com]

Interesting webpage. I'm still early on in my Rader research and your page was very helpful. Thanks. I have one correction though - that is in the family of Christopher and Anna Marie (Rader) Brown. They had six children not five as show in the second generation of Casper Rader. The sixth was John A Brown (born abt 1818). John A Brown, along with Rufus Repass, was named as an executor of Christopher Brown's will (Wythe Co, VA, Will Book 7, p 201-202; LDS Film 0034226).

Samie Melton

Will of Christopher Brown: In the name of God Amen. I Christopher Brown of Wythe County Virginia being advanced in years but of sound mind and disposing memory think proper to make this my last will and testament in manner and form following to wit.

I desire my debts and funeral expenses be paid. It being my desire that all my children be made equal in the distribution of my estate, I hereby will and direct that each be charged with the several sums heretofore given as advancements to wit to my daughter Lydia Repafs widow of Jefse Repafs deceased, the sum of three thousand six hundred and fifty dollars - to my son Daniel Brown the sum of three thousand two hundred and seventy dollars - to my son James A Brown the sum of six thousand one hundred and ninety four dollaes - to my daughter Rosanna Repafs wife of Stephen Repafs the sum of one thousand seven hundred and seventy nine dollars to my daughter Sally Repafs wife of Rufus Repafs the sum of two thousand five hundred and thirteen dollars and to my son John A Brown the sum of six thousand eight hundred and fifty nine dollars which latter sum includes the price of the land herein after devised to my said son John A Brown - it being understood that the sum herein before stated include all the money, lands and other property heretofore given to my children and that all notes, accounts or other evidences of debt heretofore subsisting against my children or the husbands of my daughters are to be cancelled being included in the above mentioned sums charged as advancements.

I give and devise to my son John A Brown the plantation and tract of land on which I reside with all the lands adjoining and containing three hundred and seventy three acres be the same more or

p 202 lefs, to him the said John A Brown and his heirs forever. It is my will and I hereby direct that all the remainder of my estate both real and personal be sold by my executors herein after named on a reason able credit at their discretion and that the proceeds be devided amongst my children, each being first charged with advancements, so that all be made equal in the distribution of my estate.

I constitute and appoint my son John A Brown and my son in law Rufus Repafs executors of this my last will and testament. In the testomony whereof I have hereto set my hand and affixed my seal this sixteenth day of May one thousand eight hundred and fifty (1850). Signed sealed published and declared Christopher Brown (S) by the testor on and for his last will and testament in our presence who have subscribed our names as entranfser A----- in his presences and at his request. William H Foster Charles A Haller J B Mathews

Virginia: At a court held for Wythe County at the Court house on Monday the 14 October 1851 This the last will and testament of Christopher Brown decd was presented in Court proved by the oaths of William H Foster and Charles A Haller two of the subscribing witnefses thereto and ordered to be recorded. And on the motion of John A Brown and Rufus Repafs the executors named in said will who made oath thereto and together with Robert Gibbiney Andrew Hufford, Adam Cafsell, William Repafs, Isaac J Left wich and Eli Xavis their securities entered into and acknowledged a bond in the penalty of $26000 conditioned as the law directs certificate is granted them for obtaining a probate of the said will in due form. Teste H S Mathews CL

Facts about this person:

Burial   September 1850 St. Johns Lutheran Cemetery, Wythe Co. VA.

Military service   1812 Captain during the war of 1812.

The following information was copied from the Virginia W.P.A. Historical Inventory Project dated March 3, 1937 and researched by Regina M. Coughlan from Wytheville, Wythe County, Virginia

1. SUBJECT:

W. A. Umberger Home

2. LOCATION:

4.5 miles north from Wytheville, Virginia on Route #21, to home and log barn on the East Side of the road.

3. DATE:

Unknown

4. OWNERS:

(NOTE Christopher Brown owned several tracts or parcels of land on Sally Run, branch of Reed Creek, acquired both by patent and by purchase).

Christopher Brown, by patent, 200 acres prior to 1800

Christopher Brown by conveyance from William Finley, 396 acres, $3000. Probably the homes site.

Tracing I Finley tract of 396 acres

John McFarland, by patent, 327 acres, June 20, 1754

David and Samuel Finley, 327 acres, Deed book 1, page 95, 1792

William Finley, 327 acres, L-55, Deed book 1, page 95, 1792 - 1812

Christopher Brown, 396 acres, $3000 including above, Deed book 5, page 480, 1812-1850

John A Brown 373 acres, Will book 7, page 241, 1850-1890

John Williams and James Cassell, 435 acres, $15,000., Deed book 38, page 201, 1890-1904

W. A. Umberger, 218 and 2.5 acres, $13,329.45, Deed book 50, page 283, 1904-1938

Christopher Brown by patent, purchase and entry acquired more than one thousand acres of land on Sally run.

DESCRIPTION:

This house is "L" shaped, two and one half stories, full length front porch, also full length back porch, gabled roof with gable in front, big stone chimney at east end, a brick chimney five feet in thickness in center of the front section and another in the center of the L section. There are ten rooms, partly plastered and partly ceiled with wide beaded boards, and fireplaces in each room and in each of the three cellars. A straight enclosed stairway with three landings leads from the second room which little flights of steps lead to bedrooms on east and west sides, the treads are worn off of at the edges. There are the chair rails, and tall wide walnut mantels with shelves supported ornamental brackets. The entry between the front and back sections lead to the kitchen and dining room, main entrance has six-paneled door with sidelights eight by ten inches, a shelf protrudes from the base of the sidelight panel on each side.

The house was apparently built at different times. Eight windows in the second story part five of them show three levels of place-ment in a horizontal row.

An old spring house northwest of house is constructed of brick which had been used in an old house that stood east of the present one built of logs and now covered with weathered boarding. It is said that John A. Brown was owner of many slaves and that the slave quarters was removed years ago. An immense log barn stands just east of the house. It is said that when it was raised to the roof plates the workmen themselves felt some timidity about ascending. Some of them more timorous said, "I would not walk around that plate for a farm", "Nor would I for a horse" etc. Mrs. Brown climbed the ladder, balanced herself on the edge and walked fearlessly around the entire roof plate. The date of erection is unknown but it is thought to be between 1790 and 1820.

HISTORICAL SIGNIFICANCE:

Christopher Brown and his family were prominent in the religious and civil-life of the county. He was deacon of Old ST. John's Lutheran Church 1808 again in 1820. Captain Christopher Brown was an elder in 1825. His son John A. Brown was an elder in 1840. Another son James A, Brown was assistant pastor 1842-1845 and pastor 1850- - 1862. He organized Luther Chapel, Washington County, 1845, and Rosenbau Chapel, Wythe County, 1875; served as trustee of Roanoke College; served as one of a committee, which included Doctor D. F. Bittle and L. D. Hancock, Esq., that selected what is now known as Gibboney Hall, Main Street, as a location for a school for young ladies. Doctor Brown gave unsparingly of both time and material resources to the success of the school, which was organized under the auspices of the Southwest Virginia Lutheran Synod. He was trustee of Marion Junior College organized in 1871, five or six years after the close of the Wytheville School. Christopher Brown- was sheriff of the county in 1846.

There were two Christopher Browns, contemporaries for a number of years in Wythe, father and son perhaps.

In his will, probated in 1851, Christopher Brown named heirs (Each of them charged with sums given as advancement); to DT. Lydia wife of Jesse Repass, $3650; to DT. Rosanna, wife of Stephen Repass, $1779; to DT, Sally, wife of Rufus Repass, $2573: to son, John A. $6859; "which included price of land hereinafter conveyed to said John A; to Daniel $3270; to James A, $6194.

To son John A. the "plantation on which I reside Exors- John A. Brown and Rufus Brown Witnesses William H. Foster, Charles A. Holler and John P. Mathews.

Christopher Browns sale included farming tools and implements of -all kinds, grain, horses, cows, etc. in large numbers. Other item of interest included:

    Surveyor's Compass, John Sharritts $30.25
    Flohr's Sermons and Gazetteer, John Brunty   1.75
    Book case, John A. Brown   14.40
    Clock, Daniel Brown   5.20
    Corner Cupboard, Stephen Repass 11.50
Pewter ware, James Felty   1.50
Dulcimer, Samuel Felty   .20
  Blacksmith tools, John A. Brown 40.50
  German Bible, John A. Brown   1.10
  English Bible, Josiah Leedy   2.00
  Sale top, Andrew Catron   6.00
One lot of German books, John Kegley .25
One lot of German Books, John Kegley .50
Four horse wagon, Isaac Kegley 40.62 1/2
Numerous hogsheads, kettles, pots

Tombstone Inscriptions:

Christopher Brown
Born Nov. 17, 1774
Died. Sept. 20, 1850
Aged 75 years 10 MISSOURI 13 days

 Anna Maria
 Consort of Christopher Brown
 Born July, 4, 1778
 Died Dec., 19, 2 1849
 Aged 71 Years 5 MISSOURI 15 days

Rufus Repass

Born May 8, 1805
Died July 31, 1878

Christopher Brown
Died July 16, 1816
Aged 65 years

Maria Brown
Consort of Christopher Brown
Died May 10, 1822

Sally
Wife of Rufus Repass
Born October 22, 1807
Died December 14, 1891
Note: Sally, daut. of Christopher Brown

Rev. James A. Brown
Born Dec. 22, 1815
Died March 4, 1900
Aged -84 years, 2 MISSOURI 12 days

Ellenora C.
Wife of the Late Rev. James A. Brown
Daughter of the late Rev. T, Herbert
-Born in Gettysburg, PENNSYLVANIA,
Aug, 1, 1819
Died in her home In Wythe County, Virginia
July 20, 1879
Aged 59 years 1 MISSOURI 19 days,

8. SOURCES OF INFORMATION:

Court Records Wythe County.
Church Records of St. John's Lutheran Church
History of the Lutheran Church in Southwest Virginia and Tennessee by Rev. C. W. Cassell.
Tombstone Inscriptions St. John's Lutheran Cemetery

Noted events in his life were:

Military: CAPT. DURING THE WAR OF 1812

Alt Birth: 1751, Lancaster Co. PA..[17, 18, 19, 22]

He appeared on the census in 1810. WYTHE COUNTY, VIRGINIA CENSUS PAGE 822

Alt Death: 16 Jul 1816, Wythe County, Virginia.[17, 18, 19, 22]

Census 1: 1820. WYTHE COUNTY, VIRGINIA CENSUS PAGE 207
Census 2: 1830. WYTHE COUNTY, VIRGINIA CENSUS PAGE 314

Census 3: 1850. WYTHE COUNTY, VIRGINIA PAGE 301 LINE 1072
He has conflicting death information of 20 Sep 1850.

Children from this marriage were:

+ 78 M i. **Esq. Daniel Brown**[19,22] was born on 4 Apr 1803 in Sally Run, Wythe Co, Virginia,[19,22] died on 6 Sep 1856 in Wythe County, Virginia[19,22] at age 53, and was buried in St. Johns Lutheran Cemetery, Wythe County, Wytheville, Virginia.

Daniel married **Theresa Stanger** (b. 27 Feb 1797, d. 9 Nov 1879) on 26 Dec 1822.

+ 79 F ii. **Sally 'Salome' Brown**[19,22,56,57,58] was born on 22 Oct 1806 in Sally Run, Wythe Co, VA,[22] died on 4 Dec 1891 in Wytheville, Wythe County, Virginia[22] at age 85, and was buried in St. Johns Lutheran Cemetery, Wythe County, Wytheville, Virginia.

Sally married **Captain Rufus Repass**[19,22,56,57,58,59] (b. 8 May 1805, d. 31 Jul 1878) on 23 Sep 1827 in Wythe County, Virginia.[22]

+ 80 M iii. **Jesse Brown**[19,22] was born on 16 Jun 1808 in Wytheville, Wythe County, Virginia.[19,22]

+ 81 F iv. **Lydia Brown**[19,22] was born on 11 Jan 1809 in Sally Run, Wythe Co, Virginia,[22] died on 14 Jul 1897 in Wythe County, Virginia[22] at age 88, and was buried in St. Johns Lutheran Cemetery, Wythe County, Wytheville, Virginia.

Lydia married **Jesse Repass**[22,59] (b. 4 Aug 1802, d. 3 Nov 1849) on 24 Oct 1824 in Wythe County, Virginia.

+ 82 F v. **Rosanna Brown**[19,22] was born on 4 Jun 1810 in Sally Run, Wythe Co, Virginia, died on 7 Oct 1901 in Wytheville, Wythe County, Virginia[19,22] at age 91, and was buried in St. Johns Lutheran Cemetery, Wythe County, Wytheville, Virginia.

Rosanna married **Stephen Repass**[22] (b. 2 Aug 1805, d. 7 Aug 1876) on 20 Oct 1829 in Wythe County, Virginia.

+ 83 M vi. **John A. Brown** was born in 1819 in Wythe County, Virginia, died in 1905 in Wythe County, Virginia at age 86, and was buried in St. Johns Lutheran Cemetery, Wythe County, Wytheville, Virginia.

John married **Sarah Tartar** (b. 27 Nov 1820, d. 28 Feb 1900).

+ 84 M vii. **Rev., James Andrew Brown**[19,22] was born on 22 Dec 1815 in Sally Run, Wythe Co, VA,[19,22] died on 4 Mar 1900 in Wythe County, Virginia[19,22] at age 84, and was buried in 1900 in St. John Cemetery, Wytheville, Wythe Co., VA.[19,22]

James married **Eleonora "Ellen" C. Herbst** (b. 1 Aug 1819, d. 20 Jul 1879) on 9 Jul 1843 in Virginia.

Source Citations

James next married **Alice Virginia Sharitz** (b. 4 May 1856, d. 23 Nov 1931) on 19 Sep 1880 in Rosenbaum Chapel, Wythe County Virginia.

+ 85 M viii. **John Ahaz Brown**[19,22] was born before 12 Apr 1818 in Wytheville, Wythe County, Virginia[19,22] and died in Feb 1905 in Wytheville, Wythe County, Virginia.[19,22]

+ 86 M ix. **Joseph Washington Brown**[19,22] was born on 22 Mar 1820.[19,22]

Catherine stayed in Wythe county Virginia

11. Catherine Rader[1,2,3,5,6,7,8,9,10,11,12,13,14,15,16,18] (*Casper Sr*[1]) was born in 1781 in East Pennsboro Twp, Cumberland Co., PA[17] and died in 1844 in Wythe County, Virginia[17,18] at age 63.

General Notes: It is not known if Catherine and Jonathan Lady moved to Greene County, Tennessee with her brothers. The St. John's Lutheran Church record of Wytheville, Virginia indicated that Catherine Lady sponsored Nancy Rader the daughter of Conrad Rader and Elizabeth Rader Rader. Jonathan was probably the son of Abraham Lady of Wythe County, Virginia. Elizabeth Lady, the widow of Abraham Lady, in 1797 relinquished her right of administration of her late husband's estate because she desired to leave the state of Virginia (Wythe County Deed Book No. 2, page 33). This information is listed in hopes that a positive identification of Jonathan's father will eventually be made.

CATHERINE WAS RELATED, IT HAS BEEN SAID, TO GEORGE MASON OF VIRGINIA, AUTHOR OF THE BILL OF RIGHTS, 1ST 10 AMENDMENTS TO THE U.S. C ONSTITUTION, THROUGH HER MOTHER, A MASON.

Noted events in her life were:

   Alt Birth: Abt 1771, East Pennsboro Twp, Cumberland Co., PA.[17]
   Alt Birth: Abt 1781, East Pennsboro Twp, Cumberland Co., PA.
   Alt Birth: 1784, Virginia.[16]
   Alt Birth: 1784, Virginia.[18]
   She appeared on the census in 1810. WYTHE COUNTY, VIRGINIA CENSUS PAGE 842
   Census 2: 1820. WYTHE COUNTY, VIRGINIA CENSUS PAGE 217
   Census 3: 1830. WYTHE COUNTY, VIRGINIA CENSUS PAGE 340

Catherine married **Jonathan Leady**,[18] son of **Unknown** and **Unknown**, before 18 Jun 1805 in Wythe County, Virginia.[17,36] Jonathan was born in 1779 in Wytheville, Wythe County, Virginia[17,18] and died in 1852 in Wythe County, Virginia[18] at age 73. Other names for Jonathan were Johnathan Leedy, and Jonathon Leedy.

   General Notes: Drafted for the War of 1812, he paid John Wyrick $1,200.00 dollars to go in his place.

   HIS DESCENTS REPORTED THAT JONATHAN'S HOUSE "ON A CONSIDERABEL EMINENCE ABOUT 3 MILES NORTH OF WYTHEVILLE WAS STILL STANDING IN 1930, WHEN A TOTAL OF 8 GOOD DWELLINGS STILL STOOD ON THE OLD FARM, BY THEN BROKEN INTO 9 TRACTS.

Source Citations

UNDER A SYSTEM THEN IN EFFECT, JONATHATN PAID $1200. TO JOHN WYRICK TO BE HIS SUBSTITUTE FOR THE WAR OF 1812.[17]

Noted events in his life were:

Alt Birth: 1779, Montgomery County, Virginia.

Alt Birth: Abt 1785, Montgomery , VA..

He appeared on the

census in 1810. WYTHE COUNTY, VIRGINIA CENSUS PAGE 842
Census 2: 1820. WYTHE COUNTY, VIRGINIA CENSUS PAGE 217
Census 3: 1830. WYTHE COUNTY, VIRGINIA CENSUS PAGE 340
Census 4: 1850. WYTHE COUNTY, VIRGINIA #658 LIVING WITH SON SAMUEL
Alt Death: Abt 1855, Wythe County, Virginia.

Children from this marriage were:

+ 87 M i. **Dr. Joel Leedy**[9] was born on 9 Mar 1806 in Wythe County, Virginia, died on 2 Jul 1882 in Lee, Virginia at age 76, and was buried in Sugar Run, Lee County, Virginia.

Joel married **Mary Magdalena "Polly" Kegley** (b. 20 Feb 1801, d. 26 May 1860) in 1828 in Black Lick District, Wythe County, Virginia.

Joel next married **Alvira Cress** (b. 1832, d. Unknown) on 23 Oct 1866 in Lee Co., Virginia.

Joel next married **Mary Magdalena "Polly" Kegley** (b. 20 Feb 1801, d. 26 May 1860) WFT Est 1820.

Joel next married **Elvira A. Crass** after 1860.

+ 88 F ii. **Rachel K. Leedy**[9] was born on 20 Jun 1807 in Wythe County, Virginia and died in 1861 in Stark, Elliott County, KY. at age 54.

Rachel married **Abraham Kegley** (b. 4 Aug 1806, d. After 1880) in 1828 in Wytheville, Wythe County, Virginia.

+ 89 F iii. **Anna Mary Leedy**[9] was born on 26 Sep 1808 in Wythe County, Virginia and died on an unknown date.

Anna married **James Repass** on 8 Sep 1825 in Wythe County, Virginia.

Anna next married **James "Rippas" Repass** (b. 1801, d. Unknown) on 8 Sep 1825 in Wythe County, Virginia.

+ 90 F iv. **Salome "Sally" Leedy**[9] was born on 4 Jun 1810 in Wythe County, Virginia and died on an unknown date.

Salome married **Enoch Bales** (b. Unknown, d. Unknown) on 10 Oct 1833 in Wythe County, Virginia.

Salome next married **Enoch T. Bails** on 10 Oct 1833 in Wythe County, Virginia.

+ 91 M v. **Josiah Leedy**[9] was born on 5 Sep 1813 in Wythe County, Virginia, died on 24 Dec 1903 in Wytheville, Wythe County, Virginia at age 90, and was buried in East End Cemetery, Wytheville, Wythe County, Virginia.

Josiah married **Sally Kegley** (b. 4 Apr 1818, d. 27 Nov 1894) on 8 Oct 1837 in Wytheville, Wythe County, Virginia.

+ 92 M vi. **Isaac Leedy**[9] was born about 1815 in Wythe County, Virginia and died on an unknown date.

+ 93 F vii. **Malinda Leedy**[9] was born on 14 Apr 1818 in Wythe County, Virginia and died in Jun 1880 at age 62.

Malinda married **Abram Ebenezer Yonce** (b. 1815) on 13 Sep 1838 in Wythe County, Virginia.

+ 94 F viii. **Rosina Leedy**[9] was born on 14 May 1820 in Wythe County, Virginia and died on an unknown date in Wythe County, Virginia.

+ 95 M ix. **Samuel Leedy**[9] was born on 4 Mar 1822 in Wythe County, Virginia and died on 13 Mar 1890 in Stark, Elliot County, KY. at age 68.

Samuel married **Mary Polly Adeline Repass** (b. Abt 1821, d. Unknown) on 8 Dec 1842 in Wythe County, Virginia.

Samuel next married **Susan Pennington** (b. Unknown, d. Unknown) on 25 Dec 1875.

Samuel next married **Susannah** (b. 1843) about 1860.

+ 96 F x. **Rebecca Leedy**[9] was born on 5 Aug 1824 in Wythe County, Virginia and died on an unknown date in Wythe County, Virginia.

+ 97 F xi. **Sophia Leedy**[9] was born about 1826 in Wythe County, Virginia, died on 19 Mar 1908 in Wythe County, Virginia about age 82, and was buried in St. Johns Lutheran Cemetery, Wythe County, Wytheville, Virginia.

Sophia married **Steward Dabney Painter** (b. 15 May 1828, d. 6 Jun 1890) on 24 May 1849 in Wythe County, Virginia.

+ 98 F xii. **Nancy Leedy**[9] was born on 2 Feb 1828 in Wythe County, Virginia and died on 24 Feb 1904 in Wytheville, Wythe County, Virginia at age 76.

Nancy married.

+ 99 F xiii. **Catherine Leedy**[9] was born on 4 Oct 1830 in Wythe County, Virginia, died on 7 Jun 1901 in Wythe County, Virginia at age 70, and was buried in Fairview Methodist Cemetery, Wythe County, Virginia.

Catherine married **Daniel M. Sharitz** (b. 23 Oct 1829, d. 3 Jan 1900) on 17 Jul 1852 in Wythe County, Virginia.

Daniel lost a farm in Madison Co., AL then moved to De Soto Co., Mississippi

12. Daniel Rader[1, 2, 3, 5, 6, 7, 8, 10, 11, 12, 13, 14, 15, 16, 18, 37, 38] (*Casper Sr*[1]) was born about 1782 in East Pennsboro Twp, Cumberland Co., PA[16, 17, 18, 38] and died on 27 Oct 1827 in Madison County, Alabama[17, 38] about age 45.

General Notes:

Daniel and Elizabeth probably did not move to Greene County, Tennessee with the other members of his family. The St. John's Lutheran Church record of Wytheville, Virginia indicated that Daniel and Elizabeth Rader were the parents of Samuel Rader born April 20, 1805.

He lost a farm in Madison Co., AL before his death. After that the family moved to De Soto Co., MI.

HE MARRIED ELIZABETH DAVIS, CIRCA 1804 BORN 1789 IN VA DIED MARY 1849 IN DE SOTO CO, MS., CHILDREN: SAMUEL, MALINDA, GEORGE W, REBECCA, JAMES D, MARIA, MARY ANN "JAKE", SARAH C, ELIZA JANE, ELANORE ELIZABETH.

Facts about this person: Burial May 1849 DeSoto Co. MS.

Noted events in his life were:

He was employed. FARMER
Alt Birth: 1790, Montgomery, VA.
Fact 2: Fact 2, 1 Jun 1805, Baptised Samuel Their Oldest Son.
Fact 1: Fact 1, 1814, Moved To Madison County, Alabama.
Alt Death: 27 Oct 1828, Madison County, Alabama.

Daniel married **Elizabeth Davis**,[38] daughter of **George Armprister** and **Barbara**, about 1804 in Wythe County, Virginia.[17, 18, 38] Elizabeth was born in 1789 in VA [17, 38] and died in May 1849 in DE Soto County, Mississippi [17, 38] at age 60. Other names for Elizabeth were Elizabeth Armbrewster, Elizabeth Armbrister, Elizabeth Armbrister, and [18] Elizabeth Armprister.

Noted events in her life were:

Alt Birth: 1790, Montgomery, VA.
Alt Birth: 1790, Wytheville, Wythe County, Virginia.[18]
Alt Death: 1850, Desoto County, Mississippi.[18]

Children from this marriage were:

+100 M i. **Samuel Emerey Rader**[5, 13, 18, 37, 38] was born on 20 Apr 1805 in Wytheville, Wythe County, Virginia,[17, 18, 32, 38] died on 22 Nov 1895 in Union, Fulton County, Arkansas[17, 18, 38] at age 90, and was buried in 1895 in Wesley's Chapel, Union, Fulton County, Arkansas.[17]

Samuel married **Elizabeth Franks**[18, 38] (b. Dec 1821, d. 29 Apr 1903) on 11 Jul 1854 in DE Soto County, Mississippi.[17, 18, 38, 60, 61]

Samuel next married **Elizabeth Byram**[18, 38] (b. 26 Feb 1812, d. 4 Nov 1852) on 27 Aug 1829 in Madison County, Alabama.[17, 18, 38, 62]

+101 F ii. **Malinda Rader**[5, 13, 18] was born about 1807 in Wythe County, Virginia [17, 18] and died in Desoto County, Mississippi.[17, 18]

Malinda married **John Baker** (d. 1844) on 15 Dec 1831 in AL.

+102 M iii. **George W. Rader**[5, 13, 18] was born about 1809 in Wythe County, Virginia [17] and died in 1861 in Kaufman County, Texas [17, 18] about age 52.

Source Citations

George married **Larinda Or Lucinda Larinda** (b. 1818, d. Feb 1860) about 1861 in ?.

+103 F iv. **Rebecca Rader**[5, 13, 18] was born about 1811 in Wythe County, Virginia[17, 18] and died about 1860 in Senatobia, Mississippi[17, 18] about age 49.

Rebecca married **Alfred Bryam** (b. 1808) on 5 May 1831 in Madison County, AL.

(Duplicate Line. See Person 18)

+104 M v. **James Daniel Rader**[5, 13] was born on 13 Nov 1813 in Tennessee, died on 20 Aug 1887 in Wilson County, Texas[17, 18] at age 73, and was buried in 1887 in Steele Branch Cemetery, Stockdale, Wilson County, Texas.

James married **Nancy Ann Caroline Montgomery** (b. 12 Nov 1823, d. 23 Feb 1908) on 4 Oct 1842 in Desoto County, Mississippi.

+105 F vi. **Martha "Marie" Rader**[5, 13, 18] was born about 1815 in Wythe County, Virginia.[17]

Martha married **Wesley Whitsel** (b. Abt 1809, d. Bef 1864).

Martha next married **Allen Rader** (b. Abt 1838, d. 1922).

+106 F vii. **Mary Ann 'Jake' Rader**[5, 13, 18] was born about 1816 in Tennessee[17, 18] and died in 1860[17, 18] about age 44.

+107 F viii. **Sarah C. Rader**[5, 13, 18] was born about 1821 in Madison County, Alabama[17] and died about 1854 in Madison County, Alabama[17, 18] about age 33.

Sarah married **John D. Gann** (b. Abt 1845, d. Abt 1863) WFT Est 1835-1857.

Sarah next married **Samuel Gann** (b. 1822, d. 1861).

+108 F ix. **Eliza Jane Rader**[18] was born about 1825 in Madison County, Alabama[17, 18] and died before 1860 in Desoto County, Mississippi.[17, 18]

Eliza married **Samuel Turner** on 31 Jan 1850.

Eliza next married **William Kader** (b. 1843).

+109 F x. **Eleanor Elizabeth Rader**[5, 13, 18] was born in 1828 in Madison County, Alabama[17, 18] and died in Desoto County, Mississippi Senatobia, Mississippi.[17, 18]

Eleanor married **William C. Gann** (b. 1826) on 28 Sep 1847 in DE Soto County, Mississippi.

+110 F xi. **Nancy C. Rader** was born in 1830 in Desoto County, Mississippi and died WFT Est 1844-1924 at age 14.

Nancy married **William R. Robinson** (b. WFT Est 1813-1833, d. WFT Est 1847-1919) WFT Est 1844-1877.

Third Generation (Grandchildren)

Map of the Rader family land on Lick Creek

They dominated the northern Mohawk area in the third generation

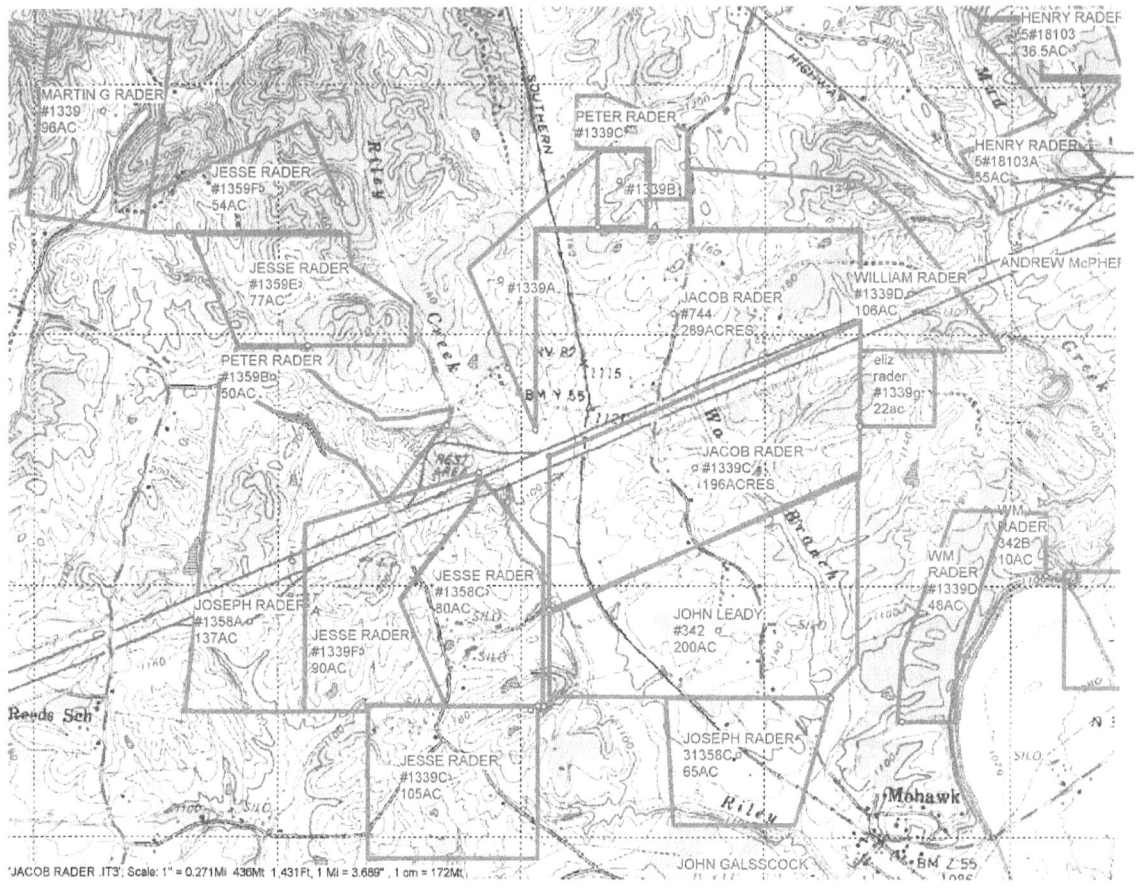

Tax records Greene County 1840 - 1862

	1840	1841	1842	1843	1844	1845	1846	1847
District # 3								
James M	86	147	147	147				
Eli		1 poll	1 poll	1 poll	1 poll	1 poll	1 poll	1 poll
Mrs Catherine				150	150	150	150	150
Jacob				1 poll	112	112	112	254
Samuel								1 poll
Hannah (widow)					147	147	147	
Joseph								1 poll
Abraham								1 poll
District #5								
Andrew	100	100	107	107	107	107	432	325
William					20	1 poll	1 poll	1 poll
District #6								

Name								
Andrew						1 poll	1 poll	1 poll
Casper	1 poll	1 poll						
Daniel						1 poll	1 poll	1 poll
Elizabeth	172							
Henry Jr.	108	108	138	138	137	137	137	79
Henry sr	132	132	132	132	132	132	132	132
Henry Sr slaves	2 slaves	2 slaves	2 slaves	2 slaves	2 slaves	2 slaves	3 slaves	3 slaves
Jesse	260	260	353	356	350	455	455	455
Jesse of Jno				1 poll				
John Dec		125	125	44	48			
John Jr.	school	625		625	600	600	600	600
John sr.	125							
Joseph	76	141	278	278	278	278	278	278
Martin G	163	155	69	69	1 poll	1 poll		
Peter R		172	212	212	262	262	250	250
Reuben M				1 poll	1 poll	1 poll	70	70
Samuel		1 poll	1 poll					
Valentine S						1 poll	1 poll	1 poll	1 poll
William	124	124	299	299	418	420	420	420
William S			1 poll					

District #7
Andrew						1 poll		

District #8
William Sr.	208	211	211	211	211	521	521	796
William Jr.	33.5	33.25	33.25	33.25	1 poll			
John						1 poll	180	

District # 10
Peter R						1 no poll		9

District # 12
Rheetor, Franklin								98

District # 19
Samuel						1 poll		1 poll

	1848	1849	1850	1851	1852	1853	1854
No 3							
Abraham C.C.	1 p	1 p				25	
Andrew					1 p		
Catherine wid	150	150	156	156	156		
Daniel				1 p	1 p		
Eli						1 p +156	156
Elis	1 p						
Hannah wid	147	147	147	147	147	147	147
Jacob	266	292	292	292		294 overseer	294
James M				84		1 p	84

John	1 p			1 p						+84 1 p		
Joseph	1 p								330			
Peter					1 p		1 p		1 p			
Samuel					1 p		1 p				1 p	

District No 5

Andrew	325	325	325	325	325	325	325
William	1 p	1 p	1 p				

District No 6

Andrew G		600	600	595	600	600	600
Casper	1 p	1 p					
Daniel	1 p	1 p					
Henry Jr	137	137	137	137	137	137	237
Henry Sr	132	132	132	132			
Henry sr slave	3	2	1	1			
James H	1 p						
Jesse Jr	1 p	1 p	1 p	1 p		1 p	
Jesse sr.	455	446	466	455			455
Jesse sr.slave						1	1
Jesse of John				1 p	1 p		
Jesse of William					1 p		
Jesse of Jacob					455	455	
John Jr			1 p				
John	600						
Joseph	278	278	278				
Lemuel						1 p	
Martin G est			100	100	100		
Mary						96	96
Peter R	250	250	250	250	250	250	250
Peter R	1 p					1p	1p
Reuben M	70	70	70	70	70	1 p +62	1 p +62
Valentine S	1 p						
Valentine S	44						
William	420	420	420	496	496	496	496
William	77						

District No 7

John sqr			1 p			140	

District No 8

William	796	817	817	817	817	817	817
William slaves	1	0	1	1	1	2	2
Andrew	1 p	1 p	1 p	1 p	1 p	1 p	
John		130	130		130	130	130
John slaves		1	1		1	1	1
Joseph						1 p	1 p
Henry						1 p	

District No 9

Henry						1 p	

District No 10

Peter R	9	8.5	8.5	2 ?	?	town lot 50	

District No 13							
Alexander J.			1 p	1 p	1 p		
District No 19							
Samuel	1 poll	1 p	1 p				
Valentine S		170	170	170	170	170	170

	1855	1856	1857	1858	1859	1860	1861	1862
District No. 3								
Catharine widow								
Andrew							97	
Jacob	1p 292	1p 292	1 p				1p 292	
Noah			1 p					
Eli	1p 126	1p 126	1 p				1p 289	
James M overseer	1p 84	1p 84	1 p				84	
Daniel							1p 74	
Hannah wid		147					1p 53	
Samuel	1p	1p	1 p					
District No. 5								
Andrew		325	1p 462.75	1 p			459	
William							1 p	
District No. 6								
Cornelius								
William			1 p					
William		500	500				500	
William slaves		1	1	1			1	
John A		140	140					
Peter R	1p 250	1p 250	1 p				1p 300	
Jesse V Isley							74	
Jesse Sr		455	509				477	
Jesse Sr slaves		1	1	1			2	
Henry	1 p							
Andrew G	1p 500	1p 400	1 p				1p 309	
Mary		96	96				96	
Lemuel	1p 50	1p 50	1 p				1p 127	
Reuben M		1p 156	1 p				1p 280	
James T							1p	
john of john							94	
John A of Jesse							1p	
Cornelius							1p	
Lewis F							1p	
							1p	
District No. 8								
John	1p 130	1p 130	1 p				1p 258	
John Slaves	2	2	2	2			1	
Andrew	1p 390	1p 390						
Joseph	1p						1 p	
William	817	817	---				369	
William slaves	2	0		2				
Henry		1 p 163	1 p					
Casper							1 p	

District No. 9
Henry   1 p

District No. 10
Peter A.   city lot

District No. 12
Joseph   1 p   1 p

District No. 18
Noah   1 p   50 1/4

District No. 19
Valentine S   1 p 170   1 p 100   190
Valentine Slaves   1
Andrew   7 1/4

District No. 25
Henry   1p 159

Raders in the 1860 Greene county Agricultural census

Name of Owner Agent, or Manager of the	Acres of Land imp	unimp	cash value of Farm	Value of Farming Implements Machinery	Live stock June 1, 1860							Value of Livestock	Produce		
					Horses	Asses & Mules	Milch Cows	Working Oxen	Other Cattle	Sheep	Swine		Wheat bushels	Rye bushels	Indian corn bushels
Caney Branch															
Andrew Rader	70	25	600	20	3		3	1	7	6	300	97		200	20
Jacob Rader	100	160	2500	100	5		4		5	7	10	600	200		500
Daniel Rader	100	49	1400	300	2		2		4		15	300	150		250
James M Rader	65	23	1000	150	2	1	2		3		25	300	140		500
Warrensburg															
Casper Rader	150	100	3000	15	3		1		2	4	8	300	290		1400
John Rader	100	70	4000	150	2	4	3	2	4		80	1000	280		500
Gasterus post office															
Mary Rader	25	78	1000	10	2		2	2	2	5	5	200	40		300
Andrew G Rader	50	95	1200	100	3	1	2		2	16	12	400	104		200
Peter Rader	140	160	4000	120	2	1	4	2	13	22	14	500	45		500
Jesse Rader	100	300	3000	275	4		5		15	36	25	600	100		400
William Rader	200	300	4000	150	8	18	9		7	13	53	3400	200		1000
R. R. Rader	40	33	1500	200	1	1	3	2	6	10	41	400	50		200
Newmansville															
Joseph Rader	60	60	2000	140	4		3		7	9	15	600	112		300
Limestone Springs															
John R Rader	20	30	1500	75	1		2	2	2		2	250	58		75
Caney Branch															
Eli Rader	100	70	1200	50	2		2	2	6	8	20	350	140		200
Blue Springs															
Valentine Rader	100	90	3000	150	3	2	4		6	25	8	600	200		500

Name of Owner Agent, or Manager of the	During the year ending June 1 1860														
	Oats bushel	Rice pound	Tobac pound	Ginned Cotton 400# bales	Wool Pound	peas beans bushels	Irish potatoes bushels	Sweet Potatoes bushels	Barley bushels	Buck wheat bushe	Value of Orchard Products	Wine gallons	Value of produce market garden	Butter pounds	cheese pounds	Hay tons
Caney Branch																
Andrew Rader				15		6	10					100		1		
Jacob Rader	50		10		15	1	12	8						150		
Daniel Rader					10			10						100		
James M Rader					12			10						105		
Warrensburg																
Casper Rader	175					1	40	40						200		9
John Rader	100						10							150		5
Gasterus post																
Mary Rader						2	5							150		
Andrew G Rader	40				14	2	10	20						150		
Peter Rader	40				40	5	10	15						50		6
Jesse Rader	20				40	5	5							200	100	5
William Rader	300				30	1		5						200		10
R. R. Rader					30	1	6							150		1
Newmansville																
Joseph Rader	200		75		51	1	40	4						200		5
Limestone Sp																
John R Rader	25						30	50						50		
Caney Branch																
Eli Rader	25				15		6	50								
Blue Springs																
Valentine Rader	100				45	2	50							100		8

Name of Owner Agent, or Manager of the				Produce During the year ending June 1 1860										
	clover seed bushels	Grass seed bushels	Hops pound	Hemp (tons) Dew rotted	Water rotted	other hemp	Flax pounds	Flax seed bushe	Silk pound	Maple sugar pound	Cane sugar 1,000	Molasses gallons made from	Beeswa pounds	Honey pound	Value of homemade manufacture	Value anamals slaughter
Caney Branch																
Andrew Rader							10				8	40		30	50	180
Jacob Rader											s	35	3	25	10	95
Daniel Rader											s	40			10	60
James M Rader											s	20			10	70
Warrensburg																
Casper Rader											s	40			4	215
John Rader														10	30	375
Gasterus post																
Mary Rader							10	2			s	60			25	50
Andrew G Rader							20	5			s	40		40	30	115
Peter Rader											s	20			30	100
Jesse Rader											s	60			50	485
William Rader											s	94		30	30	140
R. R. Rader											s	40			15	140
Newmansville																
Joseph Rader	7	1					10	3				15			30	100
Limestone Sp																
John R Rader							15									55
Caney Branch																
Eli Rader							25				s	30			20	15
Blue Springs																
Valentine Rader			3								s	40			20	95

13. Catherine Rader (*Conrad^2, Casper Sr^1*) was born about 1789 in Wythe County, Virginia.[16] Another name for Catherine was Caty Rader.[16]

    Noted events in her life were:

    She appeared on the census in 1850. OHIO TOWNSHIP, CLERMONT COUNTY, OHIO LINE 1930 PAGE 413B

Catherine married **Jacob T Fishback** on 19 Jun 1815 in Wythe County, Virginia. Jacob was born in 1765 in France. Another name for Jacob was Jacob F. Fishback.

    Noted events in their marriage were:

    Alt Marriage: 2 Feb 1815, Wytheville, Wythe County, Virginia.

General Notes: This marraige record is the only evidence I currently have. This Jacob was suposed to have fathered a child Sally Wyrick in 1821. On 11 Sept 1827 he was appointed to settle with Casper Yost and Christopher Brown, executors of John Houndshell and his name does not appear again in Wyth County records

It appears that he moved to Tazwell Co., VA where he became deputy clerk March 1820. He testified in a wythe county case in 1821 giving his place of residence as Jeffersonville, Tazwell, VA. He is still in that county in 1823 when he made a deed.

There are Jacob T Fishback's in Johnson co, Indiana in 1824. There is also a family in Clark Co., Illinois which may be connected

===============

Jacob T Fishback was in Wythe county 1811 and could have been the child of Dorthea Christian married Dr. Fishback. He could of left in 1815 but he was named in 2 later legal matters

Early Adventures on The Western Waters
Vol I by F.B. Kegley Page 342 Dorthea Christian married Dr. Fishback (circa 1790)
Vol II   Page 223 Dec 11, 1815 Jacob T. Fishback signed a petition
Vol III   Page 748 Caty Rader (daughter of Conrad) married Jacob T Fishback in 1815
Wythe county will book   Jacob T Fishback signs county documents as recorder Dec 10, 1811 - Oct 8, 1816
Wythe county marriages   Jacob T & Caty Rader 2 Feb 1815 min - John Stranger - 1 Jan 1816 bond 2 Feb 1815 d of Conrad bondsman George Ory
July 14, 1814 Jacob T Fishback was in the militia
June 10 1817 Lewis Able gave Jacob T Fishback power of Attorney to collect some money for him
1816-1817 he served in the general assembly of Virginia
1821 he is the alleged father of Sally Wyrick
1827 he settles John Hounshell's estate
    ================

Hello Jim:

I have been researching the Fishback/Rader/Wyrick dilemma for some time and also found a court record that Jacob T. sued for custody of Jacob his son from George Wyrick, the boy's grandfather. Also, I found in a Census record a Catherine Fishback with kids the right age etc. in

Johnson Co., Indiana. Interesting stuff heh? Don't have time to put it all together right now but will keep in touch with you. KURT

Fishback Photography
8234 Scrub Oak Way
Antelope, CA 95843
916.334.7041
<www.fishbackphotography.com>

Noted events in his life were:

He appeared on the census in 1810 in Wythe County, Virginia. Fishback, Jacob Tl

State: Virginia Year: 1810   County: Wythe Roll: M252_71
Township: Page: 832   Image: 542

He is alone and between 16 and 26 years old

He appeared on the census in 1820 in Tazewell, VA. Fishback, Jacob

State: Virginia Year: 1820   County: Tazewell Roll: M33_133
Township: Unknown Townships Page: 248   Image: 286

Fishback, Jacob

State: Virginia Year: 1820   County: Tazewell Roll: M33_133
Township: Unknown Townships Page: 248   Image: 286

1 age 0-10, 0 age 10-16, 1 age 16-18, 1 age 16-26, 1 age 26-45
0 over 45

1 female 0-10, 0 age 10-16, 1 age 16-26

He appeared on the census in 1830 in White River, IN. Fishback, Jacob T.

State: Indiana Year: 1830   County: Johnson Roll: M19_27
Township: White River Page: 17   Image: 34

3 under 5, 1 5 to 10, 1 age 30-40, 1 female 10-15, 1 female 20-30
1 female 50-60

He appeared on the census in 1840. Fishback, Jacob

State: Illinois Year: 1840   County: Clark Roll: M704_56
Township: Unknown Townships Page: 79   Image: 170

Fishback, Jacob F.

State: Indiana Year: 1840   County: Johnson Roll: M704_84
Township: Unknown Townships Page: 301   Image: 164

Fishback, Jacob

State: Ohio Year: 1840   County: Clermont Roll: M704_384
Township: Ohio Page: 223   Image: 222

He appeared on the census in 1850. OHIO TOWNSHIP, CLERMONT COUNTY, OHIO LINE 1930 PAGE 413B

Source Citations

The child from this marriage was:

+111 F i. **Harriett E. Fishback** was born in 1832 in Pennsylvania.

14. Conrad Rader (*Conrad^2, Casper Sr^1*) was born about 1790.

15. James Rader (*Conrad^2, Casper Sr^1*) was born in 1801.

Noted events in his life were:

He appeared on the census in 1810. WYTHE COUNTY, VIRGINIA CENSUS PAGE 852
Census 1: 1820. WYTHE COUNTY, VIRGINIA CENSUS PAGE 221
Census 2: 1850. WYTHE COUNTY, VIRGINIA CENSUS PAGE 470 LINE 328

James married **Nancy L.**. Nancy was born in 1816.

She appeared on the census in 1850. WYTHE COUNTY, VIRGINIA CENSUS PAGE 470 LINE 328

Children from this marriage were:

+112 F i. **Rebecca Rader** was born in 1834.

+113 M ii. **Jesse H. Rader** was born in 1837.

+114 F iii. **Catherine Rader** was born in 1838.

+115 M iv. **James A. Rader** was born in 1839.

+116 F v. **Malinda J. Rader** was born in 1843.

16. Nancy O. Rader[16] (*Conrad^2, Casper Sr^1*) was born on 18 Jun 1805 in Wytheville, Wythe County, Virginia,[17,32] died on 6 Sep 1885 in Wytheville, Wythe County, Virginia[16,17,40] at age 80, and was buried in St. Peters', Lutheran Cem.[40]

General Notes: Burial St. Peter's Lutheran Cemetery

The St. John's Lutheran Church record of Wytheville, Virginia recorded the birth of Conrad and Elizabeth's daughter Nancy Rader On June 18, 1805.

Noted events in her life were:

She was baptized on 25 Aug 1805. WYTHEVILLE, WYTHE CO VIRGINIA
She was baptized on 25 Aug 1805 in Wytheville, Wythe County, Virginia. St John's Lutheran||
She appeared on the census in 1860. WYTHE COUNTY, VIRGINIA 68TH. DISTRICT
Census 1: 1870. WYTHE COUNTY, VIRGINIA SPEEDWELL TOWNSHIP
Census 2: 1880. WYTHE COUNTY, VIRGINIA PAGE 8 LINE 70
Alt Death: 6 Sep 1883, Wytheville, Wythe County, Virginia.

Nancy married **James Seagle**[16] on 22 Oct 1822 in Wytheville, Wythe County, Virginia.[16,40] James was born on 14 Oct 1801 in Botetourt County, Virginia,[16] died on 16 Jan 1883 in

Wytheville, Wythe County, Virginia[16] at age 81, and was buried on 16 Jan 1883 in St. Peters', Lutheran Cem.

General Notes: Facts about this person:

Burial St. Peter's Lutheran Cemetery

Noted events in his life were:

He appeared on the

census in 1860. WYTHE COUNTY, VIRGINIA 68TH. DISTRICT
Census 1: 1870. WYTHE COUNTY, VIRGINIA SPEEDWELL TOWNSHIP
Census 2: 1880. WYTHE COUNTY, VIRGINIA PAGE 8 LINE 70
He appeared on the census in 1880 in Black Lick, Wythe, Virginia. Census Place: Black Lick, Wythe, Virginia

Source: FHL Film 1255394 National Archives Film T9-1394   Page 354D

Name	Relation	Sex	Marr	Race	Age	Birthplace	Occ	Father/Mother
George A. SEAGLE	Self	M	M	W	30	VA	Carpenter	Fa: VA Mo: VA
Bettie E. SEAGLE	Wife	F	M	W	25	VA	Keeping House	Fa: VA Mo: VA
Jettie K. SEAGLE	Dau	F	S	W	6	VA		Fa: VA Mo: VA
Cora B. SEAGLE	Dau	F	S	W	4	VA		Fa: VA Mo: VA
Blanch C. SEAGLE	Dau	F	S	W	3	VA		Fa: VA Mo: VA
Viola G. SEAGLE	Other	F	S	W	1	VA		Fa: VA Mo: VA
James SEAGLE	Father	M	M	W	79	VA	Boarder	Fa: VA Mo: VA
Nancy O. SEAGLE	Mother	F	M	W	75	VA	Boarder	Fa: VA Mo: VA

Children from this marriage were:

+117 F   i.   **Elizabeth Seagle**[16] was born on 27 Sep 1824 in Wytheville, Wythe County, Virginia.[16]

+118 F   ii. **Maria Wax Seagle**[16] was born on 6 Mar 1827 in Wytheville, Wythe County, Virginia[16] and died on 15 Sep 1884 at age 57.

Maria married **James A. Johnson** (b. 16 Feb 1830).

+119 M   iii. **Jacob C Seagle**[16] was born on 22 Oct 1829 in Wytheville, Wythe County, Virginia[16] and died on 24 Jan 1833 in Wytheville, Wythe County, Virginia at age 3.

+120 F   iv. **Judith Angelina 'Judie' Seagle**[16] was born on 23 Aug 1832 in Wytheville, Wythe County, Virginia[16] and died on 8 Jul 1883 in Washington City, TN at age 50.

Judith married **Jonas Spraker** on 24 Nov 1852 in Wythe County, Virginia.

+121 F   v.   **Mary Jane Seagle**[16] was born on 11 Jan 1835 in Wytheville, Wythe County, Virginia.[16]

Mary married **Clarke S. Whitman** on 9 Dec 1857.

+122 M vi. **Henry Lee Seagle**[16] was born on 16 Aug 1837 in Wytheville, Wythe County, Virginia,[16] died on 3 Mar 1853 in Wytheville, Wythe County, Virginia at age 15, and was buried in St. Peters Lutheran Cemetery, Wytheville, Wythe County, Virginia.

+123 F vii. **Isabella Foster Seagle**[16] was born on 30 Dec 1841 in Wytheville, Wythe County, Virginia.[16]

+124 M viii. **John Sanders Seagle** was born on 15 Mar 1844 in Wytheville, Wythe County, Virginia, died on 9 May 1864 in Battle Of Mccloyd Mountain, Civil War at age 20, and was buried in St. Peters Lutheran Cemetery, Wytheville, Wythe County, Virginia.

+125 M ix. **George Augustus Seagle**[16] was born on 14 Apr 1850 in Speedwell, Wythe Co, VA.[16]

George married **Betty E. Welsh** (b. 28 Aug 1855) on 29 Jan 1873 in Speedwell, Wythe County, Virginia.

+126 M x. **James Brown Seagle** was born on 6 Feb 1847 in Wythe County, Virginia, died on 24 Mar 1912 in Wythe County, Virginia at age 65, and was buried in East End Cemetery, Wytheville, Wythe County, Virginia.

James married **Isabella E. Hines** (b. 21 Oct 1854, d. 27 Sep 1939).

17. Judith Ora Rader[41] (*Conrad*[2], *Casper Sr*[1]) was born on 11 May 1811 in Wythe County, Virginia and died on 28 Jun 1887 in Wythe County, Virginia at age 76. Another name for Judith was Judith Ory Rader.

Noted events in her life were:

She appeared on the

census in 1840. WYTHE COUNTY, VIRGINIA CENSUS PAGE 89
Census 1: 1850. WYTHE COUNTY, VIRGINIA   PAGE 319B-320A   LINE 1327
Census 2: 1860. WYTHE COUNTY, VIRGINIA   PAGE 30   LINE 246
Census 3: 1870. WYTHE COUNTY, VIRGINIA   FORT CHISWELL TOWNSHIP
Census 4: 1880. WYTHE COUNTY, VIRGINIA BLACK LICK DISTRICT LINE 292 PAGE 32

Judith married **Absolom Fisher**, son of **David Fisher** and **Rachael Fernsler Peters**, on 23 May 1833 in Wythe County, Virginia. Absolom was born on 27 Jan 1808 in Wythe County, Virginia and died on 3 Jun 1887 in Wythe County, Virginia at age 79. Another name for Absolom was Absalon Fisher.

> Source: FISHER-L@rootsweb.com
> Subject: Re: Julian D. Fisher
> This is a Message Board Post that is gatewayed to this mailing list.
> Classification: Query Message Board URL:
> http://boards.ancestry.com/mbexec/msg/rw/YVW.2ACEB/4924.4
> Message Board Post:
> Looks like Jason is Roberts Father.
> Virginia 1910 Census Miracode Index Record

Name: Jason A Fisher Birthplace: Virginia State: VA
Age: 48 Color: W Enumeration District: 0149 Visit: 0151
County: Wythe, Wytheville Relation: Head of Household
Other Residents: Relation Name Age Birth Place Wife Dorsey(Dovey) A 46 Virginia
Daughter Arizona S 29 Virginia Son Benten O 24 Virginia Son Robert P 13 Virginia
Son Frank O 16 Virginia Son William W 12 Virginia Daughter Lillian R 10 Virginia

Family Data Collection - Individual Records Record

Name: Jason Alfred Fisher Spouse: Dovey Ann Housman
Parents: Thomas Winton Fisher , Frances Ann Fisher Birth Place: Wythe, VA Birth
Date: 13 August 1860 Death Place: Max Meadows, Wythe, VA Death Date: 16
December 1943

Millennium File Record

Name: Jason Alfred Fisher
Parents: Thomas Winton Fisher, Frances Ann Fisher
Other: Frank Odell Sr. Fisher Arizona Summers Fisher Emmett M. Fisher N
Birth: 13 Aug 1860 - Wythe, Virginia, USA
Death: 16 Dec 1943 - Max Meadows, Wythe, Virginia, USA
Name: Jason Alfred Fisher

Spouse: , Dovey Ann Housman

, Mary Colegate Birth Date: 13 Aug 1860 : Wythe: Virginia: USA
Death Date: 16 Dec 1943: Max Meadows: Wythe: Virginia: USA
Parents: Thomas Winton Fisher, Frances Ann Fisher
Children: Frank Odell Sr. Fisher Arizona Summers Fisher Emmett M. Fisher
N Jason Alfred Fisher
Life Events
  Birth: 13 AUG 1860, WYTHE, VA
  Death: 16 DEC 1943: MAX MEADOWS, WYTHE, VA
  Burial: 08 DEC 1943: MAX MEADOWS, WYTHE, VA

U.S. and International Marriage Records, 1560-1900 Record

Name: Jason Alfred Fisher Spouse: Dovey Ann Houseman
Birth: 1860 – VA Birth: 1864 – VA Marriage: 1880 - VA

You can e-mail me at tammymay21498@comcast.net

Noted events in his life were:

He appeared on the census in 1840. WYTHE COUNTY, VIRGINIA CENSUS PAGE 89
  Census 1: 1850. WYTHE COUNTY, VIRGINIA   PAGE 319B-320A LINE 1327
  Census 2: 1860. WYTHE COUNTY, VIRGINIA   PAGE 30 LINE 246
  Census 3: 1870. WYTHE COUNTY, VIRGINIA FORT CHISWELL TOWNSHIP

Children from this marriage were:

+127 M   i.   **Augustus Fisher** was born in 1835 in Wythe County, Virginia and died in 1835 in Wythe County, Virginia.

+128 M ii. **Thomas Wilson Fisher** was born on 9 Jun 1837 in Wythe County, Virginia and died on 2 Nov 1921 in Wythe County, Virginia at age 84.

Thomas married **Frances Ann Fisher** (b. 28 Jun 1843, d. 11 Nov 1862) on 11 Nov 1857 in Wythe County, Virginia.

Thomas next married **Louisa Lenora Spranker** (b. 1848, d. 1920) about 1869.

+129 F iii. **Elizabeth Fisher** was born in 1840 in Wythe County, Virginia and died in 1921 at age 81.

Elizabeth married **Alex Simmerman**.

+130 F iv. **Nancy Ory Fisher** was born in 1843 in Wythe County, Virginia and died in 1862 at age 19.

+131 M v. **James R. Fisher** was born in 1847 in Wythe County, Virginia and died in 1862 at age 15.

+132 M vi. **Andrew Clark Fisher** was born in 1850 and died in 1850.

+133 M vii. **Isaac Melville Fisher** was born on 1 Feb 1853 in Wythe County, Virginia and died on 28 Jul 1857 in Wythe County, Virginia at age 4.

18. Rebecca Rader[5, 13, 18] ($Conrad^2$, $Casper\ Sr^1$) was born about 1811 in Wythe County, Virginia[17, 18] and died about 1860 in Senatobia, Mississippi[17, 18] about age 49.

Noted events in her life were:
Alt Birth: 1811, Tennessee.
She appeared on the census in 1850. THE SOUTHERN DIST., DESOTO COUNTY, MISSISSIPPI PAGE 362 LINE 698
Alt Death: Bef 1860, Desoto County, Mississippi.

Rebecca married **Alfred Bryam** on 5 May 1831 in Madison County, AL. Alfred was born in 1808 in Alabama.

Noted events in his life were:
Alt Birth: Abt 1843.
He appeared on the census in 1850. THE SOUTHERN DIST., DESOTO COUNTY, MISSISSIPPI PAGE 362 LINE 698

Children from this marriage were:

+134 F i. **Hannah M. Byram** was born in 1832 in Alabama.

+135 F ii. **Susan S. Byram** was born in 1839.

+136 F iii. **Julia F. Byram** was born in 1841.

+137 F iv. **Martha A. Byram** was born in 1846.

+138 F v. **Susan E. Byram** was born in 1849.

19. John Rader[1, 2, 3, 6, 8, 10, 11, 12, 14, 15, 16, 43] ($Heinrich\ 'Henry'\ Sr^2$, $Casper\ Sr^1$) was born on 11 Sep 1793 in Wytheville, Wythe County, Virginia,[16] died on 8 Nov 1839 in Caney Branch, Greene County, Tennessee[16] at age 46, and was buried in Old St. James, Lutheran.

Death Notes: He was in court in 1847 therefore He must not be dead and buried

General Notes: John Rader - Hannah Scott -- Henry Misemer, James Scott the children of John and Hannah Rader were obtained from records in GREENE COUNTY, TENNESSEE County Court minutes volumn 1844 to 1858, page 250 dated February 4, 1856; same volumn pages 287 and 288 dated April 4, 1856 and April 8, 1856 respectively; and volumn 1868 to 1874, page 176 dated July 24, 1871.

Both John and Hannah are buried in the Old St. James Lutheran Church cemetery.

DECREE OVER LAND DISPUTE BETWEEN NOAH CATE, GUARDIAN
OF SAMUEL LEE HEIRS AS. RADER & GUTHRIE
Greene County   State of Tennessee   Book 22 page 412
Be it remembered that at the February Term 1837 of the Chancery Court at Greeneville Tennessee, the following decree was pronounced by said court in the suit of Noah Cate Guardian of the minor heirs of Samuel J. Lee deceased vs. John Rader and James G. Guthrie - to wit

Friday 17th February 1837

Noah Cate Guardian of the Minor Heirs of Samuel J. Lee deceased vs. John Rader & James G. Guthrie

This cause came on for hearing the 16th day of February 1837 before the Hon. Thomas L. Williams Chancellor upon the Bill, answers, replication & proofs and the Chancellor being of the opinion that the complainants are entitled to be vested with the legal title to the tract of land discribed in the deed of trust as containing ninety acres situate in the counties of Greene, Jefferson and Hawkins, bounded as follows viz. Beginning at a dogwood on a corner of said Readers line, Bulls Gap, thence with said line north thirty one degrees E seventy five poles to a dogwood thence north to a cherry tree the distance not known, but on William Keels line thence east ninety two poles to a stake thence south one hundred and fifty poles to a stake thence east Eighty seven poles to a stake, south sixty five degrees west one hundred and twenty five poles to a stake thence seventy five poles to the beginning.

It is therefore ordered adjudged and decreed by the court that the title legal and equitable to the above described tract of land be and the same hereby is divested out of the said James G. Guthrie and John Reader Sr. and also out of all others persons and the same is hereby vested in the said James Lee and Caroline Lee the minor heirs at law of said Samuel J. Lee deceased their heirs and assignes in fee simple and it is further ordered that said James and Caroline Lee on the application of their guardian may have a writ of possession requiring the Sheriff of Greene County to put them in the immediate possession of said premises and it being suggested that the said John Rader has been in the possession of the said premises or a part thereof - and also in receipt of the rents and profits thereof - since the 31st July 1827 the date of the Trustees Sale up to this time or a portion of said time at least. And the Chancellor being of opinion that defendant Reader is liable to account to complainants for the reasonable rent of said premises during the time which he may have occupied and possessed the same and that his is also liable to account for any rents and profits which he may have received from others holding, using or occupying the same under him. It is further ordered that it be referred to the master to take an account and state - 1st what would be a reasonable allowance per annum for the use and occupation of said premises from the 31st July 1827 to the time of taking said account - 2nd What portion of the time during said period have said premises been used and occupied by the respondent in doing which the master shall distinquish between the time respondent used and occupied the same as ostensible owner - and the time when he may have held the same or any portion thereof under any other person during a claim thereto under complainants - 3rd The master shall also enquire whether desponant Reader has ever received any rents profits or issues in any way from any other person or persons under the License or authority of said defendant and that the clerk and master also enquire what part of the said ninety acre tract the said John Reader did occupy and how long and it is furthered ordered by the court that each party that is the guardian and defendant Reader in there cause pay their own costs.

Clerks Certificate

I David Sevier Clerk and Master of the Chancery Court at Greeneville Tennessee do hereby certify that the foregoing is a full true and perfect copy of the decree pronounced by said court in the foregoing cause remaining of record in my office.

Witness my hand and private seal having no public seal of office at office in Greeneville the 24th day of march 1847

David Sevier Clerk and Master

Registers Certificate State of Tennessee Greene County

Registers office this deed or decree received this 24th day of March 1847 at 4 o'clock afternoon and with the clerks certificate registered in said office in Book 22 page 412 and noted in Book 1 page 91. Thomas Lane RGC

Noted events in his life were:

Military: 14 Oct 1813, War of 1812. 1812 John enlisted in the U S Army and served in the War of 1812 from October 14, 1813 to February 8, 1814. He was a private in Captain Robert McCalpins Company, 2nd Regiment of Tennessee Volunteers commanded by Colonel William Lillard.

Resided: 1839, Caney Branch, Greene Co, TN. 1839 John and Hannah lived in Caney Branch, Tennessee in Greene County until his death in 1839.

Alt Death: 3 Feb 1840, Greene County, Tennessee.

Resided: 1850, Caney Branch in Greene County. 1850 Hannah was living in in the 1850 census. Hannah was still living in Greene County, Tennessee

Affidavit: 16 Apr 1855. on April 16, 1855 according to an affidavit in the pension records relating to John's military service.

Resided: 1860, Caney Branch, Greene Co, Tennessee. In 1860 Hannah lived there until her death in 1871.

Resided: 29 Mar 1871, Caney Branch, Greene Co, TN. On March 29, 1871 she was living in Cocke County about 2 miles from the post office in Caney Branch, Tennessee in Greene County. Both John and Hannah are buried in the Old St. James Lutheran Church cemetery. Facts about this person:

John married **Hannah Scott**[16] on 25 Aug 1814 in Greene County, Tennessee.[16] Hannah was born on 10 Feb 1795 in TN,[16] died on 24 Jul 1871 in Cocke County, Tennessee[16] at age 76, and was buried in Old St. James Lutheran, Greene County, Tennessee. Another name for Hannah was Hanna Scott.

Marriage Notes: 1814 Greene Co., Marriages #1656 Aug 22, 1814 John Rader - Hannah Scott -- Henry Misemer, James Scott The children of John and Hannah Rader were obtained from records in Greene County, Tennessee County Court minutes volumn 1844 to 1858, page 250 dated February 4, 1856; same volumn pages 287 and 288 dated April 4, 1856 and April 8, 1856 respectively; and volumn 1868 to 1874, page 176 dated July 24, 1871.

General Notes: Burial Old St. James Lutheran Cemetery

John and Hannah lived in Caney Branch, Tennessee in Greene County until his death in 1839.

He died on 8 Nov 1839 in Caney Branch, Greene Co, TENNESSEE He was buried in Old St. James, Lutheran.

Hannah was living in Caney Branch in Greene County in the 1850 census.

Hannah was still living in GREENE COUNTY, TENNESSEE on April 16, 1855 according to an affidavit in the pension records relating to John's military service.

In 1860 Hannah was living in Caney Branch, Tennessee in Cocke County and lived there until her death in 1871.

On March 29, 1871 she was living in Cocke County about 2 miles from the post office in Caney Branch, Tennessee in Greene County.

Noted events in her life were:

Alt Birth: 10 Feb 1795, Virginia.
She has conflicting birth information of Alt. Birth, 10 Feb 1795 and TN. Alt Birth: 16 Feb 1795.
She appeared on the census in 1830. GREENE COUNTY, TENNESSEE PG. 188
Census 1: 1840. GREENE COUNTY, TENNESSEE
Census 2: 1850. GREENE COUNTY, TENNESSEE PG211B #1092
Census 3: 1860. COCKE COUNTY, TENNESSEE PAGE 79 LINE 568
She appeared on the census about 1870 in Cocke County, Tennessee.
She appeared on the census in 1870 in Parrotsville, Cocke County Tennessee. COCKE COUNTY, TENNESSEE

RADER ANNA ,1815,55,F,W,TN ,TN ,COCKE ,PARROTSVILLE P O M593,1519,0,354
RADER ,HANAH MC ,1795,75,F,W,VA,TN,COCKE ,PARROTSVILLE PO M593,1519,0,354
RADER ,POWELL ,1844,26,M,W,TN,TN,COCKE ,PARROTSVILLE PO M593,1519,0,354

She has conflicting death information of Alt. Death, 24 Jul 1871 and TN.

Alt Death: 24 Jul 1891.

Children from this marriage were:

+139 F i. **Mariah Rader**[16] was born on 10 Feb 1817 in Caney Branch, Greene County, Tennessee[16] and died on 18 Jan 1895 in Cocke County, Tennessee[16] at age 77.

Source Citations

Mariah married **John D. Ottinger**[16] (b. 6 Feb 1820, d. 15 Dec 1900) on 27 Oct 1842 in Greene County, Tennessee.[16]

+140 M ii. **James M. Rader**[43] was born in 1816 in Greene, Tennessee.

James married **Ruma Mace** (b. 1818) on 24 Nov 1842.

+141 F iii. **Elizabeth Rader**[16] was born before 1818 in Caney Branch, Greene County, Tennessee[16] and died before 1856 in Greene County, Tennessee.

Elizabeth married **Jacob Eusebius Summitt** (b. 2 Feb 1815, d. 25 Mar 1873) on 24 Dec 1835 in Jefferson Tennessee.[63]

+142 M iv. **James Rader**[16] was born in 1819 in Caney Branch, Greene County, Tennessee[16] and died after 1871.

James married **Ruhama Mace** (b. 1823) on 24 Nov 1842 in Greene County, Tennessee.

+143 M v. **Samuel Rader**[16, 43] was born in 1824 in Caney Branch, Greene County, Tennessee,[16] died on 22 May 1899 in Boone County, Indiana at age 75, and was buried in 1899 in Neese Cemetery, Whitestown, Indiana.

Samuel married **Elizabeth Mace** (b. 1820) in Tennessee.

Samuel next married **Christina P. Dodson** (b. Abt 1824) on 30 Apr 1889 in Boone County, Indiana.

+144 M vi. **Jesse Rader**[43] was born in 1822 in Greene, Tennessee.

+145 M vii. **John Wesley Rader Sr.**[1, 2, 3, 6, 8, 10, 11, 12, 14, 15, 16, 43] was born on 23 Oct 1826 in Caney Branch, Greene County, Tennessee,[16] died on 28 May 1889 in Caney Branch, Greene County, Tennessee at age 62, and was buried in Old St. James, Lutheran.

John married **Elizabeth Ottinger** (b. 13 Dec 1831, d. 10 Jun 1874) on 4 Sep 1849 in Parrotsville, Tennessee.

John next married **Mary M. Rader**.

+146 F viii. **Hannah Rader** was born in 1827.

Hannah married **Henry Ottinger** on 11 Aug 1850.

+147 F ix. **Emaline Rader**[43] was born in 1824 in Greene, Tennessee.

+148 F x. **Hanna G. Rader** was born on 23 Oct 1826 in Caney Branch, Greene County, Tennessee.[16]

Hanna married **Henry Ottinger** (b. 1829, d. WFT Est 1890-1938) on 11 Aug 1850 in Greene County, Tennessee.

+149 M xi. **Daniel Rader**[16, 43] was born in 1829 in Caney Branch, Greene County, Tennessee,[16] died on 6 Aug 1864 in Utoi Creek Battle-Field, Atlanta, Georgia Civil War at age 35, and was buried in Marietta National Cemetery, 500 Washington Ave. Marietta, GA. Section F, Grave #F5296.

Daniel married **Susan A. Borden** (b. 17 Nov 1831, d. 28 Jan 1915) on 9 May 1852 in Cocke County, Tennessee.

+150 M xii.   **George W. Rader**[16] was born on 25 Jan 1831 in Caney Branch, Greene County, Tennessee[16] and died on 9 Jul 1870 in Michigantown, Michigan Township, Clinton County, Indiana at age 39.

George married **Mary Ann Ottinger** (b. 26 May 1836, d. 13 May 1913) on 28 Nov 1854 in Whitestown, Boone, IN.

+151 M xiii.   **William Rader**[16] was born in 1836 in Caney Branch, Greene County, Tennessee[16] and died in Cowley County, Kansas.

William married **Margaret Ottinger** (b. 1839) on 8 Aug 1857 in Boone County, Indiana.

+152 F xiv.   **Mary Ann Rader**[16] was born on 27 Sep 1837 in Caney Branch, Greene County, Tennessee,[16] died on 15 Jun 1900 in Greene County, Tennessee at age 62, and was buried in Pine Grove, Greene Co., TN.

Mary married **Lewis Barney Ottinger** (b. 22 May 1836, d. 20 Jun 1901) on 25 Dec 1859 in Greene County, Tennessee.

20. Mary Rader[1, 2, 3, 6, 8, 10, 11, 12, 14, 15] (*Heinrich 'Henry' Sr*[2]*, Casper Sr*[1]) was born about 1794 in Wythe County, Virginia and died on 6 Mar 1848 in Greene County, Tennessee about age 54.

General Notes: Mary and John were living on Lick Creek in Greene County, Tennessee in 1830. They owned 74 acres of land. Mary was deceased when her father made his Will on December 21, 1846.

Noted events in her life were:

Fact 2: Fact 2, And 5 Girls. Not On 1840 Or 1850 Census ..
Alt Birth: 1794, Wythe County, Virginia.
Alt Birth: Abt 1794, Wythe County, Virginia.
Fact 1: Fact 1, 1830, Was In Green County, Tennessee. Had 2 Boys.
Alt Death: Abt 1846, Unk..

Mary married **John Lauchner**, son of **Christian Laughner** and **Catharine "Katie" Fore**, on 8 Feb 1816 in James Guthrie Jp, Greene Co, TN.[44] John was born in 1790 in , , , Pennsylvania[42] and died in 1849 in Greene County, Tennessee[28] at age 59. Other names for John were John Lauchner, and John Laughner.

General Notes: John was living in Greene County, Tennessee in 1830 (Census 110001-131001) and 1840 (Census 0200001-0102101). John was living in Greene County, Tennessee in 1830 and owned 74 acres of land in Captain McPheron's Company [1].

References: 1. Greene County, Tennessee Tax Record.

Noted events in his life were:

He worked as a Blacksmith.[28]

Alt Birth: Abt 1796, , , , Pennsylvania. Place Lived (3): Between 1830 and 1840, Greene County, Tennessee.[28] Alt Death: 1849.

Children from this marriage were:

+153 M   i.   **Daniel Laughner**[1,2,3,6,8,10,11,12,14,15] was born in 1819 in , , Greene, Tennessee and died in 1846 in Greene County, Tennessee at age 27.

Daniel married **Catherine Ketron** (b. 1822, d. 8 Dec 1896) on 27 Aug 1841 in Sinking Springs.

Daniel next married **Catharine (Ketron) Catron** (b. Abt 1823, d. 8 Dec 1896) on 2 Sep 1841 in , Wm Rader, Jp, Greene.

+154 M   ii. **Valentine 'Val' Laughner**[1,2,3,6,8,10,11,12,14,15] was born on 12 Sep 1829 in , , Greene, Tennessee, died on 17 Nov 1871 at age 42, and was buried in , Laymon Cem, Clinton, Indiana.

Valentine married **Catherine Miller** (b. 1 Oct 1829, d. 25 May 1900) in 1850.

+155 F   iii. **Catherine Laughner**[1,2,3,4,6,7,10,11,12,14,15] was born in 1823 in , , Greene, Tennessee, died on 9 Dec 1896 in Greene County, Tennessee at age 73, and was buried in Mt. Hope Methodist Cemetery, Greene County, Tennessee.

Catherine married **Aquilla Jackson** on 29 Jan 1864 in Greene County, Tennessee.

Catherine next married **Jesse Rader** (b. 1804, d. 1890) on 14 Oct 1875 in Greene County, Tennessee.

(Duplicate Line. See Person 48)

+156 F   iv. **Eliza J. Laughner**[1,2,3,6,8,10,11,12,14,15] was born between 26 Mar 1822 and 1826 in , , Greene, Tennessee, died on 15 Mar 1903 in , , Greene, Tennessee, and was buried in Midway, Bibles Chapel C., Greene, Tennessee.

Eliza married **Joseph Kirk Jr.** (b. 1819, d. 22 Apr 1884) on 7 Oct 1845 in Greene County, Tennessee.

+157 F   v.   **Mary Ann Laughner**[1,2,3,6,8,10,11,12,14,15] was born about 1830 in , , Greene, Tennessee, died about 1899 about age 69, and was buried in , Pleasant Hill C, Ste. Genevieve, Missouri.

Mary married **James C. Collett** (b. 7 Mar 1829, d. 12 Mar 1911) on 26 Jul 1849 in Greene County, Tennessee.

+158 F   vi. **Margaret Laughner**[1,2,3,6,8,10,11,12,14,15] was born on 1 Apr 1822 in Greene County, Tennessee, died on 5 May 1891 at age 69, and was buried in , Pleas Hills Ch, Ste. Genevieve, Missouri.

Margaret married **James Edward Bowling** (b. 25 Aug 1824, d. 14 Apr 1904) on 29 Mar 1845 in Greene County, Tennessee.

+159 F   vii. **Catharine Laughner**[8,11,14] was born in , , Greene, Tennessee.

Catharine married **Aquilla Jackson** on 29 Jan 1864.

+160 M viii. **William Laughner**[1,2,3,6,8,10,11,12,14,15] was born on 3 Aug 1832 in , , Greene, Tennessee and died on 26 Nov 1909 in Indiana at age 77.

William married **Elizabeth Ottinger** (b. 3 Dec 1832, d. 7 Sep 1908) in 1853 in Boone County, Indiana.

+161 F ix. **Louisa Laughner**[1,2,3,6,8,10,11,12,14,15] was born in 1825 in Greene County, Tennessee.

Louisa married ( ) **Beyers**.

21. Elizabeth 'Betsey' Rader[1,2,3,6,8,10,11,12,14,15,20] (*Heinrich 'Henry' Sr*[2], *Casper Sr*[1]) was born on 15 Apr 1795 in Wythe County, Virginia,[20] died on 29 Sep 1866 in Warrensburg, Greene Co, TN at age 71, and was buried in Sinking Springs, Lutheran, Greene Co, TN.

General Notes: The children of Elizabeth and Jonas can be verified by referring to the Greene County, Tennessee Chancery Court Minutes of 1847, page 595. It has many references to death dates of various family members and also their whereabouts around 1847. This case dealt with the settlement of the estate of Christian Bowers, Jonas Bowers' father, and was heard in court on October 15, 1847. Both Elizabeth and Jonas are buried in the Sinking Springs Lutheran Church cemetery. Jonas was the son of Christian and Elizabeth Bowers.

Facts about this person:

Burial Sinking Springs Lutheran Church, Greene County, Tennessee

Elizabeth 'Betsey' Rader was born on 15 Apr 1795 in Wythe Co, Virginia.

She died on 29 Sep 1866 in Warrensburg, Greene Co, Tennessee She was buried in Sinking Springs, Lutheran, Greene Co, Tennessee. The children of Elizabeth and Jonas can be verified by referring to the Greene County, Tennessee Chancery Court Minutes of 1847, page 595. It has many references to death dates of various family members and also their whereabouts around 1847. This case dealt with the settlement of the estate of Christian Bowers, Jonas Bowers' father, and was heard in court on October 15, 1847. Both Elizabeth and Jonas are buried in the Sinking Springs Lutheran Church cemetery. Jonas was the son of Christian and Elizabeth Bowers.

Noted events in her life were:

Alt Death: 29 Feb 1866, , , Greene, Tennessee.

She appeared on the census on 7 Sep 1850 in Greene County, Tennessee. 1850 Greene County, TN US Census 10th division page 317

361 Elizabeth Bowers 53 F 400 acres born VA
  Caroline 18 F the rest born TN
  Martha 16 F
  John 12 M
  Leah Cobble 15 F

She appeared on the census in 1860. 25TH. DISTRICT, GREENE COUNTY, TENNESSEE PAGE 451 & 452 LINE 779

Alt Death: 28 Feb 1866, Greene County, Tennessee.

Elizabeth married **Jonas Bowers**,[20,45] son of **Christian Bower Jr.** and **Elizabeth Andes**, on 20 Aug 1818 in Jos. E. Bell, M.G., Greene Co, TN. Jonas was born on 31 Aug 1796 in Timberville, Rockingham Co, VA,[20,45] died on 21 Dec 1838 in Greene County, Tennessee[20,45] at age 42, and was buried in , Sinking Springs, Greene, Tennessee.

Marriage Notes: Bowers, Jonas Rader, Betsy 20 Aug 1818 Tennessee

General Notes: Greene Co., Marriages #1962 Aug 13, 1818 Jonas Bowers -- Betsey Rader -- Henry Rader md 20 Aug 1818 Jos E. Bell M.G.
Facts about this person:

Burial
Sinking Springs Lutheran Church, Greene County, Tennessee
The Chancery Court Minutes of Greene County, Tennessee lists childre n of Jonas Bowers and wife Elizabeth as William, Christian, Henry, Sam uel, LEWIS, Catharine, Caroline, John B. and maybe an infant (who woul d probably be Elizabeth) and does not list Martha (who could have died).

Henry married Sarah Elizabeth Cobble, 26 Jan 1843, Greene Co., TN
William - ?
Christian married Jemima Catron, 4 Feb. 1840, Greene Co., TN
Samuel - ?
Lewis* married Barbary A. Cobble, 16 Sept. 1847, Greene Co, TN
Caroline married John A. Wampler, 19 Dec. 1850, Greene Co., TN
Martha - ?
John A. married Hyla Ann Myers, 19 July 1860, Greene Co., TN
Catherine married Henry Smith, 23 Apr 1859, Greene Co., TN
Elizabeth - ?
Jonas Bowers died intestate and the inventory of his estate is recorded
in the Greene County, Tennessee Inventory of estates Volume 1828 to 1854, page 514 dated March 4, 1839. Jonas and Elizabeth's children are recorded in the Greene County, Tennessee Chancery Court Record Volume 1841 to 1848, pages 595 to 599 dated July 7, 1847.

Noted events in his life were:

Alt Death: 22 Dec 1838, Greene County, Tennessee.
Alt Death: 24 Dec 1839.
He has conflicting death information of 24 Dec 1839 and Sinking Springs.

Children from this marriage were:

+162 M   i.   **William Bowers**[20] was born on 11 Jul 1816 in Greene County, Tennessee[20] and died on 29 Apr 1909 in Jackson County, Tennessee at age 92.

William married **Elizabeth C Hull**.

+163 M ii. **Henry Bowers**[1,2,3,6,8,10,11,12,14,15,20] was born on 18 Mar 1818 in Greene County, Tennessee, died on 22 Dec 1901 in Cape Girardeau County, Missouri[20,64] at age 83, and was buried in New Salem Cemetery, Daisy, Missouri.

Henry married **Sarah Elizabeth Cobble**[20] (b. 31 Aug 1825, d. 14 Dec 1891) on 26 Jan 1843 in Greene County, Tennessee.

+164 M iii. **Christian Bowers**[20] was born about 1 Jan 1820 in Greene County, Tennessee.[20]

Christian married **Jemima Catron** (b. 1818) on 4 Feb 1840 in Greene County, Tennessee.

+165 M iv. **Samuel Bowers**[20] was born in 1824 in Greene County, Tennessee.[20]

+166 M v. **Lewis Bowers**[20] was born on 22 Jan 1826 in Greene County, Tennessee[20] and died on 21 Apr 1911 in Washington, D.C.[20] at age 85.

Lewis married **Barbara Cobble**[20] (b. 2 Oct 1822, d. 20 Feb 1910) on 16 Sep 1847 in Greene County, Tennessee.

+167 F vi. **Elizabeth Bowers**[1,2,3,6,8,10,11,12,14,15] was born in 1832 in , , Greene, Tennessee.

+168 F vii. **Caroline J. Bowers**[20] was born in 1832 in Greene County, Tennessee.[20]

Caroline married **John A. Wampler** on 19 Dec 1850 in Greene County, Tennessee.

Caroline next married **Andrew Wampler** (b. 1831) on 19 Dec 1850 in Greene County, Tennessee.

+169 F viii. **Martha Bowers**[1,2,3,6,8,10,11,12,14,15,20] was born in 1834 in Greene County, Tennessee.[20]

+170 M ix. **John A. Bowers**[1,2,3,6,8,10,11,12,14,15,20] was born about 1837 in Greene County, Tennessee.[20]

John married **Hyla Ann Myers** (b. 1838) on 19 Jul 1860 in Greene County, Tennessee.

+171 F x. **Catherine D. Bowers** was born about 1847 in Greene County, Tennessee.

Catherine married **Henry Smith** on 23 Apr 1859 in Greene County, Tennessee.

22. William W. Rader[1,2,3,6,8,10,11,12,14,15] (*Heinrich 'Henry' Sr*[2], *Casper Sr*[1]) was born on 15 Jun 1798 in Wythe County, Virginia,[46] died on 16 Apr 1880 in Greene County, Tennessee at age 81, and was buried in , Timber Ridge Cem, Greene, Tennessee.

Death Notes: William Rader   15 Jun 1798 16 Apr 1880   In memery of William Rader Greene County Timber Ridge Cemetery Located ten miles west of Greeneville, Tennessee. Northern Presbyterian Church. Copied by Daley S. Bowman, of Greeneville, Tennessee, October 12, 1937.

will of William Rader 3 May 1880 mem 29, page 133 will and Testament of William Rader dec was produced - probate with D.B. Reed and S. Wamples subscribing witnesses whom the same was duly proven, and that came thereafter said will be recorded. In the name of God Amen. Wm Rader of the county of Greene and State of Tennessee being of - and considering the uncertainty of this frail and transitory life make ordain publish and declare this to be my last will - , that is to say first after all of my lawful debts are discharged the residue of my estate Real and persarval and condition - Wife Barbara Rader should out live me I will and bequithe for her sole use and benifit during her lifetime the homestead - reside and personal property to wit. All necessary household furnature that is necessary to be laid off by A Jury appointed by the - and one hendred dollars in money and after her death whatever the property is to be sold and divided together with all moneys that - kept by her, I also allow my wife Barbara Rader what ever - asside of the personal property for use and benifit she may sale at it durring the time she may thow any away she may think least asserapar my death I hereby direct my Administrator to sell all of my personal estate as soon as possible outside of what is - - - the use of my wife Barbara Rader, and ---- and also my Administrator is directed to collect - - - in general and - - - I want a sit-off made against - - - of fiur hundred dollars in consideration of - - twenty years ago - - - him, I hereby make him - - - of what of - - - My administrators hands to - of three hundred dollars, and the remainder of his intrest is to - devided between his five first children that is now living to - - and the two daughters by his second wife (Anna Cobble) - - Son Andrew Rader children to wit Franklin Rader heirs, Two dollars And Elbert Rader Two hundred dollars And my son Henry heirs, to wit Andrew Rader two hundred dollars, and J L Rader two dollars and Reubin Rader two hundred dollars and Lafayett two hundred dollars and Mary Rader two hundred dollars. My son Joseph Rader I want a sett-off maid against him for - hundred dollars as A Segatio for money and favors I have bestowed heretofor and then make him equal as a Legatio grani therein, my son Madison Rader I want all of his notes and legal claims against him counted and taken out of his part, and pay the balance - that he is heirs to, and my Daughter Sarah Hartman made Equal - Thier Heirs (I hold no claim against her) and my daughter Margaret camp- be paid two hundred dollars, and if after all the proceeds of - state haus poked into my Administrators hands and have been - and still is surplus, their to be divided pro ratatly - as set forth in the first payment, and in case of failure to be enough - each and all proratably as set forth the their they are to remand back - to their several amounts, and after the death of my wife, if she - survive me in living I want the homestead that is named for the - for her to live in which she may live in attum mars after death of myself and wife Barbara Rader, I want the homestead - - sold and divided as set forth in this will, and after - I want to be burried in a plain decent maner and I hereby direct - Administrator to purchase a good and suitable tomb stone for - and also my wife Barbara Rader all to be paid for out of my estate. Witness thereof I have hereto subscribed my name and - this March 16th 1878 William Rader Facts about this person:

Name (Facts Pg) William W. Rader

Burial Timber Ridge Cemetery, Greene County, Tennessee

William married Barbara Hauff in Greene Co, TENNESSEE, May 17, 1821 by Rev Phil Henkel. Barbara was born May 19, 1803 in VIRGINIA She was the daughter of Joseph Hauff and Margaret. Barbara died April 24, 1883 in Timber Ridge, Greene Co, TENNESSEE, at 79 years of age. Her body was interred in Timber Ridge. For information about the Huff family see "Timber Ridge Church: A Two Hundred Year Heritage of Presbyterian Faith 1786-1986" by Harry B. Roberts and others.

Burial Notes: William and Barbara are both buried in the Timber Ridge Church cemetery. Barbara was the daughter of Joseph and Margaret Huff. For information about the Huff family see "Timber Ridge Church: A Two Hundred Year Heritage of Presbyterian Faith 1786-1986" by Harry B. Roberts and others.

General Notes: Greene County Marriage # 2272 May 14, 1821 William Rader -- Barbara Hauff -- Joseph Hauff md 17 May 1821 Philip Henkle, M.G. William was living in Timber Ridge, Tennessee in Greene County in 1860(census).

William and Barbara are both buried in the Timber Ridge Church cemetery.

Barbara was the daughter of Joseph and Margaret Huff. For information about the Huff family see "Timber Ridge Church: A Two Hundred Year Heritage of Presbyterian Faith 1786-1986" by Harry B. Roberts and others.

Conflicting evidence states that he died in Timber Ridge, March 6, 1880. William was living in Timber Ridge, Tennessee in Greene County in 1860 (census).

Noted events in his life were: He was employed. FARMER & JUSTICE OF THE PEACE

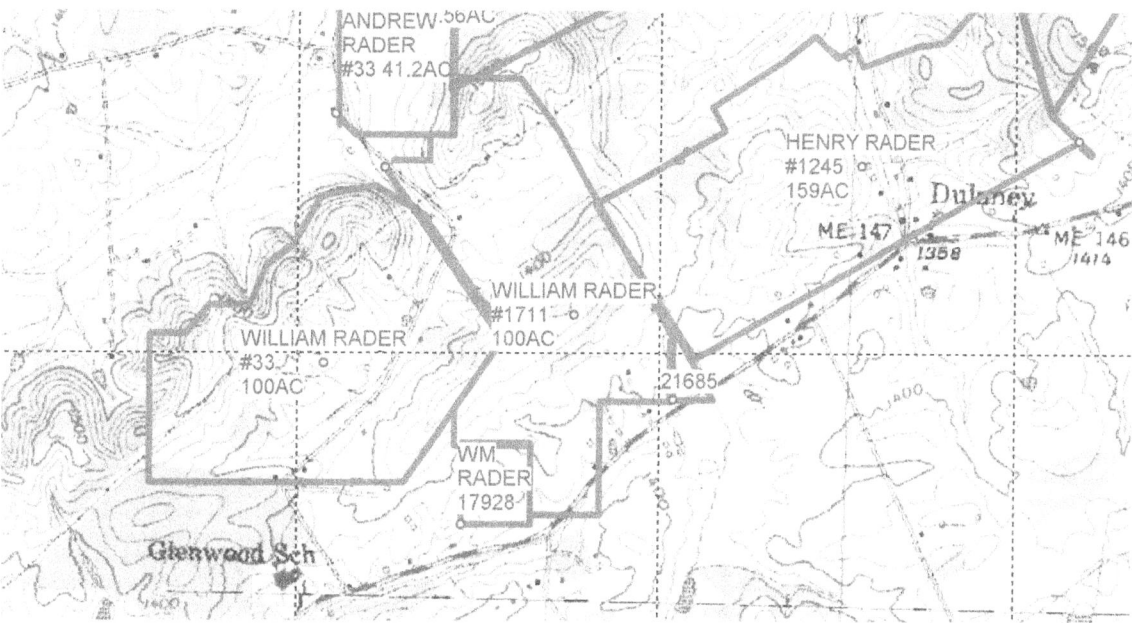

Map of Williams first 100 acre parcel #33 is the first purcase and in 1848 his residence (1821)

He owned land in 1821 in Greenwood School, Greene County, Tennessee.[65] This purchase parcel #33 containing 100 acres from Samuel Dunwoody on the waters of Little Chuckey

He owned land in 1821 in Greenwood School, Greene County, Tennessee.[65] This purchase parcel #33 containing 100 acres from Samuel Dunwoody on the waters of Little Chuckey

[Caption: 310 Glenwood Road - Rader - Roberts house]

He owned land in 1821 in Greenwood School, Greene County, Tennessee.[65] This purchase parcel #33 containing 100 acres from Samuel Dunwoody on the waters of Little Chuckey

He appeared on the census in 1830 in Greene County, Tennessee. Greene Co. TN 1830 Federal Census

Tax list: 1830-1841, Little Chuckey, Greene Co, TN. He paid taxes from 1830 through 1841 for 100 acres.

He owned land on 1 May 1836 in Little Chuckey, Greene Co, TN.[66] He purchased Parcel #17928 containing 10.5 acres from James Patterson

He owned land on 3 Jul 1837 in Little Chuckey, Greene Co, TN. He obtained a Tennessee land grant #21685 for 2 acres

He owned land on 30 Sep 1837 in Little Chuckey, Greene Co, TN.[67] #1711 purchase from Henry Feezel of 100 acres

He owned land on 30 Sep 1837 in Little Chuckey, Greene Co, TN.[67] #1711 purchase from Henry Feezel of 100 acres

He owned land on 5 Apr 1841 in Little Chuckey, Greene Co, TN. #1358 he purchased 21 acres from Alfred Russell (Love)

"to william son of Henry"

Tax list: 1842-1845, Little Chuckey, Greene Co, TN. District 5 taxes paid on 107 acres

[Caption: 4200 Dulaney Rd - Wilburn Rader]

He owned land in 1844.

[Caption: 4304 Dulaney Road]

He owned land in 1844. 4304 Dulaney Road

He owned land in 1844.

He owned land in 1844.

[Caption: 4055 Dulaney Rd. John Reed]

He owned land on 21 Aug 1844 in Dulaney, Greene County, Tennessee. Purchased Plot #1272 containing 310 acres from Adam Profit

He owned land on 21 Aug 1844 in Dulaney, Greene County, Tennessee. Purchased Plot #1272 containing 310 acres from Adam Profit

He owned land on 21 Aug 1844 in Dulaney, Greene County, Tennessee. Purchased Plot #1272 containing 310 acres from Adam Profit

Tax list: 1846, Little Chuckey, Greene Co, TN. District #5 taxes for 432 acres

He owned land on 27 Oct 1846 in Dulaney, Greene County, Tennessee. Purchased parcel #1913 containing 250 acres from John Nelson (Geo T Gilispie)

[Caption: 1046 Hartman Rd]

He owned land on 27 Oct 1846 in Dulaney, Greene County, Tennessee. Purchased parcel #1913 containing 250 acres from John Nelson (Geo T Gilispie)

[Caption: 1000 Hartman Rd.]

He owned land on 27 Oct 1846 in Dulaney, Greene County, Tennessee. Purchased parcel #1913 containing 250 acres from John Nelson (Geo T Gilispie)

He appeared on the census in 1850 in Greene County, Tennessee. RADER WILLIAM 52 M W VA GREENE 10 sub 880 306

    RADER BARBARY   47 F W VA GREENE 10 sub 880 306
    RADER HENRY   21 M W TN GREENE 10 sub 880 306
    RADER JOSEPH   19 M W TN GREENE 10 sub 880 306
    RADER MARTIN   15 M W TN GREENE 10 sub 880 306
    RADER CASPER   12 M W TN GREENE 10 sub 880 306
    RADER MADISON   8 M W TN GREENE 10 sub 880 306
    RADER MARGARET 4 F W TN GREENE 10 sub 880 306

He appeared on the census on 25 Jun 1860 in Timber Ridge, Greene Co, TN. Wm Rader found in: Census Microfilm Records: Tennessee, 1860
    Age: 62   Gender: M   Race: W   Birthplace: VA
    State: Tennessee   County: GREENE   Locale: TIMBER RIDGE P O
    Series: M653   Roll: 1252   Part: 1   Page: 423A
    25 june 1860
    789 789 Wm Rader 63 M farmer 3000 Virginia
           Barbary   57 F   "
           Margt   13 f   "

He appeared on the census on 8 Sep 1870 in Bulls Gap, Greene County, Tennessee. William Rader found in: Census Microfilm Records: Tennessee, 1870
    Age: 71   Gender: M   Race: W   Birthplace: VA
    State: Tennessee   County: GREENE   Locale: BULLS GAP P O
    Series: M593   Roll: 1531   Part: 1   Page: 228A
    civil district #6 8th day September 1870
    51 51 Rader, William 71 M W farmer 5000 1500 Virginia
           Elizabeth 71 F W keeping house   "
           Mary E   10 F B   Tennessee

He signed a will on 16 Mar 1878.

Alt Death: 6 Mar 1880, , , Greene, Tennessee.

He had an estate probated on 3 May 1880. GREENE COUNTY, TENNESSEE

William married **Barbara Hauff**, daughter of **Joseph Hauff** and **Margaret**, on 17 May 1821 in Rev Phil. Henkel, Greene Co, TN.[44] Barbara was born on 19 May 1803 in VA,[21,46] died on 24 Apr 1883 in Timber Ridge, Greene Co, TN at age 79, and was buried in , Timber Ridge Cem, Greene, Tennessee. Other names for Barbara were Huff, and Barbara Hauff.

Marriage Notes: Greene County Marriage # 2272 May 14, 1821 William Rader -- Barbara Hauff -- Joseph Hauff md 17 May 1821 Philip Henkle, M.G.

Hauff, Barbara Rader, William 17 May 1821 Tennessee

Noted events in their marriage were:

Alt Marriage: 14 May 1821, Greene County, Tennessee.

Source Citations

General Notes: The HAUFF family - Barbara's ancestors Peter Hauff. Born in Philadelphia co, Pa. Died, 1784 in Philadelphia, PA. He married Anna the only child I know about was Andrew Hauff.

SECOND GENERATION Andrew Hauff born in Keezletown. Died in Rockingham Co, VA. He married Barbara. Children: Elias Hauff, Benjamin Hauff, Leonard Hauff, Sally Hauff, Jacob Hauff, Henry Hauff, Joseph Hauff.

THIRD GENERATION Joseph Hauff Born, 21 Apr 1781, in Pennsylvania. Died, 5 May 1852, in Ely, Green, Tn. 1824, He married Margaret. Born, 1785, in Pennsylvania. Children: Barbara Hauff, Sally Huff. Born, 1805. She married Martin Welty, Elias Huff. Born, 1807, in VA., Elizabeth Huff. Born, 1809. She married Jno C. Welty, 7 Sep 1837., Peter Huff., Andrew Jackson Huff. Born, 1816., William Huff. Born, 14 Jun 1818. Died, 17 Feb 1883, buried in Timber Ridge, Greene, TN. He married Mariah Thompson 17 Sep 1839

FOURTH GENERATION Barbara Hauff Born, 19 May 1803, in Va. Died, 24 Apr 1883, buried in Timber Ridge, Greene, TN. She married William W. Rader, son of Henry Rader and Catherine Etter, 17 May 1821, in Green Co, Tenn. Born, 15 Jun 1798, in Wythe Co, Va. Died, 16 Apr 1880, in Green Co. Tn. Death(2): 6 Mar 1880, in Timber Ridge. William was living in Timber Ridge, Tennessee in Greene County in 1860(census). William wrote his Will on March 16, 1878 and it was probated in Greene County, Tennessee on May 3, 1880. William and Barbara are both buried in the Timber Ridge Church cemetery. Barbara was the daughter of Joseph and Margaret Huff. For information about the Huff family see "Timber Ridge Church: A Two Hundred Year Heritage of Presbyterian Faith 1786-1986" by Harry B. Roberts and others. Children: John Rader, Sarah Rader, Andrew Rader, Henry Rader, Joseph James Rader, Martin Rader. Born, 12 Nov 1831, Died, 3 Mar 1853, buried in Timber Ridge, Casper Rader. Born, 26 Jan 1838. Died, 27 Mar 1863, in Mt Pleasant, Green, Tn. He married Nancy Davis, 4 Jan 1857 in Greene Co., TN., Dr. Madison Rader., Margaret Rader. Born, 27 Sep 1846, in Greene Co., Tn, Died, 23 Apr 1870, Burial in Timber Ridge. She married George W. Campbell, 12 Mar 1867.

Peter Huff Born, 21 Aug 1810, in Keezletown, Rockingham Co., VA. Died, 27 Sep 1889, in Hauff, Greene, Tn. He married Barbara Elizabeth Welty, 5 May 1831 Born, 1804 in Greene Co., TN. Children: Andrew Huff. Born, 1832, in Greene Co., TN., John Huff. Born, 14 Jan 1833 in Greene Co., TN. He married Margaret An Smith, 1 May 1900, in Hartman Chapel., Joseph Huff. Born, 1835, in Greene Co., TN., Noah Huff. Born, 1838 in Greene Co., TN., Elizabeth Huff. Born, 1843, in Greene Co., TN., Jonas Huff. Born, 1845, in Greene Co., TN. Facts about this person:

> Burial Timber Ridge Cemetery, Greene County, Tennessee
> !Bobby Carter gives also an alternate spelling of Hauff as does Elizabeth Rader McNew of 708 York St., Rocky Mount, NC 27801.

Noted events in her life were:
Fact 1: Fact 1, See Note Page.
Alt Death: 24 Apr 1843, , , Greene, Tennessee.
Alt Death: 24 Apr 1843, , , Greene, Tennessee.[21, 68]
She appeared on the census in 1850. GREENE COUNTY, TENNESSEE   PAGE 306A #196
Census 1: 1860. GREENE COUNTY, TENNESSEE   PAGE 423 #789
Census 2: 1870. TIMBER RIDGE, GREENE COUNTY, TENNESSEE DIST. 25 PAGE 448 #19

Children from this marriage were:

+172 F   i.   **Elizabeth J. Rader** was born WFT Est 1819-1848 and died WFT Est 1824-1930 at age 5.

+173 M ii.   **John Rader**[1, 2, 3, 6, 8, 10, 11, 12, 14, 15] was born on 15 Feb 1822 in Greene County, Tennessee, died on 25 Dec 1900 in Murdered, Blountville, TN at age 78, and was buried in Greene County, Tennessee.[28]

John married **Jane P. Britton** (b. 1827, d. Abt 1855) on 15 Dec 1842 in Greene County, Tennessee.[44, 69]

John next married **Anna Cobble** (b. 4 Dec 1831, d. After 1880) on 28 Oct 1856 in Greene County, Tennessee.[42, 44, 70]

John next married **Mary Elizabeth Stafford** (b. 9 Sep 1856, d. 1895) on 7 Sep 1876 in Greene County, Tennessee.

John next married **Eunice Emaline Hood** (b. Apr 1851) on 10 Sep 1896 in Greene County, Tennessee.

+174 M iii. **Joseph Rader** .[8, 11, 14]

+175 F iv. **Sarah 'Sallie' Rader** was born on 24 Jun 1824 in Greene County, Tennessee, died on 24 Apr 1902 in Greene County, Tennessee at age 77, and was buried in Mt. Pleasant Methodist Church Cemetery, Greene County, Tennessee.

Sarah married **Marshall Hartman Jr** (b. 26 Oct 1820, d. 8 Mar 1887) on 7 Mar 1844 in Greene County, Tennessee.

+176 M v.   **Andrew Rader** was born in 1828 in Greene County, Tennessee and died in 1856 in Greene County, Tennessee at age 28.

Andrew married **Rebecca Amelia Britton** (b. 1834, d. Abt 1855) on 14 Mar 1848 in Greene County, Tennessee.[44]

Andrew next married **Loisa P** (b. 1838).

+177 M vi.   **Henry L. Rader**[1, 2, 3, 6, 8, 10, 11, 12, 14, 15] was born on 17 Feb 1829 in Dulaney, Greene County, Tennessee, died on 25 Jul 1864 in Camp Douglas, Union Prison, Cook County, Illinois at age 35, and was buried in Chicago, Oak Woods Cem, , Illinois.

Henry married **Mary Ann 'Pollyan' Bowers** (b. 15 Feb 1831, d. 7 Dec 1895) on 3 Oct 1850 in , , Greene, Tennessee.[44]

+178 M vii. **Joseph James Rader**[1, 2, 3, 6, 10, 11, 12, 14, 15] was born on 10 Apr 1831 in Greene County, Tennessee, died on 21 Jul 1918 in Sullivan County, Tennessee at age 87, and was buried in Boy Cemetery, Sullivan County, Tennessee.

Joseph married **Susannah Stein** (b. 31 Mar 1832, d. 6 Apr 1908) on 20 Jan 1853 in Greene County, Tennessee.[44]

+179 M viii. **Martin Rader**[1, 2, 3, 6, 8, 10, 11, 12, 14, 15] was born on 12 Nov 1831 in , , Greene, Tennessee,[46] died on 3 Mar 1853 in Timber Ridge, Greene Co, TN at age 21, and was buried in , Timber Ridge Cem, Greene, Tennessee.

+180 M ix. **Casper Rader**[1, 2, 3, 6, 8, 10, 11, 12, 14, 15] was born on 26 Jan 1838 in , , Greene, Tennessee, died on 27 Mar 1863 in Big Creek Gap Civil War at age 25, and was buried in Mt. Pleasant Methodist Church Cemetery, Greene County, Tennessee.

Casper married **Nancy J. Davis** (b. 1840) on 4 Jan 1857 in Greene County, Tennessee.[44]

+181 M x. **Doctor Madison Rader**[1, 2, 3, 6, 8, 10, 11, 12, 14, 15] was born on 23 May 1842 in , , Greene, Tennessee,[71] died on 1 Aug 1913 in Greene County, Tennessee at age 71, and was buried in 1913 in Bruners Grove United Methodist Church, Cocke County, Tennessee.

Madison married **Emily Jane Meyers** (b. 30 Jul 1841, d. 4 Apr 1880) on 19 Jan 1860 in Greene County, Tennessee.[44]

Madison next married **Laura R Henderson** (b. 16 Sep 1861, d. 1932) on 23 Jun 1895 in Timber Ridge, Greene County, Tennessee.

Madison next married **Mary Jane Earnest Harrison** (b. 21 Mar 1858, d. 11 Jun 1894) on 10 Oct 1880.

+182 F xi. **Margaret Rader**[1, 2, 3, 6, 8, 10, 11, 12, 14, 15] was born on 27 Sep 1846 in Greene County, Tennessee,[46] died on 23 Apr 1870 in Timber Ridge, Greene Co, TN at age 23, and was buried in Timber Ridge, Greene Co, TN.

Margaret married **George W. Campbell** (b. 1840) on 12 Mar 1867 in Greene County, Tennessee.

Margaret next married (_____) **Campbell**.

Raders Gap plot #3573

23. Casper J. Rader Jr. [1, 2, 3, 6, 8, 10, 11, 12, 14, 15] (*Heinrich 'Henry' Sr* [2], *Casper Sr* [1]) was born on 19 Apr 1801 in Greene County, Tennessee, died on 6 Oct 1883 in Brizil, Clay Co, IN, Or MO [47] at age 82, and was buried in 1883 in Mc Cullough, Washington Twp, Potnam Co, IN.

General Notes: Casper was mentioned in his father's estate settlement in 1859 however part of his inheritance apparently was shared by his nephew George W. Rader, son of his brother John Rader. No record of Casper can be found in the Greene County, Tennessee census after 1840. For Casper,s children see the publication "Rader Relatives" Vol. II Number 3 Winter, pages 36 and 37.

The Saint James Lutheran Church record indicated that Casper took Communion on Sunday May 4, 1817.

Facts about this person: Burial McCullough Cemetery, Washington Township, Putnam County, Indiana

Facts about this person: Burial   October 1883 McCullough, Washington Twp., Putnam Co. IN.

Casper Rader was born on 19 Apr 1801 in Greene COUNTY, TENNESSEE He was baptized on 22 Sep 1805 in Sinking Springs. He was buried in 1883 in Mc Cullough, Washington Twp, Potnam Co, IN. He died on 6 Oct 1883 in Brizil, Clay Co, IN , or MISSOURI Casper was mentioned in his father's estate settlement in 1859 however part of his inheritance apparently was shared by his nephew George W. Rader, son of his brother John Rader. No record of Casper can be found in the GREENE COUNTY, TENNESSEE census after 1840. Mary McKamey of Cloverdale Indiana is a descendant of Casper and she says he moved his family to Clay County, Indiana about 1852. For Casper,s children see the publication "Rader Relatives" Vol. II Number 3 Winter, pages 36 and 37. Casper was living in McPherson's district on Lick Creek in GREENE COUNTY, TENNESSEE in 1830 and owned 200 acres of land. He was living in the same location in 1828 but owned no land (Tax list). The Saint James Lutheran Church record indicated that Casper took Communion on Sunday May 4, 1817.

See note on Casper's brother Henry.

Noted events in his life were:
Fact 1: Fact 1, See Note Page.

Alt Birth: 9 Apr 1801, Greene County, Tennessee.
Alt Birth: 22 Sep 1805, , , Greene, Tennessee.
He was baptized on 22 Sep 1805. SINKING SPRINGS LUTHERAN, GREENE COUNTY, TENNESSEE

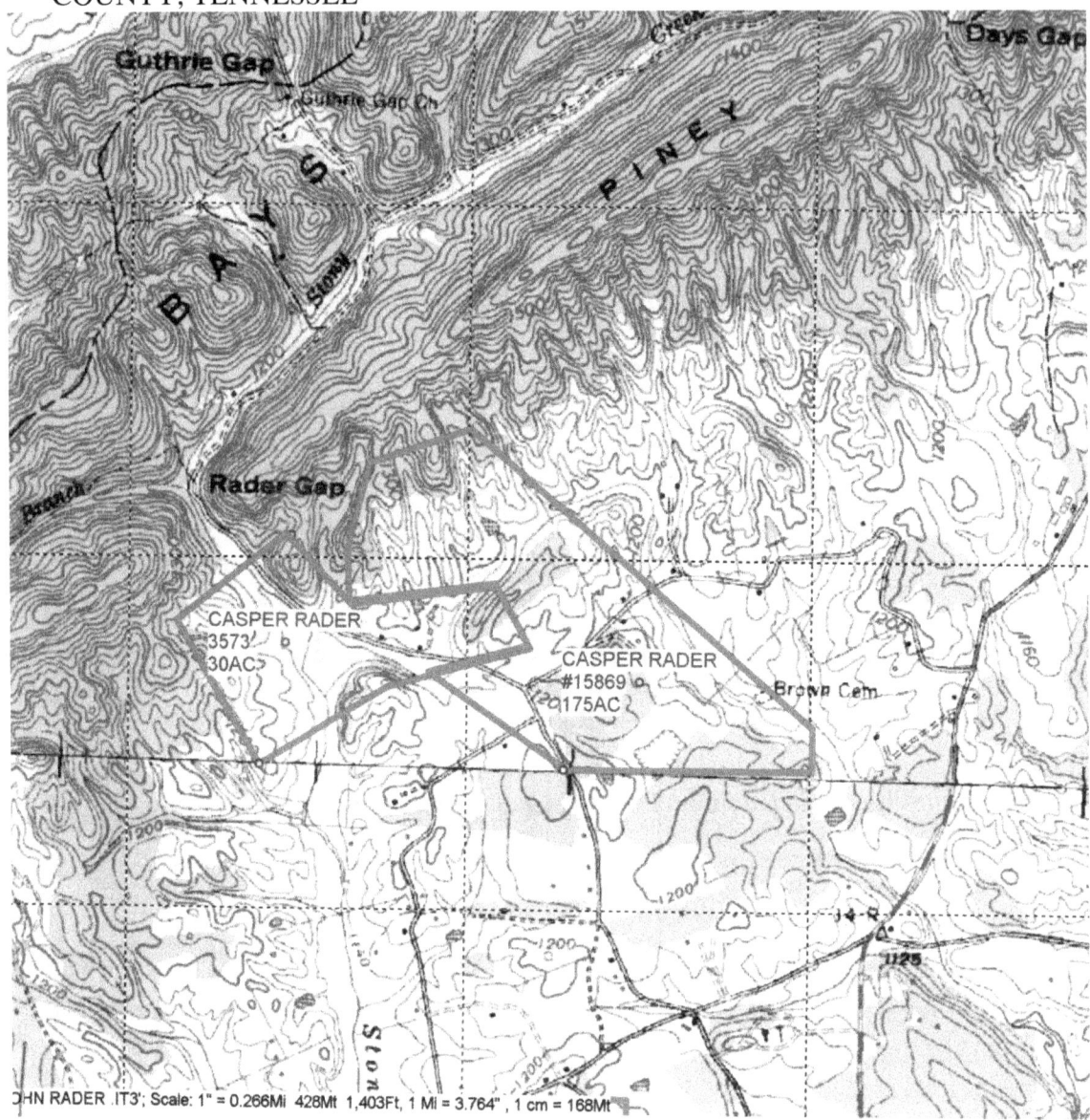

Map of Land in Rader's Gap purchased by Casper Rader 1828

He owned land in 1828 in Raders gap, Greene county, Tennessee. Casper purchased 30 acres from Jesse Self on Stoney creek ft of Bays Mt 27 Oct 1827 and he purchased 175 acres from Isaac Mace on stoney creek 1 Nov 1829

[Caption: rader's gap]

He owned land in 1828 in Raders gap, Greene county, Tennessee. Casper purchased 30 acres from Jesse Self on Stoney creek ft of Bays Mt 27 Oct 1827 and he purchased 175 acres from Isaac Mace on stoney creek 1 Nov 1829

He owned land on 27 Oct 1828 in Lick Creek Valley, Greene County Tennessee. Purchased 30 acres from Jesse Self #3573

He owned land on 1 Nov 1829 in Lick Creek Valley, Greene County Tennessee. Purchased 175 acres of land from Isaac Mace #15869

He appeared on the census in 1830 in Lick Creek Vly, Greene Co, TN. Casper was living in McPherson's district on Lick Creek in Greene County, Tennessee in 1830 and owned 200 acres of land. He was living in the same location in 1828 but owned no land(Tax list).

Census 1: 1840. GREENE COUNTY, TENNESSEE PAGE 73
Census 2: 1850. WILLIAMSON COUNTY, ILLINOIS LINE 875   PAGE 275
Resided: 1852, Clay County, Indiana. Mary McKamey of Cloverdale Indiana is a descendant of Casper and she says he moved his family to Clay County, Indiana about 1852.
Census 3: 1860. CASS TOWNSHIP, CLAY COUNTY, INDIANA LINE 88
Census 4: 1870. CASS TOWNSHIP, CLAY COUNTY, INDIANA   LINE 807 PAGE 41

He appeared on the census in 1880 in Washington, Clay, Indiana. Census Place:Washington, Clay, Indiana

Source: FHL Film 1254270 National Archives Film T9-0270   Page 502C
RelationSexMarrRaceAgeBirthplace
Casper RADER   Self M M W 79 TN Occ:FarmerFa: VAMo: VA
Annie RADER   Wife F M W 68 TN Occ:Keeping HouseFa: TNMo: TN
Nicholas M. RADER Son M S W 25 IN Occ:FarmerFa: TNMo: TN
Census 5: 1880. WASHINGTON TOWNSHIP, CLAY COUNTY, INDIANA LINE 59
Alt Death: Oct 1885, Cass Twp., Putnam Co, Indiana.
MARRIAGE # 1: 2975. M. G. WILSON JP (BROWN)
MARRIAGE # 2: 3622. JEPSE W. HAILE L.D.

Casper married **Anny Brown** on 29 Nov 1828 in M.G. Wilson, Jp, Greene Co, TN.[44] Anny was born in 1805 in Tennessee, died about 1833 in Pilot Knob, Greene County, Tennessee about age 28, and was buried in Pilot Knob Cemetery, Greene County, Tennessee. Another name for Anny was Anna Brown.

> General Notes: Greene County Marriage # 2975 Nov 21, 1828 Casper Rader -- Anny Brown -- md 29 NOV 1828 -- M.G. Wilson, J.P.

Noted events in her life were:
She appeared on the census in 1830. GREENE COUNTY, TENNESSEE PG. 188
MARRIAGE # 1: 2975. M. G. WILSON JUSTICE OF THE PEACE

Children from this marriage were:

+183 M   i.   **George Washington Rader**[72] was born on 15 Aug 1829 in Greene County, Tennessee[72] and died on 27 Apr 1881 in Centerpoint, Clay County, Indiana at age 51.

George married **Mary E. Jenkins**[72] (b. 1839) on 5 Feb 1860 in Clay County, Indiana.

+184 F   ii. **Elizabeth Jane Rader** was born on 16 Nov 1831 in Greene County, Tennessee and died on 11 Jan 1915 in Brazil, Clay County, Indiana at age 83.

Elizabeth married **Francis Asberry Bridewell** (b. 1825) on 1 Sep 1849 in Greene County, Tennessee.

+185 M   iii. **Henry Rader** was born on 9 Oct 1833 in Greene County, Tennessee and died on 6 Sep 1865 in Washington Twp, Putnam, IN at age 31.

Henry married **Mary C. Grable** (b. 15 Mar 1835, d. 3 Mar 1919) on 13 Aug 1854 in Greencastle, Putnam County, Indiana.

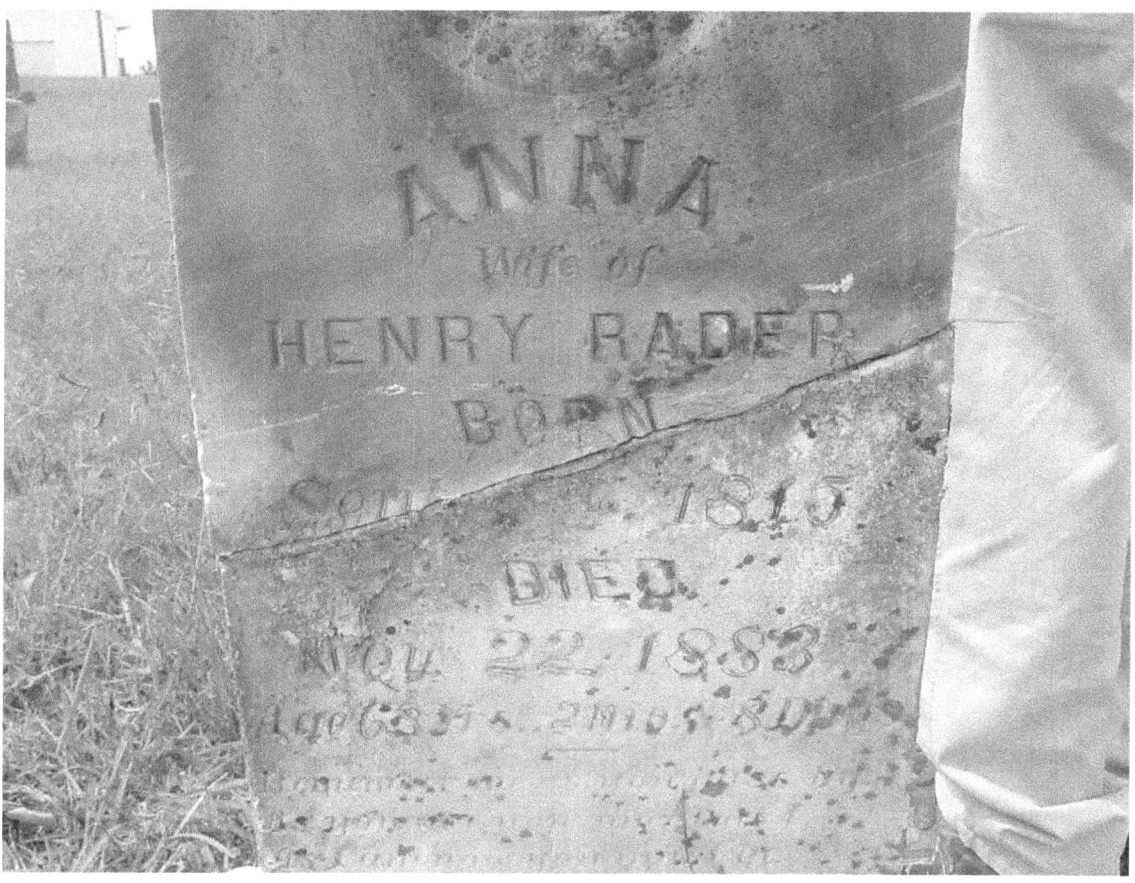

Casper next married **Anna Mary Mace**, daughter of **Henry Mace** and **Unknown**, on 31 Jul 1834 in , Jesse W Haile, Ld, Greene, Tennessee.[44] Anna was born on 15 Oct 1816 in Greene County, Tennessee, died on 22 Nov 1883 at age 67, and was buried in , Pilot Knob. Another name for Anna was Anna Mary Mace.

General Notes:

Greene Co Marriage # 3622 Jul 31, 1834 Casper Rader -- Anna Mace md 31 Jul 1834 Jepse W. Haile, L.D. Greene County marriage # 3861 July 18, 1836 Henry Rader --

Anna Mace -- Henry Mace -- md 21 JUL 1836 -- Geo Easterly, M.G.

19. Casper3 Rader (Heinrich 'Henry'2, Casper (Roeder)1) was born in Greene Co, TN April 19, 1801. Casper died October 6, 1883 in Brizil, Clay Co, IN, or MO, at 82 years of age.(43) His body was interred 1883 in Mc Cullough, Washington Twp, Potnam Co, IN.

He married twice. He married Anny Brown in M.G. Wilson, jp, Greene Co, TN, November 29, 1828.(44) Anny was born 1805 in TN. Anny died circa 1833 in Greene Co, TN. He married Anna Mace July 31, 1834.(45) Anna was born October 15, 1816 in Greene Co, TN. Anna died September 16, 1908 in Clay Co, IN, at 91 years of age. Her body was interred in McCullough cem, Washington Twp, Putnam Co, IN.

He was baptized in Sinking Springs, September 22, 1805.

Casper Rader and Anna Mace had the following family:

+ 130 i. Catherine4 Rader was born before February 19, 1863, the first event for which there is a recorded date.

+ 131 ii. Philip Rader was born September 29, 1835.

132 iii. Malinda Jane Rader was born in Greene Co, TN July 20, 1839. Malinda died November 5, 1862 at 23 years of age. Her body was interred in Risley, Poland, Clay Co, IN. She married Elisha Dalgarn in Clay Co, IN, May 21, 1859.

133 iv. William 'Bill' Rader was born in Greene Co, TN March 12, 1841. William died after 1915 in Montrose, Effingham Co., IL. He married Helen Wallace East April 14, 1864. Helen was born September 24, 1847. Helen died August 27, 1870 at 22 years of age. Her body was interred in McCullough, Washington Twp, Putnam Co, IN.

+ 134 v. John Nelson Rader was born October 10, 1843.

+ 135 vi. Andrew Thomas Jackson Rader was born December 26, 1846.

136 vii. Martha Ann 'Matt' Rader was born in Greene Co, TN September 27, 1848. Martha died May 8, 1934 in Terre Haute, Vigo Co, IN, at 85 years of age. She married Jesse Fritts December 11, 1879.

+ 137 viii. Casper Rader,Jr. was born November 10, 1851.

+ 138 ix. Isaac Newton Rader was born May 17, 1855.

+ 139 x. Nicholas Marion Rader was born May 17, 1855.

140 xi. Dulsena Candace Rader was born in Clay Co, IN August 17, 1858. Dulsena died November 19, 1860 in Clay Co, IN, at 2 years of age. Her body was interred in McCullough cem.

Casper Rader and Anny Brown had the following family:

141 xii. George W. Rader was born in Greene Co, TN August 15, 1829. George died April 27, 1881 in Centerpoint, Clay Co, IN, at 51 years of age. He married Mary E. Jenkins in Clay Co, IN, February 5, 1860.

142 xiii. Elizabeth Jane Rader was born in Greene Co, TN November 16, 1831. Elizabeth died January 11, 1915 in Brazil, Clay Co, IN, at 83 years of age. She married Francis Asberry Bridewell.

+ 143 xiv. Henry Rader was born October 9, 1833.

Anna was listed as a resident in the census report in Cocke Co, Tn., 1870 (a widow age 55 living next door to son Powell, Granville & Sarah Worelock).

Noted events in her life were:

Alt Burial: McCullough cem, Washington Twp, Putnam Co, IN.
Alt Buried: Pilot Knob Cemetery, Greene County, Tennessee.
Alt Birth: 14 Sep 1815, Greene County, Tennessee.
Alt Birth: 15 Oct 1816, Greene County, Tennessee.
She appeared on the census in 1840. GREENE COUNTY, TENNESSEE PAGE 73

Census 1: 1850. WILLIAMSON COUNTY, ILLINOIS LINE 875   PAGE 275
Census 2: 1860. CASS TOWNSHIP, CLAY COUNTY, INDIANA LINE 88

Census 3: 1870. CASS TOWNSHIP, CLAY COUNTY, INDIANA   LINE 807 PAGE 41
She appeared on the census in 1870 in Parrotsville, Cocke County Tennessee. RADER
    ANNA   ,1815,55,F,W,TN ,TN ,COCKE ,PARROTSVILLE P O
    ,M593,1519,0,354
    RADER ,HANAH MC ,1795,75,F,W,VA ,TN ,COCKE ,PARROTSVILLE P O
    ,M593,1519,0,354
    RADER ,POWELL   ,1844,26,M,W,TN ,TN ,COCKE ,PARROTSVILLE P O
    ,M593,1519,0,354
    Anna Rader , District 2, Cocke, TN , abt 1815 Tennessee , White, Female ,93,
    Granville Rader , District 2, Cocke, TN , abt 1848 Tennessee , White, Male ,93,
    Sarah J Rader , District 2, Cocke, TN , abt 1855 Tennessee , White, Female ,93,
Census 4: 1880. WASHINGTON TOWNSHIP, CLAY COUNTY, INDIANA   LINE 59

She appeared on the census in 1880 in Greene County, Tennessee. Census Place: District
    7, Greene, Tennessee
    Source: FHL Film 1255258 National Archives Film T9-1258   Page 113B
    Relation   Sex   Marr   Race   Age   Birthplace
  Henry MOORELOCK Self M M W 30 TN   Occ: Farmer Fa: TN Mo: TN
  Sarah MORELOCK   Wife F M W 24 TN   Occ: Keeping House Fa: TN Mo: TN
  Anna RADER MotherL F W W 66 TN   Occ: At Home   Fa: TN Mo: TN
  Joseph CHESSER Other M S W 16 TN   Occ: Laborer   Fa: TN Mo: TN

Alt Death: 22 Nov 1883, Greene County, Tennessee.
Alt Death: 22 Nov 1883, Pilot Knob, Greene County, Tennessee.
Census 5: 1900. WASHINGTON TOWNSHIP, CLAY COUNTY, INDIANA PAGE 350
    LIVING W/PHILIP
Alt Death: 6 Sep 1908, Clay County, Indiana.
Alt Death: 16 Sep 1908, Clay County, Indiana.
MARRIAGE # 1: 3622. JESSE W. HAILE, L. D.

   Children from this marriage were:

+186 M   i.   **Philip Rader** was born on 29 Sep 1835 in Greene County, Tennessee, died on
                30 Jan 1915 in Clay County, Indiana at age 79, and was buried in Clearview
                Cemetery, Centerpoint, Clay County, Indiana.

        Philip married **Elizabeth Murbargar** (b. 18 May 1842, d. 19 Dec 1884) on 20 Oct
        1861 in Clay County, Indiana.

        Philip next married **Sarah Ann Davis** (b. 12 Dec 1840, d. 12 May 1921) on 10 Oct
        1889.

        Philip next married **Darlina** (b. Dec 1840).

+187 F   ii.   **Mary Rader** was born in 1836.

        Mary married **John Burroughs**.

+188 F   iii. **Catherine Rader** was born on 28 Feb 1838 in Greene County, Tennessee,
                died on 15 Jul 1933 in Vanburen Twp, Clay Co, IN at age 95, and was buried
                in Cottage Hill, Brazil, Clay Co, IN.

Catherine married **John 'Pap' Murbargar III** (b. 4 Sep 1838, d. 4 Jul 1918) on 19 Feb 1863 in Clay County, Indiana.

+189 F iv. **Malinda Jane Rader** was born on 20 Jul 1839 in Greene County, Tennessee, died on 5 Nov 1862 in Clay County, Indiana at age 23, and was buried in Risley, Poland, Clay County, IN.

Malinda married **Elisha Dalgarn** on 21 May 1859 in Clay County, Indiana.

+190 M v. **William 'Bill' Rader** was born on 12 Mar 1841 in Greene County, Tennessee and died in 1916 in Montrose, Effingham Co., IL at age 75.

William married **Helen Wallace East** (b. 24 Sep 1847, d. 27 Aug 1870) on 14 Apr 1864 in Putnam Co. In.

+191 M vi. **John Nelson Rader** was born on 10 Oct 1843 in Greene County, Tennessee, died on 10 Mar 1889 in Council Grove, Morris, Kansas at age 45, and was buried in Council Grove, Morris, Kansas.

John married **Mary Catherine Acrea** (b. 1 Jul 1850, d. 8 Jul 1923) on 24 Aug 1865 in Putnam County, Indiana.

+192 M vii. **Andrew Thomas Jackson Rader** was born on 26 Dec 1846 in Greene County, Tennessee,[73] died on 23 Jul 1922 in Cass Township, Clay County, Indiana at age 75, and was buried in Matkins, Rr1, Reelsville, Putnam Co., IN.

Andrew married **Mary Elizabeth Johnson** (b. 26 Mar 1852, d. 7 Mar 1912) on 3 May 1868 in Putnam Co Indiana.

+193 F viii. **Martha Ann 'Matt' Rader** was born on 27 Sep 1848 in Greene County, Tennessee and died on 8 May 1934 in Terre Haute, Vigo Co, IN at age 85.

Martha married **Jesse Fritts** on 11 Dec 1879 in Clay County, Indiana.

+194 M ix. **Casper J Rader Jr.**[47] was born on 10 Nov 1851 in Illinois, died on 18 Sep 1888 in Harrison Township, Clay County, Indiana at age 36, and was buried about 23 Sep 1888 in Greewwell, , Harrison Twp., Clay County, Indiana.

Casper married **Clara Belford** (b. 12 Jul 1860, d. 20 Mar 1948) on 12 Jun 1875 in Clay County, Indiana.

Casper next married **Clarinda "Clara"** (b. WFT Est 1837-1860, d. WFT Est 1880-1949) on 26 Jul 1875.

+195 M x. **Isaac Newton Rader** was born on 17 May 1855 in Clay County, Indiana, died on 3 Jul 1926 in Brazil, Clay County, Indiana at age 71, and was buried in Risley, Poland, Clay Co, IN.

Isaac married **Sarah Jennie Dalgarn** on 21 Nov 1881 in Clay County, Indiana.

Isaac next married **Clara E. Cole** (b. 1874) on 31 Dec 1891 in Clay County, Indiana.

+196 F xi. **Elizabeth Rader** was born in 1852 in Greene County, Tennessee.

+197 M xii. **Nicholas Marion Rader** was born on 17 May 1855 in Clay County, Indiana, died on 20 Jan 1935 in Clay County, Indiana at age 79, and was buried in Union Cemetery, Clay County, Indiana.

Nicholas married **Rhoda Ann Sanderson** (b. Jun 1865) on 31 Jul 1883 in Putnam, IN.

+198 F xiii. **Dulsena Candace Rader** was born on 17 Aug 1858 in Clay County, Indiana, died on 19 Nov 1860 in Clay County, Indiana at age 2, and was buried in McCULLOUGH, WASHINGTON TOWNSHIP, PUTNAM COUNTY INDIANA.

24. Rachel Rader[1,2,3,6,8,10,11,12,14,15] (*Heinrich 'Henry' Sr*[2], *Casper Sr*[1]) was born about 1803 in Wythe County, Virginia, died in 1855 in Williamson Co, IL about age 52, and was buried in , Frank Campbell F, Williamson, Illinois.

General Notes: Rachel and Michael were living on Paint Creek in Greene County, Tennessee in 1830. They owned 120 acres of land.

Rachel married **Michael Basinger Jr.**, son of **Unknown** and **Unknown**, on 30 Dec 1823 in Rev Phil Henkel, Greene Co, TN. Michael was born on 24 Aug 1806 and died on 29 Jul 1855 in Williamson County, Illinois at age 48.

Noted events in his life were:

He signed a will on 14 Aug 1846 in Greene Co.TN, Phillip 116Ac. Isaac 80 Ac. And Grist Mill, Children- Jacob, George, William, Betsy Porter, Sally Champlin.

Children from this marriage were:

+199 M i. **William Basinger** was born in 1826 in Greene County, Tennessee.

William married **Susan** (b. 1833).

+200 M ii. **Jacob Basinger** .

+201 M iii. **Hamilton Basinger** was born on 6 Dec 1827 in Greene County, Tennessee and died in Williamson County, Illinois.

Hamilton married **Elizabeth "Lizzy" Swatzell** (b. 1825) on 18 Mar 1848 in Greene County, Tennessee.

Hamilton next married **Gracia Latham** in 1883.

+202 M iv. **George Basinger** .

George married **Jane Peters** (b. Abt 1810) on 13 May 1830 in Greene County, Tennessee.

+203 M v. **George William Basinger** was born on 12 Sep 1832 in Greene County, Tennessee and died on 23 Oct 1865 in Williamson County, Illinois at age 33.

George married **Sally Ann Reiss** (b. 1 Sep 1836, d. 21 Jan 1897) on 16 Feb 1854 in Williamson County, Illinois.

+204 F vi. **Sally Basinger** .

Sally married **Alexander Champlin** on 10 Oct 1836 in Greene County, Tennessee.

+205 F vii. **Margaret Ann Basinger** was born in 1834 and died in 1856 at age 22.

+206 M viii. **Phillip Basinger** .

+207 F ix. **Mary E. Basinger** was born in 1840 and died in 1857 in Williamson County, Illinois at age 17.

    Mary married **Goslin**.

+208 F x. **Elizabeth Betsy Basinger** was born in 1816 in Greene County, Tennessee.

    Elizabeth married **John Porter** (b. Abt 1815) on 10 May 1837 in Greene County, Tennessee.

+209 F xi. **Samuel Basinger** was born in 1848.

+210 M xii. **Isaac Basinger** was born in 1824 in Greene County, Tennessee.

    Isaac married **Nancy Lister** (b. 1829) on 21 Oct 1846 in Greene County, Tennessee.

+211 M xiii. **John Basinger** was born on an unknown date.

+212 M xiv. **Michael Basinger** was born in 1824.

+213 F xv. **Levina Basinger** was born on 12 Nov 1830 in TN and died on 26 Mar 1886 in MO at age 55.

    Levina married **Ezekiel 111 Smith**[74] (b. 15 Sep 1821, d. 13 Jan 1900) on 12 Nov 1830 in TN.

25. Daniel Rader[1, 2, 3, 6, 8, 10, 11, 12, 14, 15] (*Heinrich 'Henry' Sr*[2], *Casper Sr*[1]) was born on 9 Jan 1808 in Greene County, Tennessee and died on 25 Jul 1854 in Greene County, Tennessee at age 46.

General Notes: Daniel was living in McPherson's district in Greene County, Tennessee in 1830 but owned no land(Tax list).

Noted events in his life were:

He was baptized on 5 Jun 1808 in Sinking Springs, Greene Co, TN.

Alt Death: 13 Oct 1830, Greene County, Tennessee.

Daniel married **Nancy Mathews** on 13 Oct 1830 in Greene County, Tennessee. Nancy was born on 14 Sep 1808 and died on 23 Oct 1894 at age 86. Another name for Nancy was Nancy Matthews.

    Marriage Notes: <u>WPA Marriage License Index</u>
    3204 Oct 1, 1830
    Daniel Reader   to   Nancy Mathews
    A. Patterson C G C V Sevier D C
    <u>Greene County Tennessee Marriages, 1783-1868</u>
    <u>by Goldine Fillers Burgner</u>
    3204 October 1, 1830 David Reader - Nancy Matthews -- William Etter
    md 13 Oct 1830 -- Wm Senter M.G.

Children from this marriage were:

+214 M   i.   **Louis Franklin Rader** was born in Apr 1847 in TN and died on 22 Apr 1933 at age 86.

Louis married **Sarah J.** (b. 1827).

Louis next married **Amanda Ella Minton** (b. Nov 1869, d. 17 Feb 1943).

+215 M   ii. **Henry J Rader** was born in 1835 in Missouri.

+216 F   iii. **Margaret J. Rader** was born in 1838 in Missouri.

+217 M   iv. **Joseph M Rader** was born in 1842 in Illinois.

+218 F   v.   **Isabella Rader** was born in 1845 in Illinois.

26. **Henry Thomas Rader Jr.**[1, 2, 3, 6, 8, 10, 11, 12, 14, 15] (*Heinrich 'Henry' Sr*[2], *Casper Sr*[1]) was born on 28 May 1810 in , , Greene, Tennessee and died on 3 Jul 1860 in , , Cooke, Tennessee at age 50.

General Notes: Henry's brother Casper must have died about 1835 for Henry married Anna Mace on 21 July 1836 in Greene Co. by George Easterly, Lutheran Minister with Henry Mace as Surety. Henry and Anna show in 1850 census with Anna as age 35.

Noted events in his life were:
Alt Birth: 14 Sep 1815, Greene County, Tennessee.
He appeared on the census in 1840. GREENE COUNTY, TENNESSEE PAGE 77
Census 1: 1850. GREENE COUNTY, TENNESSEE PG 325A & 325B
He appeared on the census in 1850 in P 325A, Greene Co, TN. Database: :2156009
Individual: I20015

Link: http://worldconnect.genealogy.rootsweb.com/cgi-bin/igm.cgi?op=GET&db=:2156009&id=I20015

Name: Florene Hutchens Westenhover Email: fwestenhov@aol.com

Note: Henry RADER, son of Johann Casper (Roeter) Rader, was born in 1768 in PA and married only one time---to Catherine ETTER. Catherine died before Henry, her husband.

 In the 1850 census for Greene Co. TN (10th Div. E. Dist. page 325), Henry was shown to be 82. Listed with him are: Kithy (Hithy), age 28, a mulatto b. SC, shown as free; his son Henry, age 40 b. TN, farmer; Anna, age 35, b.TN (*who Henry, the younger, married in 1836, maiden name MACE); Powell age 6; Granville, age 3. (sons of Henry and Anna) (Henry and Anna later had 2 daughters:

Mary Elizabeth Rader who mar. Ben Ottinger

and Sarah J. who mar. Henry S. Morelock). The above Granville Rader is my great-grandfather. Granville's 1st marriage was to *Mary E. SHAW--no issue. Granville's 2nd marriage was to *Susan N. SHAW-sister of 1st wife after 1st wife died. Children born to Granville and Susan RADER were Martha Ellen, 1874; Henry Thomas, 1875; Louisa Lulu, 1879; Jennie West, 1880 (my grandmother); William Powell, 1884; and Hester E. RADER Granville Rader's 3rd marriage (after the death of 2nd wife after moving family to Williamson Co. TX) was to Harriett PITTS. Granville and Harriett's children are Joseph A., 1899; John Granville, 1901; Anny Blanche, 1903; Mary Lee, 1905; Jessie and Bessie, 1908 (Jessie died at birth.

*Marriage records in Greene Co. TN

Sincerely, Florene Hutchens Westenhover

He was employed in 1850. FARMER

He owned property in 1850. VALUE $1,400.00

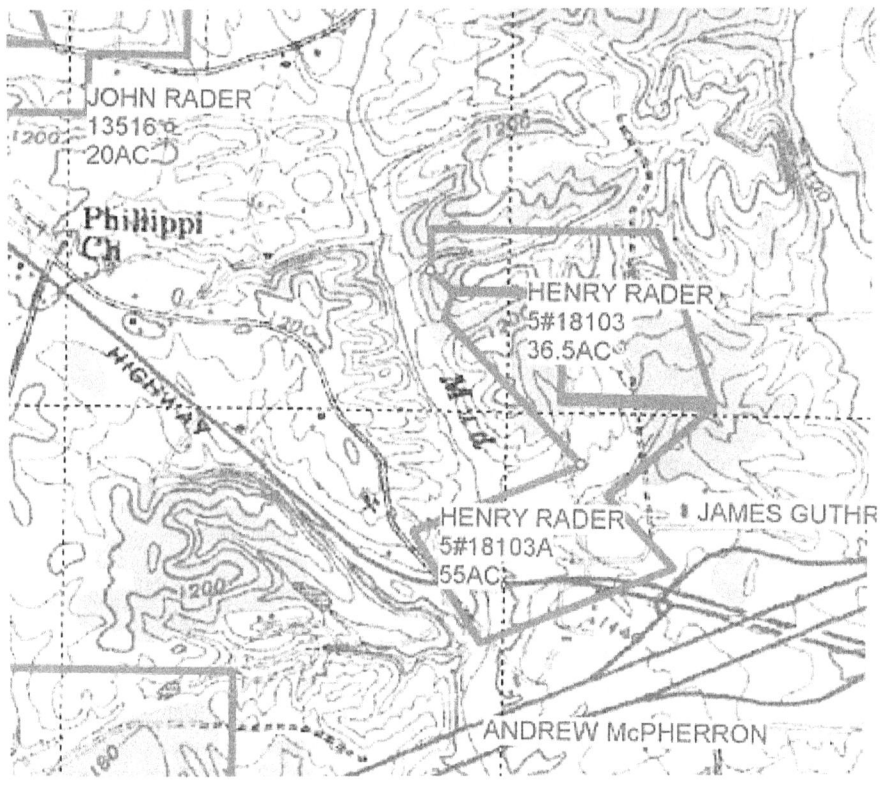

Map of Land Henry owned in Lick Creek 1853

> He owned land on 23 Aug 1853 in Lick Creek Valley, Greene County Tennessee. Henry purchased two parcels which total 91.5 acres from Samuel L. Jenkins in the 6th district of Greene county

Census 2: 1860. COCKE COUNTY, TENNESSEE PAGE 411 LINE 566
Alt Death: 22 Nov 1883.
MARRIAGE # 2: 3861. HENRY MACE (SPONSOR)

Henry married **Anny Brown**. Anny was born in 1805 in Tennessee, died about 1833 in Pilot Knob, Greene County, Tennessee about age 28, and was buried in Pilot Knob Cemetery, Greene County, Tennessee. Another name for Anny was Anna Brown.

> General Notes: Greene County Marriage # 2975 Nov 21, 1828 Casper Rader -- Anny Brown -- md 29 NOV 1828 -- M.G. Wilson, J.P.

Noted events in her life were:

She appeared on the census in 1830. GREENE COUNTY, TENNESSEE PG. 188

MARRIAGE # 1: 2975. M. G. WILSON JUSTICE OF THE PEACE

Henry next married **Anna Mary Mace**, daughter of **Henry Mace** and **Unknown**, on 21 Jul 1836 in , Rev G. Easterly, Greene, Tennessee.[44] Anna was born on 15 Oct 1816 in Greene County, Tennessee, died on 22 Nov 1883 at age 67, and was buried in , Pilot Knob. Another name for Anna was Anna Mary Mace.

Marriage Notes: Reference Number:690661

Henry Mace signed as sponsor at their marriage.

> General Notes: Greene Co Marriage # 3622 Jul 31, 1834 Casper Rader -- Anna Mace md 31 Jul 1834 Jepse W. Haile, L.D.
> Greene County marriage # 3861 July 18, 1836 Henry Rader --
> Anna Mace -- Henry Mace -- md 21 JUL 1836 -- Geo Easterly, M.G.
> 19. Casper3 Rader (Heinrich 'Henry'2, Casper (Roeder)1) was born in Greene Co, TN April 19, 1801. Casper died October 6, 1883 in Brizil, Clay Co, IN, or MO, at 82 years of age.(43) His body was interred 1883 in Mc Cullough, Washington Twp, Potnam Co, IN.

He married twice. He married Anny Brown in M.G. Wilson, jp, Greene Co, TN, November 29, 1828.(44) Anny was born 1805 in TN. Anny died circa 1833 in Greene Co, TN. He married Anna Mace July 31, 1834.(45) Anna was born October 15, 1816 in Greene Co, TN. Anna died September 16, 1908 in Clay Co, IN, at 91 years of age. Her body was interred in McCullough cem, Washington Twp, Putnam Co, IN.

He was baptized in Sinking Springs, September 22, 1805.

Casper Rader and Anna Mace had the following family:

+ 130 i. Catherine4 Rader was born before February 19, 1863, the first event for which there is a recorded date.

+ 131 ii. Philip Rader was born September 29, 1835.

132 iii. Malinda Jane Rader was born in Greene Co, TN July 20, 1839. Malinda died November 5, 1862 at 23 years of age. Her body was interred in Risley, Poland, Clay Co, IN. She married Elisha Dalgarn in Clay Co, IN, May 21, 1859.

133 iv. William 'Bill' Rader was born in Greene Co, TN March 12, 1841. William died after 1915 in Montrose, Effingham Co., IL. He married Helen Wallace East April 14, 1864. Helen was born September 24, 1847. Helen died August 27, 1870 at 22 years of age. Her body was interred in McCullough, Washington Twp, Putnam Co, IN.

+ 134 v. John Nelson Rader was born October 10, 1843.

+ 135 vi. Andrew Thomas Jackson Rader was born December 26, 1846.

136 vii. Martha Ann 'Matt' Rader was born in Greene Co, TN September 27, 1848. Martha died May 8, 1934 in Terre Haute, Vigo Co, IN, at 85 years of age. She married Jesse Fritts December 11, 1879.

+ 137 viii. Casper Rader, Jr. was born November 10, 1851.

+ 138 ix. Isaac Newton Rader was born May 17, 1855.

+ 139 x. Nicholas Marion Rader was born May 17, 1855.

140 xi. Dulsena Candace Rader was born in Clay Co, IN August 17, 1858. Dulsena died November 19, 1860 in Clay Co, IN, at 2 years of age. Her body was interred in McCullough cem.

Casper Rader and Anny Brown had the following family:

141 xii. George W. Rader was born in Greene Co, TN August 15, 1829. George died April 27, 1881 in Centerpoint, Clay Co, IN, at 51 years of age. He married Mary E. Jenkins in Clay Co, IN, February 5, 1860.

142 xiii. Elizabeth Jane Rader was born in Greene Co, TN November 16, 1831. Elizabeth died January 11, 1915 in Brazil, Clay Co, IN, at 83 years of age. She married Francis Asberry Bridewell.

+ 143 xiv. Henry Rader was born October 9, 1833.

Anna was listed as a resident in the census report in Cocke Co, Tn., 1870 (a widow age 55 living next door to son Powell, Granville & Sarah Worelock).

Noted events in her life were:

Alt Burial: McCullough cem, Washington Twp, Putnam Co, IN.
Alt Buried: Pilot Knob Cem, Greene Co, TN.
Alt Buried: Pilot Knob Cemetery, Greene County, Tennessee.
Alt Birth: 14 Sep 1815, Greene County, Tennessee.
Alt Birth: 15 Oct 1816, Greene County, Tennessee.
She appeared on the census in 1840. GREENE COUNTY, TENNESSEE PAGE 73
Census 1: 1850. WILLIAMSON COUNTY, ILLINOIS LINE 875 PAGE 275
Census 2: 1860. CASS TOWNSHIP, CLAY COUNTY, INDIANA LINE 88
Census 3: 1870. CASS TOWNSHIP, CLAY COUNTY, INDIANA LINE 807 PAGE 41

She appeared on the census in 1870 in Parrotsville, Cocke County Tennessee.

RADER ANNA ,1815,55,F,W,TN ,TN ,COCKE ,PARROTSVILLE P O ,M593, 1519, 0,354

RADER ,HANAH MC ,1795,75,F,W,VA ,TN ,COCKE ,PARROTSVILLE P O ,M593, 1519 ,0,354

RADER ,POWELL ,1844,26,M,W,TN ,TN ,COCKE ,PARROTSVILLE P O ,M593,1519, 0,354

Anna Rader , District 2, Cocke, TN , abt 1815 Tennessee , White, Female ,93,
Granville Rader , District 2, Cocke, TN , abt 1848 Tennessee , White, Male ,93,
Sarah J Rader , District 2, Cocke, TN , abt 1855 Tennessee , White, Female ,93,
Census 4: 1880. WASHINGTON TOWNSHIP, CLAY COUNTY, INDIANA LINE 59

She appeared on the census in 1880 in Greene County, Tennessee. Census Place: District 7, Greene, Tennessee Source: FHL Film 1255258 National Archives Film T9-1258 Page 113B

Relation Sex Marr Race Age Birthplace
Henry MOORELOCK Self M M W 30 TN Occ: Farmer Fa: TN Mo: TN

Sarah MORELOCK Wife F M W 24 TN   Occ: Keeping House   Fa: TN Mo: TN
Anna RADER MotherL F W W 66 TN   Occ: At Home   Fa: TN Mo: TN
Joseph CHESSER Other M S W 16 TN   Occ: Laborer   Fa: TN Mo: TN

   Alt Death: 22 Nov 1883, Greene County, Tennessee.

   Alt Death: 22 Nov 1883, Pilot Knob, Greene County, Tennessee.

   Census 5: 1900. WASHINGTON TOWNSHIP, CLAY COUNTY, INDIANA PAGE 350 LIVING W/PHILIP

   Alt Death: 6 Sep 1908, Clay County, Indiana.

   Alt Death: 16 Sep 1908, Clay County, Indiana.

   MARRIAGE # 1: 3622. JESSE W. HAILE, L. D.

Children from this marriage were:

+219 M   i.   **Powell Rader**[8, 11, 14] was born about 1844 in , , Greene, Tennessee.

+220 M   ii. **David Powell Rader**[1, 2, 3, 6, 10, 11, 12, 14, 15] was born on 11 Oct 1844 in Midway, Greene Co, TN and died on 27 May 1918 in Crowell, Foard County, Texas at age 73.

   David married **Narcissa Neas** (b. 25 May 1844, d. 19 Apr 1885) on 4 Oct 1866 in Cocke County, Tennessee.

   David next married **Emma Prisilla Barnes** (b. Aug 1859, d. 26 Aug 1927) on 25 Jun 1887 in Georgetown, Williamson County, Texas.

+221 M   iii. **Granville Rader**[1, 2, 3, 6, 8, 10, 11, 12, 14, 15] was born on 17 Aug 1847 in Midway, Greene Co, TN and died on 21 Oct 1928 in O'brien, Texas at age 81.

   Granville married **Susan N Shaw** (b. 6 Jul 1848, d. 12 Feb 1894) on 21 Mar 1872 in Greene County, Tennessee.

   Granville next married **Harriet Pitts** (b. Abt 1867) about 1898.

   Granville next married **Mary E. Shaw** on 21 Mar 1872 in Greene County, Tennessee.

   Granville next married **Harriett** (b. May 1868) about 1885.

+222 F   iv. **Sarah J. Rader** was born in 1854 in Midway, Greene Co, TN.

   Sarah married **Henry Morelock** (b. 1850, d. 21 Oct 1928).

+223 F   v.   **Mary Elizabeth Rader** was born in 1850 in Greene County, Tennessee and died before 1900 in TX..

   Mary married **Benjamin Ottinger** (b. 10 Oct 1845, d. 12 Jan 1897) on 6 Sep 1868.

27. Andrew W. S Rader[1, 2, 3, 6, 8, 10, 11, 12, 14, 15] (*Heinrich 'Henry' Sr*[2], *Casper Sr*[1]) was born on 23 Nov 1812 in Greene County, Tennessee,[28, 48] died on 10 Sep 1889 in Timber Ridge, Greene Co, TN at age 76, and was buried in Timber Ridge, Greene Co, TN.[21]

   General Notes: Greene Co. Marriages # 3595 Apr 1 1834 Andrew Rader -- Lydia Andes -- Jefferson Etter

   The will of Andrew Rader. To my wife - $600.50, one bureau and safe, all she brought with her when we married and all she has made in the house since she came hear. I want to burried at Timber Ridge by the side of my first wife, and berry me in a coffin just like your mother was burried in and put up Toom Stones about the same quality of hers. All my money and personal property eaculey divided between: William Rader, George Rader, Andrew Rader, Carline Taylor and Lyda Bordon. I want iron palings around my first wife's grave with room for myself. Executor: son William Rader. Dated: September 4, 1889. Witnesses: J.G. Greer, W.P. Bradford. Signed: Andrew Rader

Noted events in his life were:

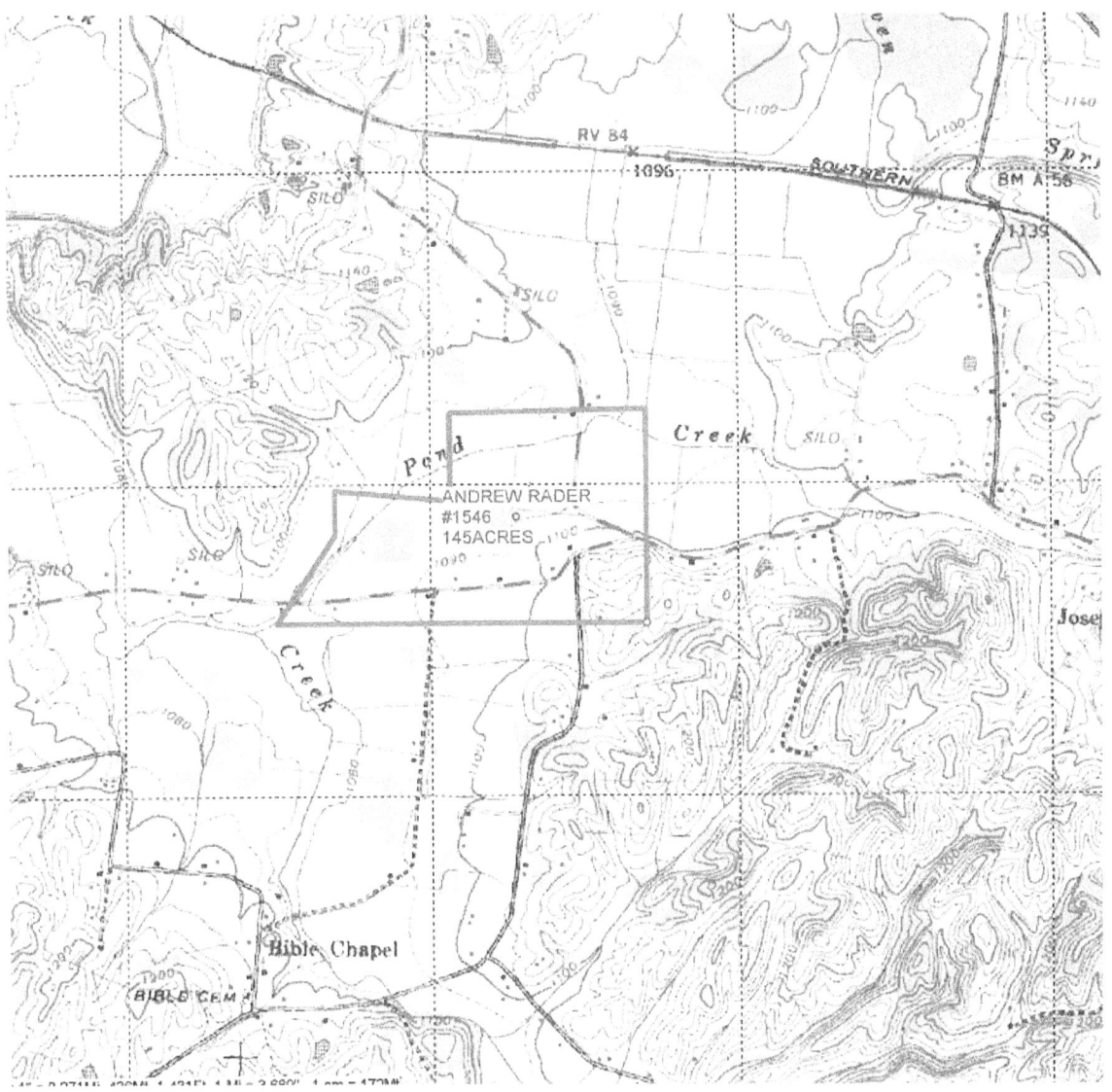

Map of land Andrew owned on 14 Feb 1835 in Lick Creek Valley near Bible Chapel

, Greene County Tennessee. Greene County Tennessee Deed book 17 page 339

146 Acres from Adam Kinser on Swan Pond neighbors Kinser and Kelly
Church: 10 Jul 1837, sinking springs Lutheran church, greene co, TN. Andrew Rader & wife
 their daughter Sara Jane born 22 Apr, 1835
 their daughter Barbara Emaline born 11 Oct 1836
baptised 10 Jul 1837

Map of land Andrew owned on 2 Nov 1839 in Bright Hope,

Greene County, Tennessee. Purchased parcel # 545 containing 100 acres from Isaac N Magill

Swan Pond Creek

> He appeared on the census in 1840 in Greene County, Tennessee. Andrew and Lydia were living in Greene County, Tennessee in 1840 (Census)

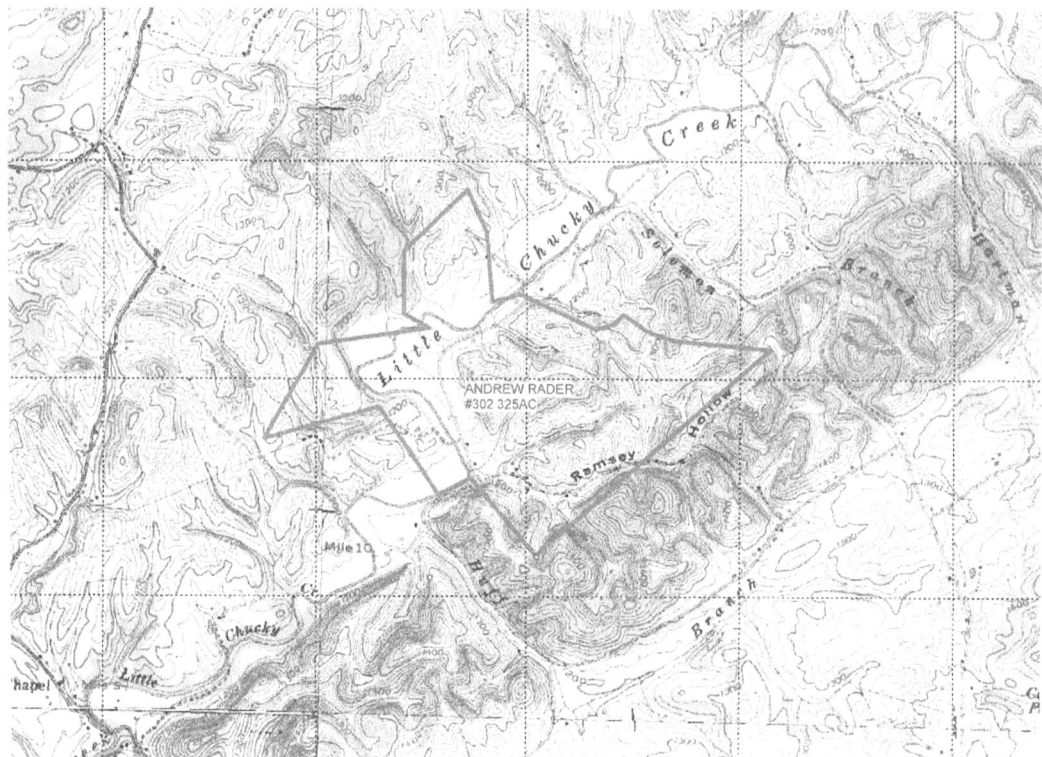

Map of land Andrew owned on 15 Feb 1848 in Little Chuckey, Greene Co, TN.

Purchased parcel #302 containing 325 acres from George Andes

Site of Rader Mill parcel #302]

He appeared on the census in 1850 in Greene County, Tennessee.

```
RADER WILLIAM    52 M W VA GREENE10 sub880306
    RADER BARBARY   47 F W VA GREENE10 sub880306
    RADER ANDREW    22 M W TNGREENE10 sub880306
    RADER HENRY     21 M W TN GREENE10 sub880306
    RADER JOSEPH    19 M W TNGREENE10 sub880306
    RADER REBECCA   16 F W TNGREENE10 sub880306
    RADER MARTIN    15 M W TN GREENE10 sub880306
    RADER CASPER    12 M W TN GREENE10 sub880306
    RADER MADISON    8 M W TN GREENE10 sub880306
    RADER MARGARET 4 F W TN GREENE10 sub880306
    RADER JAMES      0 M W TN GREENE10 sub880306
```

Site of Rader Mill parcel #302]

He was employed in 1850. MILLER

Swan Pond Creek Parcel #1546]

He appeared on the census in 1850. GREENE COUNTY, TENNESSEE   PAGE 317B #366

Site of Rader Mill parcel #302]

He owned property in 1850. VALUE $1,500.00

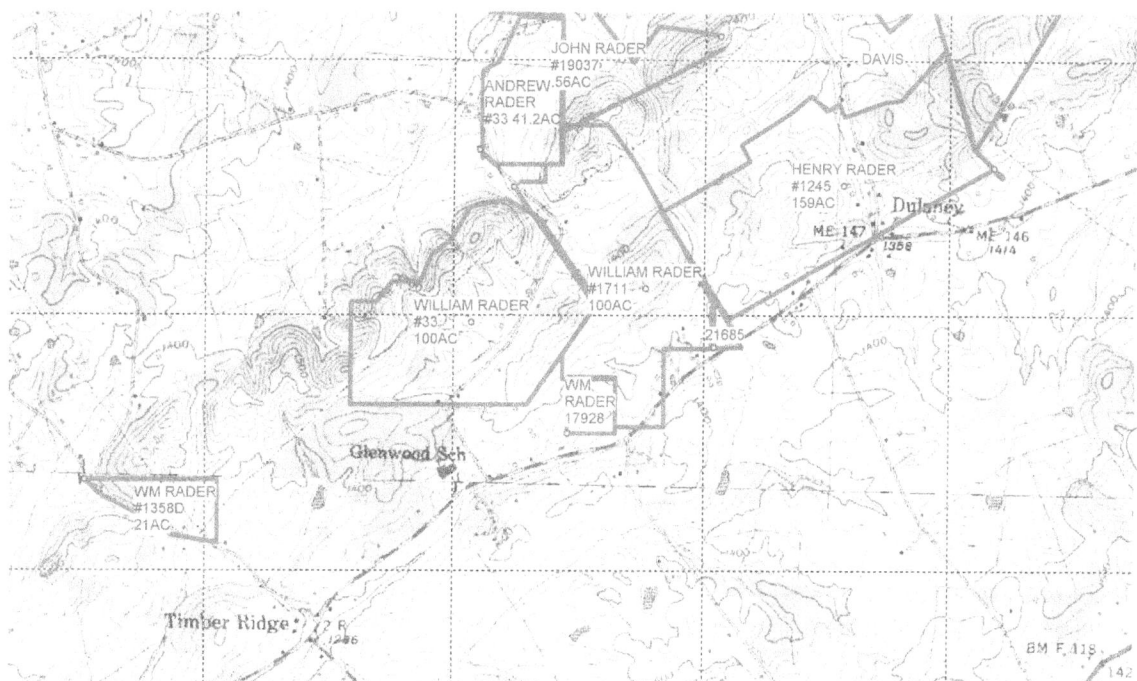

Map of Dulaney Rader's Land

He owned land in Dec 1855 in Dulaney, Greene County, Tennessee. Purchased parcel #33 containing 41.25 acres from Samuel Donwoody (dec)

[Caption: Site of Rader Mill parcel #302]

Census 1: 1860. GREENE COUNTY, TENNESSEE   PAGE 379 #1126

Glennwod Road]

He owned land in 1860 in Days Gap, Greene County, Tennessee. obtained Tennessee Grand #30049 for 384 acres

[Caption: Wheeler Road parcel #30049]

Resided: 1860.

Wheeler Road parcel #30049]

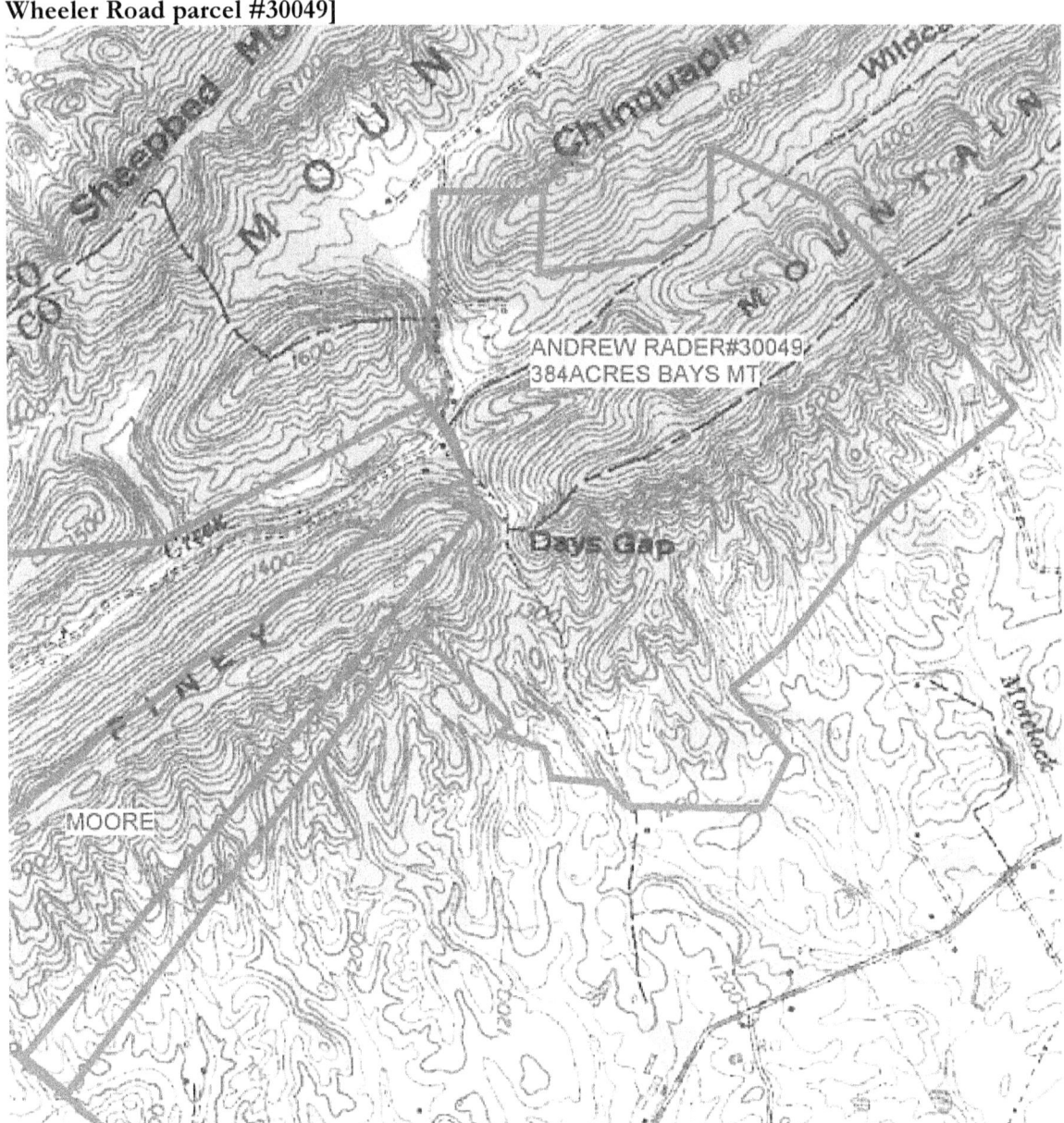

Map of land Andrew owned in Days Gap parcel #30049 – 384

Resided: 1860.

210 Glenwood Rd.]

Census 2: 1870. GREENE COUNTY, TENNESSEE PAGE 223 LINE 111

Timber Ridge road parcel #545

He appeared on the census in 1880 in District 25, Greene, Tennessee. Census Place:District 25, Greene, Tennessee Source:FHL Film 1255258 National Archives Film T9-1258 Page 80B   RelationSexMarrRaceAgeBirthplace

Andrew RADER Self M M W68 TN Occ:FarmerFa: VAMo: VA
Lydia RADER Wife F M W 68 TN Fa: TNMo: TN
Lydia RADER Dau F S W 22 TN Fa: TNMo: TN

[Caption: Timber Ridge road parcel $545]
Census 3: 1880. GREENE COUNTY, TENNESSEE PAGE 80B LINE 77
Alt Death: 11 Sep 1889, Greene County, Tennessee.[21]

Andrew married **Lydia Andes**, daughter of **George Andes** and **Barbara Roller**, on 1 Apr 1834 in Greene County, Tennessee.[28] Lydia was born on 16 May 1813 in , , Greene, Tennessee, died on 18 Jun 1880 in Timber Ridge, Greene Co, TN[48] at age 67, and was buried in Timber Ridge, Greene Co, TN.[21]

Marriage Notes: Fact 1:PLAC Marriage Bond Date was 4/1/1834, Jefferson Etter security.SOUR @S11298@NOTE 1. Greene County, Tennessee Marriage Book.1. Greene County, Tennessee Marriage Book.

Noted events in their marriage were:

Alt Marriage: 13 Apr 1834, Greene County, Tennessee.[28] Marriage Notes: Fact 1:PLAC Marriage Bond Date was 4/1/1834, Jefferson Etter security.SOUR @S11298@NOTE 1. Greene County, Tennessee Marriage Book.1. Greene County, Tennessee Marriage Book.

Alt Marriage: 13 Apr 1834, Greene County, Tennessee.
   General Notes: Housewife
Noted events in her life were:
She was employed.
Place Lived: Greene County, Tennessee.
She was religious. Presbyterian

Alt Birth: 1812, , , Greene, Tennessee.

She appeared on the census in 1850. GREENE COUNTY, TENNESSEE   PAGE 317B #366

Census 1: 1860. GREENE COUNTY, TENNESSEE   PAGE 379 #1126

Census 2: 1870. GREENE COUNTY, TENNESSEE PAGE 223 LINE 111

Census 3: 1880. GREENE COUNTY, TENNESSEE PAGE 80B LINE 77

Children from this marriage were:

+224 F   i.   **Sarah Jane Rader**[1, 2, 3, 6, 8, 10, 11, 12, 14, 15] was born on 22 Apr 1835 in , , Greene, Tennessee,[28, 75] died on 13 Feb 1859 in Mosheim, Greene Co, TN[21] at age 23, and was buried in Blue Springs.

Sarah married **Frederick W. Cobble** on 9 Sep 1851.

Sarah next married **Frederick Washington Cobble** (b. 24 Oct 1826, d. 19 Dec 1908) on 9 Sep 1851 in Greene County, Tennessee.[28]

+225 F   ii. **Barbara Emmeline Rader**[1, 2, 3, 6, 8, 10, 11, 12, 14, 15] was born on 11 Oct 1836 in Greene County, Tennessee and died on 24 Nov 1887 in Indiana at age 51.

Barbara married **Andrew Baughard** (b. 1828) on 1 Jul 1856 in Greene County, Tennessee.

+226 M iii. **William M. 'Bill' Rader**[1, 2, 3, 4, 6, 8, 10, 11, 12, 14, 15] was born on 30 Sep 1838 in , , Greene, Tennessee, died on 28 Sep 1897 in , , Greene, Tennessee at age 58, and was buried in , Timber Ridge Cem, Greene, Tennessee.

William married **Nancy Elizabeth Rader** (b. 23 Mar 1836, d. 3 Mar 1913) on 12 Jul 1860 in , J K Hancher, Min, Greene, Tennessee.

+227 F   iv. **Caroline Rader**[1, 2, 3, 6, 8, 10, 11, 12, 14, 15] was born on 11 Feb 1841 in , , Greene, Tennessee.

Caroline married **James Anderson Taylor** (b. 1837, d. 1901) on 25 Jan 1859 in Greene County, Tennessee.

+228 F   v.   **Mary Ann Rader**[1, 2, 3, 6, 8, 10, 11, 12, 14, 15] was born on 18 Oct 1842 in Greene County, Tennessee.

Mary married **Wes Harmon**.

+229 M vi. **George Alexander Rader**[1, 2, 3, 6, 8, 10, 11, 12, 14, 15] was born on 7 Nov 1844 in Little Chuckey, Greene Co, TN,[48] died on 11 Jul 1908 in Greene County, Tennessee[48] at age 63, and was buried in Mohawk Cemetery, Mohawk, Tennessee.

George married **Sarah Angeline Bradford** (b. 26 Feb 1844, d. 19 Jun 1917) on 22 Dec 1870 in Mosheim, Greene Co, TN.[48]

+230 F   vii. **Molly Rader** was born in 1846 in Greene County, Tennessee, died in 1917 in Indiana at age 71, and was buried in Mt. Hope Methodist Cemetery, Greene County, Tennessee.

Molly married **Valentine 'Von' Baughard** (b. 1842).

Source Citations

+231 F viii. **Martha Conmella Rader**[1,2,3,6,8,10,11,12,14,15] was born on 11 Aug 1848 in Greene County, Tennessee, died before 1860 in Greene County, Tennessee, and was buried in Sinking Springs Lutheran Cemetery, Greene County, Tennessee.

Martha married **Joseph Washington Cobble** (b. Jan 1849, d. 6 Jun 1937).

+232 F ix. **Lydia Angeline 'Ann' Rader** was born on 20 Mar 1850 in Greene County, Tennessee, died on 16 Jul 1919 in Timber Ridge, Greene Co, TN at age 69, and was buried in Pine Grove Or, Timber Ridge.

Lydia married **Morgan J. Pittman** on 29 Dec 1872.

Lydia next married **Henry C. Borden** (b. 25 Oct 1848, d. 31 May 1890) on 30 Sep 1881.

Lydia next married **Ruben J. Gammon** (b. Nov 1851, d. 1930) in 1891 in Greene County, Tennessee.

+233 M x. **Andrew Jackson 'Big Andy' Rader** was born on 11 May 1852 in Greene County, Tennessee, died on 11 Mar 1917 in Greene County, Tennessee at age 64, and was buried in Piney Crove Cem, Greene Co, TN.

Andrew married **Lavina Elizabeth Rader** (b. 29 Aug 1857, d. 21 Feb 1936) on 23 Dec 1875 in Greene County, Tennessee.

Andrew next married **Elizabeth Gammon** on 20 Jan 1881. Elizabeth was born on 19 Dec 1824 and died on 6 Nov 1892 at age 67.

Andrew next married **Lillie Kinser**, daughter of **George Kinser** and **Unknown**. Lillie was born in 1813 in Greene County, Tennessee.

28. Catherine M. Rader[1,2,3,6,8,10,11,12,14,15] (*Heinrich 'Henry' Sr*[2], *Casper Sr*[1]) was born on 19 Jan 1816 in Sinking Springs, Greene County, Tennessee and died before 1859 in Greene County, Tennessee.

General Notes: Moved to Ste. Genevieve County, Missouri.

Noted events in her life were:

She was baptized on 19 Jan 1816 in Sinking Springs, Lutheran, Greene Co, TN.

She appeared on the census in 1850. GREENE COUNTY, TENNESSEE PAGE 166B TO 167 #420

She appeared on the census in 1880 in Saline, St. Genevieve, Missouri. Census Place:Saline, St. Genevieve, Missouri

Source:FHL Film 1254715   National Archives Film T9-0715   Page 629A
RelationSexMarrRaceAgeBirthplace
G. W. SMITHSelfMMW67TN Occ:FarmerFa: VAMo: VA
Catharine SMITHWifeFMW65TN Occ:Keeping HouseFa: PAMo: VA
James W. SMITHSonMMW23MO Occ:Works On FarmFa: TNMo: TN

Rhoda R. SMITHDauLFMW19MO Occ:At HomeFa: TNMo: MO
Philip SMITHGSonMSW11MMO Fa: MOMo: MO

Catherine married **John F. Washington Smith** on 24 Mar 1836 in , Rev G. Easterly, Greene, Tennessee. John was born in 1813 in Greene County, Tennessee, died in 1896 in Libertyville Chr, St. Francis Co., MO at age 83, and was buried in Libertyville Church, St. Francis County, Missouri. Another name for John was John F. Washington Smith.

> General Notes: Greene County marraige # 3833 Mar 22, 1836 Washington Smith -- Catharinr Rader -- md 24 Mar 1836 -- George Easterly, M.G.

Noted events in his life were:
Alt Birth: 1815, Greene County, Tennessee.
He appeared on the census in 1850. GREENE COUNTY, TENNESSEE PAGE 166B TO 167 #420
He was employed in 1850. JUSTICE OF THE PEACE & CARPENTER

Children from this marriage were:

+234 M i. **James W. Smith** was born in 1857 in MO.

James married **Rachael Rhoda Henderson** (b. 1861).

+235 F ii. **Martha A. Smith** was born in 1837 in Greene County, Tennessee.

+236 F iii. **Margaret E. Smith** was born in 1839 in Greene County, Tennessee.

+237 M iv. **William C. Smith** was born in 1840 in Greene County, Tennessee.

+238 M v. **George A. Smith** was born in 1842 in Greene County, Tennessee.

+239 M vi. **Mckindrie Smith** was born in 1845 in Greene County, Tennessee.

+240 M vii. **Alfred H. Smith** was born in 1847 in Greene County, Tennessee.

29. Issabella Rader[1, 2, 3, 6, 8, 10, 11, 12, 14, 15] (*Heinrich 'Henry' Sr*[2], *Casper Sr*[1]) was born on 24 Jun 1819 in Greene County, Tennessee and died on 1 Sep 1879 at age 60. Other names for Issabella were Isabell Rader, and Isabelle Rader.

> General Notes: Believe buried in Missouri. Bobby Carter gives birth date as 8 May 1823 and date of death as 1889.

Noted events in her life were:
She was baptized on 24 Jun 1819 in Sinking Springs, Lutheran, Greene Co, TN.
Alt Birth: 1830, Greene County, Tennessee.
She appeared on the census in 1850. GREENE COUNTY, TENNESSEE PAGE 325 TO 335B #470
She appeared on the census in 1880 in Saline, St. Genevieve, Missouri. Census Place: Saline, St. Genevieve, Missouri
Source: FHL Film 1254715   National Archives Film T9-0715   Page 636C
Relation   Sex   Marr   Race   Age   Birthplace
Isaac L. SMITH Self M   M   W   26   MO   Occ: FarmerFa: TN Mo: TN
Mary J. SMITH Wife F M W 23   TN   Occ: Keeping House   Fa: TN Mo: TN
Isabella SMITH Mother F D W   62   TN   Occ: At Home   Fa: --- Mo: ---

Issabella married **Isaac Smith**, son of **Unknown** and **Unknown**, on 9 Sep 1845 by William Rader, Jp, Greene Co, TN. Isaac was born on 8 Mar 1823 in Greene County, Tennessee.

Noted events in their marriage were:
Bond: Jacob Cobble. J. P.: William Rader.
Alt Marriage: 7 Sep 1845, Greene County, Tennessee.
General Notes: Greene County marriage # 1045 Sept. 9, 1845 Isaac Smith -- Isabella Rader -- Jacob Cobble -- md 9 Sep 1845 -- Wm Rader J.P.
Noted events in his life were:
He appeared on the census in 1850. GREENE COUNTY, TENNESSEE PAGE 325 TO 335B #470

Children from this marriage were:

+241 F i. **Candesa Smith** [1, 2, 3, 6, 8, 10, 11, 12, 14, 15] was born in 1846 in , , Greene, Tennessee.

+242 M ii. **Arthur Smith** [1, 2, 3, 6, 8, 10, 11, 12, 14, 15] was born in 1849 in , , Greene, Tennessee.

30. Johannes Pieter Richard Rader [1, 2, 3, 6, 8, 10, 11, 12, 14, 15] (*Heinrich 'Henry' Sr* [2], *Casper Sr* [1]) was born on 2 Jun 1820 in , , Greene, Tennessee and died on 2 Jun 1820 in Greene County, Tennessee. Another name for Johannes was John Peter Richard Rader.

Noted events in his life were:

He has conflicting birth information of Alt. Birth and 2 Jun 1820.

31. John Rader Jr. [1, 2, 3, 6, 8, 10, 11, 12, 14, 15] (*John* [2], *Casper Sr* [1]) was born in 1795 in Wythe County, Virginia and died after 1860 in Greene County, Tennessee.

General Notes: Greene Co., Marriages #1980 Oct 16, 1818 John Rader --

Ethelinda Smiley -- Andrew Smiley -- md 28 Oct 1818 – Joseph Davis J.P.

John and Ethelinda were living in Greene County, Tennessee in 1850(census) but she had apparently died before the 1860 census was taken since John was living alone in district number 6 of Greene County. Living with them in 1850 was Anna Smiley, born in 1796. The relationship of Anna to Ethelinda is not known. The Greene County, Tennessee County Court Minutes volumn 1838 to 1856, page 438 and dated April 3, 1848 indicated that Anna Smiley, one of the poor, was placed in the care of John Rader.

Noted events in his life were:

He appeared on the census in 1820. WYTHE COUNTY, VIRGINIA CENSUS PAGE 221

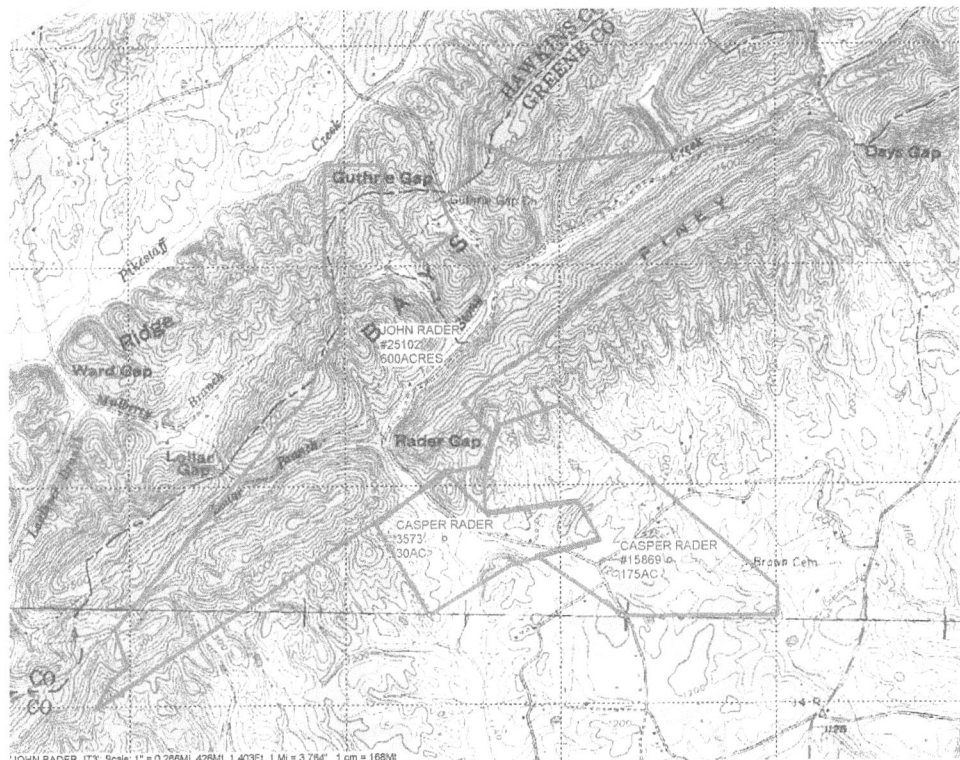

Map of Land John owned land on 16 Feb 1839 in Rader gap,

Greene County, Tennessee. Tennessee Land Grant #25102 600 Acres on Stoney Creek

He appeared on the census in 1850 in Greene County, Tennessee. John Raider 55 M wagonmaker TN Ethe M 54 F TN Mary S. 16 NC Anna Smiley 56 F TN

He owned land on 16 Feb 1839 in Rader gap, Greene County, Tennessee. Tennessee Land Grant #25102

600 Acres on Stoney Creek

John married **Ethelinda M. Smiley** on 29 Oct 1818 in Greene County, Tennessee. Ethelinda was born in 1796 and died before 1860 in Greene County, Tennessee.

Marriage Notes: Rader, John Smiley, Ethelinda 29 Oct 1818 Tennessee

Noted events in her life were:

She appeared on the census in 1820. WYTHE COUNTY, VIRGINIA CENSUS PAGE 221 Census 2: 1850. GREENE COUNTY, TENNESSEE PG 245B #1581

Children from this marriage were:

+243 M i. **William Rader** [1, 2, 3, 6, 8, 10, 11, 12, 14, 15] was born in 1822 in Greene County, Tennessee.

William married **Sarah Peterson** (b. 1815).

+244 M ii. **Reuben M. Rader** [1, 2, 3, 6, 8, 10, 11, 12, 14, 15] was born in 1822 in Greene County, Tennessee and died on 23 Apr 1887 in Bulls Gap, Hawkins County, Tennessee at age 65.

Reuben married **Cynthia Adaline Hunter** (b. 1823, d. 4 Feb 1901) on 10 Aug 1843 in Greene County, Tennessee.[44]

+245 M iii. **Andrew G. Rader** [1, 2, 3, 6, 8, 10, 11, 12, 14, 15] was born in 1823 in Greene County, Tennessee and died on 5 Aug 1863 in Nashville, Tennessee at age 40.

Andrew married **Arenas "Anna" Matilda Miles** (b. 15 Mar 1825, d. 8 Nov 1907) on 16 Nov 1847 in Greene County, Tennessee.[44]

+246 M iv. **James H. Rader** [1, 2, 3, 6, 8, 10, 11, 12, 14, 15] was born about 1825 in Greene County, Tennessee.

James married **Elizabeth** (b. 1836).

+247 M v. **John Anderson Rader** [1, 2, 3, 6, 8, 10, 11, 12, 14, 15] was born on 8 Nov 1827 in Greene County, Tennessee and died on 5 Jul 1901 in Whitehorn, Hawkins Co, TN at age 73.

John married **Nancy Isabelle Crosier** (b. 1 Nov 1824, d. 2 Jul 1910) on 17 Jan 1850 in Whitehorn, Hawkins Co, TN.

+248 F vi. **Mary S. Rader** [1, 2, 3, 6, 8, 10, 11, 12, 14, 15] was born in 1834 in Greene County, Tennessee.

32. Catherine "Caty" Rader [1, 2, 3, 6, 8, 10, 11, 12, 14, 15] ($John^2$, $Casper\ Sr^1$) was born about 1797 in , Wythe, Virginia.

General Notes: . James and Catherine were living in Greene County in 1844 according to the Chancery Court case mentioned earlier dealing with the estate of John Rader her father.. On April 3, 1848 Catherine and James purchased items at the sale of the personal estate of her mother Mary Rader.

Noted events in her life were:

She appeared on the census in 1830. GREENE COUNTY, TENNESSEE PG. 188

Catherine married **James Altom** on 7 May 1814 in , , Greene, Tennessee. James was born about 1794 in , , , Tennessee.

General Notes: data as interpreted from 1850 census Boone Co., Indiana. I believe the census taker got the dates of birth of James and Catharine reversed.

Noted events in his life were:

Alt Birth: 1790, Germany.

He appeared on the census in 1830 in Captain McPherons Company, Greene County, Tennessee.

Children from this marriage were:

+249 M i. **Riley Altom**[1, 2, 3, 6, 8, 10, 11, 12, 14, 15] was born about 1815 in , , Greene, Tennessee and died on 4 Jun 1855 in , , Howard, Indiana about age 40.

Riley married **Mary Keesling** on 27 Nov 1833 in , , Greene, Tennessee.

+250 M ii. **Joseph Altom**[1, 2, 3, 6, 8, 10, 11, 12, 14, 15] was born about 1818 in , , Greene, Tennessee and died after 1885.

Joseph married **Margaret Pickard** on 5 Sep 1838 in , , Greene, Illinois.

+251 M iii. **John Altom**[1, 2, 3, 6, 8, 10, 11, 12, 14, 15] was born about 1820 in , , Greene, Tennessee and died in Lebanon, , Boone, Indiana.

John married **Sarah ( )**.

John next married **Susanna Keesling** on 27 May 1840 in , , Greene, Tennessee.

+252 M iv. **Ervin Altom**[2, 6, 8, 11, 14] was born about 1820 in , , Greene, Tennessee and died in Lebanon, , Boone, Indiana.

Ervin married **Susanna Keesling** on 27 May 1840 in , , Greene, Tennessee.

+253 F v. **Elizabeth Altom**[1, 2, 3, 6, 8, 10, 11, 12, 14, 15] was born about 1826 in , , Greene, Tennessee.

Elizabeth married **Thomas Wallace** on 20 May 1848 in , , Greene, Tennessee.

+254 M vi. **Jesse Altom**[1, 2, 3, 6, 8, 10, 11, 12, 14, 15] was born about 1832 in , , , Tennessee.

+255 F vii. **Betty Altom**[1, 2, 3, 6, 8, 10, 11, 12, 14, 15] was born about 1833 in , , , Tennessee.

+256 F viii. **Martha Ann Altom**[1, 2, 3, 6, 8, 10, 11, 12, 14, 15] was born about 1837 in , , , Tennessee.

Martha married **George Thomas** in , , Greene, Illinois.

Source Citations

+257 F ix. **Susan Altom**[1, 2, 3, 6, 8, 10, 11, 12, 14, 15] was born about 1840 in , , , Tennessee.

Susan married **George Sipes**.

+258 M x. **James Altom**[1, 2, 3, 6, 8, 10, 11, 12, 14, 15] was born about 1841 in , , , Tennessee.

+259 M xi. **George Altom**[1, 2, 3, 6, 8, 10, 11, 12, 14, 15] was born about 1843.

33. Elizabeth Rader[1, 2, 3, 4, 6, 7, 8, 10, 11, 12, 14, 15] (*John*[2], *Casper Sr*[1]) was born on 3 May 1799 in Wythe County, Virginia and died on 13 Sep 1871 in Mohawk, Greene Co, TN at age 72.

General Notes: Elizabeth and William were first cousins! They lived where the city of Mohawk is now. They were strict Presbyterians. Bible Family, Terri Strotman, World Connect Project

Noted events in her life were:

She owned land on 5 Oct 1829 in Lick Creek Valley, Greene County Tennessee. Purchased parcel #1339G containing 22 acres from John Love the same day her husband (first cousin) did

She appeared on the census in 1840. GREENE COUNTY, TENNESSEE PAGE 77
Census 1: 1850. GREENE COUNTY, TENNESSEE PAGE 335B #619
Census 2: 1860. GUSTAVUS DIST. 6, GREENE COUNTY, TENNESSEE PAGE 182 LINE 244
Census 3: 1870. GREENE COUNTY, TENNESSEE ROLL 1531 PAGE 228
Alt Death: 13 Sep 1877, Mohawk, Greene County, Tennessee.

Elizabeth married **William Rader**, son of **Jacob Rader** and **Elizabeth Woods Been Hedrick**, on 23 Nov 1820 in Gap Creek, Greene County Tennessee.[4] William was born on 28 Jun 1799 in Wytheville, Wythe County, Virginia and died on 25 Nov 1877 in Mohawk, Greene Co, TN at age 78.

Marriage Notes: William and Elizabeth were first cousins. His father, Jacob, and her father, John, were brothers.[4]

Noted events in their marriage were:

Alt. Marriage:

General Notes: William was the son of Jacob and Elizabeth Rader. Jacob was the brother of John Rader, Elizabeth's father. The children of Elizabeth and William Rader was obtained from census records and from a Greene County, Tennessee County Court record dated June 4, 1878, volumn 1875 to 1879, pages 195, 198, 199, 245, 246 and 247. This court case recorded the petition of the children and grandchildren of William Rader deceased to sell the landed estate of William Rader containing 440 acres located in district number 6 and situated along Lick Creek in Greene County, Tennessee. Elizabeth was the daughter of John Rader and Mary Etter Rader. John Rader and Jacob Rader were brothers. The record of William and Elizabeth Rader can be found in the section under John Rader and Mary Etter Rader. In 1860(census) William was living in Gustavus District number 6 in Greene County, Tennessee. Marriage # 2222 Nov 23, 1820 William Reader -- Elizabeth Reader -- witn. John Reader A letter from William Rader 1877

I recieved this letter by way of Jan Maddux of the Greene County, TN Genealogical society, Thanks Jan !!

13 Jul 1994 Dear Friends, I have been to your county, researching my own Bridewell and Reed families, some time back. I did not have an opportunity to visit your genealogy group, or library, but am aware of the wonderful work you have all published on Green County. . . . . . My good friend and neighbor, Dania Sue Chambers, has furnsihed this letter, which had belonged to her paternal grandmother, Dania Rader, who had recived it from her father, Valentine Rader and wife, Elira, to whom it had beed written by Valentine's father, William Rader, of Greene County, TN .. Dania Sue tells me her grandmother was from Piedmont, KS and that other relatives lived in a nearby town. Interested persons may contact her; Dania Sue Chambers, 3102 Coffey St., Victoria, TX 77901-7427 (512) 578-7330

Sincerely, Billye D. Jackson 3101 Coffey St. Victoria, TX 77901-7426

September 15, 1877 Greene County Tennessee Dear Son and Daughter I seat myself to drop you a few lines. I feel it my duty to give you the painfull news of the death of your mother . she died the day before yesterday and was buried yesterday at the buring ground at P.R. Raders ???. She was very unwell at times all through the summer and on the 26th day of August she vomited a full pint of Blood. There was clods of Blood amongst it as large as hulled walnuts. On the next day she vomited blood three different times. The last time in the evening she vomited about a quart of blood. Then she was free from bleeding for several days but afterwards volited Blood again at different times until she died, lived 19 days from the time that she first vomited Blood and was intirely confined to her bed during that time.. During the time she scarcely eat anything except drank a little coffee, she was in her proper mind all the time. Doctor Rader says there was a cancer in her stomach. One night she was very bad we were standing around her bed she told us she was going to heaven and requested us all to meet her in heaven. I asked her if she felt reconciled to die she said yes, and said she was proud to see her friends standing around her. let us all try to live in that way that will enable us when we come to die to meet her in that glory land where parting is nomore. She told your sister Lurina Drake that she wished to live to see Valentine and Elira one time more but said she knowed she couldnot. Your Brothers and sister and families are all well Luvina and Lemuels wife are both here with me to day I feel very lonesome I expect to try to keep house me and mary the colored girl. I am as well at present as common hope these lines may find you all enjoying reasonable health I wish you to answer as soon as it comes to hand I have not sent your and Eliras money yet your mother was so poorly I could not leave home and now the time is coming close that you said you and Elvira was comming to Tennessee I would be very glad to see you both so will wait to see you or an answer from you Your uncle Joseph Rader is as well as common at present and still living with me yet and says he expects to go back to kansas Baxter Springs some time in the forepart of October as he wishes to stay and hear Brother Petens funeral preached on the last sabbath in this month and EM. Drakes funeral is to be preached on the fourth sabbath in this month which be tomorrow a week I will close by saying I remain your affectionate father as ever Wm Rader To V.S. Rader + Elina J. Rader Your sister Livina says that they wrote you a long letter some time last spring and has been looking for an answer from you ever since.

1870 GREENE COUNTY CENSUS LISTS A BLACK FEMALE CHILD 10 YEARS OF AGE BY THE NAME OF MARY E. RADER LIVING WITH WILLIAM AND ELIZABETH RADER.

WILLIAM AND ELIZABETH ARE 1ST. COUSINS

Bible Family, Terri Strotman, World Connect Project

Noted events in his life were:

Alt Birth: 1793.

Alt Birth: Abt 1798, , Wythe, Virginia.

He owned land on 15 Mar 1829 in Lick Creek Valley, Greene County Tennessee. Purchased parcel #1339D containing 48 acres from John Love

He appeared on the census in 1840. GREENE COUNTY, TENNESSEE PAGE 77

He owned land on 31 Mar 1841 in Lick Creek Valley, Greene County Tennessee. Purchased parcel # 342 containing 10 acres from Alfred Russell

Census 1: 1850. GREENE COUNTY, TENNESSEE PAGE 335B #619

He appeared on the census in 1850 in Greene County, Tennessee.

RADER	WILLIAM	51	M	W	VA	GREENE	10 sub 880	335
RADER	ELIZABETH	51	F	W	VA	GREENE	10 sub 880	335
RADER	JESSEE	21	M	W	TN	GREENE	10 sub 880	335
RADER	LEMUEL	18	M	W	TN	GREENE	10 sub 880	335
RADER	CORNELIUS	15	M	W	TN	GREENE	10 sub 880	335
RADER	LEWIS	13	M	W	TN	GREENE	10 sub 880	335
RADER	MELVINA	15	F	W	TN	GREENE	10 sub 880	335

He was employed in 1850. FARMER

He owned property in 1850. VALUE $1,500.00

Census 2: 1860. GUSTAVUS DIST. 6, GREENE COUNTY, TENNESSEE PAGE 182 LINE 244

He appeared on the census in 1860 in Gustavus Dist 6, Greene Co, TN.

Alt Death: Abt 1870, Mohawk, , , Tennessee.

Census 3: 1870. GREENE COUNTY, TENNESSEE ROLL 1531 PAGE 228

He has conflicting death information of 25 Nov 1878.[76]

Children from this marriage were:

+260 M i. **Valentine Sevier Rader**[1, 2, 3, 4, 6, 7, 8, 10, 11, 12, 14, 15] was born on 31 Jan 1822 in Mohawk, Greene Co, TN, died on 19 Feb 1902 in Piedmont, Greenwood Co., KS at age 80, and was buried in Piedmont Cemetery, Greenwood Co., KS.[4]

Valentine married **Louisa "Eliza" J. Bible** (b. 13 May 1823, d. 12 Aug 1856) on 8 Oct 1845 in Greene County, Tennessee.

Valentine next married **Eliza Jane Moore** (b. 6 Nov 1824, d. 1 Feb 1901) on 3 Jan 1857 in Knox Co, KY.

+261 F ii. **Louvina Rader**[7, 8, 11, 14] was born on 22 Sep 1824 in Mohawk, Greene County, Tennessee, died on 17 Apr 1909 in Greene County, Tennessee at age 84, and was buried in Gap Creek, Willoughby Cem, , Tennessee.

Louvina married **Edward M. Drake** (b. 1818, d. 21 Feb 1877) on 10 Jan 1849 in Greene County, Tennessee.

Louvina next married **Estell M. Drake** (b. Abt 1818, d. 21 Feb 1877) on 10 Jan 1849.

+262 F iii. **Lovinia Rader**[1, 2, 3, 4, 6, 10, 11, 12, 14, 15] was born in 1818 in Mohawk, , Greene, Tennessee, died on 21 Feb 1877 in Greene County, Tennessee at age 59, and was buried in Gap Creek, Willoughby Cem, , Tennessee.

Lovinia married **Estel M Drake** (b. 22 Sep 1824, d. 17 Apr 1909) on 10 Jan 1849 in Greene County, Tennessee.

+263 M iv. **Estel M Drake**[1, 2, 3, 6, 10, 11, 12, 14, 15] was born on 22 Sep 1824 in Mohawk, Greene Co, TN, died on 17 Apr 1909 in Greene County, Tennessee at age 84, and was buried in Drake Family Bulls Gap, Greene Co, TN.

Estel married **Lovinia Rader** (b. 1818, d. 21 Feb 1877) on 10 Jan 1849 in Greene County, Tennessee.

(Duplicate Line. See Person 262)

+264 F v. **Eliza Jane Rader**[1, 2, 3, 4, 6, 8, 10, 11, 12, 14, 15] was born in May 1826 in Mohawk, Greene Co., TN and died on 20 Oct 1827 in Mohawk, Greene Co., TN at age 1.

+265 M vi. **Jesse Rader**[1, 2, 3, 4, 6, 8, 10, 11, 12, 14, 15] was born on 25 May 1829 in Mohawk, Greene Co, TN, died on 30 Jun 1900 in Canon City, Fremont, Colorado at age 71, and was buried in Greenwood Cem.

Jesse married **Elizabeth D. Bell** (b. 1837) on 22 Jun 1854 in Greene County, Tennessee.

+266 M vii. **Samuel Rader** was born in 1832.

+267 M viii. **Lemuel Rader**[1, 2, 3, 4, 6, 8, 10, 11, 12, 14, 15] was born on 25 May 1832 in Greene County, Tennessee, died on 23 Sep 1899 in Hamblen County, Tennessee at age 67, and was buried in 1899 in Whitesburg, Bent Creek Cem, Hamblen, Tennessee.

Lemuel married **Elizabeth Ann Myers** (b. 23 Sep 1831, d. 1 May 1856) on 30 Nov 1853 in Greene County, Tennessee.

Lemuel next married **Melvina A. Kirpatrick** (b. 5 Oct 1834, d. 4 Sep 1911) on 3 Aug 1857 in Jefferson Co, TN.

Lemuel next married **Melvina Kirkpatrick** on 3 Aug 1857.

+268 M ix. **S. Cornelius Rader**[1, 2, 3, 4, 6, 8, 10, 11, 12, 14, 15] was born on 11 Feb 1835 in Mohawk, Greene Co, TN, died on 17 May 1863 in Vicksburg, Mississippi

Civil War at age 28, and was buried in Mt. Hope Cemetery, Greene County, Tennessee.

S. married **Sarah 'Sally' Crosby** (b. 8 Jun 1839, d. 24 Jul 1916) on 16 Feb 1860 in Lick Creek Vally, Greene County Tennessee.[77]

+269 M x. **Lewis Franklin Rader**[1, 2, 3, 4, 6, 8, 10, 11, 12, 14, 15] was born on 4 Apr 1837 in Mohawk, Greene Co, TN, died on 1 Mar 1914 in Greene County, Tennessee at age 76, and was buried in George Jackson Cemetery, Mowhawk, Greene County, Tennessee.

Lewis married **Sarah M. 'Sallie' Jackson** (b. 29 Jan 1841, d. 26 Oct 1907) on 22 Sep 1859 in Greene County, Tennessee.

+270 F xi. **Sarah Melvina Rader**[4] was born about 1843 in Greene County, Tennessee and died about 1860 in Greene County, Tennessee about age 17.

34. Sarah 'Sally' A. Rader[1, 2, 3, 6, 8, 10, 11, 12, 14, 15] (*John*[2], *Casper Sr*[1]) was born on 22 Aug 1801 in Wythe County, Virginia and died on 18 Aug 1886 in McMINN COUNTY, TENNESSEE at age 84. Another name for Sarah was Sarah 'Sally' A Rader.

General Notes: She appears on the 1860 census for McMinn Co., Tennessee as widow of Washington Etter.

She appeared on the census in 1850. McMINN COUNTY, TENNESSEE PAGE 319 LINE 1345

Sarah married **Fredrick Washington Etter**, son of **John Etter** and **Phobe Michaels**, on 29 Nov 1828 in Greene County, Tennessee. Fredrick was born on 15 May 1805 in Wythe County, Virginiowa and died on 31 Oct 1856 in McMINN COUNTY, TENNESSEE at age 51.

General Notes: Greene County Marriage # 2978 Nov 24, 1828 Frederick W. Etter -- Sally Rader -- md 29 Nov 1828-- M.G. Wilson, J.P. !License was issued 24 November 1828 at a cost of $0.75.

He appears on 1850 census for McMinn Co., Tennessee and Sarah Ann shows on the 1860 census as his widow. While the children are indicated as being born in McMinn Co. another source states Greene Co. and it really isn't known when Frederick went to McMinn and just where the children were born.

He appeared on the census in 1850. McMINN COUNTY, TENNESSEE PAGE 319 LINE 1345

Children from this marriage were:

+271 M i. **James Goodan Etter**[1, 2, 3, 6, 8, 10, 11, 12, 14, 15] was born on 14 Apr 1830 in , , Greene, Tennessee.

+272 M ii. **Martin Luther Etter**[1, 2, 3, 6, 8, 10, 11, 12, 14, 15] was born on 2 Oct 1831 in McMINN COUNTY, TENNESSEE, died in 1916 in Brown County, MN at age 85, and was buried on 12 Mar 1916 in Brown County, MN.

Martin married **Lourena Long** (b. 8 Mar 1835, d. 14 Aug 1915) on 3 May 1851 in , , Mcminn, Tennessee.

+273 M iii. **Valentine Etter**[1, 2, 3, 6, 8, 10, 11, 12, 14, 15] was born in Jan 1833 in McMINN COUNTY, TENNESSEE.

Valentine married **Citha P. Willhite** on 21 Nov 1856 in , , Mcminn, Tennessee.

+274 M iv. **Samuel Etter**[1, 2, 3, 6, 8, 10, 11, 12, 14, 15] was born in 1834 in McMINN COUNTY, TENNESSEE.

+275 M v. **George W. Etter**[1, 2, 3, 6, 8, 10, 11, 12, 14, 15] was born in 1839 in McMINN COUNTY, TENNESSEE.

George married **Eliza Jane (   )** (b. Abt 1844).

+276 F vi. **Elizabeth Etter**[1, 2, 3, 6, 8, 10, 11, 12, 14, 15] was born in 1841 in McMINN COUNTY, TENNESSEE.

+277 F vii. **Mary Etter**[1, 2, 3, 6, 8, 10, 11, 12, 14, 15] was born about 1839 in McMINN COUNTY, TENNESSEE.

Sarah next married **Valentine Patton** on 7 Apr 1820.

35. William Rader[1, 2, 3, 6, 8, 10, 11, 12, 14, 15] (*John*[2], *Casper Sr*[1]) was born about 1805 in , , Greene, Tennessee.

General Notes: Marriage # 2503 Jan 26, 1824 Wm. Rader -- Peggy Paysinger --

Peter Catrin A double check of the book shows Paysinger

He appeared on the census in 1840. GREENE COUNTY, TENNESSEE PAGE 87

William married **Peggy Baysinger**, daughter of **Jacob Dreher Basinger** and **Catherine Cash**, on 26 Jan 1824 in , , Greene, Tennessee. Peggy was born about 1805 in Greene County, Tennessee. Other names for Peggy were Peggy Basinger, and Peggy Paysinger.

Marriage Notes: Paysinger, Peggy Rader, William 26 Jan 1824 Tennessee

Noted events in her life were:

She appeared on the census in 1840. GREENE COUNTY, TENNESSEE PAGE 87

36. Mary Rader[1, 2, 3, 6, 8, 10, 11, 12, 14, 15] (*John*[2], *Casper Sr*[1]) was born on 27 Feb 1806 in Wythe County, Virginia and died before 1847.

Noted events in her life were:

She was baptized on 6 Apr 1806 in Wytheville, Wythe County, Virginia. St John's Lutheran||

Mary married **Jessie Rader** before 1844 in , , Greene, Tennessee. Jessie was born in 1816 in Greene County, Tennessee.

Noted events in his life were:

He appeared on the census in 1850. GREENE COUNTY, TENNESSEE PAGE 336 #629

He appeared on the census in 1850 in Greene County, Tennessee.

| RADER | JESSE | 34 | M | W | TN | GREENE | 10 sub 880 | 336 |
| RADER | MARY | 42 | F | W | NC | GREENE | 10 sub 880 | 336 |

He was employed in 1850. LISTED AS TENNANT

37. Sophia Rader[1, 2, 3, 6, 8, 10, 11, 12, 14, 15] (*John*[2], *Casper Sr*[1]) was born on 22 Jul 1808 in Botetourt County, Virginia and died on 13 Feb 1868 in Coles Co. Illinois at age 59. Another name for Sophia was Sarah Rader.

General Notes: According to the referenced Chancery Court record of 1844, the

location of Sophia and Leander was unknown.

Ref: Marriage Records Greene Co. Tennessee

Ref: Goldene Fillers Burgner, Chancery Court Minutes Greene Co. Tennessee November 1825 - January 1831, Southern Historical Press, Inc - Easley, South Carolina 29641 Copyright 1987 SEE HUSBAND NOTES

Noted events in her life were:

Alt Birth: Abt 1800, , , Greene, Tennessee.

Sophia married **Leander M. Hudson**, son of **Unknown** and **Unknown**, on 22 Oct 1832 in Greene County, Tennessee. Leander was born on 5 Sep 1809 in Carter Co., TN and died on 19 Dec 1879 in Coles Co. Illinois at age 70.

Noted events in their marriage were:

Alt Marriage: 22 Oct 1832, Greene County, Tennessee.

General Notes: NOT CONFIRMED TO BE A CHILD OF WILLIAM J. HUDSON, BUT MOST LIKELY

REF: "EARLY EAST TENN MARRIAGES VOL 1 & 2 GREENE CO. TENN"

LEANDER HUTSON TO SOPHIA READER 22 OCT 1832 (NOTE: SHE WAS A "RADER" DAUGHTER OF JOHN RADER, SR)

Ref: Coles Co. Illinois lookup
Subj: Re: Coles Co. Illinois look up
Date: 6/26/01 4:45:40 PM Central Daylight Time
From: keyrse@msn.com (Kelly Roley) To: Atsissie@aol.com
Carolyn,
I have looked through the 1840, 1850, and 1860 in Coles and there are no listings for any Hudsons. The 1870 does show your family though:
Hudson,
Leander 61 M Farmer TN (born 1809 - SEE MARRIAGE RECORD BELOW 1866)
Delilah 33 F IN (born 1837)
Rosetta 11 F IL (Note: This is a child by her prior marriage and last name of Rutherford)
David 7 M IL (Note: This is a child by her prior marriage and last name of Rutherford)
Braden, Marion 22 M Farm Laborer IN
I did find a marrige record that might be of interest to you:
Hudson, Mrs. Delilah J Samuel H Ashmore 18 Jan 1881 by Wm Hunt. H-491 (I don't know for sure, but I think this refers to a roll of film or a book of marriages at Coles County Courthouse.)
Good luck and if there is anything else, just let me know!
Kelly
NOTE: ONE OF TWO THINGS HAPPENED - EITHER SARAH RADER DIED A DIFFERENT YEAR OR THEY DIVORCED AND HE REMARRIED.

REF: GREENE CO TENN QUERIES

HUDSON/RADER

Would like to corresponde with anyone doing research on line of Leander HUDSON b. 5 Sept. 1809, Tenn. d. 19 Dec. 1879, Coles Co. Il. married to Sophia RADER on 23 Oct. 1833 in Greene Co. Tenn. She was b. 22 July 1808 in Boutetourt Co., Va. and died on 13 Feb. 1868 in Coles co. Il. Thank you
Annette Thompson
wbt@swbell.net (as of June, 2001 email no long valid, got returned mail)
Annette Thompson Mon, 24 Nov 1997

Ref: Illinois Statewide Marriages - Coles Co. Illinois -Index 1763 - 1900
GROOM   BRIDE   CNTY   DATE   VOL/PAGE LIC
HUDSON, GEORGE to CLARK, SARAH E LINCH (MRS) COLES 12/12/1891 /75
HUDSON, GEORGE M to PARKER, MINNIE COLES 11/14/1892 /96
HUDSON, HENRY M to LAWYER, CHRISTINA COLES 02/25/1886 00J/0391
HUDSON, J P to MOHLER, MARY C COLES 01/21/1875 00G/0081

HUDSON, JOHN H to SIDENER, ZELNORA COLES 01/30/1878 00H/0100
HUDSON, JOHN W to HAGAN, RENCIA A COLES 03/05/1885 00J/0246
HUDSON, LEANDER M to RUTHERFORD, DELIAH JANE MRS COLES 08/25/1866 E/ 59
See 1870 census
HUDSON, LEMUEL to MCKINNEY, MARY F COLES 05/23/1857 B/ 137
HUDSON, WILL to LEWIS, SARAH COLES 02/21/1898 /226
HUDSON, WILLIAM to WOODRUM, JANE COLES 08/08/1884 00J/0145
ASHMORE, SAMUEL H to HUDSON, DELILAH J (MRS) COLES 01/18/1881 00H/0491
ASHMORE, SAMUEL H to HUDSON, DELILAH J MRS COLES 01/18/1881 00H/0491
MINER, GIDEON to HUDSON, ELIZABETH COLES 04/07/1886 00J/0409
MODRELL, GEORGE G to HUDSON, EMMA COLES 11/18/1882 00I/0352
CRAIG, JOSEPH E to HUDSON, EMMA COLES 11/26/1890 00K/0482
FRANTZ, E W to HUDSON, HARRIET COLES 03/24/1898 /234
STIFF, WILLIAM R to HUDSON, LAURA B COLES 11/06/1889 002/0018
CLARK, WILLIAM C to HUDSON, LUCY M COLES 12/11/1899 /271
QUIMBY, ALL to HUDSON, MARY COLES 01/01/1875 00G/0084
GOODMAN, WILLIAM to HUDSON, MARY C COLES 09/27/1860 B/ 214
WILSON, WILLIAM to HUDSON, MARY H COLES 09/01/1875 00G/0162
STARK, FRANCIS MARION to HUDSON, MARY JANE COLES 12/22/1862 C/ 58
RAY, SAMUEL to HUDSON, MELINDA COLES 10/09/1878 00H/0179
POWERS, JONATHAN W to HUDSON, MINERVY COLES 12/27/1852 B/ 46
HITE, URIAH to HUDSON, NANCY JANE COLES 02/21/1866 E/ 29

Edgar Co. Illinois marriages
GROOM   BRIDE   CNTY   DATE   VOL/PAGE   LIC

HUDSON, ALEXANDER to MAPES, MARGARET EDGAR 12/01/1864 B/ 56
HUDSON, CHARLES to RYON, ADA EDGAR 12/18/1894 0II/0091
HUDSON, JED. WEBSTER to TRIGGS, HANNAH J. EDGAR 11/22/1875 01A/0010
HUDSON, JESSE to STARK, HARRIET EDGAR 10/10/1861 B/ 41
HUDSON, JOHN to WALL, MATILDA EDGAR 11/28/1865 B/ 61
HUDSON, LEMUEL to CARY, ALICE (DICKSON) (MRS) EDGAR 06/27/1894 0II/0079
HUDSON, LEVI H to ALLEN, MARGARET J EDGAR 11/06/1864 B/ 55
HUDSON, SAMUEL to RIGHT, ELIZABETH EDGAR 04/14/1861 B/ 39
HUDSON, THOMAS to WYNN, VIOLIA EDGAR 05/04/1876 01A/0014
HUDSON, WILLIAM W to ALLEN, MARTHA (LA 158) EDGAR 04/03/1840 SA/ 48 Lic #SA 754
FONCANNON, ORVALL to HUDSON (HUTSON), NANNIE EDGAR 02/07/1899 0II/0181
CRAWFORD, BRUCE N. to HUDSON, ANNA B. EDGAR 07/28/1892 0II/0037
VERMILLION, HARVEY to HUDSON, DELILA MRS EDGAR 08/16/1865 B/ 60
MASON, GEORGE H to HUDSON, DELILAH EDGAR 01/03/1864 B/ 51
BAKER, ALONZO to HUDSON, DORA EDGAR 04/05/1897 0II/0140
ALLAN, BENJAMIN (4/20/1850 OR) to HUDSON, NANCY H (4/21/1850 LA 218) EDGAR 04/25/1850 SA/ 108 SA 1692 ALLISON, THOMAS to HUDSON, NORA EDGAR 05/23/1894 0II/0077
KIRBY, JAMES A. to HUDSON, NORA A. EDGAR 03/01/1896 0II/0117
SWINFORD, HUGH to HUDSON, ROSA EDGAR 10/08/1896 0II/0128
FLYNN, JAMES to HUDSON, SUSIE EDGAR 12/13/1891 0II/0026

Ref: Coles Co. Illinois Mortality Schedule 1860
East Oakland Township, Enumerated by H.L. Taylor, page 1
Mary F. Hudson age25 f Born Va. Died Apr Cause of death: Peratum Eastus Days Ill 12 days
Ref: Genforum - Hudson Family
Top of Form 1 Leander M Hudson (1809-1879) TN/IL
Posted by: David </cgi-genforum/email.cgi?918492421>Date: October 27, 2000 at 20:12:29
of 4305
Bottom of Form 1
I'm looking for any information on the parents of Leander M Hudson, born 5 September 1809 in Tennessee and died 19 December 1879 in Coles County, Illinois. He married Sophia Rader on 22 October 1832 in Greene County, Tennessee.
Ref: Subj: Re: Leander Hudson
Date: 6/26/01 8:44:44 AM Central Daylight Time
From: schanbac@yahoo.com (D C Schanbacher) To: Atsissie1@aol.com
Good morning Carolyn, I need to tell you up front that most of the information I have came either from family documents or the Internet. I take both with a grain of salt. When it comes to the Hudsons, I suppose the only thing of which I am completely sure is that Emma May Hudson was my great grandmother. I didn't know her -- she died five years before I was born -- but she was well know to my mother. Emma and my great grandfather (Joseph Edward Craig) lived in Coles County, Illinois. A lot of my family history passed through Coles County -- my mother was born there and where I still have several relatives living there. The information I have about Emma's parents and grandparents came from a Stark family website and the Mormons. I'll believe it until I find credible conflicting information.
I believe that Jesse Hudson was Emma's father and Leander was Jesse's father. That said, here is the information I have on Leander forward: Leander M Hudson (b.5 Sep 1809; d.19 Dec 1879 in Coles County, Illinois) married Sophia Rader (b.22 Jul 1808 in Botetourt County, Virginia; d.13 Feb 1868 in Coles County, Illinois) on 22 Oct 1832 in Greene County, Tennessee. Their son, Jesse Hudson (1840-1888) married Harriet Stark (1842-1902) on 10 Oct 1861 in Edgar County, Illinois. This marriage was verifed with records maintained by the Illinois State Genealogy Society. Harriet was born in Indiana. I found her family listed in the 1850 census for Fayette Township in Vigo County, Indiana. Jesse and Harriet Stark Hudson had the following children: 1) Laura Hudson (1869 - ?) who married William Riley Stiff on 6 Nov 1889 (according to Illinois State Genealogy Society). 2) Emma May Hudson (8 Nov 1871 - 13 Jun 1950) who married Joseph Craig (13 Feb 1866 - 23 Aug 1948) on 26 Nov 1890 in Coles County Illinois. 3) Jesse Therman Hudson (1880-1941) who married Besse Jane Cook (?-1961) 4) Alva Roscoe Hudson (29 Jun 1881-Jan 1969) who married Anna Bell James (23 Sep 1881 - Feb 1966)

David Schanbacher

Noted events in his life were:

Alt Birth: 5 Sep 1809, Greene County, Tennessee.

Children from this marriage were:

+278 F i. **Minerva Hudson** was born on 14 Aug 1835 in Tennessee, died on 24 Nov 1917 in Illinois at age 82, and was buried in Oakland Cemetary, Illinois.

Minerva married **Jonathan W. Powers II** (b. 5 Jun 1829, d. 28 Sep 1905) on 27 Dec 1852 in Coles Co. Illinois.

+279 M ii. **Jesse Hudson** was born on 27 Jun 1840 in Jasmine co., KY and died in 1888 at age 48.

Jesse married **Harriett Stark** (b. 1842, d. 1902) on 10 Oct 1861 in Edgar Co. Illinois.

38. Samuel Rader[1, 2, 3, 6, 8, 10, 11, 12, 14, 15] (*John*[2], *Casper Sr*[1]) was born about 1810 in , , Greene, Tennessee and died before 1850 in , , Greene, Tennessee.

General Notes: Greene County marriage # 3493 July 11, 1833 Samuel Rader -- Delilah Kinser -- Jacob Cobble -- md 11 July 1833 -- Peter Cobble J.P.

Noted events in his life were:

Alt Birth: 1810, Wythe County, Virginia.

Samuel married **Delilah Kinser** on 11 Jul 1833 in , , Greene, Tennessee. Delilah was born in 1812 in TN.

Noted events in her life were:

She appeared on the census in 1850 in Greene County, Tennessee.

RADER	DELILA	38	F	W	TN	GREENE	10 sub 880	323
RADER	JAMES	16	M	W	TN	GREENE	10 sub 880	323
RADER	ELIZA	14	F	W	TN	GREENE	10 sub 880	323
RADER	MALVINA	11	F	W	TN	GREENE	10 sub 880	323
RADER	WILLIAM	8	M	W	TN	GREENE	10 sub 880	323
RADER	CAROLINE	6	F	W	TN	GREENE	10 sub 880	323
RADER	LEWIS	3	M	W	TN	GREENE	10 sub 880	323
RADER	MARY	0	F	W	TN	GREENE	10 sub 880	323

She appeared on the census in 1850. GREENE COUNTY, TENNESSEE PAGE 323B #450

Children from this marriage were:

+280 M i. **James C. Rader**[1, 2, 3, 6, 8, 10, 11, 12, 14, 15] was born in 1834 in , , Greene, Tennessee.

+281 F ii. **Eliza Rader**[1, 2, 3, 6, 8, 10, 11, 12, 14, 15] was born in 1836 in , , Greene, Tennessee.

+282 F iii. **Melvina Rader**[1, 2, 3, 6, 8, 10, 11, 12, 14, 15] was born in 1839 in , , Greene, Tennessee.

+283 M iv. **William A. Rader**[1, 2, 3, 6, 8, 10, 11, 12, 14, 15] was born in 1842 in , , Greene, Tennessee, died in 1928 at age 86, and was buried in Susong Cemetery, Washington County, Virginia.

William married **Teresa E.** (b. 1837, d. 1901).

+284 F v. **Caroline Rader**[1, 2, 3, 6, 8, 10, 11, 12, 14, 15] was born in 1844 in , , Greene, Tennessee.

+285 M vi. **Lewis Rader**[1, 2, 3, 6, 8, 10, 11, 12, 14, 15] was born in 1847 in , , Greene, Tennessee.

+286 F vii. **Margaret Rader**[1,2,3,6,8,10,11,12,14,15] was born in 1849 in , , Greene, Tennessee.

39. Isabella 'Ibbie' Rader[1,2,3,6,8,10,11,12,14,15] ($John^2$, $Casper\ Sr^1$) was born in 1813 in Greene County, Tennessee, died in Feb 1884 in Hawkins County, Tennessee at age 71, and was buried in Cumberland Presbyterian Cemetery, Hawkins County, Tennessee.

General Notes: Isabella and Andrew were living in Greene County, Tennessee in 1844. They were living there also in 1850(census). They probably moved to Hawkins County, Tennessee after this date. Isabella and Andrew are mentioned in Goodspeed page 1228 of the Hawkins County edition. It is probable that they are buried in the Cumberland Presbyterian Church cemetery in Hawkins County, Tennessee.

Noted events in her life were:

Alt Birth: 1813, Wythe County, Virginia.
Census 1: 1850. GREENE COUNTY, TENNESSEE PAGE 245 LINE 1579
Census 2: 1860. GREENE COUNTY, TENNESSEE
Census 3: 1870. DISTRICT 6, GREENE COUNTY, TENNESSEE LINE 123
She appeared on the census in 1880 in Greene County, Tennessee. Census Place: District 6, Greene, Tennessee   Source: FHL Film 1255258   National Archives Film T9-1258   Page 81B

Name	Relation	Sex	Marr	Race	Age	Birthplace	Occ	Fa	Mo
John GUTHRIE	Self	M	M	W	37	TN	Farmer	TN	TN
Elenden GUTHRIE	Wife	F	M	W	38	TN	Keeping House	TN	VA
Martha Jane GUTHRIE	Dau	F	S	W	14	TN	At Home	TN	TN
Mary Isebel GUTHRIE	Dau	F	S	W	12	TN	At Home	TN	TN
Lewis E. GUTHRIE	Son	M	S	W	9	TN	At Home	TN	TN
Lillie P. GUTHRIE	Dau	F	S	W	4	TN	At Home	TN	TN
William Lauson GUTHRIE	Son	M	S	W	1	TN	At Home	TN	TN
Anderson Dauson GUTHRIE	Son	M	S	W	1	TN	At Home	TN	TN
Isebella GUTHRIE	Mother	F	W	W	65	TN	Keeping House	TN	TN
Mary An GUTHRIE	Dau	F	S	W	43	TN	At Home	TN	TN

Isabella married **Andrew Guthrie**, son of **James Guthrie** and **Isabella King**, on 11 Sep 1832 in Greene County, Tennessee. Andrew was born on 18 Dec 1801 in Hawkins County, Tennessee, died on 3 Aug 1867 in Greene County, Tennessee at age 65, and was buried in Cumberland Presbyterian Cemetery, Hawkins County, Tennessee.

General Notes: Greene County Marriage #3397 Sept. 11, 1832 Andrew Guthrie -- Isabella Rader -- Jas G. Guthrie.

Noted events in his life were:
Census 1: 1850. GREENE COUNTY, TENNESSEE PAGE 245 LINE 1579
Census 2: 1860. GREENE COUNTY, TENNESSEE
Census 3: 1870. DISTRICT 6, GREENE COUNTY, TENNESSEE LINE 123

Children from this marriage were:

Source Citations

+287 M i. **Lewis W. Guthrie**[1, 2, 3, 6, 8, 10, 11, 12, 14, 15, 78] was born on 11 Feb 1834 in Greene County, Tennessee, died on 13 Jul 1914 in Hawkins County, Tennessee at age 80, and was buried in Hawkins County, Tennessee.

Lewis married **Rhoda N. Moore** (b. 1843) on 3 Nov 1859 in Hawkins County, Tennessee.

+288 M ii. **James C. Guthrie** was born on 4 Oct 1834 in Greene County, Tennessee, died on 7 Dec 1862 in Greene County, Tennessee at age 28, and was buried in Drake Cemetery, Greene County, Tennessee.

+289 M iii. **William Guthrie**[1, 2, 3, 6, 8, 10, 11, 12, 14, 15] was born in 1835 in Greene County, Tennessee.

+290 F iv. **Emeline Guthrie**[1, 2, 3, 6, 8, 10, 11, 12, 14, 15] was born about 1838 in , , Greene, Tennessee.

+291 F v. **Mary A. Guthrie**[1, 2, 3, 6, 8, 10, 11, 12, 14, 15] was born in 1836 in Greene County, Tennessee.

+292 F vi. **Emaline Guthrie** was born in 1838 in Greene County, Tennessee.

Emaline married **Joseph Bullenton** on 9 Oct 1872 in Hawkins County, Tennessee.

+293 M vii. **John A. Guthrie**[1, 2, 3, 6, 8, 10, 11, 12, 14, 15] was born on 10 Apr 1841 in Greene County, Tennessee, died on 25 Mar 1923 in Greene County, Tennessee at age 81, and was buried in Speedwell Baptist Cemetery, Tennessee.

John married **Ellendine Moore** (b. 13 Apr 1840, d. 22 Apr 1900) on 18 May 1865 in Hawkins County, Tennessee.

John next married **Susan Walker** (b. 12 Nov 1877, d. 6 Sep 1952).

+294 M viii. **Andy Andrew Guthrie** was born in May 1846 in Greene County, Tennessee, died on 20 Aug 1916 in Greene County, Tennessee at age 70, and was buried on 21 Aug 1916 in Mt. Hope Methodist Cemetery, Greene County, Tennessee.

Andy married **Sarah Ann Moore** (b. 17 Jul 1842, d. 17 Jul 1920) on 8 Sep 1868 in Greene County, Tennessee.

+295 F ix. **Laney J. Guthrie**[1, 2, 3, 6, 8, 10, 11, 12, 14, 15] was born in 1845 in Greene County, Tennessee.

Laney married **Thomas A. Solomon** on 26 Nov 1868 in Greene County, Tennessee.

+296 M x. **Andrew "Andy" Guthrie**[1, 2, 3, 6, 8, 10, 11, 12, 14, 15] was born in 1846 in Greene County, Tennessee and died on 20 Aug 1916 in Greene County, Tennessee at age 70.

Andrew married **Sarah Ann Moore** on 8 Sep 1868 in Greene County, Tennessee.

+297 M xi. **Joseph Guthrie**[1, 2, 3, 6, 8, 10, 11, 12, 14, 15] was born on 4 Aug 1846 in Greene County, Tennessee, died on 25 Aug 1919 in Greene County, Tennessee at age 73, and was buried on 26 Aug 1919 in Drake Cemetery, Greene County, Tennessee.

Joseph married **Martha Ann Ward** (b. May 1855) on 25 Sep 1872 in Hawkins County, Tennessee.

+298 F xii. **Malinda A. Guthrie** was born on 15 Apr 1852 in Greene County, Tennessee and died on 31 Jan 1928 in Dickinson County, Kansas at age 75.

Malinda married **David Bullington** (b. 20 Dec 1852, d. 27 May 1924) on 19 Nov 1873 in Hawkins County, Tennessee.

+299 F xiii. **Isabel Guthrie** was born in 1851 in Greene County, Tennessee.

+300 F xiv. **Nancy Guthrie** was born in 1852.

+301 M xv. **Linda A. Guthrie** was born on 15 Apr 1852 in Greene County, Tennessee and died on 31 Jan 1928 in Dickinson County, Michigan at age 75.

40. Lucinda Rader[1, 2, 3, 6, 8, 10, 11, 12, 14, 15] ($John^2$, $Casper\ Sr^1$) was born in 1819 in Greene County, Tennessee, died on 3 Aug 1893 in Tennessee at age 74, and was buried in Phillips Cem, St Clair, TN.

General Notes: interred Phillips Cem, St. Clair, TN
Noted events in her life were:
Alt Birth: 1819, Wythe County, Virginia.
She appeared on the census in 1880 in Hawkins County, Tennessee. Census Place: District 1, Hawkins, Tennessee   Source: FHL Film 1255260   National Archives Film T9-1260   Page 170B

	Relation	Sex	Marr	Race	Age	Birthplace		
Wm. COLIER	Self	M	M	W	62	VA	Occ: Farmer	Fa: VA Mo: NC
Lucinda COLIER	Wife	F	M	W	65	TN	Occ: Keeping H.	Fa: VA Mo: VA
Martha FAWBUSH	GDau	F	S	W	16	TN		Fa: TN Mo: TN

Lucinda married **William Colyer** on 14 Jan 1839.[50] William was born on 9 Jan 1818 in Virginia, died on 9 Aug 1893 in Tennessee at age 75, and was buried in Phillips Cemetery, St. Clair, Tennessee.

41. Emaline Rader[1, 2, 3, 6, 8, 10, 11, 12, 14, 15] ($John^2$, $Casper\ Sr^1$) was born in 1820 in Wythe County, Virginia.

Noted events in her life were:
Alt Birth: 1820, Greene County, Tennessee.
Alt Birth: After 1820, Greene County, Tennessee.

Emaline married **William Jenkins** on 8 Oct 1840 in John Walker, Jp, Greene Co, TN. William was born in 1815 in Tennessee.

General Notes: Greene Co. Marriage # 358 Oct 5, 1840 William Jenkins -- Emeline Rader -- William Rader -- 8 Oct. 1840 -- John Walker,J.P.

Children from this marriage were:

+302 F i. **Mary Jenkins**[1, 2, 3, 6, 8, 10, 11, 12, 14, 15] was born about 1841 in , , Hawkins, Tennessee.

+303 M ii. **Jackson Jenkins**[1, 2, 3, 6, 8, 10, 11, 12, 14, 15] was born about 1844 in , , Hawkins, Tennessee.

+304 F iii. **Catherine Jenkins**[1, 2, 3, 6, 8, 10, 11, 12, 14, 15] was born about 1846 in , , Hawkins, Tennessee.

+305 F iv. **Jane Jenkins**[1, 2, 3, 6, 8, 10, 11, 12, 14, 15] was born about 1848 in , , Hawkins, Tennessee.

42. Mary Ann Rader (*William^2, Casper Sr^1*) was born in 1800 in Wythe County, Virginia.

General Notes: bound out to Christopher Brown (son of Christopher) and on
April 12, 1815 she chose him as her guardain at an age upwards
of 14
APRIL 10, 1805 The court appointed John Rader guardian for Samuel, Anne, and Susanna Rader, orphans of William Rader, deceased, in 1805.
APRIL 12, 1815 Anna chose Christopher Brown as her guardian.
NOVEMBER 15, 1809 Anna was bound over to Christopher Brown.

Mary married **William Stowers** in 1834 in Bland, Virginia.[51] William was born on 27 Nov 1812 and died on 25 Jan 1902 at age 89.

Mary next married **John Cregan** on 19 Jun 1815.

43. Susan "Susannah" Rader (*William^2, Casper Sr^1*) was born in 1800 in Wythe County, Virginia. Another name for Susan was Susannah Reeder.

General Notes: She chose John Repass as her guardian she was upwards of age 14
APRIL 10, 1805 The court appointed John Rader guardian for Samuel, Anne, and Susanna Rader, orphans of William Rader, deceased, in 1805.
APRIL 12, 1815 Susannah chose John Repass as her guardian.
Noted events in her life were:
Alt Birth: 1801, Wythe County, Virginia.
She appeared on the census in 1850. BOONE COUNTY, VIRGINIA PAGE 29 LINE 388
Census 1: 1860. BALLARDSVILLE, BOONE COUNTY, VIRGINIA LINE 635 PAGE 99
Census 2: 1870. WASHINGTON TOWNSHIP, KANAWHA COUNTY, WEST VIRGINIA PAGE 279 LINE 54
Census 3: 1880. JEFFERSON TOWNSHIP, LINCOLN COUNTY, WEST VIRGINIA PAGE 182 LINE 81

Susan married **James "Black Jim" Hager Jr.**, son of **Unknown** and **Unknown**, on 31 Dec 1822 in Tazewell Co., Virginia. James was born in 1791 in Fayette Co., Kentucky Or Pennsylvania and died on 15 Oct 1859 in Boone County, Virginia at age 68.

General Notes: Facts about this person:

Census 1840
Logan Co., VA-#M704/Roll 566: p. 80
Noted events in his life were:
Fact 1: Fact 1, See Note Page.
Alt Birth: 1791, Boone County, Virginia (West Virginia).
He appeared on the census in 1840. LOGAN COUNTY VIRGINIA ROLL 566 PG. 80
He appeared on the census in 1840 in Logan Co., VA-#M704/Roll 566: P. 80.
Census 1: 1850. BOONE COUNTY, VIRGINIA PAGE 29 LINE 388

Children from this marriage were:

+306 F i. **Elizabeth Hager** was born WFT Est 1814-1841 and died WFT Est 1831-1924 at age 17.

Elizabeth married **Bejamin Vannatter** WFT Est 1831-1875.

+307 F ii. **Malvina Hager** .

Malvina married **Francis Thompson**.

+308 F iii. **Lavina Melvina Hager** was born in 1824 in Wythe County, Virginia and died after 1900 in Lincoln County, West Virginia.

Lavina married **Francis "Frank" Thompson** (b. 1812, d. Bef 1900).

+309 M iv. **Joseph Hager** was born about 1818 in Virginia.

Joseph married **Rachel Pauley** (b. 1821) on 10 Feb 1838.

+310 M v. **William P. Hager** was born in 1823 in Tazwell County, Virginia and died in 1865 at age 42.

William married **Sarah Parsons Or Payne** (b. Abt 1829).

William next married **Sarah Parsons** (b. 1826).

+311 M vi. **Henderson Hager** was born in 1824 in Tazewell Co., Virginia.

Henderson married **Martha Ellen Mcneely** (b. 23 Jul 1832, d. 26 Feb 1896) on 18 Feb 1848 in Boone County, West Virginia.

Henderson next married **Eliza Adkins**.

Henderson next married **Leanna Fry** about 1880.

+312 F vii. **Mary Elizabeth Hager** was born in 1830 in Tazwell County, Virginia.

Mary married **Benjamin Franklin Vannatter** (b. 1828, d. After 1900) before 1850 in Boone County, West Virginia.

+313 M viii. **Russell Hager Sr.** was born on 25 Jan 1829 in Tazwell County, Virginia and died on 9 Feb 1917 in Morrisville, Boone County, Virginia (West Virginia) at age 88.

Russell married **Delona Delaney Adkins** (b. 1831, d. 2 Dec 1915) on 25 Jul 1846 in Coal River, Boone County, West Virginia.

Russell next married **Permelia Ann Hill** (b. 1852) after 1878.

+314 M ix. **John Hager** was born in 1832 in Logan County, Virginia (West Virginia).

John married **Nancy** (b. 1832).

+315 F x. **Sarah Hager** was born about 1833 in Logan County, Virginia (West Virginia).

Sarah married **Andrew Elkins** (b. 1824) in 1853 in Boone County, West Virginia.

+316 F xi. **Rebecca Hager** was born about 1836 in Logan County, Virginia (West Virginia).

Rebecca married **William L Price** (b. Jan 1856).

Rebecca next married **Luke G. Adkins**.

Rebecca next married **Allen Vannatter** (b. 1827).

+317 F xii. **Eliza Hager** was born about 1837 in Logan County, Virginia (West Virginia) and died on 15 Feb 1914 in Lincoln County, West Virginia about age 77.

Eliza married **Silas Hager** (b. 1828, d. 27 Jan 1906) in 1855 in Boone County, West Virginia.

Eliza next married **Bejamin Vannatter**.

Susan next married **Nathan Turley**, son of **John Turley Sr.** and **Martha**, on 31 Dec 1862 in Kanawha County Virginia. Nathan was born in 1797 in Pittsylvania County Virginia.

Noted events in his life were:

He appeared on the census in 1870. WASHINGTON TOWNSHIP, KANAWHA COUNTY, WEST VIRGINIA PAGE 279 LINE 54

44. Samuel Rader ($William^2$, $Casper\ Sr^1$) was born in 1802 in Wythe County, Virginia. Other names for Samuel were Samuel Reeder, and Samuel Reeder.

General Notes:
APRIL 10, 1805 The court appointed John Rader guardian for Samuel, Anne, and Susanna Rader, orphans of William Rader, deceased, in 1805.
NOVEMBER 15, 1809 Samuel was bound over to Christopher Oury to be trained as a tailor. Was bound out to Christopher Oury to learn the trade as a taylor
Noted events in his life were:
Alt Birth: 1802.

45. William Rader[1, 2, 3, 4, 6, 7, 8, 10, 11, 12, 14, 15] ($Jacob^2$, $Casper\ Sr^1$) was born on 28 Jun 1799 in Wytheville, Wythe County, Virginia and died on 25 Nov 1877 in Mohawk, Greene Co, TN at age 78.

General Notes: William was the son of Jacob and Elizabeth Rader. Jacob was the brother of John Rader, Elizabeth's father. The children of Elizabeth and William Rader was obtained from census records and from a Greene County, Tennessee County Court record dated June 4, 1878, volumn 1875 to 1879, pages 195, 198, 199, 245, 246 and 247. This court case recorded the petition of the children and grandchildren of William Rader deceased to sell the landed estate of William Rader containing 440 acres located in district number 6 and situated along Lick Creek in Greene County, Tennessee. Elizabeth was the daughter of John Rader and Mary Etter Rader. John Rader and Jacob Rader were brothers. The record of William and Elizabeth Rader can be found in the section under John Rader and Mary Etter Rader. In 1860(census) William was living in Gustavus District number 6 in Greene County, Tennessee. Marriage # 2222 Nov 23, 1820 William Reader -- Elizabeth Reader -- witn. John Reader A letter from William Rader 1877

I recieved this letter by way of Jan Maddux of the Greene County, TN Genealogical society, Thanks Jan !!

13 Jul 1994 Dear Friends, I have been to your county, researching my own Bridewell and Reed families, some time back. I did not have an opportunity to visit your genealogy group, or library, but am aware of the wonderful work you have all published on Green County. . . . . . My good friend and neighbor, Dania Sue Chambers, has furnsihed this letter, which had belonged to her paternal grandmother, Dania Rader, who had recived it from her father, Valentine Rader and wife, Elira, to whom it had beed written by Valentine's father, William Rader, of Greene County, TN .. Dania Sue tells me her grandmother was from Piedmont, KS and that other relatives lived in a nearby town. Interested persons may contact her; Dania Sue Chambers, 3102 Coffey St., Victoria, TX 77901-7427 (512) 578-7330

Sincerely, Billye D. Jackson 3101 Coffey St. Victoria, TX 77901-7426

September 15, 1877 Greene County Tennessee Dear Son and Daughter I seat myself to drop you a few lines. I feel it my duty to give you the painfull news of the death of your mother . she died the day before yesterday and was buried yesterday at the buring ground at P.R. Raders ???. She was very unwell at times all through the summer and on the 26th day of August she vomited a full pint of Blood. There was clods of Blood amongst it as large as hulled walnuts. On the next day she vomited blood three different times. The last time in the evening she vomited about a quart of blood. Then she was free from bleeding for several days but afterwards volited Blood again at different times until she died, lived 19 days from the time that she first vomited Blood and was intirely confined to her bed during that time.. During the time she scarcely eat anything except drank a little coffee, she was in her proper mind all the time. Doctor Rader says there was a cancer in her stomach. One night she was very bad we were standing around her bed she told us she was going to heaven and requested us all to meet her in heaven. I asked her if she felt reconciled to die she said yes, and said she was proud to see her friends standing around her. let us all try to live in that way that will enable us when we come to die to meet her in that glory land where parting is nomore. She told your sister Lurina Drake that she wished to live to see Valentine and Elira one time more but said she knowed she couldnot. Your Brothers and sister and families are all well Luvina and Lemuels wife are both here with me to day I feel very lonesome I expect to try to keep house me and mary the colored girl. I am as well at present as common hope these lines may find you all enjoying reasonable health I wish you to answer as soon as it comes to hand I have not sent your and Eliras money yet your mother was so poorly I could not leave home and now the time is coming close that you said you and Elvira was comming to Tennessee I would be very glad to see you both so will wait to see you or an answer from you Your uncle Joseph Rader is as well as common at present and still living with me yet and says he expects to go back to kansas Baxter Springs some time in the forepart of October as he wishes to stay and hear Brother Petens funeral preached on the last sabbath in this month and EM. Drakes funeral is to be preached on the fourth sabbath in this month which be tomorrow a week   I will close by saying I remain your affectionate father as ever Wm Rader To V.S. Rader + Elina J. Rader Your sister Livina says that they wrote you a long letter some time last spring and has been looking for an answer from you ever since.

1870 GREENE COUNTY CENSUS LISTS A BLACK FEMALE CHILD 10 YEARS OF AGE BY THE NAME OF MARY E. RADER LIVING WITH WILLIAM AND ELIZABETH RADER.

WILLIAM AND ELIZABETH ARE 1ST. COUSINS
Bible Family, Terri Strotman, World Connect Project
Noted events in his life were:
Alt Birth: 1793.
Alt Birth: Abt 1798, , Wythe, Virginia.

Map of land William owned on 15 Mar 1829 in Lick Creek Valley

Greene County Tennessee. Purchased parcel #1339D containing 48 acres from John Love

> He appeared on the census in 1840. GREENE COUNTY, TENNESSEE PAGE 77
>
> He owned land on 31 Mar 1841 in Lick Creek Valley, Greene County Tennessee. Purchased parcel # 342 containing 10 acres from Alfred Russell

Census 1: 1850. GREENE COUNTY, TENNESSEE PAGE 335B #619

He appeared on the census in 1850 in Greene County, Tennessee.

RADER	WILLIAM	51	M	W	VA	GREENE	10 sub 880	335
RADER	ELIZABETH	51	F	W	VA	GREENE	10 sub 880	335
RADER	JESSEE	21	M	W	TN	GREENE	10 sub 880	335
RADER	LEMUEL	18	M	W	TN	GREENE	10 sub 880	335
RADER	CORNELIUS	15	M	W	TN	GREENE	10 sub 880	335
RADER	LEWIS	13	M	W	TN	GREENE	10 sub 880	335
RADER	MELVINA	15	F	W	TN	GREENE	10 sub 880	335

He was employed in 1850. FARMER

He owned property in 1850. VALUE $1,500.00

Census 2: 1860. GUSTAVUS DIST. 6, GREENE COUNTY, TENNESSEE PAGE 182 LINE 244

He appeared on the census in 1860 in Gustavus Dist 6, Greene Co, TN.

Alt Death: Abt 1870, Mohawk, , , Tennessee.

Census 3: 1870. GREENE COUNTY, TENNESSEE ROLL 1531 PAGE 228

He has conflicting death information of 25 Nov 1878.[76]

William married **Elizabeth Rader**, daughter of **John Rader** and **Mary Etter**, on 23 Nov 1820 in Gap Creek, Greene County Tennessee.[4] Elizabeth was born on 3 May 1799 in Wythe County, Virginia and died on 13 Sep 1871 in Mohawk, Greene Co, TN at age 72.

Marriage Notes: William and Elizabeth were first cousins. His father, Jacob, and her father, John, were brothers.[4]

Noted events in their marriage were:

Alt. Marriage:

General Notes: Elizabeth and William were first cousins! They lived where the city of Mohawk is now. They were strict Presbyterians.Bible Family, Terri Strotman, World Connect Project

Noted events in her life were:

She owned land on 5 Oct 1829 in Lick Creek Valley, Greene County Tennessee. Purchased parcel #1339G containing 22 acres from John Love the same day her husband (first cousin) did

She appeared on the census in 1840. GREENE COUNTY, TENNESSEE PAGE 77

Census 1: 1850. GREENE COUNTY, TENNESSEE PAGE 335B #619

Census 2: 1860. GUSTAVUS DIST. 6, GREENE COUNTY, TENNESSEE PAGE 182 LINE 244

Census 3: 1870. GREENE COUNTY, TENNESSEE ROLL 1531 PAGE 228

Alt Death: 13 Sep 1877, Mohawk, Greene County, Tennessee.

(Duplicate Line. See Person 33)

46. **John Rader**[4,7] (*Jacob*[2], *Casper Sr*[1]) was born about 1800 in Wythe County, Virginia and died before 1822.

General Notes: Not listed in fathers probate. Must of died before 1822 childless !

47. Joseph Rader[1,2,3,4,6,7,8,10,11,12,14,15] (*Jacob*[2], *Casper Sr*[1]) was born about 1801 in , Wythe, Virginia and died in Clay County, Illinois.

General Notes: Joseph was living in Greene County, Tennessee in Captain McPherons Company along Lick Creek in 1830 and owned 170 acres of land. Joseph was living in District number 10 in Greene County, Tennessee in 1850(Census). Living with his family at this time was Mary Matthews born 1795 in Tennessee and Lucinda Slate born 1810 in Tennessee. Joseph and his family apparently moved sometime after 1850 since no record has been found indicating their whereabouts in Tennessee after this date. The family history says he went west. (E.C. Rader 13 SEP 1936 for family reunion) Query in Greene County Pioneer May 1993 by Richard M. Breidenthal (800 Meadowlark Lane, Sandpoint, ID 83864) "They went to Clay Co., IL ca 1850"

Noted events in his life were:

Alt Birth: 1791, , , Wythe, Virginia, USA.

Alt Birth: 1791, Wythe County, Virginia.

He appeared on the census in 1840. GREENE COUNTY, TENNESSEE PAGE 77

He owned land on 17 Aug 1840 in Lick Creek Valley, Greene County Tennessee.
   Purchased Parcel # 1358C containing 65 acres from Vincent Jackson

[Caption: 089]

He owned land on 9 Dec 1841 in Lick Creek Valley, Greene County Tennessee. purchased parcel #1358a containing 137 acres from Alfred Russell

Census 2: 1850. GREENE COUNTY, TENNESSEE PAGE 335B #625

He appeared on the census in 1850 in Dist 10, Greene Co, TN.

RADER JOSEPH   49   M   W   VA   GREENE   10 sub 880   335

RADER TENNESSEE	45	F	W	TN	GREENE	10 sub 880	335
RADER ALEXANDER	21	M	W	TN	GREENE	10 sub 880	335
RADER ELBERT	19	M	W	TN	GREENE	10 sub 880	336
RADER JAMES	16	M	W	TN	GREENE	10 sub 880	336
RADER MARY	14	F	W	TN	GREENE	10 sub 880	336
RADER REBECCA	12	F	W	TN	GREENE	10 sub 880	336
RADER PENELOPE	9	F	W	TN	GREENE	10 sub 880	336
RADER JACOB	7	M	W	TN	GREENE	10 sub 880	336
RADER TENNESSEE	5	F	W	TN	GREENE	10 sub 880	336

He was employed in 1850. FARMER

He owned property in 1850. VALUE $1,271.00

Joseph married **Tennessee Tennessee** about 1825 in Tennessee.[4] Tennessee was born about 1805 in Tennessee.[42]

Noted events in her life were:
She appeared on the census in 1840. GREENE COUNTY, TENNESSEE PAGE 77
Census 2: 1850. GREENE COUNTY, TENNESSEE PAGE 335B #625
Children from this marriage were:

+318 M i. **Alexander Rader**[4] was born about 1829 in Greene County, Tennessee.

+319 M ii. **Elbert J. Rader**[4] was born in Apr 1831 in Greene County, Tennessee.

Elbert married **Mary C. Stansbury** (b. Apr 1850) on 13 Feb 1853 in Clay County, Illinois.[4]

+320 M iii. **James Rader**[4] was born about 1834 in Greene County, Tennessee.

James married **Jane Farmer**.

James next married **Augusta** (b. 1835).

+321 F iv. **Mary Rader**[4] was born about 1836 in Greene County, Tennessee.

Mary married **Robert Mccollum**.[4]

+322 F v. **Rebecca Jane Rader**[4] was born about 1838 in Greene County, Tennessee.

Rebecca married **Charles Hoffman** on 14 Dec 1854 in Clay County, Illinois.[4]

+323 F vi. **Penelope Ann Rader**[4] was born about 1841 in Greene County, Tennessee.

Penelope married **Moses H. Monical** (b. 1836) on 25 Jan 1860 in Clay County, Indiana.[4]

+324 M vii. **Jacob W. Rader**[4] was born about 1843 in Greene County, Tennessee.

Jacob married **Anna** (b. 1839).

+325 F viii. **Tennessee Rader**[4] was born about 1845 in Greene County, Tennessee.

48. Jesse Rader[1, 2, 3, 4, 6, 7, 8, 10, 11, 12, 14, 15] (*Jacob^2, Casper Sr^1*) was born in 1804 in VA and died in 1890 in Greene County, Tennessee at age 86.

General Notes: Marriage # 2956 Oct 4, 1828 Jesse Rader -- Elizabeth Willoughby md 22 Oct 1828 -- Peter Cobble, J.P. In 1850, 1860 and 1870(census) Jesse and Elizabeth were living in Gustavus District number 6 in Greene County, Tennessee and in 1880(census) he was living in the same district with his second wife Catherine. Catherine is buried in the Mount Hope Church cemetery. Jesse Rader's children can be found in the Greene County, Tennessee County Court minutes, volumn 32 and page 512 dated June 10, 1891.

Catherine (Ketron) Laughner could have been the wife of Daniel Laughner. From census records the two women were born about the same year and it is known that Daniel Laughner died around 1850. Daniel Laughner was the son of John Laughner and Mary Rader Laughner. For more on Mary's family see the Mary Rader Family of Henry.

CATHERINE AND JESSE WERE FIRST COUSINS ONCE REMOVED. THEY MARRIE LATE IN LIFE AND HAD NO CHILDREN.

Bible Family, Terri Strotman, World Connect Project

Noted events in his life were:

He owned land on 13 Apr 1833 in Lick Creek Valley, Greene County Tennessee. Purchased 80 acres Plot #1358c from John Love

[Caption: Mt Valley Rd   087]

He owned land on 13 Apr 1833 in Lick Creek Valley, Greene County Tennessee. Purchased 80 acres Plot #1358c from John Love

He appeared on the census in 1840. GREENE COUNTY, TENNESSEE PAGE 76

He owned land on 19 Jun 1841 in Lick Creek Valley, Greene County Tennessee. Purchased 90 acre plot #1339F from Alfred Russell

[Caption: Mt Valley Road] [Description: 088]

He owned land on 2 Nov 1846 in Lick Creek Valley, Greene County Tennessee. purchased 105 acre plot # 1339C from Henderson Lady

He owned land on 2 Nov 1846 in Lick Creek Valley, Greene County Tennessee. purchased 105 acre plot # 1339C from Henderson Lady

He was employed in 1850. FARMER

He owned property in 1850. VALUE $1,700.00

Census 1: 1850. GREENE COUNTY, TENNESSEE PAGE 335B #623

He owned land on 24 Dec 1855 in Lick Creek Valley, Greene County Tennessee. Purchased parcel #1359F containing 54 acres from Thomas P Morgan

[Caption: on ridge 092]

He owned land on 24 Dec 1855 in Lick Creek Valley, Greene County Tennessee. Purchased parcel #1359F containing 54 acres from Thomas P Morgan

Census 2: 1860. GREENE COUNTY TENNESSEE PAGE 244 LINE 1225

He owned land on 18 Jun 1860 in Lick Creek Valley, Greene County Tennessee. Purchased parcel # 1359E containing 77 acres from Franklin Pinkston

[Caption: Mt valley rd 091]

He owned land on 18 Jun 1860 in Lick Creek Valley, Greene County Tennessee. Purchased parcel # 1359E containing 77 acres from Franklin Pinkston

Census 3: 1870. GREENE COUNTY, TENNESSEE PAGE 229 LINE 67

He appeared on the census in 1880 in Greene County, Tennessee. Census Place:District 6, Greene, Tennessee

Source:FHL Film 1255258 National Archives Film T9-1258   Page 89B

1880 Census for District 6,Greene,Tennessee

RelationSexMarrRaceAgeBirthplace

Jessee Rader Self M Male W 76 VA Farmer VA VA

Catherine Wife M Female W 58 TN Keeping House VA VA

He owned land on 2 Nov 1846 in Lick Creek Valley, Greene County Tennessee. purchased 105 acre plot # 1339C from Henderson Lady

Jesse married **Catharine (Ketron) Catron**, daughter of **Valentine Catron** and **Eve Missemer**. Catharine was born about 1823, died on 8 Dec 1896 in , , Greene, Tennessee about age 73, and was buried in , MT Hope Cem, Greene, Tennessee.

Jesse next married **Elizabeth Willoughby** on 22 Oct 1828 in Greene County, Tennessee.[4] Elizabeth was born about 1810 in TN and died on 10 Mar 1875 in Greene County, Tennessee about age 65.

Noted events in their marriage were:

Alt Marriage: 26 Oct 1828, Greene County, Tennessee.[4]
Alt Marriage: 26 Oct 1828.
Noted events in her life were:
She appeared on the census in 1840. GREENE COUNTY, TENNESSEE PAGE 76
Census 1: 1850. GREENE COUNTY, TENNESSEE PAGE 335B #623

Census 2: 1860. GREENE COUNTY TENNESSEE PAGE 244 LINE 1225
Census 3: 1870. GREENE COUNTY, TENNESSEE PAGE 229 LINE 67
Alt Death: 1872, Greene County, Tennessee.

Children from this marriage were:

+326 F   i.   **Mary Ann Rader**[4,7] was born about 1830 in Greene County, Tennessee and died before 1891 in Greene County, Tennessee.

Mary married **Seymore Haun** (b. 9 May 1825, d. 5 Oct 1879) on 11 Dec 1851 in Greene County, Tennessee.[79]

+327 M   ii.   **Dr. John Asberry Rader**[4,7] was born on 31 Jan 1835 in Greene County, Tennessee, died on 6 Dec 1894 in Greene County, Tennessee at age 59, and was buried in George Jackson Cemetery, Mowhawk, Greene County, Tennessee.

John married **Lollie Laura Jackson** (b. 26 Feb 1847, d. 27 Aug 1909) on 14 Jul 1868 in Greene County, Tennessee.

+328 F   iii. **Martha J. Rader**[4,7] was born on 18 May 1839 in Greene County, Tennessee, died on 2 Jul 1919 in Greene County, Tennessee at age 80, and was buried in Bible's Chapel Cemetery, Greene County, Tennessee.

Martha married **Marion B. Vance** (b. 13 Dec 1830, d. 7 Feb 1897) on 17 Nov 1859 in Greene County, Tennessee.[4]

+329 F   iv.   **Emiline Jane Rader**[4,7] was born on 11 Feb 1846 in Greene County, Tennessee,[21] died on 27 Feb 1899 in Greene County, Tennessee[21] at age 53, and was buried in Bible's Chapel, Greene Co., TN.[21]

Emiline married **Phillip M. (K.) Bible** (b. Abt 1845) on 16 Aug 1868 in Greene County, Tennessee.

+330 F   v.   **Nancy C. Rader**[4,7] was born on 29 Apr 1847 in Greene County, Tennessee, died in 1929 in Greene County, Tennessee at age 82, and was buried in Crosby Cemetery, Greene County, Tennessee.

Nancy married **James A. Riley Day** (b. 1 Oct 1842, d. 14 Feb 1916) on 7 Feb 1867 in Greene County, Tennessee.

+331 F   vi.   **Elizabeth Laura Jane 'Eliza' Rader**[4,7] was born on 14 May 1849 in Mohawk, Greene County, Tennessee, died on 27 May 1932 in Bible's Chapel, Greene Co., TN at age 83, and was buried in Bible's Chapel, Greene Co., TN.

Elizabeth married **William Harrison Bible** (b. 15 Jan 1843, d. 22 Apr 1925) on 19 Sep 1869 in Greene County, Tennessee.

Jesse next married **Eliza J. 'Hannah' Willoughby**, daughter of **John M. Willoughby** and **Elizabeth 'Eliza' Rader**, on 26 Oct 1828. Eliza was born on 10 Aug 1854 in Bulls Gap, Greene County, Tennessee and died on 26 Nov 1938 at age 84.

Noted events in her life were:

Census 1: 1870. DISTRICT 6, GREENE COUNTY, TENNESSEE LINE 141

Jesse next married **Catherine Laughner**, daughter of **John Lauchner** and **Mary Rader**, on 14 Oct 1875 in Greene County, Tennessee. Catherine was born in 1823 in , , Greene, Tennessee, died on 9 Dec 1896 in Greene County, Tennessee at age 73, and was buried in Mt. Hope Methodist Cemetery, Greene County, Tennessee.

General Notes: CATHERINE AND JESSE WERE FIRST COUSINS ONCE REMOVED. THEY MARRIE LATE IN LIFE AND HAD NO CHILDREN.

Catherine was mentioned in the settlement document for the estate of Henry Rader in 1859 and she was not married at that time. It is not confirmed that she married Aquilla Jackson and the marriage date above is only the bond date.

1880 Census for District 6,Greene,Tennessee

Jessee Rader Self M Male W 76 VA Farmer VA VA

Catherine Wife M Female W 58 TN Keeping House VA VA

Noted events in her life were:

She appeared on the census in 1850. GUSTAVUS DIST. 6, GREENE COUNTY, TENNESSEE,

Census 1: 1880. GREENE COUNTY, TENNESSEE PAGE 18B LINE 157

49. Sarah 'Sally' Rader $^{1, 2, 3, 4, 6, 7, 8, 10, 11, 12, 14, 15}$ ($Jacob^2$, $Casper\ Sr^1$) was born on 21 Mar 1806 in Wythe County, Virginia ^{32} and died before 1860 in Midway, Greene Co., TN. Another name for Sarah was @I508848@.

General Notes: The birth date of Sarah is not known but her baptisimal date was March 21, 1806 and is recorded in the St. Johns Lutheran Church record of Wytheville, Virginia. Sarah and Jacob were living in Greene County, Tennessee in 1850 and Jacob's occupation was blacksmith(Census). In 1860 Jacob had apparently died and Sarah was living with her children in Greene County, Tennessee. Jacob Cobble lived in Midway, Tennessee in the house where Ethel Cobble lived for many years. The house is located at the headwaters of the spring which feeds Muddy Creek in front of the Solan Keicker place. After Jacob and Sarah died their house became the property of their daughter Martha Jane Cobble. Martha Jane lived here all her life and raised a large family. Jacob Cobble not only operated a blacksmith shop but also ran a tavern and produced his own alcohol for sale. His blacksmith shop and tavern were located across the road from his house and near the spring.

Lutheran Housewife

Noted events in her life were:
Baptisimal: 21 Mar 1806, St. Johns Lutheran Church, Wytheville, Wythe Co., VA.
She was baptized on 6 Jul 1806 in St. John's, Lutheran, Wytheville, Wythe Co, VA.
She appeared on the census in 1850 in Greene County, Tennessee. PG. 324 #458
Place Lived (2): Between 1850 and 1860, Greene County, Tennessee.^{28}
Alt Death: After 1860.

Sarah married **Jacob 'Jake' Cobble**, son of **Unknown** and **Unknown**, on 2 Sep 1825 in Greene County, Tennessee.[28] Jacob was born in 1798 in Greene County, Tennessee and died before 1860 in Midway, Greene County, Tennessee. Another name for Jacob was @I508846@.

Noted events in their marriage were:

Alt Marriage: 26 Sep 1825, , , Greene, Tennessee, USA.

Alt Marriage: 26 Sep 1825, Greene County, Tennessee.[28]

>General Notes: December 5, 1820, John Cobble to Peter Cobble, both of Greene County, Tennessee, 104 acres of land being where Michael Cobble now lives, witnessed by Jacob Cobble, Phillip Cobble.

Farmer, Blacksmith, Tavern Owner

Noted events in his life were:

He was employed. BLACKSMITH & TAVERN OWNER

He was employed.[80]

Place Lived (2): Between 1830 and 1850, Greene County, Tennessee.

He appeared on the census in 1850. GREENE COUNTY, TENNESSEE PG. 324 #458

Children from this marriage were:

+332 M   i.   **John Cobble**[4,7] was born in 1831 in Midway, Greene County, Tennessee.

+333 M   ii. **Unknown Cobble**[4] was born between 1825 and 1830 in Midway, Greene Co., TN.

+334 F   iii. **Polly Ann Cobble**[4,7] was born in 1833 in Midway, Greene Co, TN.

Polly married **Thomas Clifford** (b. 1830) on 23 Jul 1853 in Greene County, Tennessee.

+335 F   iv. **Unknown Cobble** was born between 1825 and 1830 in Midway, Greene Co., TN.

+336 F   v.   **Elizabeth 'Bets' Cobble**[4,7] was born in 1835 in Midway, Greene County, Tennessee.

Elizabeth married **Unknown Haun**.

Elizabeth next married **Patrick Clifford** (b. Abt 1823) on 31 Jul 1854 in Greene County, Tennessee.[81]

Elizabeth next married **Christopher A. Haun** (b. 1825, d. 17 Dec 1861).

+337 M   vi. **James Cobble**[4,7] was born on 18 Aug 1836 in Midway, Greene County, Tennessee, died on 13 May 1916 in Greene County, Tennessee at age 79, and was buried on 14 May 1916 in Mt. Hope Cemetery, Greene County, Tennessee.

James married **Nancy Susong Isley** (b. 1837) on 13 May 1860 in Greene County, Tennessee.

James next married **Margaret D. Masoner** (b. 28 Jan 1845, d. 10 Feb 1889) on 13 May 1877 in Greene County, Tennessee.

James next married **Martha Tulley** (b. 3 Feb 1850, d. 2 May 1913).

+338 F vii. **Martha Jane Cobble**[4,7] was born on 16 Sep 1838 in Midway, Greene Co., TN,[21,82] died on 13 Mar 1925 in Midway, Greene Co., TN[21,83] at age 86, and was buried on 15 Mar 1925 in Midway, Greene Co., TN.[83]

Martha married.

Martha married **Adam Lonas** (b. Mar 1821, d. 18 May 1905).

+339 F viii. **Anna Cobble**[4,7] was born in 1842 in Midway, Greene County, Tennessee and died before 1860 in Midway, Greene Co., TN.

+340 F ix. **Tennessee Cobble**[4,7] was born in 1846 in Midway, Greene County, Tennessee.

Tennessee married **Elbert Hall** (b. Abt 1848) on 2 Aug 1867 in Greene County, Tennessee.

50. Elizabeth 'Eliza' Rader[1,2,3,4,6,7,8,10,11,12,14,15] (*Jacob*[2], *Casper Sr*[1]) was born on 15 Jul 1808 in Wytheville, Wythe County, Virginia,[52] died on 27 Dec 1893 in Greene County, Tennessee[52] at age 85, and was buried in Willoughby Cem, Gap Creek, Greene Co, TN. Other names for Elizabeth were @I508877@, and ??? Elizabeth.

> General Notes: They lived near Devil's Nose, Greene County, owned large amount of land had several girls and one son. The land was divided and made several good homes.
> Noted events in her life were:
> She was baptized on 25 Sep 1808 in Wytheville, Wythe County, Virginia. St John's Lutheran
> She appeared on the census in 1850. GREENE COUNTY, TENNESSEE
> Census 2: 1870. DISTRICT 6, GREENE COUNTY, TENNESSEE LINE 141
> She appeared on the census in 1880 in Greene County, Tennessee. Census Place:District 6, Greene, Tennessee
> Source:FHL Film 1255258 National Archives Film T9-1258 Page 83A
> RelationSexMarrRaceAgeBirthplace
> Eliza WILLOUGHBYSelfFWW72VA
> Occ:Keeping HouseFa: VAMo: VA
> She has conflicting death information of 27 Dec 1899 and Greene County, Tennessee.

Elizabeth married **John M. Willoughby** on 23 Apr 1829 in Greene County, Tennessee.[53] John was born on 12 May 1805 in Tennessee[52] and died on 18 Sep 1869[52] at age 64.

> General Notes: Greene County marriage # 3024 Apr 20, 1829 John Willoughby -- Eliza Rader -- William Willoughby -- md 23 Apr 1829 -- John G. Stout.

Noted events in his life were:

He appeared on the census in 1850. 9TH. DISTRICT, GREENE COUNTY, TENNESSEE

Census 2: 1870. DISTRICT 6, GREENE COUNTY, TENNESSEE LINE 141

Children from this marriage were:

+341 F i. **Elizabeth Willoughby**[4] was born on 9 Jan 1830 in Bulls Gap, Greene County, Tennessee and died on 31 Jul 1908 at age 78.

Elizabeth married **James Wesley Myers** (b. 1829).

+342 F ii. **Mary Willoughby**[4,7] was born on 11 Apr 1832 in Bulls Gap, Greene County, Tennessee.

Mary married **John Barlow** on 8 Nov 1855 in Greene County, Tennessee.[84]

+343 M iii. **William Willoughby**[7] was born about 1837.

+344 F iv. **Anna Willoughby**[4,7] was born on 24 Aug 1835 in Bulls Gap, Greene County, Tennessee[52] and died on 23 May 1921[52] at age 85.

Anna married **John Tivis Myers** (b. 1830, d. 1902) on 28 Oct 1856 in Greene County, Tennessee.[85]

+345 M v. **William R. Willoughby**[4] was born on 11 Dec 1838 in Bulls Gap, Greene County, Tennessee and died in 1884 at age 46.

William married **Candace Harmon** (b. 1849).

+346 M vi. **Bedford Willoughby**[7] was born about 1843.

+347 M vii. **Granville Willoughby**[4,7] was born on 26 Apr 1841 in Bulls Gap, Greene County, Tennessee and died on 24 May 1863 at age 22.

+348 M viii. **John Bedford Willoughby**[4] was born on 3 Jun 1843 in Bulls Gap, Greene County, Tennessee and died on 3 Sep 1865 at age 22.

+349 F ix. **Winnie Willoughby**[4] was born on 8 Aug 1845 in Bulls Gap, Greene County, Tennessee and died on 25 Sep 1845 in Bulls Gap, Hawkins County, Tennessee.

+350 F x. **Nancy Willoughby**[4,7] was born on 6 Apr 1847 in Bulls Gap, Greene County, Tennessee, died on 17 Aug 1928 in Greene County, Tennessee at age 81, and was buried in Willoughby Family Cemetery, Greene County, Tennessee.

Nancy married **James Taylor Harmon** (b. 15 Apr 1847, d. 26 Jun 1917) on 17 Oct 1867 in Greene County, Tennessee.

+351 F xi. **Sarah 'Sadie' Jane Willoughby**[1,2,3,4,6,7,8,10,11,12,14,15] was born on 30 Nov 1849 in Bulls Gap, Hawkins County, Tennessee, died on 3 Feb 1938 in Greene County, Tennessee at age 88, and was buried in Willoughby Cemetery, Greene Co., TN.

Sarah married **William Minnis Rader**[86] (b. 26 Aug 1851, d. 10 Mar 1935) on 1 Nov 1877 in Greene County, Tennessee.

+352 F xii. **Eliza J. 'Hannah' Willoughby**[2,4,6,11,14] was born on 10 Aug 1854 in Bulls Gap, Greene County, Tennessee and died on 26 Nov 1938 at age 84.

Eliza married **Eli Haun** on 15 May 1879.[4]

Eliza next married **Jesse Rader** (b. 1804, d. 1890) on 26 Oct 1828.

(Duplicate Line. See Person 48)

51. **Jacob Rader**[4, 7] ($Jacob^2$, $Casper\ Sr^1$) was born about 1809 in Greene County, Tennessee and died before 1822.

   General Notes: Not listed in fathers probate. Must of died before 1822 childless !

52. **Martin George Rader**[1, 2, 3, 4, 6, 7, 8, 10, 11, 12, 14, 15] ($Jacob^2$, $Casper\ Sr^1$) was born on 23 Feb 1811 in Mohawk, Greene Co, TN and died before 1850 in Capt. Mcpherons, Greene Co, TN. Another name for Martin was Martin George.

   General Notes: Greene Co., Marriage # 3490 July 2, 1833 Martin G. Rader --Polly Lady -- George Jones -- md 16 JUL 1833 -- Jepse McCaile, L.D.

   Noted events in his life were:

   He owned land on 9 Sep 1852 in Lick Creek Valley, Greene County Tennessee. Purchased 96 acres from Alfred Russell #1339

Tom White Holler 093]

   He owned land on 9 Sep 1852 in Lick Creek Valley, Greene County Tennessee. Purchased 96 acres from Alfred Russell #1339

Martin married **Mary A. 'Polly' Lady** on 16 Jul 1833 in Greene County, Tennessee. Mary was born on 10 Dec 1815 and died on 11 Dec 1895 in Greene County, Tennessee at age 80.

Noted events in her life were:

She appeared on the census in 1850. GREENE COUNTY, TENNESSEE PAGE 336 #628

She appeared on the census in 1850 in Greene County, Tennessee.

RADER	MARY	36	F	W	TN	GREENE	10 sub 880	336
RADER	JAMES	14	M	W	TN	GREENE	10 sub 880	336
RADER	OLENA	9	F	W	TN	GREENE	10 sub 880	336
RADER	LAWSON	7	M	W	TN	GREENE	10 sub 880	336
RADER	MARY	6	F	W	TN	GREENE	10 sub 880	336

She owned property in 1850. VALUE $150.00

Census 1: 1860. GREENE COUNTY, TENNESSEE PAGE 384 #1199
Census 2: 1870. GREENE COUNTY, TENNESSEE PAGE 231 LINE 96

Children from this marriage were:

+353 F i. **Melvina Rader**[4] was born on 28 Jan 1835 in Tennessee.

Melvina married **William Lady** (b. 1829) on 29 Jun 1851 in Greene County, Tennessee.

+354 F ii. **Nancy Elizabeth Rader**[1, 2, 3, 4, 6, 8, 10, 11, 12, 14, 15] was born on 23 Mar 1836 in Greene County, Tennessee, died on 3 Mar 1913 in Greene County, Tennessee at age 76, and was buried in , Timber Ridge Cem, Greene, Tennessee.

Nancy married **William M. 'Bill' Rader** (b. 30 Sep 1838, d. 28 Sep 1897) on 12 Jul 1860 in , J K Hancher, Min, Greene, Tennessee.

(Duplicate Line. See Person 226)

Nancy next married **Jacob Mcnew** (b. Nov 1837) after 1897.

+355 M iii. **James Polk Rader**[4] was born on 14 Jul 1837 in Greene County, Tennessee, died on 25 Jul 1863 in Fort Delaware, Del. Civil War at age 26, and was buried in Salem, New Jersey Finn's Point, National Cemetery.

+356 F iv. **Sarah Jane Rader**[4] was born on 14 Mar 1839 in Greene County, Tennessee.

Sarah married **William Lynch** on 26 Jul 1857 in Greene County, Tennessee.

+357 F v. **Arlena 'Orlena' Rader**[4] was born on 3 Nov 1840 in Greene County, Tennessee.

Arlena married **Isaac Lane** on 19 Jan 1860 in Greene County, Tennessee.

+358 M vi. **Lawson G. Rader**[4] was born on 11 Dec 1843 in Greene County, Tennessee and died in Civil War.

+359 F vii. **Mary T. Rader**[4] was born on 10 Mar 1845 in Greene County, Tennessee.

+360 F viii. **Lourinda E. Rader**[1, 2, 3, 4, 6, 8, 10, 11, 12, 14, 15] was born on 7 Jul 1850 in Greene County, Tennessee, died on 2 Sep 1923 in , , Greene, Tennessee at age 73, and was buried in MT Hope.

Lourinda married **Andrew Jackson G. Rader** (b. 17 Mar 1853, d. 28 Jun 1891) on 16 Dec 1871 in Greene County, Tennessee.

Lourinda next married **Strand**.

Lourinda next married **James Sutre Stroud** (b. 23 Aug 1834, d. 18 Feb 1916) on 28 Dec 1913 in Greene County, Tennessee.

+361 F ix. **Louisa C. Rader**[4] was born on 11 Jan 1854.

+362 F x. **Elizabeth Louise Rader**[4] was born on 11 Jan 1855 in Greene County, Tennessee, died on 29 Jul 1909 in Greene County, Tennessee at age 54, and was buried in Mt. Hope Cemetery, Greene Co., TN.

Elizabeth married **Joseph O. Lane** (b. 17 Sep 1849, d. 10 Mar 1910) on 17 Oct 1869 in Greene County, Tennessee.

53. Susannah Rader[4,7] (*Jacob*[2], *Casper Sr*[1]) was born about 1812 in Greene County, Tennessee and died in 1892 about age 80.

General Notes: Greene Co marr # 3200 Sept 17, 1830 William Etter -- Susanna Rader -- William Laughner -- md 19 Sep 1830 -- Philip Henkel
Noted events in her life were:
She appeared on the census in 1850. BOONE COUNTY, INDIANA   PAGE 185   LINE 1764
Census 1: 1860. MONTGOMERY COUNTY, RIPLEY TWP., INDIANA PAGE 214 LINE 163
Census 2: 1870. MONTGOMERY COUNTY, RIPLEY TWP., INDIANA PAGE 167 LINE 99
Census 3: 1880. MONTGOMERY COUNTY, RIPLEY TWP., INDIANA PAGE 19 LINE 186

Susannah married **William Etter**, son of **John Etter** and **Phobe Michaels**, on 19 Sep 1830 in Greene County, Tennessee.[54] William was born on 21 Apr 1806 in Greene County, Tennessee and died on 29 Aug 1860 in Montgomery, Daviess Co., IN at age 54.

Noted events in his life were:

Alt Birth: 21 Apr 1806, Wythe County, Virginia.

He appeared on the census in 1850. BOONE COUNTY, INDIANA PAGE 185 LINE 1764

Census 1: 1860. MONTGOMERY COUNTY, RIPLEY TWP., INDIANA PAGE 214 LINE 163

Children from this marriage were:

+363 F i. **Martha Ann Etter**[4] was born on 24 Apr 1832 in Greene County, Tennessee.

Martha married **Andrew J. Lucas** (b. 1831) on 22 Nov 1858 in Boone, IN.

+364 F ii. **Mary Jane Etter**[4] was born on 29 Aug 1834 in Greene County, Tennessee.

Mary married **Hugh A. Hickey** on 7 Nov 1853 in Boode, IN.

+365 M iii. **Jefferson Etter**[4] was born on 14 Feb 1837 in Boone County, Indiana.

Jefferson married **Mary Elizabeth Denman** (b. Aug 1846) on 3 Aug 1862.

+366 F iv. **Amanda C. 'Mandy' Etter**[4] was born on 6 Mar 1842 in Boone County, Indiana.

+367 M v. **Andrew Etter**[4] was born on 17 Aug 1844 in Boone County, Indiana.

Andrew married **Mary M.** (b. Feb 1852).

+368 M vi. **John Etter**[4] was born on 26 Jan 1847 in Boone County, Indiana.

+369 F vii. **Eliza Emmeline Etter**[4] was born on 10 Jan 1850 in Boone County, Indiana.

Eliza married **Josephus Brown** (b. Sep 1855) on 28 Jan 1874.

+370 M viii. **William Laughner Etter**[4] was born on 11 Dec 1852 in Indiana and died on 7 Apr 1857 at age 4.

+371 M ix. **Joseph Etter**[4] was born on 11 Jun 1857 in Indiana.

Joseph married **Amanda J. Hebarger** (b. 1858) on 6 Jan 1879.

54. Peter R. Rader[1, 2, 3, 4, 6, 7, 8, 10, 11, 12, 14, 15] (*Jacob*[2], *Casper Sr*[1]) was born on 15 Oct 1819 in Mohawk, Greene Co, TN and died on 16 May 1877 in Bulls Gap, Greene County, Tennessee at age 57.

Death Notes: Peter died at his home in Bulls Gap, Tennessee on May 16, 1877(Greene County, Tennessee Chancery Court record in volumn 1876 to 1884, page 243 states he died on November 20, 1877). Much of the information on Keziah and Peter Rader was obtained from Peter's military file.

Noted events in his life were:

Alt Birth: 1822, Mohawk, Greene County, Tennessee.

Bound out: 28 Jul 1834, Greene County, Tennessee. Peter Rader was bound to William Rader his guardian(Greene County, Tennessee Guardians and Orphans Court, page 414 dated July 28, 1834).

He appeared on the census in 1840 in Greene County, Tennessee. He apparently was living with his mother in Greene County, Tennessee in 1840(Census).

He owned land on 3 Aug 1841 in Lick Creek Valley, Greene County Tennessee. He purchased parcel #1359C containing 25 acres from Alfred Russell

Map of land Peter R Rader owned on 13 Mar 1845 in Greeneville,

Greene County, Tennessee. He purchased parcel #1018 containing 7.5 acres in Greeneville

He appeared on the census in 1850. GREENE COUNTY, TENNESSEE PAGE 335A #611

He appeared on the census in 1850 in Greene County, Tennessee.

| RADER PETER R | 28 | M | W | TN | GREENE | 10 sub 880 | 335 |
| RADER KIZIAH | 26 | F | W | TN | GREENE | 10 sub 880 | 335 |

Source Citations

RADER GEORGE	5	M	W	TN	GREENE	10 sub 880	335
RADER DAWSON	1	M	W	TN	GREENE	10 sub 880	335
RADER ELIZABETH	76	F	W	VA	GREENE	10 sub 880	335

He was employed in 1850. FARMER

He owned property in 1850. VALUE $700.00

Census 1: 1860, Greene County, Tennessee. DIST. 6, GREENE COUNTY, TENNESSEE PAGE 180 & 181 #1219

In 1860(census) Peter was living with his wife in Blue Springs District number 19 in Greene County, Tennessee.

He owned land in 1860 in Lick Creek Valley, Greene County Tennessee. purchased parcel #1359B from Riley Wallace

Military: 15 Apr 1863, Greeneville, Tennessee. CORP. COUNTY F 4TH. REG. TENNESSEE VOLUNTEER INF. REG. UNION

Peter Rader enlisted in the U S Army in Greeneville, Tennessee on April 15, 1863. He was mustered in at Nashville, Tennessee on June 15, 1863 as a Corporal in F Company of the 4th Regiment Tennessee Infantry Volunteers. He was captured at Morristown, Tennessee on February 4, 1865 and taken to Lynchburg, Virginia and subsequently to Richmond arriving March 23, 1865. He was paroled at Boulware and Core's wharf in Virginia on March 26, 1865 and was sent to Camp Chase in Ohio on March 29, 1865 and remained there until April 1, 1865. Peter was mustered out in Nashville, Tennessee on August 2, 1865.

MILITARY DISCHARGE DATE: 12 Aug 1865. CORP. COUNTY F 4TH. REG. TENNESSEE VOLUNTEER INF. REG. UNION

Census 2: 1870. GREENE COUNTY, TENNESSEE PAGE 226 LINE 16

Peter married **Kegish S. 'Kissiar' Rhea Ray?**, daughter of **Unknown** and **Unknown**, on 31 Dec 1844 in Greene County, Tennessee. Kegish was born about 1824 in Greene County, Tennessee and died on 3 Jan 1903 in Greene County, Tennessee about age 79. Other names for Kegish were @I509018@, Kissiar Ray, and Kegish S. 'Kissiar' Rhea.

Marriage Notes: Greene County Marriage # 950 Dec 31, 1844 Peter R. Rader -- Kezia S. Rhea -- Jesse Rader md 31 Dec 1844 -- Wm McDonald J.P. Keziah was the daughter of John and Mary Rhea. At his death John Rhea owned considerable property in the town of Greeneville, Tennessee located on Main and Ash streets. He raised a large family consisting of eleven children. For records relating to the Rhea family see Greene County, Tennessee Chancery Court volumn 1844 to 1857, page 44 dated November 10, 1845; page 74 dated May 11, 1846; page 134 dated May 13, 1847; page 182 dated May 10, 1848(contains the children and son in laws of John Rhea).

Noted events in her life were:

Census 1: 1850. GREENE COUNTY, TENNESSEE PAGE 335A #611
Census 2: 1860. DIST. 6, GREENE COUNTY, TENNESSEE PAGE 180 & 181 #1219
Census 3: 1870. GREENE COUNTY, TENNESSEE PAGE 226 LINE 16

Resided: 23 Jun 1877, Bulls Gap, Greene County, Tennessee. Keziah was living in Bulls Gap, Tennessee in Greene County on June 23, 1877 according to an affidavit she signed on that date.

She appeared on the census in 1880 in District 6, Greene, Tennessee. Census Place:District 6, Greene, Tennessee
Source:FHL Film 1255258 National Archives Film T9-1258   Page 90C
RelationSexMarrRaceAgeBirthplace
Keziah RADERSelfFWW55TN Occ:Keeping HouseFa: NCMo: TN
Sarah A. RADERDauFSW18TN Occ:At HomeFa: TNMo: TN
Ulyesses G. RADERSonMSW15TN Occ:Farm LaborerFa: TNMo: TN
Isac N. RADERSonMSW12TN Occ:Farm LaborerFa: TNMo: TN
Census 5: 1900. GREENE COUNTY, TENNESSEE DIST. #6 LINE 114

Children from this marriage were:

+372 M i. **George H. Rader**[4] was born on 25 Nov 1845 in Mohawk, Greene Co, TN, died on 11 Mar 1910 in Mohawk, Greene Co, TN at age 64, and was buried in Bible Family Cemetery, Concord, Greene County, Tennessee.

George married **Hannah Elizabeth Haun** (b. 30 Nov 1846, d. 5 Apr 1889) on 1 Nov 1866 in Greene County, Tennessee.

George next married **Martha A. 'Mattie' Melton** (b. 31 Aug 1863, d. 14 Jun 1928) on 27 Jan 1892 in Whitesburg, Hamblen Co., TN.

+373 M ii. **Dawson R. Rader**[4] was born on 10 Jul 1849 in Mohawk, Greene Co, TN, died on 19 Nov 1929 in Greene County, Tennessee at age 80, and was buried in Willoughby Cemetery, Greene Co., TN.

Dawson married **Melissa Jemima Phillips** (b. 15 Jan 1848, d. 10 Jul 1918).

+374 F iii. **Mary Jane 'Mollie' Rader**[1, 2, 3, 4, 6, 8, 10, 11, 12, 14, 15] was born about 1851 in Mohawk, Greene Co., TN and died on 14 Mar 1906 about age 55.

Mary married **John T. Rader** (b. Mar 1846, d. 8 Apr 1904) on 9 Apr 1869 in Greene County, Tennessee.

+375 M iv. **Carroll Drake Rader**[4] was born on 23 Feb 1855.

Carroll married **Mattie** (b. 1858).

+376 F v. **Florence E. Rader**[4] was born on 5 Aug 1851.

Florence married **John Haun** on 16 Sep 1878 in Greene County, Tennessee.

+377 F vi. **Sarah Alice Rader**[4] was born on 2 Jan 1862 in Mohawk, Greene County, Tennessee.

Sarah married **J. W. Bullen** on 3 Apr 1880 in Greene County, Tennessee.

+378 F vii. **Melissa A. Rader**[4] was born about 1863 in Mohawk, Greene Co, TN and died before 1877.

+379 M viii. **Ulysses Grant Rader**[4] was born on 24 Jul 1864 in Mohawk, Greene County, Tennessee, died on 11 Sep 1939 in Greene County, Tennessee at age 75, and was buried in Phillippi Church, Greene County, Tennessee.

>Ulysses married **Sudie Davis** on 12 Jan 1911 in Bulls Gap, Greene County, Tennessee.

+380 M ix. **Isaac Newton Rader**[4] was born on 10 May 1866 in Mohawk, Greene Co, TN, died in 1903 in Greene County, Tennessee at age 37, and was buried in Oak Grove Cem, Greeneville, Greene Co, TN.

>Isaac married **Jennie Click** (b. Sep 1869, d. 1917) on 14 Jun 1893 in Greene County, Tennessee.

Peter next married **Kezia S. Rhea** on 31 Dec 1844. Kezia was born on 28 Jun 1824 and died on 3 Jan 1903 at age 78.

55. Henry Rader (*Casper Jr.*[2], *Casper Sr*[1]) died on 16 Aug 1826 in Sevier County, Tennessee and was buried in Fox Cemetery, Sevier County, Tennessee.

56. Casper Rader (*Casper Jr.*[2], *Casper Sr*[1]) was born on 8 Aug 1829, died on 27 Jun 1834 in Sevier County, Tennessee at age 4, and was buried in Fox Cemetery, Sevier County, Tennessee.

57. Synthia Rader[34] (*Phillip Sr.*[2], *Casper Sr*[1]) was born on 13 Jan 1812 in Ohio.[34] Another name for Synthia was Cynthia Rader.

>Synthia married **Julien Murden**[34,34]. Julien was born in 1818 in Ohio.[34]

58. Henrietta Rader[34] (*Phillip Sr.*[2], *Casper Sr*[1]) was born on 7 Mar 1818 in Montgomery County, Ohio.[34]

>General Notes: Henrietta Rader….born in Ohio. Married ? Murden. No further info

>(Info submitted by A. Shepherd)

>§"Children of Philip Rader, Sr…..Henrietta, b. 1818 Ohio, m. 1837 to Joseph Fentres (Source 1)

>§"Henrietta, dau of Philip, St., and Elizabeth (Siddon) Rader, m. September

>22, 1837 to Joseph Fentress (L.D.M. Brien, Montgomery Co Ohio Marriages 1803-1851). Joseph Fentres age 34, b. Ohio, & Henrietta, 33, householders of Henry Twp, Fulton Co Ind, in Census 1850 had children: Philip, 10 b. Ohio; (J. or I.) A.,

>8 b. Ohio; Jas., 6 b. Ind; Catherine, 5 b. Ind; Elizabeth, 3 b. Ind; and Davis, 10 months b. Ind. There was not found a record of this Fentres family in Henry Twp, Census 1860. There is a record of a Joseph Fenters marriage to Clarissa Strong, March 14, 1858 (Fulton Co Ind M.R.). Joseph & Clarissa, both 54, and both b. Ohio, were householders of Henry Twp, Fulton Co Ind, in the Census, 1870, with Davis 20, and Martha E. 10. Joseph Fenters, age 64, b. Ohio (parents both b. So. Car) "widowed" was living with the household of Isaac & Lydia Sears in Henry Twp, Fulton Co Ind, in Census 1880." (Source 1)

>§CHILDREN

- Philip…b. Ohio
- (J. or I.) A…b. Ohio
- Jas…b. IN
- Catherine…b. IN
- Elizabeth…b. IN
- Davis…b, IN

Henrietta next married **Joseph Fortress** on 22 Sep 1837 in Montgomery County, Ohio.

59. Francis J. Rader (*Phillip Sr.^{2}, Casper Sr^1*) was born in 1819 in Ohio.

Noted events in his life were:

He appeared on the census in 1850. NOBLE TOWNSHIP, WABASH COUNTY, INDIANA PAGE 419 LINE 182

Francis married **Harriet Palmer**. Harriet was born in Ohio.

Noted events in her life were:

She appeared on the census in 1850. NOBLE TOWNSHIP, WABASH COUNTY, INDIANA PAGE 419 LINE 182

Children from this marriage were:

+381 F i. **Elizabeth Rader** was born in 1844 in Ohio.

+382 F ii. **Martha A. Rader** was born in 1845 in Ohio.

+383 M iii. **William J. Rader** was born in Aug 1847 in Fulton County, Indiana.

William married **Emma** (b. Sep 1849) in 1873.

+384 M iv. **Austin Rader** was born in 1849 in Indiana.

60. Mary Rader^{34} (*Phillip Sr.^{2}, Casper Sr^1*) was born on 3 May 1820 in Ohio ^{34} and died in 1899 in Miami co, Indiana ^{34} at age 79.

General Notes: · 1860 Census lists: William N. Pearson, age 41, Farmer, b in OH; Mary Pearson, age 42, b. in OH; Eli H, age 18, farm hand, b. in Montgomery Co, OH; William W. age 16, b. in Cass Co, IN; Phillip, age 14, b. in Cass Co, IN; Noah, age 12, b. in Cass Co, IN; Martha J. age 8, b. in Cass Co, IN (1860 Census, Indiana, Cass, Miami)

· 1880 Census lists: Noah Pearson, born approx 1847, farm laborer, son (relationship to head-of-household), widower (marital status), Mary Pearson (mother's name), OH (mother and father's birthplace), Miami, Cass, IN. NOTE: Others listed was Eldora and Mary; however, I was unable to obtain a copy. I will go to LDS and obtain a copy in the near future.) (1880 Census, Miami, Cass, IN)

· Indiana WPA Death Record: Mary Pearson, died February 3, 1899, Peru, IN

Book CH-9, page 13) NOTE: This needs to be investigated for additional information in order to document that this is Mary Rader.

· Cemetery records, Eel River Chapel, Jefferson Twp, Miami Co, IN NOTE: Further investigation is needed; however the following is listed at this cemetery:

Pearson, Mary, wife of Wm. (stone under ground)
Pearson, Joseph, son of Wm. & Mary, d. in the U.S.S., Nov 20, 1862, age 21y-9m-23d
Pearson, William N., d. Oct 7, 1875, age 54y-9m-1d.
Pearson, Philip, son of Wm. N. & M., d. in the U>S>S>, April 1, 1862, age 16y-5m-14d
 Also in the same cemetery and same vicinity are:
Pearson
(1)   Hannah, Nov. 4, 1813 - Dec 10, 1900
(2)   William, Jan 30, 1814 - May 23, 1887
(NOTE: Phillip was listed in the 1860 census, age 14. Joseph was not listed but may have been out of the household during the 1860 census due to his age. Death date of William N. corresponds to age listed in the 1860 census. William N. is not listed in the 1880 census.)

· (Rochester Union-Spy, Fri. Dec. 25, 1874) "Mrs. Pearson, of New Waverly, IN, is visiting her brother, David Rader, at this place."

· (Rochester Union-Spy, Fri. Mar. 26, 1875) "Mrs. Philip Rader, of Akron, is visiting in the vicinity of New Waverly, Cass county."

· (Rochester Union-Spy, Fri. Oct. 15, 1875) "Marshall Rader last Thursday received intelligence of the death of a brother-in-law at New Waverly, IN. He left for that place the day following." NOTE: Capt. David Rader was Marshall of Rochester at this time.

Mary married **William N. Pearson**[34 34].   Another name for William was Pierson.

General Notes: CHILDREN OF MARY AND WILLIAM N. PEARSON;
 Joseph b. Feb 1841, died Nov. 20, 1862. (Born in OH?)
 Eli H.   born Abt 1841, Montgomery Co, OH
 William W. b. Abt 1843, Cass Co, IN
 Phillip b. Abt 1845, Cass Co, IN
  Noah   b. Abt 1847, Cass Co., IN
  Martha J. b. Abt 1851, Cass Co., IN

The child from this marriage was:

+385 M   i.   **John Pearson** was born in 1836 in Dayton, Montgomery County, Ohio.

John married **Lydia Wilkinson**.

61. Catherine Rader[34] (*Phillip Sr.*[2], *Casper Sr*[1]) was born on 4 Feb 1822 in Ohio.[34]

General Notes: ·   Census 1870 lists the following: David C. Jenkins, age 48, occupation "teaming" b. in OH;

Catherine, age 48, b. in OH; Olive C. age 18, b. in IN; Eliza B., age 13, b. in IN. (Census 1870, Cass, Miami)

·   Census 1880 lists the following info: David C. Jenkins, age 57, occupation "Keeps boarders", b. in OH, both parents born in S. Carolina; Catherine, age 58, wife, "keeps house", b. in OH, father b. in VA, mother b. in S. Carolina; Scholly, age

---

OBITUARY.
David Clarkson Jenkins, son of David and Ann Jenkins, was born in Miami county, Ohio, June 30, 1822, and died at New Waverly, Ind., August 12, 1892, aged 70 years, 1 months and 12 days.
He was married to Catharine Rader July 4, 1841, and to them were given seven children, four of whom with the mother have passed over the river.
The funeral was from the M. E. church, conducted by the G. A. R., of which the deceased was a member. The number of comrades in line showed that the deceased was held in high esteem by them. A goodly number of the Wm. B. Reyburn Post of Peru attended the funeral. Comrade Jenkins served in the 46th Indiana Volunteer Infantry, which regiment experienced some hard service while in the Southwest. Rev. McNeely, of Tiosa, delivered the address, and he, having been a member of the same regiment, seemed to be touched.
One by one the boys of '61-'65 are dropping out of the ranks; one by one are they answering the last roll call. Not many years more will there be one left to tell of the hardships and privations of a soldier's life.
On behalf of the relatives we would return thanks to those who so kindly assisted in this sad bereavement and to the G. A. R. who were in attendance.

28, "boarder", b. in IN, both parents b. in OH. (1880 Census, New Waverly, Cass Co, Indiana, Roll T9_268, Family History film 1254268, page 240B, enumeration District 26, image 0117; enumerated June 3, 1880) NOTE: Olive C. Jenkins, daughter of David and Catherine, married John K. Schooley on Sept. 24, 1879. Could she have been their "boarder". Was not able to fine David or Catherine in any other census records. No additional info regarding Eliza B.

· Olive C. Jenkins married John K. Schooley on Sept 24, 1879, Cass Co, IN

(Index to Marriage Record 1850-1920 Inclusive Volume III Letters N-Z Inclusive. Record location: Cass County. WPA Original record located County Clerk's Office, Logansport compiled by Indiana WPA 1940) Book 7, page 110 (NOTE: Checked 1870, 1880, 1900, 1920, 1930 for John Schooley....was not able to locate only one record. Possible in household of Onevi and Priscilla E. Schooley, IN, Owen Co, Washington Twp)

· NOTE: A "Mary Jenkins" age 16, was listed in the household of Philip & Margaret Rader in the 1860 Census, Fulton Co, Henry Twp.

Catherine married **David C. Jenkins**[34] in 1841-Jul 1841.[34]

General Notes: CHILDREN OF MARY AND DAVID JENKINS:

Olive C. Jenkins….. born Abt 1852, IN

Eliza B. Jenkins…. born Abt 1857, IN

Catherine next married **David Clarkson Jenkins**, son of **David Jenkins** and **Ann**, on 4 Jul 1841. David was born on 20 Jun 1822 in Miami County, Ohio and died on 12 Aug 1892 in New Waverly, Indiana at age 70.

Noted events in his life were:

Military:46 TH. INDIANA VOLUNTEER INFANTRY CIVIL WAR

62. Hanna J. Rader (*Phillip Sr.*[2], *Casper Sr*[1]) was born about 1823 in Montgomery County, Ohio.

Hanna married **Jeremiah Cupp** on 23 Mar 1845 in Montgomery County, Ohio.

63. Philip Rader Jr.[33, 34] (*Phillip Sr.*[2], *Casper Sr*[1]) was born on 7 Jul 1824 in Montgomery County, Ohio,[34] died on 28 Aug 1899 in Akron, Henry Township, Fulton County, Indiana[34] at age 75, and was buried in 1899 in Akron, Henry Township, Fulton County, Indiana.

General Notes: Regarding Philip Jr this is what it says: Was born in OH July 7, 1824 (parents Philip and Elizabeth (Siddon) Rader....he was German, she Irish) He came to IN with his parents 1842-1843. He worked for his father one year....so Philip Sr did live in the Fulton Co area.

1880 United States Census

Name Relation Marital Status Gender Race Age Birthplace Occupation Father's Birthplace Mother's Birthplace

Philip RADER Self M Male W 55 OH Retired Farmer VA SC
Margaret RADER Wife M Female W 54 DE Keeping House DE DE
Clara L. RADER Dau S Female W 15 IN At Home OH DE

Source Information:
 Census Place Henry, Fulton, Indiana
 Family History Library Film   1254278
 NA Film Number   T9-0278
 Page Number   53A   NA Film Number   T9-0278   Page Number   47B

Philip Jr. lived with his father and step-mother until he was 18. He worked on farms for small pay until 1844 when he rode to Fulton County, Indiana and back on horseback. His enthusiasm for the Hoosier State caused the entire family to move to Akron, Indiana. However, Philip remained in Ohio and taught school during the 1844-45 and 1845-46 terms. He then moved to Indiana where he met the "idol of his heart", Margaret Stradley.

Philip was a splendid marksman with a rifle and killed many wild turkeys and deer. He also loved to ofish and would often get up and catch a string of sunfish before breakfast.

"Pictorial History of America, The Fulton County Edition" by Elia Peattie - published in 1896

PHILIP RADER is a retired farmer and pioneer of Henry township, who has devoted the best energies of his life to the improvement of the lands of Fulton County, transforming the wild tracts into rich fields, whose productiveness adds materially to the properity of the county. He came to Indiana from Ohio, his native state, his birth having occurred in Montgomery County, July 4, 1824. His father, Philip Rader, who was born in Wythe County, Virginia, moved to Ohio in an early day. He was of German descent and married Miss Cress for his first wife and after her death wedded Elizabeth Siddon, of English lineage. With an ax upon his shoulder, Philip Rader, of this sketch, left home to carve out his own fortune, and by working in this way he started in life. After working for one year for his father for $100, he was married Dec. 28, 1846, to Margaret Stradley, and with his bride and his small capital began housekeeping a mile east of Akron on a forty-acre farm which he had purchased. Five years later he sold this place with the intention of removing to Illinois, but circumstances prevented and he purchased his father's farm, which in 1863 he exchanged for 170 acres of land in henry township, two miles east of the village. There he profitably carried on farming until 1886, when with the handsome competence acquired through his own labors he removed to Akron, where he has since lived retired. Mrs. Rader, who has been his faithful helpmeet for many years, was born in Delaware and her father, Caleb Stradley, was among the pioneers who opened up this locality to civilization. He was the first justice of the peace of Henry township, and for several years did his judicial business in his log cabin, two and one-half miles southwest of where Akron now stands. Mr. and Mrs. Rader are the parents of the following named children: W.N., of Henry township; Sarah E., wife of Joseph Nelson, of Disco; Schuyler, of Henry township; Albert W., of Huntingon, Indiana; and Clara, wife of William Morrett, of Henry township. Deeply interested in America, Mr. Rader has traveled quite extensively over this country, thus gaining a knowledge of his native land that could not be acquired from history. Accompanied by his wife, he visited the Centennial exposition in 1876, returning by way of the Atlantic states and visiting New York, Niagara and other points of interest. Some years later they took a six months' trip through the west, at length reaching San Diego, Cal., and returning by way of the Central Pacific route. They thus visited some twenty-six states and territories, and viewed the grandeur of the Rocky mountains and other magnificent scenery of the west. After a life well spent in fruitful toil they are now enjoying rest from labor in their pleasant home in Akron, and Mrs. Rader is now the oldest living resident of Henry township. Her brother, Luther Stradley, was the first white child born in the township.

· "NOTE: Philip, son of Philip, Sr., of Montgomery Co, OH, removed to Henry Twp, Fulton Co, IN, 1842 and married 1846 Margaret M. Stradley

Margaret, born Delaware, daughter of Caleb & Sarah Stradley, migrated to Ohio 1828 - 31, then to IN 1836 - 38. Children of Phillip & Margaret were: Charles Holdiay, Jacob Harrison, Caleb Stradley, Wm. Nelson, Sarah Elizabeth, Schuyler Colfax, Albert Wilbur and Clara Luella. (Source: Family records of Ralph Rader, Akron, IN and of Jean C. Tombaugh; Peattie, "History of Fulton Co IN" pp. 118-119)

· Obituary and Biographical: "Philip Rader was born in Montgomery County, Ohio July 7th 1824; died at his home in Akron, Monday, Aug. 28, 1899, aged 75 years, 1 month and 21 days.

The subject of this sketch came with his parents to this community in early life, in 1845. Having received a fair education for the opportunities afforded in those early days, and by close application and an indomitable will he secured sufficient qualification which enabled him to employ his time several winters teaching school.

December 18, 1946, he was united in marriage with Miss Margaret M. Stradley, his now bereaved widow. To this union eight children were born, three eldest of which were boys who died in infancy. The living children are, W.N. Rader, Sarah E. Nelson, Schuyler C. Rader, A.W. Rader and Clara L. Morrett.

He successfully engaged in farming and stock raising until 1886, when they sold their valuable farm and retired from active business and rendered substantial financial aid to each of his sons and daughters. He purchased a handsome home in Akron where, together they enjoyed their declining days.

He was an extensive traveler, a close observer and thus gained a fund of information which made his company interesting and his conversations profitable to his many friends. In 1876 with Mrs. Rader he visited the Centennial exposition at Philadelphia, and many other places of interest in the eastern part of the U.S. Ten years later they spent a half year in the west and on the Pacific coast, visiting many states and territories and viewing the scenery. He was enthusiastically patriotic which led him to be an exceptional admirer of his country and nation. After the organization of the G.A.R. (Grand Army Republic) by General Logan, being disqualified to join the order by reason of the face that he never served in the army, yet he was a constant contributor to the G.A.R. support, and a regular attendant at all their social meetings. For this, he was chosen by the Post of his town as an honorary member a distinction he particularly enjoyed to the day of his death.

Uncle Philip, as he was familiarly called, was a man of great intellectual force, strong upright character and his word was as good as his bond.

Thus he lived and died teaching us by example the principles of noble manhood, the "noblest works of God".

In the death of Mr. Rader, the community loses an upright citizen, his family a wise councilor, and indulgent husband and father.

The funeral occurred Wednesday from the home conducted by Rev. R.H. Smith in the presence of a large concourse of friends and his body laid peacefully away in the Odd-fellows cemetery." (Source: Akron News, Friday, Sept 1st 1899, S.N. Suesier, Editor & Publisher)

· PHILIP RADER. This well-known farmer and stockman was born in Ohio July 7, 1824, being the oldest son of Philip and Elizabeth (Siddon) Rader; he is on the paternal side of German descent and of the Irish descent on his mother's side.

The education acquired by young Philip was similar to that received by most boys of that period.

Coming with his parents to Indiana, the family settled on the place now owned by Abner Thompson, in 1842-43. Upon reaching the age of eighteen, Philip commenced the battle of life for himself, working as a farm hand for the sum of $8 per month, losing no time. For the first nine months he received no pay, his employer proving to be an irresponsible person.

After coming to Indiana, he was in the employ of his father one year, receiving therefore the sum of $100. Soon after, he purchased a small farm and on December 18, 1846, was married to Margaret Stradley, a daughter of C. Stradley, a pioneer of this county. Mrs. Rader was born June 21, 1827.

The first purchase of land made by Mr. Rader caused his going in debt to the amount of $300. To pay this caused him serious difficulty, which he surmounted by continual borrowing and promptly meeting his former obligations; finally he sold his place for $1,100. Paying all his debts, he purchased a property originally settled by his father, again going in debt to the amount of $2,100. After a long experience of short crops and continued sickness, he mortgaged his property for $800, with which he engaged in the purchase and shipping of cattle, a speculation that at first very nearly proved disastrous; however, the trade turned, every venture proved a success, prosperity followed, and he exchanged his property for the premises upon which he now resides in 1864. This farm consists of 170 acres, now fully improved with numerous and convenient farm buildings and a handsome commodious residence.

The lesson of Mr. Rader's life is an instructive one to the young men of the present day, without capital, save that of a good constitution, industry, ambition and strict integrity, he presents a fair type of the hardy race of pioneers to whom the present generation is so deeply indebted.

The marriage of Mr. and Mrs. Rader was blessed with eight children, of whom William N., Sarah Elizabeth, Schuyler C., Albert W. and Clara L. are still living, and are all married, residing in the immediate vicinity of their parents, with the exception of A.W. Rader. (Source: Historical Atlas, Fulton Co, IN, by Kingman Bros, 1883, page 40)

· PHILIP RADER is a retired farmer and pioneer of Henry township, who has devoted the best energies of his life to the improvement of the lands of Fulton county, transforming the wild tracts into rich fields, whose productiveness adds materially to the prosperity of the county. He came to Indiana from Ohio, his native state, his birth having occurred in Montgomery county, July 4, 1824. His father, Philip Rader, who was born in Wythe county, VA, moved to Ohio in an early day. He was of German descent and married Miss Cress for his first wife and after her death weeded Elizabeth Siddon, of English lineage. With an ax upon his shoulder, Philip Rader, of this sketch, left home to carve out his own fortune, and by working in this way he started in life. After working for one year for his father for $100. he was married Dec. 18, 1846, to Margaret Stradley, and with his bride and his small capital began housekeeping a mile east of Akron on a forty-acre farm which he had purchase. Five years later he sold this place with the intention of removing to Illinois, but circumstances prevented and he purchased his father's farm, which in 1863 he exchanged for 170 acres of land in Henry township, two miles east of the village. There he profitably carried on farming until 1886, when with the handsome competence acquired through his own labors he removed to Akron, where he has since lived retired. Mrs. Rader, who has been his faithful helpmate for many years, was born in Delaware and her father, Caleb Stradley, was among the pioneers who opened up this locality to civilization. He as the first justice of the peace of Henry township, and for several years did his judicial business in his log cabin two and one-half miles southwest of where Akron now stands. Mr. and Mrs. Rader are the parents of the following named children: W.N., of Henry township; Sarah E., wife of Joseph Nelson, of Disco; Schuyler, of Henry township; Albert W., of Huntington, Ind.; and Clara, wife of William Morrett of Henry township. Deeply interested in American, Mr. Rader has traveled quite extensively over this country, thus gaining a knowledge of his native land that could not be acquired from history. Accompanied by his wife, he visited the Centennial exposition in 1876, returning by way of the Atlantic states and visiting New York, Niagara and other points of interest. Some years later they took a six months' trip by way of the Central Pacific route. They thus visited some twenty-six states and territories, and viewed the grandeur of the Rocky mountains and other magnificent scenery of the west. After a life well spent in fruitful toil they are now enjoying rest from labor in their pleasant home in Akron, and Mrs. Rader is now the oldest living resident of Henry township. Her brother, Luther Stradley was the first white child born in the township. (Source: Elia W. Peattie, Histor of Fulton Co Ind, 1896, pp 118-119)

· "Philip Jr. lived with his Father and Step-Mother, attending school until he was eighteen, when he took up life's battle for himself. He worked on farms for small pay until 1844, when he rode to Fulton County, Indiana and back, on horseback. His enthusiasm for the Hoosier State, caused the entire family to move to Akron, Indiana, the next year, except Philip (Jr.). He remained in Ohio, and taught school the winters of 1844-45 and 1845-46 and then he came to Indiana. He soon met the "Idol of his heart" (as he called her), Miss Margaret Stradley, when he came to Indiana in 1846.

…..They (Philip Jr. and Margaret Stradley) were married December 18, 1846 and went to housekeeping on a forty acre farm, one mile east of Akron. To this union were born eight children: Charles Holiday, Sept. 22, 1847; Jacob Harrison, Feb. 11, 1849; Caleb Stradley, June 22, 1850 were born here. Philip sold the farm, in 1851 with the intentions of moving to Ohio. Circumstances prevented him and he purchased his father's farm 1 1/2 miles eat of Akron. In February of the next year, the fourth son, William Nelson, was born. The following February, the eldest son, Charles passed away and 5 days later, Caleb died. Their first daughter, Sarah Elizabeth was born in October 1854. The next two were boys, Schuyler Colfax Dec. 10, 1856 and Albert Wilbur July 19, 1858. In 1863 Philip exchanged his farm for a larger farm 2 miles east of A kron, Here their last child was born, Clara Luella, Dec. 19, 1864. (Their son Jacob was the first to die in Nov. 1852, in the Fall after William Nelson was born.

Philip was a splendid marksman with a rifle and killed many wild turkeys and deer, when he came to Indiana. He also loved to fish and would often get up and catch a string of sunfish before breakfast. Margaret had said that she would never put a frog in her skillet. So one time Philip caught frogs and cleaned the hams so they looked like fish. The children saw him laughing behind his paper but thought nothing of it. After all had eaten heartily, Philip told them they were frogs, but Margaret never believed it." (Source #3)

· " My grandparents began housekeeping on a forty-acre farm one mile East of Akron. Five years later they sold this and bought Philip Sr.'s farm West of Akron. In 1863, my grandfather exchanged this property for the 170 acre farm, two mils East of town, which came to be known as the Rader homestead. Father (Albert Wilbur Rader) was then five years old. I do not know when my grandparents moved to Akron. They were still living on the farm when my parents were married, December 30, 1880, for they went to the homestead on their honeymoon. The move had been made by the time we moved to Huntington, IN, in 1890. Father's younger sister, Clara, and her husband, William Morrett, bought the farm after their marriage.

What about the Rader Homestead? The home was a two-story white frame house, with two front doors, one leading into the parlor, the other into the dining room. At the rear was a summer kitchen and the milk house. The barn was across the road. Across a ten-acre field, was a lake, sometimes called the Rader Lake, where the family and friends enjoyed the fishing and the fish which the lake afforded.

Back of rhe house and to the West was a huckleberry marsh. In season, folks came from far and near to pick berries on the shores. I remember seeing buckets and baskets of berries waiting to be weighed and divided. There was a small porch across the two front doors. I remember that Fay (Fay Morrett) and I often set up a millinery shop there, using leaves of all shapes and sizes for the hats, trimming them with clover and other flowers."

Three years after Philip and Margaret celebrated their Fiftieth Wedding Anniversary, grandfather died August 28, 1899. He was a gentleman of whom his children and all the Raders who were to follow, could be proud. He had great integrity. Mother used to say of him, "His word was as good as his bond". After he moved to Akron, his gardens were his pride, strawberries, melons and grapes in great abundance. I remember the arbor covered with choice green grapes. I always hoped to have a nephew named Philip. Perhaps some day I will have a great, great nephew, who will be the third Philip in our family. …. Grandmother lived until January 6, 1907. ….Years bring changes in our thinking about ages. Grandfather, with his beard, seemed in spite of his spirit, a man well advanced in years….he was only seventy-five when he died, and that grandmother was only eight - how young they were." (Source #2, Lucile Rader)

· "The Rader farm while Philip and Margaret lived there, was known as the Travelor's Inn. Many travelers were welcomed.

After they moved to Akron, they traveled quite a lot for those days. In 1876 they visited the Centennial Exposition in Philadelphia and other places of interest in the east. About 1886 they spent 1/2 year in the west, to the Pacific Coast and visiting many States and Territories. On Dec 18, 1896 (almost 2 years before I was born) they celebrated their 50 Wedding Anniversary. Their 5 children and 12 grandchildren were present, to witness a short Ceremony at 12:00 performed by Rev. W.W. Brown. The daughters gave their mother a beautiful set of dishes and the sons gave their father a Gold Headed Cane. They received several gifts from friends. Mr. Rader's two sisters, Mary Pierson of Peru and Mrs. Bethany Stephens of Rochester were present." (Source: #4, Margaret Elizabeth "Morrett" Riley)

· "Philip Rader (Jr) was born July 7, 1824, in Montgomery CO, OH. His parents were

Philip and Elizabeth Siddon Rader. He was of German descent, she of English lineage."

(Source: #2, Lucile Rader)

· (Obituary...The Rochester Weekly Sentinel Tuesday, August 29, 1899)

"Phillip Rader died at Akron last night of dropsy after a long illness, aged seventy years. He was a brother of Capt. Rader, of this city. ..."

· (The Rochester Weekly Sentinel, Thursday, August 31, 1899)

"The five Philip Rader heirs met Tuesday of this week, and effected an amicable settlement of the estate among themselves without going to court. The four heirs bought Nelson (William Nelson) Rader out of the estate and he assigned all notes and chattels to them and made deed to them for the real estate."

· (Rochester Sentinel, Sat., March 14, 1874) "Mr. Philip Rader has returned from the west, where he has been visiting friends and looking at the country. He seems well pleased with portions of different States which he visited, and thinks that a farmer can make money faster there than is possible fo him to do in Indiana, and finally concluding by saying that a man having a good farm here had just as well stay if he lives only to enjoy life."

· (Rochester Sentinel, Saturday, Jan. 18, 1879) "Henry Township is one of the best of the eight in the county. It has a large German element all of whom are excellent farmers and good citizens. Among the more prominent of farmers we note, ...Philip Rader...."

Noted events in his life were:

Alt Birth: 24 Jul 1824.

Resided: Ohio, 1842, Fulton County, Indiana.[87] from the "New Historical Atlas of Fulton Co., In, 1883

    This well known farmer and stockman was born in Ohio July 7, 1824, being the oldest son of Philip and Elizabeth (Siddon) Rader; he is on the paternal side of German descent, and of Irish descent on his mother's side.

    The education acquired by young philip was similar to that received by most boys of that period.

    Coming with his parents to Indiana, the family settled on the place now owned by Abner Thompson, in 1842-42. Upon reaching the age of eighteen, Philip commenced the battle of life for himself, working as a farm hand for the sum of &8 per month, losing no time. For the first nine months he received no pay, his employer proving to be an irresponsible person.

    After coming to Indiana, he was in the employ of his father one year, receiving thereof the sum of $100. Soon after, he purchased a small farm, and on December 18, 1846, was married to Margaret Stradley, a daughter of Ca Stradley, a pioneer of this county. Mrs Rader was born June 21, 1827.

    The first purchase of land made by Mr Rader caused his going in debt to the amount of $300. To pay this caused him serious difficulty, which he surmounted by continual borrowing and promptly meeting his former obligations; finally he sold his place for $1,100. Paying all his debts, he purchased the property originally settled by his father, again going in debt to the amount of $2,100. After a long experience of short crops and continued sickness, he mortgaged his property for $800, with which he engaged in the purchase and shipping of cattle, a speculation that at first very nearly proved disastrous; however, the trade turned, every venture proved a success, prosperity followed and he exchanged his property for the premises upon which he now resides in 1864. This farm consists of 170 acres, now fully improved with numerous and convenient farm buildings and a handsome, commodious residence

The lesson of Mr. Rader's life is an instructive one to the young men of the present day, without capital, save that of a good constitution, industry, ambition and strict integrity, he presents a fair type of the hardy race of pioneers to whom the present generation is so deeply indebted.

The marriage of Mr. and Mrs Rader was blessed with eight children, of whom William N., Sarah Elizabeth, Schuyler C., Albert W. and Clara are still living, and are all married, residing in the immediate vicinity of their parents, with the exception of A.W. Rader.

He was employed winters of 1844-5-6 in Ohio. Taught school

Resided: 1846, Indiana.

He appeared on the census in 1850 in Henry Township, Fulton County, Indiana. HENRY TOWNSHIP, FULTON COUNTY, INDIANA PG. 407 LINE 92

· 1850 Census: Philip Rader, 25 yrs, M; Margaret D. 22 yrs, F; Charles H, 2 yrs, M; Jacob H, 1 yr, M; Caleb 1/2 yr, M (Source: 1850 Federal Census, Henry Twp, Fulton Co, IN)

He appeared on the census on 30 Jul 1850 in Henry, Fulton, Indiana. Henry, Fulton, IN abt 1825 Ohio

Philip Rader 25 M born OH
Margaret   22 F   Del
Charles H   2   M Ia.
Jacob H   1   M "
Caleb   1/12 M "

He appeared on the census in 1860 in Henry Township, Fulton County, Indiana. HENRY TOWNSHIP, FULTON COUNTY, INDIANA PAGE 245 LINE 1668

· 1860 Census: Philip Rader, 36 yrs, M, Farmer, born in OH; Margaret, 34 yrs, F, born in Delaware; William, 8 yrs, M, born in IN; Sarah, 6 yrs, born in IN; Colfax, 4 yrs, M, born in IN; Albert, 2 yrs, M, born in IN; Mary Jenkins, 16 yrs, F, born in IN; (Source: 1860 Federal Census, Henry Twp, Fulton Co, IN) NOTE: Mary Jenkins may be the daughter of Mary (Rader) Jenkins????

He appeared on the census in 1870 in Henry Township, Fulton County, Indiana. HENRY TOWNSHIP, FULTON COUNTY, INDIANA PAGE 34 LINE 254

· 1870 Census: Phillip Rader, 48 yrs, M, W, Farmer, born in OH; Margaret 44 yrs, F, W, Keeping house, born in Delaware; Nelson, 18 yrs, M, W, born in IN; Sarah E, 16 yrs, F, W, born in IN; Colfax, 13 yrs, M, W, born in IN; Albert W, 12 yrs, M, W, born in IN; Clara L, 5 yrs, F, W, born in IN (Source: 1870 Census, Henry Twp, Fulton Co, IN)

He appeared on the census in 1880 in Henry Township, Fulton County, Indiana. HENRY TOWNSHIP, FULTON COUNTY, INDIANA PAGE 53A LINE 296

- 1880 Census: Philip Rader, est birth 1825, born in OH; Margaret, est birth 1826, born in Delaware; Clara L, est birth 1865, born in IN

(Source: 1880 Federal Census, Henry Twp, Fulton Co, IN)

He appeared on the census in 1880 in Henry, Fulton, Indiana. 1880 United States Census

Name Relation Marital Status Gender Race Age Birthplace Occupation Father's Birthplace Mother's Birthplace

Philip RADER   Self   M   Male   W   55   OH   Retired Farmer   VA   SC
Margaret RADER   Wife   M   Female   W   54   DE   Keeping House   DE   DE
Clara L. RADER   Dau   S   Female   W   15   IN   At Home   OH   DE

Source Information:
Census Place Henry, Fulton, Indiana
Family History Library Film   1254278
NA Film Number   T9-0278
Page Number   53A
NA Film Number   T9-0278
Page Number   47B

Philip married **Margaret Stradley**,[34] daughter of **Caleb Stradley** and **Unknown**, on 18 Dec 1846 in Akron, Fulton County, Indiana.[34] Margaret was born on 21 Jun 1827 in Delaware,[34] died on 6 Jan 1907 in Disco, Fulton County, Indiana[34] at age 79, and was buried in Akron Cemetery, Akron, Fulton County, Indiana. Another name for Margaret was Margaret M. Stadley.

Marriage Notes: The following is from a history gathered by Elizabeth Morrett Riley...

When first married, Philip and Margaret purchased a forty acre farm, one mile east of Akron, Indiana. The first three of their eight children were born here. Philip sold the farm in 1851 with the intention of moving to Ohio, but circumstances prevented him from doing so. He then purchased his father's farm 1.5 miles east of Akron, Indiana. The next four children were born on this farm. Thethree eldest sons, Charles, Jacob and Caleb died there. In 1863, Philip exchanged his farm for a larger farm two miles east of Akron. Their last child was born here.

Margaret had said that she would never put a frog in her skillet. So one time Philip caught frogs and cleaned the hams so they looked like fish. The children saw him laughing behind his paper but thopught nothing of it. After all had eaten heartily, Philip told them they were frogs, but Margaret never believe it.

The Rader farm, while Philip and Margaret lived there, was known as the Travelers Inn. Many travelers were welcomed. After they moved to Akron they traveled quite a lot for those days. Ind 1876 they visited the centenial Exposition in Philadelphia and other places of interest in the east. About 1876 they spent 1/2 year in the west, to the Pacific Coast and visiting many states and territories. On December 18, 1896 they celebrated their 50 Wedding Anniversary. Their 5 children and 12 grandchildren were present, to witness a short Ceremony at 12:00 performed by Rev WW Brown. The daughters gave their mother a beautiful set of dishes and the sons gave their father a Gold Headed Cane. They received several gifts from friends. Mr. Rader's 2 sisters Mary Pierson of Peru and Mrs. Bethany Stephens of Rochester were present.

Noted events in their marriage were:

Alt Marriage: 28 Dec 1846, Akron, Fulton County, Indiana.

> General Notes: Philip Jr married Margaret Stradley (DOB 6-21-1827), daughter of C. Stradley. They had 8 children....living children are: William N, Sarah Elizabeth, Schuyler C, Albert W., Clara L, and A.W. All but A.W. live in Fulton Co area. Page 40

Margaret moved to Indiana from Delaware in 1836. They traveled in a wagen pulled by a team of oxen. Her playmates were Indian girls. One time an Indian girl told Margaret to get on her (the Indian's) pony. Margaret was afraid and the Indian girl drew her hatchet. Margaret ran and reached home safely.

After the death of her husband in 1899, Margaret continued to live in Akron, Indiana. Several young girls stayed with her and attended school. She died at the home of her daughter, Sarah Rader Nelson, where she was visiting.

Born June 21, 1827 in Delaware. Married December 18, 18, 1846. Died January 6, 1907   (Info submitted by A. Shepherd)

> Born: June 21, 1827
>
> Died: January 6, 1907
>
> · Margaret M. Stradley born June 21, 1827 (Source 6)
>
> · Philip Rader & Margaret M. Stradley was married December 18, 1846

(Source 6)

> · Philip Rader married Margaret Stradley December 18, 1846, Book (1), pg 161 (Source: Fulton Co Library Marriage Records)
>
> · "Mother" Margaret Rader, June 21, 1827 - January 6, 1907. Buried at I.O.O.F. Cemetery, Akron, Fulton Co, IN (Source: Fulton Co Library Cemetery Records)
>
> · (Obituary....The Rochester Evening Sentinel, Monday, January 7, 1907)

"Mrs. Margaret (Stradley) Rader, widow of the late Phillip Rader, of Akron, died Sunday, at the home of her daughter at Disko (IN) after a brief illness. She had been in failing health for several years but the final illness was of but a few days duration.

Mrs. Rader was the daughter of Mr. & Mrs. Caleb Stradley and was born in Delaware nearly 80 years ago. She located in Henry township more than 70 years ago and for many years last past was the pioneer of the early settlers. She married Phillip Rader in 1846 and to them eight children were born five of whom are living, viz: W.N. (Rader) and Schuyler Rader and Mrs. Wm. Morrett (Clara L. Rader), of Henry township; Mrs. Joseph Nelson (Sarah Elizabeth Rader) of Disko; and A.W. Rader of Minnesota. ......"

> · "Mr. Rader died August 28, 1899 and Mrs. Rader continued to live in Akron. Several young girls stayed with her and went to school. She died Jan 6, 1907 at the home of her daughter, Mrs. Joe Nelson (Sarah Elizabeth Rader), where she was visiting."

(Source: #4, Margaret Elizabeth "Morrett" Riley)

· Stradley's came to Indiana from Delaware in 1836 in a wagon pulled by a team of oxen, when Margaret was a little girl. She was born in Delaware June 21, 1827. Her playmates were Indian girls. One time an Indian girl told her to get on her pony. Margaret was afraid to get on and the Indian girl drew her hatchet, but Margaret ran and reached home safely. (Source 3)

· "In 1845 Philip (SR) and Catherine moved to Akron, IN. The following year, when Philip (JR) was twenty-two, he married Margaret Stradley. Grandmother (Margaret Stradley) was born in Delaware on June 21, 1827. Her father, Caleb Stradley, was one of the pioneers of Henry Township, Fulton County, the Akron community. He was the first Justice of Peace in Henry Township. For the most part he transacted his business in his log cabin home, two and one-half miles southwest of where Akron now stands. The youngest son, Luther, was the first white child born in the Township." (Source #2). NOTE: The Stradley's were prominent citizens in Fulton County. The Rochester Sentinel newspaper reported that Luther Stradley had a public sale for the intent to move to Illinois to cultivate the fertile soil there. This was published in said newspaper on Mar. 14, 1874.

· Excerpt from Biography of brother of Margaret Stradley, Charles J. Stradley: " Among the pioneer settlers of this county, whose interest and labors have found a wide field for good work, non, perhaps, have taken a greater interest in the civilization and development of the county than the man of whom this writing is concerned. He is a native of Kent Count, Delaware, and born October 14, 1814. His parents, Caleb and Susan Stradley, were natives of Delaware, and descendants of old English stock. In 1822, his mother deceased, and six years later and in 1835 became a resident of Fulton County, where he endured all the hardships of frontier life as a farmer up to 1858, when he deceased....." (Source: Historical Atlas, Fulton Co, IN, by Kingman Bros, 1883, page 26)

Noted events in her life were:
1850. HENRY TOWNSHIP, FULTON COUNTY, INDIANA PG. 407 LINE 92
1860. HENRY TOWNSHIP, FULTON COUNTY, INDIANA PAGE 245 LINE 1668
1870. HENRY TOWNSHIP, FULTON COUNTY, INDIANA PAGE 34 LINE 254
1880. HENRY TOWNSHIP, FULTON COUNTY, INDIANA PAGE 53A LINE 296
1900. HENRY TOWNSHIP, FULTON COUNTY, INDIANA PAGE 4B LINE 93

Children from this marriage were:

+386 M i. **Charles Holiday Rader**[34] was born on 22 Sep 1847 in Akron, Indiana,[34] died on 4 Feb 1853 in Akron, Indiana[34] at age 5, and was buried in Omega Cemetery, Akron, Fulton County, Indiana.

+387 M ii. **Jacob Harrison Rader**[34] was born on 11 Feb 1849 in Akron, Indiana,[34] died on 27 Nov 1852 in Akron, Indiana[34] at age 3, and was buried in Omega Cemetery, Akron, Fulton County, Indiana.

+388 M iii. **Caleb Stradley Rader**[34] was born on 22 Jun 1850 in Akron, Indiana,[34] died on 9 Feb 1853 in Akron, Indiana[34] at age 2, and was buried in Omega Cemetery, Akron, Fulton County, Indiana.

+389 M iv. **William Nelson Rader**[34] was born on 5 Feb 1852 in Akron, Indiana,[34] died on 6 Nov 1918 in Henry Township, Akron, Fulton County, Indiana[34] at age 66, and was buried in 1918 in Akron Cemetery, Akron, Fulton County, Indiana.

William married **Nancy "Jennie" Jane Hine** (b. 4 Aug 1855, d. 11 Dec 1931) on 30 Jan 1873 in Kosciusko Co, IN.[34]

+390 F v. **Sarah Elizabeth Rader**[34] was born on 20 Oct 1854 in Akron, Indiana[34] and died in Nov 1939 in North Manchester, Wabash Co, IN[34] at age 85.

Sarah married **Joseph H. Nelson**[34] (b. Jul 1850, d. 6 Jul 1916) on 10 Oct 1873 in Fulton County, Indiana.[34]

+391 M vi. **Schuyler Colfax Rader** was born on 10 Dec 1856 in Akron, Indiana,[34] died on 2 May 1934 in Fulton County, Indiana[34] at age 77, and was buried in Akron Cemetery, Akron, Fulton County, Indiana.

Schuyler married **Mary Alice Teeter** (b. 4 Aug 1856, d. 17 Aug 1913) on 9 Oct 1875 in Fulton County, Indiana.[34]

Schuyler next married **Emma J. Feree**[34] in 1890 in Fulton County, Indiana.[34]

+392 M vii. **Albert Wilber Rader**[34] was born on 19 Jul 1858 in Akron, Indiana,[34] died in Feb 1914 in Des Moines, Polk Co, Iowa[34] at age 55, and was buried in Mount Hope Cemetery, Huntington, Huntington County, Indiana.

Albert married **Jennie E. Brown**[34] (b. 14 Jul 1860, d. 1946) on 30 Dec 1880 in Akron, Indiana.[34]

+393 F viii. **Clara Luella Rader**[34] was born on 19 Dec 1864 in Akron, Fulton County, Indiana[34] and died on 22 Oct 1914 in Akron, Fulton County, Indiana[34] at age 49.

Clara married **William Michael Morrett**[34] (b. 19 Jan 1860, d. 17 Feb 1936) on 19 Oct 1882 in Akron, Fulton County, Indiana.[34]

64. William Rader (*Phillip Sr.*[2], *Casper Sr*[1]) was born in 1826 and died on 15 Sep 1895 in Kewanna, Fulton County, Indiana at age 69.

William married **Mary Ann**. Mary was born in 1828 and died on 17 Aug 1914 in Union Township Fulton County, Indiana at age 86.

Children from this marriage were:

+394 M i. **John W. Rader** was born in 1850.

+395 M ii. **Thomas J. Rader** was born in 1855.

Thomas married **Phebe J. Egman** on 26 Sep 1875 in Fulton County, Indiana.

Thomas next married **Mary M. Hill** on 19 Feb 1913 in Fulton County, Indiana.

+396 F iii. **Rosella E. Rader** was born in 1857.

Rosella married **Charles W. Hill** on 1 Mar 1881 in Fulton County, Indiana.

+397 M iv. **Daniel C. Rader** was born in 1860.

+398 F v. **Martha V. Rader** was born in 1862.

Martha married **Levi H. Matthews** (b. 1856) on 26 May 1880 in Fulton County, Indiana.

+399 F vi. **Eunice F. Rader** was born in 1866.

65. Christina Bethany Rader[34] (*Phillip Sr.*[2], *Casper Sr*[1]) was born in Jul 1826 in Ohio[34] and died on 19 Jan 1904 in Rochester, Fulton County, Indiana[34] at age 77. Other names for Christina were Christine, and Bethany.

General Notes: Margaret Elizabeth Morrett writes The youngest girl, Christine, married a Mr. Stevens and lived about 15 miles from my Mothers home. She raised a large family and I remember of mother telling, about her parents taking them to visit the Stevens Family, in bobsleds or big wagons, in the days of corduroy roads.
Christina Rader…born 1826 in Ohio. Married ? Stevens. No further info
(Info submitted by A. Shepherd)
§ Buried at I.O.O.F. Cemetery, Rochester, IN, (Section 10)
(Headstone reads: Bethany Stevens, July 4, 1826 - Jan. 19, 1904)
(Fulton Co Cemetery Records)
§ (Fulton Co Death Records) Stevens, Bethany R. (F) (W) 77, Jan 19, 1904, Rochester, IN Book C-5, pg 34
· Per history written by Lucile Rader (12-25-1961) Christina was born 1826 and often called "Bethany". Suzanne Parker has a "New Testament 1871" which has written on the front page "Presented to Miss Clara Rader by her Aunt Behany Stevens. March the 19 187_"

· M. Elizabeth Rader wrote in the Spring 1917 (Pro-German to Pro-American)

"the youngest girl, Christine, married a Mr. Stevens and lived about fifteen miles from my Mother's home. She raised a large family and I remember of Mother telling, about her parents taking them to visit the Stevens Family, in Bob Sleds or Big Wagons, in the days of corduroy roads." (Source 3)

· Bethany Christine, dau of Philip, Sr., and Katharine (Sheets) Rader, m. October 31, 1844 to Jacob Stevens (L.D.M. Brien, Montgomery Co Ohio Marriages, 1803-1851). Since Philip Rader, Sr., and his family had already gone to Ind, it is possible that Bethany remained in Ohio, but not certain. (Source 1)

· Obituary (Rochester Sentinel, Tuesday, January 19, 1904)

"Death has called another of Rochester's old people. Mrs. Bethany Stevens, aged 78 years and 6 months. She had been an invalid for several months and her passing away was indirectly the result of paralysis.

Deceased came to Fulton county with her husband, Jacob Stevens, 35 years ago and Mr. Stevens died about 17 years ago. They reared a family of one adopted son and eleven children of their own viz: James, Hezekiah, Austin, Rev. J.O. Stevens, all dead, and Mrs. Lucinda (Stevens) Cushman, Mrs. Rilla (Stevens) Cushman, and Schuyler Stevens, of Kokomo; Mrs. Mary (Stevens) Jones, of Dayton, OH; and Mrs. Al(le)ba (Stevens) Enyart, Mrs. Ida (Stevens) Carter and Mrs. Nellie (Stevens) Babcock, of this city.

She also leaves three half brothers, of whom Capt. David Rader, of this city is one. "
HUSBAND: Jacob Stevens
    (Fulton Co Cemetery Records) buried at I.O.O.F Cemetery,
    Rochester, IN (Headstone: May 15, 1824 - Oct 8, 1888)[35]
Noted events in her life were:
Moved: 1870, Rochester, Fulton Co, IN.

Christina married **Jacob Stevens Esq.**[34] in Oct 1844.[34] Jacob was born on 15 May 1824 in Dayton, Montgomery County, Ohio[34] and died about 1886 in Rochester, Fulton County, Indiana[34] about age 62.

Marriage Notes: CHILDREN:
  James....died prior to 1904
  Hezekiah....died prior to 1904
  Austin...Buried at I.O.O.F. Cemetery, Section 10, Rochester, IN
     Headstone reads: Austin I. Stevens died Oct 12, 1882
     age 30y-6m-7d (Fulton Co Cemetery Records)
  J.O. (Rev)...Buried at I.O.O.F. Cemetery, Section 10, Rochester, IN
     Headstone reads: Rev. J. O. Stevens, died Oct 18, 1883
     age 26y-9m-18-d (Fulton Co Cemetery Records)
  Lucinda....married ___Cushman
     Buried at I.O.O.F. Cemetery, Section 10, Rochester, IN
     Headstone reads: Lucinda Cushman, 1845-1926
     (Fulton Co Cemetery Records)
  Arilla.... AKA...Rilla born Aug. 1, 1861 in Germantown OH
     died Saturday, Nov 30, 1940, buried in I.O.O.F. Cemetery,
     Rochester, IN (Headstone: Arilla Cushman 1861-1940)
     (Fulton Co Cemetery Records)
     Lived in Layfayette, IN for a period of time.
     (Rochester Sentinel, Sat, Nov. 30, 1940)
     "Mrs. Arilla Cushman, aged 79, a seamstress, died at the home
     her sister, Mrs. Nellie Babcock..... The deceased was born in
     Germantown, Ohio, August 1, 1861, the daughter of Stephen
     and Bethany Rader. Her husband, Consider Cushman,
     preceded her in death.....Survivors are the sister, Mrs. Babcock
     and two sons Virgil Cushman, Muncie (IN) and Clarence
     Cushman, South Bend (IN)."
     Husband: Consider Cushman
     Children:

Virgil Cushman….Muncie, IN
Clarence Cushman…South Bend, IN
Schuyler C….lived in Kokomo, IN AKA Schuyler C., approx b. 1866,
   died, Nov. 1938
   (Rochester News Sentinel, Friday, Nov 4, 1938)
   "Mrs. Nellie Babcock, mayor of the City of Rochester,
   received word late Thursday of the death of her brother,
   Schuyler C. Stevens, 72, which occurred at his home in
   Kokomo (IN). …."
   *** Per Obit of Ida (Stevens) Carter (Rochester News Sentinel,
   Thurs, Jan 22, 1931) Schuyler, his daughter and granddaughter
   attended Ida's funeral. No information yet on his children
Mary…married ___Jones, lived in Dayton, OH AKA Mary C.
Alleba….AKA   Allebra…..lived in Rochester, IN
   born in Montgomery County, OH on Sept 27, 1854
   died July 6, 1930. Buried in I.O.O.F Cemetery, Section 9,
   Rochester, IN. Headstone reads: Alleba Enyart, Sept 27, 1854
   - July 6, 1930 (Fulton Co. Cemetery Records)
   (Rochester Sentinel, Monday, July 7, 1930)
   "Mrs. Clark Enyart, 75, resident of Rochester for over half a
   century, died at 5:30 Sunday evening in her home on West
   Eighth street, death being due to paralysis. The deceased had
   been in ill health for the past six years but her condition was
   only regarded as serious three weeks.
Allebra Stevens, daughter of Jacob and Bethany (Rader) Stevens, was born in Montgomery County, OH, on Dec. 27, 1854. Nov. 14, 1874, she married Clark Enyart and all of their married life had been spent in Rochester. She was a member of the W.R.C., Rebekah Lodge and Evangelical church. Surviving are her husband, four sisters, and one brother: Mrs. Ida Carter, of Rochester; Mrs. Arilla Cushman, of Lafayette (IN), Mrs. Mary C. Jones of Dayton, OH; Mrs. J. L. Babcock of Rochester, and Schuyler C. Stevens, of Kokomo (IN). Two children died in infancy. ….."

HUSBAND: Clark B. Enyart…married Nov 14, 1875, Book C, pg 346 (Fulton Co Marriage Records) Married Alleba Stevens

(Fulton Co Cemetery Records) Buried in I.O.O.F. Cemetery, Section 9, Rochester, IN Headstone reads: Clark B. Enyart,

Dec. 25, 1853 - Dec 30, 1934

CHILDREN:
2 died in infancy (per obit)

Ida….lived in Rochester, IN
   born Feb 16, 1859 in Montgomery Co, OH
   died Jan 19, 1931 in Rochester, IN
   buried in Antioch Cemetery, Row 24, Rochester Twp, IN,
   Headstone reads: Ida Carter, Mother, 1859-1931 (Fulton County Cemetery Records)

(Obit published by Rochester News Sentinel, Mon, Jan 19, 1931)

"Mrs. Ida Carter, 71, resident of Rochester for 60 years died Monday morning at 8:55 in the home of her daughter, Mrs. Charles Willard, 1425 Bancroft Ave, death being due to complications of diseases......

Ida (Stevens), daughter of Jacob and Bethany Stevens, was born on February 16, 1859 in Montgomery Co, OH and moved with her parents to this community when a young girl. On August 21, 1879 she was married to Lot M. Carter, who died 37 years ago.....Surviving are two daughters, Mrs. Marie Ort, of Mishawaka (IN) and Mrs. Charles Willard of Rochester; three sisters, Mrs. J.L Babcock of Rochester; Mrs. Rilla Cushman of Layfayette (IN), and Mrs. Mary C. Jones of Dayton Ohio; and one brother, Schuyler Stevens of Kokomo (IN). Two grandsons and eight great-grandchildren also survive....."

HUSBAND: Lot M. Carter born 1858, died 1893 buried at Antioch Cemetery, Rochester Twp. Headstone reads: Lot M. Carter 1858-1893 (per Fulton Co Cemetery Records)

Married Ida Stevens on Aug 21, 1879, Book D, pg 68 (Fulton County Marriage Records)

CHILDREN:
    Mrs. Marie Ort...Mishawaka, IN
    Mrs. Charles Willard, Rochester, IN
    ***per Obit, had 2 grandchildren and 8 great grandchildren

Nellie...born in Rochester, IN Dec 11, 1868...died May 7, 1957 (per Obit) buried in I.O.O.F. Cemetery, Section 10, Rochester IN Headstone: Nellie Stevens, D.D.S. 1868-1957 (Fulton Co Cemetery Records)

(Obit in Rochester Sentinel, Weds, May 8, 1957)

"Final rites for Mrs. Nellie Babcock, DDS, a native of Rochester, who once was the city's Mayor, will be at....burial will be in the Rochester I.O.O.F. cemetery. Mrs. Babcock 89, died Tuesday at the Odd Fellows home in Greensburg.... From Oct 26, 1938 to Jan. 1, 1939, Mrs. Babcock served as Mayor of Rochester after being appointed to the post by the City Council following the death in office of her husband, Dr. James L. Babcock. Dr. Babcock was elected in 1935 and died on Oct 7, 1938. Mrs. Babcock was the only woman to occupy the Rochester mayor's chair in the 47-year history of office. Born in Rochester on Dec 11, 1868, she had lived her entire life in this city and vicinity until moving to Greensburg. She was the daughter of James and Bethany (Rader) Stevens. Mrs. Babcock was a dentist by occupation, having been graduated from Northwestern University Dental School on April 2, 1897. ... She was married to James L. Babcock, DDS, on Dec. 30, 1886. Surviving are numerous nieces and nephews, among them Mrs. Charles Willard, Rochester, and Mrs. Alva Petty, Peru, and a great-nephew, Ralph Lillard, Indianapolis...."

HUSBAND: James Leonard Babcock, DDS buried I.O.O.F. Cemetery, Section 10, Rochester IN. Headstone: James Leonard Babcock, D.D.S. 1864-1938 (Fulton Co Cemetery Records)

Married Dec 30, 1886 (per Obit of Ida)

(Obit Rochester News-Sentinel, Fri, Oct 7, 1938)

"Dr. James L. Babcock, aged 76, Mayor of Rochester died at his home 1301 S. Main St. at 3:30 o'clock Friday afternoon. auto accident….resulted in his death on his fifty-first wedding anniversary……was elected Mayor of Rochester four years ago …His wife is the only immediate survivor."

General Notes: § Buried at I.O.O.F. Cemetery, Rochester, IN, (Section 10)

(Headstone reads: Bethany Stevens, July 4, 1826 - Jan. 19, 1904)

(Fulton Co Cemetery Records)

§ (Fulton Co Death Records) Stevens, Bethany R. (F) (W), housewife, 77, Jan 19, 1904, Rochester, IN (Fulton Co Death Records, Book C-5, pg 34)

· Per history written by Lucile Rader (12-25-1961) Christina was born 1826 and often called "Bethany". Suzanne Parker has a "New Testament 1871" which has written on the front page "Presented to Miss Clara Rader by her Aunt Behany Stevens. March the 19 187_"

· M. Elizabeth Rader wrote in the Spring 1917 (Pro-German to Pro-American)

"the youngest girl, Christine, married a Mr. Stevens and lived about fifteen miles from my Mother's home. She raised a large family and I remember of Mother telling, about her parents taking them to visit the Stevens Family, in Bob Sleds or Big Wagons, in the days of corduroy roads." (Source 3)

· Bethany Christine, dau of Philip, Sr., and Katharine (Sheets) Rader, m. October 31, 1844 to Jacob Stevens (L.D.M. Brien, Montgomery Co Ohio Marriages, 1803-1851). Since Philip Rader, Sr., and his family had already gone to Ind, it is possible that Bethany remained in Ohio, but not certain. (Source 1)

· Bethany gave Clara L. Rader a New Testament and wrote in the front of it, " Presented to Miss Clara Rader by her Aunt Bethany Stevens, March the 19th, 187_" (Property of Suzanne Parker)

· Obituary (Rochester Sentinel, Tuesday, January 19, 1904)

"Death has called another of Rochester's old people. Mrs. Bethany Stevens, aged 78 years and 6 months. She had been an invalid for several months and her passing away was indirectly the result of paralysis.

Deceased came to Fulton county with her husband, Jacob Stevens, 35 years ago and Mr. Stevens died about 17 years ago. They reared a family of one adopted son and eleven children of their own viz: James, Hezekiah, Austin, Rev. J.O. Stevens, all dead, and Mrs. Lucinda (Stevens) Cushman, Mrs. Rilla (Stevens) Cushman, and Schuyler Stevens, of Kokomo; Mrs. Mary (Stevens) Jones, of Dayton, OH; and Mrs. Al(le)ba (Stevens) Enyart, Mrs. Ida (Stevens) Carter and Mrs. Nellie (Stevens) Babcock, of this city.

She also leaves three half brothers, of whom Capt. David Rader, of this city is one. "

Children from this marriage were:

+400 F i. **Lucinda Stevens** was born in Oct 1845 in Ohio.

Lucinda married **Unk Cushman**.

+401 F ii. **Aleba Stevens** was born in Sep 1854 in Ohio.

Aleba married **Clark Enyart** (b. Sep 1854) on 14 Nov 1875 in Fulton County, Indiana.

+402 F iii. **Ida Stevens** was born in Feb 1859 in Fulton County, Indiana.

Ida married **Lot Carter** on 21 Aug 1879 in Fulton County, Indiana.

+403 M iv. **Austin Stevens** was born on an unknown date, died in Tolono, Illinois, and was buried in Odd Fellows' Cemetery, Fulton County, Indiana.

+404 M v. **Hezekiah M. Stevens** was born on an unknown date.

Hezekiah married **Lizzie Norris** on 21 Feb 1875 in Fulton County, Indiana.

+405 M vi. **James B. Stevens** was born on an unknown date.

James married **Minnie Wilhoit** on 2 Oct 1884.

+406 F vii. **Mary Stevens** was born on an unknown date.

Mary married **Unk Jones**.

+407 F viii. **Nellie Stevens** was born on an unknown date.

Nellie married **James L. Babcock** on 30 Dec 1886 in Fulton County, Indiana.

+408 M ix. **Rev. Jabes O. Stevens** was born on an unknown date in Fulton County, Indiana and died in Westerville, Ohio.

+409 F x. **Rilla Stevens** was born on an unknown date.

Rilla married **Unk Cushman**.

+410 M xi. **Schuyler Stevens** was born on an unknown date.

Schuyler married **Sarah Brown** on 12 Mar 1887 in Fulton County, Indiana.

66. Andrew Rader[34] (*Phillip Sr.*[2], *Casper Sr*[1]) was born on 28 Sep 1828 in Ohio and died in 1900 in Prescott, Pierce County, Wisconsin[34] at age 72.

General Notes: Andrew lived the greater part of his adult life in Prescott, Wisconsin.

Andrew served three years in Company F, 13th Regiment, Wisconsin Volunteer Infantry during the Civil War. After the war, his Company built a steamship named "Prescott" which was still running in 1899.

Andrew held a number of elected and appointed positions in his community - postmaster, for one.

Andrew was a carpenter for several years.

·(Rochester Sentinel, Sat, Nov. 25, 1882) " Mr. A. Rader, of Prescott, WI, is visiting his brother, Capt. David Rader, of this place. He is accompanied by his wife and they will remain during the winter…It has been eleven years since Mr. Rader visited here…Unlike his brothers of this country, he is an ardent Democrat…"

·"Andrew served three years in the Co. F. Thirtieth Reg. Wisconsin Volunteer Infantry in the Civil War. After the War, his Company built a steamship, named "Prescott", which was still running in 1899. He was a carpenter for several years. He died in Prescott, Wisconsin in 1900." (Source 3)

·(Source: 1890 Veterans Schedules, Wisconsin, Ancestry.com) Andrew Rader, Home in 1890 Prescott Twp, Pierce Co, WI, Rank "Private", Years of service "1862-1865", Company "F", Name of regiment "30", Infantry, time of service "Aug. 12, 1862 to Aug. 12, 1865", "3 years, no months, no days".

·"The school house, in Montgomery Co, OH, where the eleven Rader children were enrolled, was built of round logs, chinked and daubed with clay. The writing desk was a board along the wall under the window, the length of the room. The seats or benches, as they were then called, were made of slabs, with two logs of small trees at each end and one in the middle. Twenty-six days of the month the school was in session, three months of the year, with two days out for Christmas and New Years. Teachers were paid from eight to ten dollars a month, boarding among the families of their pupils. Orthography, reading, writing, arithmetic and sometimes geography were taught. I found this description of the school in a biographical sketch written by Andrew Rader. My grandfather (Philip Jr.) and Andrew both taught school very briefly."

(Source: #2)

·"Andrew Rader, the oldest son of this third marriage, lived the greater part of his adult life in Prescott, Wisconsin. He served three years in the Union Army. In his community he held a number of elected and appointed positions, among them that of Postmaster. He died at the age of ninety-two." (Source: #2, Lucile Rader)

·Census 1860: Andrew Rader, age 31, occupation Carpenter, birthplace OH, Home in 1860 Prescott Ward 1, Pierce, WI. (Source: Fed Census 1860, Post Office Prescott, Roll: M653_1426, page 137) NOTE: Further investigation needed and need to review original census from LDS. A " Louisa" was listed but could not access the following census page. Her age was listed as 32, birthplace OH, estimated year of birth 1827.

·Census 1880: Andrew Rader, age 52, birthplace OH, occupation Merchant, home in 1880 Prescott, Pierce, WI, married, white, male, spouse's name "Loisa P. Rader", father's birthplace VT, Mother's birthplace NY; Loisa P, wife, age 42, birthplace OH, father's birthplace VA, mother's birthplace NC; Almedia, female, age 15, daughter, birthplace Minnesota, father's birthplace OH, mother's birthplace OH.

(Source: 1880 Fed Census, Prescott, Pierce, WI, Roll: T9_1441: Family History Film: 1255441; page 85A, enumeration District 109) NOTE: It may that the enumerator mixed up Andrew's parents' places of birth and Loisa's parents' places of birth. Almedia's name was difficult to read....so error could be in spelling.

Noted events in his life were:

Alt Birth: 1808, Indiana.[34]

He appeared on the census in 1850. HENRY TOWNSHIP, FULTON COUNTY, INDIANA PAGE 405 LINE 62

Census 1: 1860. 1ST. WARD, PRESCOTT, PIERCE COUNTY, WISCONSIN   PAGE 137

He appeared on the census in 1860 in Prescott Ward 1, Pierce, Wisconsin. Name: Andrew Rader Age in 1860: 31 Birthplace: Ohio Home in 1860: Prescott Ward 1, Pierce, Wisconsin : Prescott Roll: M653_1426 Page: 137 Year: 1860 Head of Household: Andrew Rader

Military: 31st of August, 1861, Indianapolis, Marion County, Indiana. COUNTY "F" 13TH. REGIMENT WISCONSIN VOLUNTEER INFANTRY CIVIL WAR

· Article regarding the Civil War and Company A, 26th Regiment:

"The war of the rebellion had not long been in progress when, upon the call of the President for volunteers to enlist in the army of the Union, Fulton County responded to the call, and her sons went forth to aid the nation in the hour of its peril, nobly discharging the duty imposed by their obligations to their common country, and the purpose to maintain the supremacy of the laws. In the brief space allotted, it will be impossible to give a detailed account of the particular services of every individual thus enrolled, nor, indeed, more than a general review of the more important engagements and the incidents connected with them, as a part of the military history of the country. The first enlistments made in this county were in the month of July, and the early part of August, 1861, the volunteers thus enrolling themselves being subsequently mustered into service as Company A, of the Twenty-sixth Regiment. This company, upon being organized, was placed under the command of Capt. Milton L. Minor, with subordinate officers nearly all from this county. The following is the roster of Company A, as it appears in the report of the Adjutant General: Captain -Milton L. Minor, Percival G. Kelsey, David Rader, Archibald H. McDonald.

First Lieutenant-Percival G. Kelsey, David Rader, Alexander H. McDonald, Henry H. Carter, Joseph H. Weit.

Second Lieutenant-David Rader......(Sergeants, Corporals, Privates, Recruits, etc)

The regiment was organized and mustered into service at Indianapolis, on the 31st of August, 1861, with William M. Wheatley as Colonel. After leaving Indianapolis, on the 7th of September, it went into active service in Missouri, participating in the memorable campaign of Gen. Fremont, afterward doing guard duty at Sedalia. At a later period, it was on duty, moving with the other forces into Southern Missouri and Arkansas, and participating in the battles of Newtonia, MO., Prairie Grove and Van Buren, Ark. On the first of June, 1863, it joined the army under Gen. Grant, in the rear of Vicksburg, remaining there until the surrender of that place on the 4th of July following. The regiment was engaged in the battle of Camp Sterling, near Morganza, September 29, and suffered a defeat, losing nearly one-half of its officers and men, mostly by capture. The prisoners were taken to Tyler, Tex., and held for several months. On the 1st of January, 1864, it re-enlisted, and after enjoying a veteran furlough of one month at home, it returned to the field in Louisiana on the 1st of June.

In the latter part of March, 1865, at the opening of the campaign against Mobile, the Twenty-sixth was actively engaged for several days, participating in the siege and in the assault on Spanish Fort. After some further service in that vicinity, it returned to Indianapolis, and was honorably discharged September 18, 1865." (Source: Historical Atlas, Fulton Co, IN, by Kingman Bros, 1883, page 15)

NOTE: Capt Rader stated that he was discharged in March, which the article written in Historical Atlas, page 25 confirms.)

o   (Rochester Sentinel, Sat. Aug 24, 1861) "Headquarters, Camp Sulivan. Aug. 18th 1861. The boys, generally, since our arrival, have been in good health and spirits, with the exception of a few cases of diarrhea, ague, dysentery and desertion. ….Twenty nine of our boys were granted leave of absence for an hour, and improved their time by a bath in the White River. ….and "your own", represented by Fulton County to a T…Lieut. Rader is home on furlough, as 28 other of our company. "

o   (Rochester Sentinel, Sat. Jan 18, 1862) In camp near Otterville, MO….David Rader was 2nd Lieut then….the Capt stated that Fulton county had sent a quantity of clothing, sox, blankets, etc….stated that "Lieut. Rader, while on a scout the other day, took a severe cold and has not fully recovered….visited him and he is much improved."

o   (Rochester Chronicle, Thurs. Mar. 26, 1863) "From the 26th Regiment. Camp 26th Indiana Volunteers, Near Hazel Wood, MO, March 6th 1863: Editor Chronicle:….In conclusion we speak of Captain D. Rader and upon him too much praise cannot be bestowed….Very respectfully yours, J.L. Atkinson, Co. A., 26th Reg. Ind. Vol"

o   Rochester Chronicle, Thurs. June 25, 1863) This letter states that David was promoted or "elected" to Captain in his regiment: "A voice from Indiana in the field. At a meet of company A, 26th Regiment, Ind. Vol. Infantry, the following preamble and Resolutions were unanimously agreed to….David Rader, Captain A."

o   (Rochester Chronicle, Thurs. Oct. 29, 1863) "Losses of Co. A., 26th Ind. Vols. The following are the extent of our casualties in the 26th Indiana. There are but a few really dangerous wounds, and with few exceptions they will all recover. Company A…..Wounded: Capt. David Rader, nose, right eye and fracture of skull…"

He appeared on the census June 16th 1870, in Rochester, Fulton Co, IN,. ·   1870 Census: David Rader, 40 yrs, M, W, Farmer, born in OH; Delilah, 37 yrs, F, W, Keeping house, born in IN; Frank D., 9 months, M, W, born in IN (Source: 1870 Census, Rochester, Fulton Co, IN, enumeration date June 16th 1870, page 21)

DIED.

At Prescott, Wis., on the 13th day of November, 1890, Mrs. Louisa Rader, aged 54 years.

Mrs. Rader was born at Willoby, Ohio, on the 29th day of June, 1836, and was married to Andrew Rader, Esq., who survives her, on the 23d day of November, 1854. Her maiden name was Fish and her mother was residing with her at her death. Mrs. Rader was one of the early settlers of Prescott, coming here in 1856, where she has since resided. She was a practical Christian, and never failed to confer benefits on the needy, if within her power. She goes down to her last resting place, mourned by all her friends, as well as her bereaved husband.

Census 2: 1880, Prescott, Pierce County, Wisconsin. 2ND. WARD, PRESCOTT, PIERCE COUNTY, WISCONSIN PAGE

·   1880 Census: David Rader, age 50, born in OH, occupation "Trader", Father born in VA, Mother born in NC; Delilah, age 39, born in PA, Father born in PA, Mother born in VA; Frank D., age 10, born in IN, Father born in OH (Fulton Co Census, 1880, Family History Library Film 1254278, NA Film # T9_0278, Page 65D)

He appeared on the census on 16 Jun 1880 in Prescott, Pierce, Wisconsin. Rader, Andrew W M 53   merchant Ohio Vt NY

Louisa   W F 42   Ohio Virginia NC

Almedia   W F 15   Minnesota, OH OH

Census 3: 1900, Prescott, Pierce County, Wisconsin. 2ND. WARD, PRESCOTT, PIERCE COUNTY, WISCONSIN

PAGE 134

Census 1900 Data: Andrew Rader, born Sept 1828, age 71, married, born in OH, father born in VA, mother born in N. Carolina, occupation "Merchant Notions"; Francis M, wife, age 45, born July 1854, born in NY, father born in NY, mother born in Massachusetts, occupation "Milliner" (Source: Fed Census 1900, Prescott, Pierce, WI, Roll T623, 1811, Page 5B, Enumeration District 112) NOTE: Further investigation needed for birth, marriage and death records.

Andrew married **Louisa Fisher** on 23 Nov 1854. Louisa was born on 29 Jun 1836 in Willoby, Ohio and died on 13 Nov 1890 in Prescott, Pierce County, Wisconsin at age 54. Another name for Louisa was Louisa Fish.

Alt Birth: 1828, OH.

She appeared on the census in 1880. 2ND. WARD, PRESCOTT, PIERCE COUNTY, WISCONSIN PAGE

Died: 13 Nov 1890, Prescott, Pierce County, Wisconsin.

The child from this marriage was:

+411 F i. **Almedia Rader** was born in 1865 in Minn..

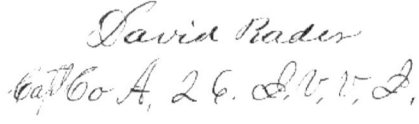

Andrew next married **Francis M.** in 1893. Francis was born in Jul 1854 in New York.

Noted events in her life were:

She appeared on the census in 1900. 2ND. WARD, PRESCOTT, PIERCE COUNTY, WISCONSIN PAGE 134

Caption: Cap David Rader]

67. David Andrew "Cap" Rader Capt.[34] (*Phillip Sr.*[2], *Casper Sr*[1]) was born on 29 Mar 1830 in Montgomery County, Ohio, died on 6 Mar 1908 in Rochester, Fulton co., Indiana[34] at age 77, and was buried in Hoover Cemetery, Fulton County, Indiana.

General Notes: 1880 United States Census

Name Relation Marital Status Gender Race Age Birthplace Occupation Father's Birthplace Mother's Birthplace

David RADER   Self   M   Male   W   50   OH   Trader   VA   NC
Delilah RADER   Wife   M   Female   W   39   PA   PA   VA
Frank D. RADER   Other   S   Male   W   10   IN   OH   ---

Source Information:

Census Place Rochester, Fulton, Indiana
Family History Library Film   1254278
NA Film Number   T9-0278
Page Number   65D

Regarding Capt David Rader, son of Philip Sr....same book, pg 89. Says he was born in Montgomery Co, OH on March 29, 1830. Mother was Catherine Sheets, a native of N. Carolina but became a resident of OH early in life. His father was born in VA and German by descent. "He came to OH in the early history of the state....."

Capt David came to Fulton Co IN in 1845....then went to the gold fields of CA.....etc

David "took part of the Indian war of 1812"....also "the" war....marched to the siege of Vicksburge till the city was taken , July 4, 1863......Received his discharge March 11, 1864. Married Delilah Dauson March 6, 1864. Had 3 children James G (died in infancy) Frank D. and Estella E (died at 2 mos)

David fought in the Civil War and lost the sight of one eye.

1880 United States Census
Name Relation Marital Status Gender Race Age Birthplace Occupation Father's Birthplace Mother's Birthplace
David RADER   Self M Male W 78 VA Farmer VA VA
Rachiel RADER Wife M Female W 76 VA Keeping House --- ---

Source Information:
 Census Place Liberty, Delaware, Ohio
 Family History Library Film   1255012
 NA Film Number   T9-1012
 Page Number   315D

David fought in the Civil War and lost the sight of one eye.

CAPT. DAVID RADER

BY O. F. MONTGOMERY.

   The above-named gentleman is a native of Ohio, born in Montgomery County March 29, 1830. His father, Philip Rader, was a Virginian by birth and a German by descent. He came to Ohio in the early history of the State, when the wigwam of the red man was to be seen nestling down among the forest trees, and the wild yell often proclaimed death to the few white settlers. He took part in the Indian war of 1812. Catharine Rader, nee Sheets, his wife, and the mother of the subject of this sketch, was a native of North Carolina, but became a resident of Ohio early in her life.

   Their family consisted of six children, all of whom are living, except one, and of whom "Cap" is the second. They died at their old home in Ohio just one year apart, the mother in 1852 and the father in 1853.

   " Cap, " as he is familiarly called, has lived a varied life. Having acquired a very meager education in the district schools he set out early in life to do for himself. He came to Fulton County in 1845, and began work on a farm. But the spirit of adventure had seized him, and the alluring stories from the gold fields of California prompted him, in the spring of 1854, to take up the journey across the plains, to find the shining treasure hidden in the debris of ancient volcanic eruptions. The journey was accomplished with ox teams, making it slow and toilsome, yet enlivened by advent-ure and new scones, and many a story is told by "

Cap " of exploits to his friendly listeners. Four years of a miner's life was sufficient to teach him that "all is not gold that glitters " so, in 1858, he returned home, and immediately engaged in the general merchandise business, at Akron, in Henry Township, under the firm named Curtis & Rader. He continued at this business until the beginning of the war, when he entered the service as Second Lieutenant in Company " A " of the Twenty-sixth Indiana Regiment. He was pro-moted to First Lieutenant, then to Captain of the compaNEW YORK The first, real engagement he was in was at the battle of Prairie Grove, Ark., on the 7tb of December, 1862. They then marched to the siege of Vicksburg, and remained theretill the city was taken, July 4, 1863, then went to Yazoo City, and captured it. They then returned to Vicksburg, and were ordered to Morganza Bend, and on the 29th day of September, 1863, while in an advance guard, to intercept the enemy at the crossing on the Chaffollia River, in a skirmish which took place, he lost his right eve by a musket ball from the enemy. He was taken to the hospital at New Orleans, and remained there till November, then came home, and received his discharge March 11, 1864.

On the 6th day of March, 1864, he was united in marriage with Delilah Dauson, daughter of James Dauson. and sister of our townsman, Jonathan Dauson. She was a native of Ohio, but at the date of marriage was a resident of Fulton County. The result of this union is three children - James G - oldest son, died in infancy - Frank D., now quite a boy, and Estella E., died in infancy at the age of two months.

Mr. Rader is a genial and very sociable gentleman; always ready in conversation; a firm friend of the soldier. He is also a very shrewd man, prompt in business relations. Is a member of the G. A. R., Post 95 He says, while he has been unfortunate in some things he has always been most successful in having, the great events of his life occur in the month of His birth, marriage and discharge from the army.

· Capt. David Rader: "Cap" as he is familiarly called, has lived a varied life. Having acquired a very meager education in the district schools, he set out early in life to do for himself. He came to Fulton County in 1845, and began work on a farm. But the spirit of adventure had seized him, and the alluring stories from the gold fields of California prompted him, in the spring of 1854, to take up the journey across the plains, to find the shining treasure hidden in the debris of ancient volcanic eruptions. The journey was accomplished with ox teams, making it slow and toilsome, yet enlivened by adventure and new scenes, and many a story is told by "Cap" of exploits to his friendly listeners. Four years of a miner's life was sufficient to teach him that "all is not gold that glitters;" so, in 1858 he returned home, and immediately engaged in the general merchandise business, at Akron, in Henry Township, under the firm named Curtis & Rader. He continued at this business until the beginning of the war, when he entered the service as Second Lieutenant in Company A of the Twenty-sixth Indiana Regiment. He was promoted to First Lieutenant, then to Captain of the company. The first real engagement he was in was at the battle of Prairie Grove, Ark., on the 7th of December, 1862. They then marched to the siege of Vicksburg, and remained there till the city was taken, July 4th, 1863; then went to Yazoo City, and captured it. They then returned to Vicksburg, and were ordered to Morganza Bend, and on the 29th day of September, 1963, while in an advance guard, to intercept the enemy at the crossing on the Chaffellia River, in a skirmish which took place, he lost his right eye by a musket ball from the enemy. He was taken to the hospital at New Orleans, and remained there till November, then came home, and received his discharge March 11, 1864.

On the 6th day of March, 1864, he was united in marriage in Delilah Dauson, daughter of James Dauson, and sister of our townsman, Jonathan Dauson. She was a native of Ohio, but at the date of marriage was a resident of Fulton County. The result of this union is three children---James G., oldest son, died in infancy; Frank D., now quite a boy, and Estella E., died in infancy at the age of two months.

Mr. Rader is genial and a very sociable gentleman; always ready for conversation; a firm friend of the soldier. He is also a very shrewd man, prompt in business relations. Is a member of the G.A.R., Post 95. He says, while he has been unfortunate in some things he has always been most successful in having the great events of his life occur in the month of March, viz.: His birth, marriage and discharge from the army." (Source: Historical Atlas, Fulton Co, IN, by Kingman Bros, 1883, page 25)

· ADDITIONAL EXCERPTS FROM VARIOUS NEWSPAPERS REGARDING CAPTAIN DAVID RADER WHICH MAY BE OF INTEREST TO HIS DESCENDANTS:

o (Rochester Chronicle, Thurs. April 2, 1868) " The members of the Union Central Committee of Fulton County will meet at the Chronicle office,….the following gentlemen compose the committee: David Rader of Henry Township…."

o (Rochester Union-Spy, Fri. May 27, 1870) Announcements: … "For Sheriff, David Rader, a wounded Union soldier…"

o (Rochester Union-Spy, Fri. May 5, 1871) "Capt. David Rader and Mr. Samuel Dawson, of this county, are now in Missouri, driving eastward a large herd of cattle. This stock will be fed on the prairies of Jasper and Newton Counties, Indiana, until fit for market."

o (Rochester Union-Spy, Thurs. Sept. 26, 1872) "Captain David Rader has accepted the agency for the Howe Sewing Machine Company in this county. Office at Dawson's Drug Store…machines, needles and attachments."

o (Rochester Union Spy, Thurs., Oct. 23, 1873) Runaway: On Tuesday last, David Rader borrowed his father-in-law's team and proceeded to Al Goodrich's cooper shop after some apple barrels…barrels rolled…frightened the horses…The runaway will only cost Dave a little pain in walking, and about $10 in cash…."

o (Rochester Union Spy, Feb 16, 1874) "David Rader, Esq., is not only a veteran soldier, but a veteran subscriber to the Union-Spy. He walked deliberately into our office last Monday and gave is the wherewith to pay for his paper three years in advance….He also subscribed one year for a brother, A. Rader at Prescott, WI"

o Rochester Sentinel, Sat., May 16, 1874) "Captain David Rader and family expect to start soon for Wisconsin and Minnesota, where they will spend the summer months among their friends and relatives."

o Rochester Sentinel, Sat., June 27, 1874) "Capt. David Rader with his family started for Minnesota on Thursday, to spend the heated-season. The recovery of the health of Mrs. Rader is the incentive for the visit."

o (Rochester Union Spy, Sept 3, 1874) "Capt. David Rader and lady returned from their extended summer visit in the west, last week, well and hearty. The Captain knows how to enjoy a western tour."

o(Rochester Sentinel, Sat., Sept. 26, 1874) "The dwelling house on the farm lying east of the lake owned by David Rader....was destroyed..." NOTE: This is the original Rader homestead purchased by Philip Rader Sr....Philip Jr, David, Fay Morrett, Elizabeth (Morrett) Riley lived there....my mother, Margel (Riley) Craig was born there. See description of homestead under Philip Rader Sr.

o(Rochester Union-Spy, Fri., May 14, 1875) " The new town council appointed Capt. David Rader, Marshall to serve one year or during good behavior."

o(Rochester Sentinel, Sat., Aug. 4, 1877) "According to an ordinance published elsewhere in this issue, a brick sidewalk is to be built on the west side of Jefferson street, extending from Fred Fromm's residence to Capt. Rader's. The necessity of such an improvement has been long been felt by many of the residents living along the line of the project and by hundreds of church goers who attend the three churches located on that street." NOTE: Before this year, David and family could have resided in Akron on the homestead. This periodical shows approximate time that he moved to Rochester permanently.

o(Rochester Union Spy, Fri., March, 28, 1879) "Capt. Rader and Wm H. C. Chinn have the agency for a self-binding reaping machine, that is said to excel all others...."

o(Rochester Sentinel, Sat., Nov. 10, 1883) "List of Pensioners in Fulton County, showing their disabilities and the amounts received per month:..........RADER, David, loss right eye, $15......"

Noted events in his life were:

Alt Birth: 1802, VA.[34]

Resided: 1845, Fulton County, Indiana. from Historical Atlas

Capt. David Rader by G. F. Montgomery

The above named gentleman is a native of Ohio, born in Montgomery County March 29, 1830. His father, Philip Rader, was a Virginian by birth and a German by descent. He came to Ohio in the early history of the state, when the wigwam of the red man was to be seen nestling down among the forest trees, and the wild yell often proclaimed death to the few white settlers. He took part in the indian war of 1812. Catharine Rader, nee Sheets, his wife, and the mother of the subject of this sketch, was a native of North Carolina, but became a resident of Ohio early in her life.

Their family consisted of six children, all of whom are living except one, and whom "Cap" is the second. They died at their old home in Ohio just one year apart, the mother in 1852 and the father in 1853.

"Cap" as he is familiarly called, has lived a varied life. Having acquired a very meager education in the District schools, he set out early in life to do for himself. He came to Fulton County in 1845, and began work on a farm.

He appeared on the census in 1850. HENRY TOWNSHIP, FULTON COUNTY, INDIANA PAGE 405 LINE 62

Resided: 1854-1858, California. But the spirit of adventure had seized him, and the alluring stories from the gold fields of California prompted him, in the spring of 1854, to take up the journey across the plains, to find the shining treasure hidden in the debris of ancient volcanic eruptions. The journey was accomplished with ox teams, making it slow and toilsome, yet enlivened by adventure and new scenes, and many a story is told by "Cap" of exploits to his friendly listeners. Four years of a miner's life was sufficient to teach him that "all is not gold that glitters"

Resided: 1858, Akron. so, in 1858 he returned home, and immediately engaged in the general merchandise business, at Akron, in Henry Township, under the firm named Curtis & Rader. He continued at this business until the beginning of the war,

Military: Between 9 Aug 1861 and 11 Mar 1864. CAPT. A COUNTY 26TH. INFANTRY REG. INDIANA

He served in the military from 1862 to 1864. At the beginning of the war, when he entered the service as Second Lieutenant in Company A of the 26th Indiana Regiment. He was promoted to First Lieutenant, then to Captain of the Company. The first real engagement he was in was at the battle of Prairie Grove, Ark., on the 7th of December, 1862. They then marched to the siege of Vicksgurg, and remained there until the city was taken, July 4, 1863; then went to Yazoo City and captured it. They then returned to vicksburg, and were ordered to Morganza Bend, and on the 29th day of September, 1863, while in an advance guard, to intercept the enemy at the crossing on the Chaffellia River, in a skirmish which took place, he lost his right eye to a musket ball from the enemy. He was taken to the hospital at New Orleans and remained there till November, then came home, and received his discharge March 11, 1864.

Census 1: 1870. HENRY TOWNSHIP, FULTON COUNTY, INDIANA PAGE 125 LINE 150

He appeared on the census on 16 Jun 1870 in Rochester, Fulton, Indiana. Rader, David 40, M W farmer born Ohio   Delilah 37 F W   born Indiana   Frank 9/12 M W

Census 2: 1880. ROCHESTER, FULTON COUNTY, INDIANA PAGE 16 LINE 165

He appeared on the census in 1880 in Liberty, Delaware, Ohio. 1880 United States Census
Name Relation Marital Status Gender Race Age Birthplace Occupation Father's Birthplace Mother's Birthplace
David RADER Self M Male W 78 VA Farmer VA VA
Rachiel RADER Wife M Female W 76 VA Keeping House --- ---

Source Information:
  Census Place Liberty, Delaware, Ohio
  Family History Library Film   1255012
  NA Film Number   T9-1012
  Page Number   315D

Retired: 1883, Fulton County, Indiana. Mr Rader is a genial and very sociable gentleman; always ready in conversation; a firm friend of the soldier. He is also a very shrewd man, prompt in business relations. Is a member of the G.A.R., post 95. He says, while he has been unfortunate in some things he has always been most successful in having the great events of his life occur in the month of March, viz: His birth, marriage and discharge from the army.

Census 3: 1900. ROCHESTER, FULTON COUNTY, INDIANA PAGE 43B LINE 379

David married WFT Est 1824-1869.[34]

David married **Rachiel**. Rachiel was born in 1804 in VA.

David next married **Delila Dawson**, daughter of **James Dawson Esq.** and **Sarah Biddle**, on 6 Mar 1864 in Fulton County, Indiana. Delila was born on 25 Jan 1839 in Rochester, Fulton County, Indiana, died on 21 May 1904 in Rochester, Fulton County, Indiana at age 65, and was buried in Hoover Cemetery, Fulton County, Indiana. Another name for Delila was Delilah Dawson.

> Marriage Notes: On the 6th day of March, he was united in marriage in Delilah Dauson, daughter of James Dauson and sister of our townsman, Jonathan Dauson. She was a native of Ohio, but at the date of the marriage was a resident of Fulton County.
>
> The result of this union is three children -- Jaes G., oldest son, died in infancy; Frank D., now quite a boy, and Estella E., died in infancy at the age of 2 months.
>
> > General Notes: · OBIT: "Mrs. David (Delilah Dawson) Rader who has been ill for the past few days suffering with a mastoid abscess that greatly affected her brain, died at about eight o'clock this morning. Following is an obituary as prepared by the relatives:
> >
> > Delilah Dawson, daughter of James and Sarah Dawson, was born on a farm near Akron, in Fulton county, IN, January 25, 1839; died in Rochester, May 21, 1904; aged 65 years, 3 months and 26 days; and was united in marriage with Captain David Rader, March 6, 1864.
> >
> > Mrs. Rader's entire life was spent in Fulton county, and until her marriage, on a farm; after marriage, in Akron, until coming to Rochester where the remainder of her life was spent. Mrs. Rader leaves her husband, Captain David Rader, one son, Frank D. Rader, of Rochester and four grandchildren, and two brothers, Jonathan Dawson, of Rochester, and Samuel B. Dawson of near Akron, and many relatives and friends. The deceased was a member of the first Baptist church for years. …Burial at Athens."
> >
> > (Published: Rochester Sentinel, Saturday, May 21, 1904)
>
> Noted events in her life were:
>
> She appeared on the census in 1870. HENRY TOWNSHIP, FULTON COUNTY, INDIANA PAGE 125 LINE 150
>
> Census 1: 1880. ROCHESTER, FULTON COUNTY, INDIANA PAGE 16 LINE 165
>
> Census 2: 1900. ROCHESTER, FULTON COUNTY, INDIANA PAGE 43B LINE 379

Children from this marriage were:

+412 M i. **James G. Rader** was born in Feb 1863 in Fulton County, Indiana, died on 3 Apr 1863 in Fulton County, Indiana, and was buried in Hoover Cemetery, Fulton County, Indiana.

+413 M ii. **Frank D. Rader** was born on 16 Aug 1869 in Rochester, Fulton County, Indiana and died on 7 Nov 1927 in Toledo, Ohio at age 58.

> Frank married **Hattie May Housley** (b. 16 Aug 1869, d. 28 Jun 1915) in Grand Rapids, Wood Co. Ohio.

+414 F   iii.   **Estella Edith Rader** was born in Jun 1878 in Fulton County, Indiana and died on 24 Aug 1878 in Fulton County, Indiana.

68. Barbara Rader[34] (*Phillip Sr.*[2], *Casper Sr*[1]) was born on 1 Jan 1832 [34] and died on 23 Feb 1898 in Pierce Co, WI [34] at age 66.

General Notes: Barbara Rader (daughter of Philip Rader, Sr and Catherine "Sheets" Rader)

Born: Abt 1832, Montgomery Co, OH

Died: February 23, 1898 Pierce Co, WI (Need additional verification)

· Born 1832-1833, Montgomery Co, Ohio (Source 1)

Died: Feb 23, 1898, Pierce County, WI (Need additional verification)

· Married A.M. Rudy, lived in PA (Source 3)

· (Rochester Union-Spy, Fri. April 28, 1876) "Miss Allie Rudy, of Prescott, WI and Mr. H. Rudy, of Harrisburg, PA, are guests of Captain Rader."

NOTE: Grandma stated that Barbara was married to a Rudy and that they visited them from PA. However, census in Pierce Co, WI show Rudy's and this is the same county in which A.W. Rader lived. Additionally, a Mary Alfaretta Rudy (maybe her nickname was "Allie" was the daughter of Barbara "Rader" and Adam Rudy or perhaps Allie was Mary Alfaretta's daughter, Aleathea. Alfaretta's husband was Harrie K. Rudy per World Family Tree: Vol 6, Tree #2279.

· Barbara (spelled "Rabara") Rudy died Feb 23, 1898, Pierce County, WI

(Source: Wisconsin Vital Records Death Index. Volume 01, page 0088, Reel 107, Image 0988, ImageNum 104545, Sequence # 330216) NOTE: Her brother, A.W. Rader lived in the same county.

HUSBAND:
Adam M. Rudy
AKA: A.M.
Born: Abt 1830, Harrisburg, Dauphin, PA
Died:

§ Barbara Rader married A.M. Rudy April 30, 1856

(Source: Rochester Library: Index to Marriage Records, Miami Co. 1850-1920 Inclusive. IREF 929.3 IND Vol 2, Book C2 page 316) Original record located County Ckerks Office, Peru, Indiana compiled by Indiana Works Progress Administration 1938

§ Census 1850 Info: Adam Rudy, age 20, Home in 1850 Harrisburg North Ward, Dauphin, PA, son of Jonas and Mary Rudy, single person, occupation "Plasterer" (Source: 1850 Fed Census, Roll M432_774, page 67) NOTE: This information corresponds to information in LDS which states his parents were Jonas and Mary Rudy and family members listed were: Adam, b. 1830; David, b. 1833; Darius, b. 1835; Ann, b. 1837; William, b. 1840; Edward, b. 1842; Jonas or James, b. 1846; and Jane, b. 1850 with all born in Harrisburg, Dauphin Co, PA. (LDS Source: Film #458158)

§ Census 1860 Info: Adam Rudy, age 29, occupation "Plasterer" born in PA; Barbara Rudy, age 27, born in OH; Mary, age 2, born in IN (Source: 1860 Fed Census, M653_1426, page 141, Prescott Ward 2, Pierce Co, WI) NOTE: Checked additional census and found no additional information. NOTE: LDS, Source: Film #458158 states they had a daughter, Mary Alfaretta Rudy.

CHILDREN OF BARBARA AND A.M. RUDY:

The following information regarding Mary Alfaretta, Harrie K. Rudy and their children were obtained from Family Tree Maker, Version 8, World Family Tree: Vol 6, Tree # 2279

unless otherwise noted.

Mary Alfaretta Rudy

Barbara married **A. M. Rudy**[34][34].

69. Eliza Jane Rader[34] (*Phillip Sr.*[2], *Casper Sr*[1]) was born on 11 Aug 1833 in Montgomery County, Ohio,[34] died on 2 Dec 1852 in Fulton County, Indiana[34] at age 19, and was buried in Omega Cemetery, Akron, Fulton County, Indiana.

Death Notes: · Cemetery record: " Ball, Eliza Jane, wife of Aaron M., d. Dec 2, 1852, age 19 yrs-3mos-25days. (Source: Omega Cemetery, Henry Twp, Fulton Co, IN.)

NOTE: Her grave in next to Katherine Rader's grave. Also, there is a grave of (----) Thomas M., 1850 (not readable). This could be her son…..so I will do further research.

· ???? Census 1880 has the following info: Eliza J. Ball, Wife of Aaron M. Ball, est year of birth 1826, age 54, married, home in 1880 Liberty, Delaware, IN, father and mother's birthplace OH, Eliza's birthplace OH; Aaron M. Ball, age 5_, occupation farmer, has bronchitis, born in IN, both parents born in TN; Elmer, age 19, son-in-law, occupation "works on farm", born in IN, father born in VA, mother born in OR; Emmencia (difficult to read), age 16, daughter-in-law, born in IN, father born in VA, mother born in OR; Sigmand S. age 1_ (difficult to read), son-in-law, born in IN, father born in VA, mother born in OR. (Source: 1880 Fed Census, Liberty, Delaware, IN; Roll T9_274; Family History Film: 1254274; Page 426D, Enumeration District 185; Image 0494, enumeration date June 8, 1880 by T.E. Harrington) NOTE: This needs further investigation to determine that this is Eliza Rader Ball due to the additional marriages of Aaron Ball in Fulton Co.

HUSBAND:

Aaron M. Ball

· Eliza J. Rader married Aaron M. Ball on March 13, 1851, Book A, pg 41

(Source: Fulton Co Library Marriage Records…married by J. Whittenberger}

NOTE: Aaron Ball also had two additional marriages listed; however, no data confirming that this is the same Aaron Ball. Marriages are: Aaron Ball married Sieneth (name difficult to read) Crocket, May 12, 1853 by Jacob Whittenberger, Fulton Co, IN marriage records, Book A, page 123. Aaron Ball married Martha Douglas May 16, 1856 by John Elam, Justice of the Peace, Fulton Co Marriage Records, Book A, page 253.

CHILDREN: No children mentioned in family notes or found in any documentation to date.

Noted events in her life were:

She appeared on the census in 1850. HENRY TOWNSHIP, FULTON COUNTY, INDIANA PAGE 405 LINE 62

Eliza married **Aaron Miller Ball**, son of **William Dyer Ball** and **Margaret Widner**, on 13 Mar 1851 in Fulton County, Indiana. Aaron was born on 3 Feb 1827 in Wayne County, Indiana.

Noted events in his life were:

Military: Between 29 Jul 1862 and 17 Apr 1863. PVT. COUNTY D INDIANA 87TH. INFANTRY

70. Henry C. Rader[34] (*Phillip Sr.*[2], *Casper Sr*[1]) was born on 25 Jan 1836 in Ohio[34] and died in Colton, CA.[34]

General Notes: Henry settled in Colton, California.

Noted events in his life were:

He appeared on the census in 1850. HENRY TOWNSHIP, FULTON COUNTY, INDIANA PAGE 405 LINE 62

He appeared on the census in 1870 in Round Valley, Mendocino Co, CA. · Census 1870: Henry Rader, age 36, b. OH, approx year of birth 1934, occupation "do", which is listed on the next line after "Laborer" from previous name written, Home in 1870 Round Valley, Mendocino, CA, post office Covelo. (Source: 1870 Fed Census, Round Valley, Mendocino Co, CA, Roll M593_74, pg 221, image 436) NOTE: This census does not list birth place of parents.

He appeared on the census in 1900 in Rowland, Los Angeles, CA. Rowland Township, Los Angeles County, California PAGE 42

· Census 1900: Henry C. Rader, age 64, approx year of birth 1836, born in OH, (cannot read places of parents birth); Sarah, wife, age 59, estimated year of birth 1841, born in Missouri, her parents both born in OH; Green C., son, age 2, estimated birth year 1898, born in CA, father born in OH, cannot read mother's place of birth (Source: Fed Census, Rowland, Los Angeles, CA, Roll: T623 92; Page 20A, Enumeration District 121) City of Pasadena??? NOTE: Further investigation needed.

He appeared on the census in 1910 in Los Angeles, Los Angeles, California. · Census 1910: Sarah Rader, age 60, estimated birth year 1849, widow, birthplace Missouri, home in 1910 Los Angeles, Los Angeles, CA, father born in OH, mother born in Maryland, (Source: Fed Census, Los Angeles, Los Angeles, CA, Series T624, Roll 80, Part 2, Page 163A) NOTE: Further investigation needed….examine birth years since Census of 1900 and 1910 do not match. Also, no child named Green on the 1910 census.

Source Citations

· NOTE: Need to investigate Colton area. Per map, it is near San Bernadino and Riverside. Is Rowland twp or Co in the Pasadena area?? Need to investigate death, marriage and birth records in CA.

Henry married **Sarah** about 1887. Sarah was born in Oct 1850 in Missouri.

Noted events in her life were:

She appeared on the census in 1900. Rowland Township, Los Angeles County, California PAGE 42

The child from this marriage was:

+415 M   i.   **Grover C. Rader** was born in Dec 1888 in California.

71. Julia Ann Rader[34] (*Phillip Sr.*[2], *Casper Sr*[1]) was born in 1838 in OH[34] and died in Jan 1898 in Iowa[34] at age 60. Another name for Julia was Julian Rader.

General Notes: ·"Julia (Rader) Sheppard"....Sheppard married name. AKA Julia (Source 3)

· "Julia Ann ...lived most of her married life in Albia, Iowa. She had one son, Oscar J. Garriett" (Source 2)

· (The Rochester Weekly Sentinel, Friday, Jan. 7, 1898) "Capt. Rader received a telegram this morning that his sister, Mrs. Julia Garrett, of Ottowa, Iowa, who has been sick for some time died yesterday. No particulars given." NOTE: Could be a misspelling....could be Ottumwa, Iowa. I checked internet and there was no "Ottowa", Iowa.

HUSBAND:

Oliver Garriott   Born:

    Died: 1871, Albia Iowa, Oak View Cemetery

§ Julia A. Rader married Oliver Garriott, March 29, 1857, Miami Co, IN

(Source: Index to Marriage Record 1850-1920 Inclusive Volume I, Letters A - L Inc.Record location: Miami CO, IN. Original Record located County Clerks Office, Peru, Indiana compiled by IN Works Progress Adm. 1938. Book C-2, page 377)

    CHILDREN OF JULIA ANN AND OLIVER GARRIOTT:
        Oscar Jm Garriott
            Born: Abt 1858, Iowa
            Died:

o 1910 Census: Oscar Jm Garriott, age 51, estimated year of birth 1858, born in Iowa. (Source: 1910 Fed Census, 3-WD Ottumwa, Wapello Co, Iowa, Series T624, Roll 426, Part 2, page 98A) NOTE: Additional information needed. Need to review original census for wife and children.

o   "O.J. Garriott, of Des Moines, was visiting with relatives over Sunday in the city. Mr. Garriott formerly resided here, but is now located in Des Moines, being a member of the firm of the O'Dea Hardware Co." (Source: Ottumwa Daily Courier, July 27, 1903.) NOTE: Father was Oliver and supposedly died in 1871. Albert Wilbur Rader lived in the Des Moines, Iowa area also. Need further investigation. I checked 1870, 1880, 1890 and 1900 census but no record until 1910 for Oscar....none for parents.)

Noted events in her life were:

Resided: Albie, Iowa.

She appeared on the census in 1850. HENRY TOWNSHIP, FULTON COUNTY, INDIANA PAGE 405 LINE 62

Julia married **Oliver Garriott**[34] WFT Est 1819-1865.[34] Oliver died in 1871 in Albie, Iowa.[34]

Marriage Notes: Julia lived most of her married life in Albia, Iowa.

The child from this marriage was:

+416 M i. **Oscar J. Carriett**[34] was born WFT Est 1825-1864 [34] and died WFT Est 1834-1941 [34] at age 9.

Julia next married **Sheppard**.

72. Eliza Rader (*Peter*[2], *Casper Sr*[1]) was born on 29 Oct 1812 in Blountville, Sullivan County, Tennessee.[32]

73. Elizabeth Rader (*Peter*[2], *Casper Sr*[1]) was born in 1812 and died WFT Est 1813-1906 at age 1.

74. James J. Rader (*Peter*[2], *Casper Sr*[1]) was born in 1814 in Blountville, Sullivan County, Tennessee.

Noted events in his life were:

He appeared on the census in 1850. SULLIVAN COUNTY, TENNESSEE PAGE 53 LINE 143

He appeared on the census in 1850 in Sullivan Co., TN.

```
RADER ELIZABETH 40    F    W    TN    SULLIVAN  1-DIVN       897   113
RADER JAS P    36    M    W    TN    SULLIVAN  1-DIVN    897       113
RADER MARTHA   14    F    W    TN    SULLIVAN  1-DIVN       897   113
RADER MARGARET 8     F    W    TN    SULLIVAN  1-DIVN       897   113
RADER ADOLPHUS 6     M    W    TN    SULLIVAN  1-DIVN       897   113
RADER INDIANA  3     F    W    TN    SULLIVAN  1-DIVN       897   113
RADER ELLEN    0     F    W    TN    SULLIVAN  1-DIVN       897   113
```

Census 1: 1860. DISTRICT 2, SULLIVAN COUNTY, TENNESSEE PAGE 16 LINE 260

Census 2: 1870. SULLIVAN COUNTY, TENNESSEE PAGE 441 LINE 114

Census 3: 1880, District 20, Sullivan, Tennessee. DISTRICT 20, SULLIVAN COUNTY, TENNESSEE LINE 150 PAGE 398

1880 United States Census   Household:
 Name Relation Marital Status Gender Race Age Birthplace Occupation Father's Birthplace Mother's Birthplace
 James J. RADER   Self M   Male   W   64   TN   Farmer   VA   VA
 P. Jane RADER   Wife M   Female W   41   VA   Keeping House   VA   VA
 Charles W. RADER   Son   S   Male   W   13   TN   On Farm   TN   VA
 James C. RADER   Son   S   Male   W   10   TN   On Farm   TN   VA

```
   Landon C. RADER   Son   S   Male     W   9   TN        TN   VA
   E. Leona RADER    Dau   S   Female   W   7   TN        TN   VA
   H. Florence RADER Dau   S   Female   W   6   TN        TN   VA
   Albert W. RADER   Son   S   Male     W   3   TN        TN   VA
   Cordelia M. RADER Dau   S   Female   W   1   TN        TN   VA
```

Source Information:
 Census Place District 20, Sullivan, Tennessee
 Family History Library Film   1255281
 NA Film Number   T9-1281
 Page Number   398C

He appeared on the census in 1880 in Lewisburg, Greenbrier, West Virginia. 1880 United States Census

Name Relation Marital Status Gender Race Age Birthplace Occupation Father's Birthplace Mother's Birthplace
```
   Jas. M. RADER     Self     S   Male   W   25   WV   Farmer   WV   WV
   Calvin B. RADER   Brother  S   Male   W   20   WV   Farmer   WV   WV
```

Source Information:
 Census Place Lewisburg, Greenbrier, West Virginia
 Family History Library Film   1255402
 NA Film Number   T9-1402
 Page Number   366D

James married **Elizabeth T. T.**. Elizabeth was born in 1810 in Tennessee.

Noted events in her life were:

She appeared on the census in 1850. SULLIVAN COUNTY, TENNESSEE PAGE 53 LINE 143

Census 1: 1860. DISTRICT 2, SULLIVAN COUNTY, TENNESSEE PAGE 16 LINE 260

Children from this marriage were:

+417 F   i.   **Martha Rader** was born in 1836 in Sullivan County, Tennessee.

+418 F   ii. **Margaret Rader** was born in 1842 in Washington, TN.

+419 M   iii. **Adolphus L. Rader** was born in May 1847 in Sullivan County, Tennessee.

Adolphus married **Georgia Reat** (b. Feb 1853) on 16 Feb 1874 in Coles Co. Illinois.[88]

+420 F   iv. **Indiana Rader** was born in 1847 in Washington, TN.

+421 F   v.   **Eleanor S. Rader** was born in 1850 in Washington, TN.

James next married **Permilia Jane**. Permilia was born in 1839 in Virginia.

Noted events in her life were:

She appeared on the census in 1870. SULLIVAN COUNTY, TENNESSEE PAGE 409 LINE 95

Census 1: 1880. DISTRICT 20, SULLIVAN COUNTY, TENNESSEE LINE 150 PAGE 398

Children from this marriage were:

+422	M	i.	**Charles W. Rader** was born in 1866 in Sullivan County, Tennessee.
+423	M	ii.	**Granville Rader** was born in 1868 in Sullivan County, Tennessee.
+424	M	iii.	**James C. Rader** was born in 1870 in Sullivan County, Tennessee.
+425	M	iv.	**Landon C. Rader** was born in 1871 in Sullivan County, Tennessee.
+426	F	v.	**E. Leona Rader** was born in 1873 in Sullivan County, Tennessee.
+427	F	vi.	**H. Florence Rader** was born in 1874 in Sullivan County, Tennessee.
+428	M	vii.	**Albert W. Rader** was born in 1877 in Sullivan County, Tennessee.
+429	F	viii.	**Cordelia M. Rader** was born in 1879 in Sullivan County, Tennessee.

75. Elkanah D. Rader (*Peter ^{2}, Casper Sr ^{1}*) was born in 1817 in Blountville, Sullivan County, Tennessee.

Noted events in his life were:

He appeared on the census in 1850. WASHINGTON COUNTY, TENNESSEE PAGE LINE 228

He appeared on the census in 1850 in Washington Co, Tennessee.

RADER E D 32 M W TN WASHINGTON 4 sub east 898 118
RADER ANGELINA 27 F W OH WASHINGTON 4 sub east 898 118
RADER JAMES P 5 M W TN WASHINGTON 4 sub east 898 118
RADER DORCUS L 2 F W TN WASHINGTON 4 sub east 898 118

Census 1: 1860. 17TH. DISTRICT, SULLIVAN COUNTY, TENNESSEE PAGE 53 LINE 146

Census 2: 1870. SULLIVAN COUNTY, TENNESSEE PAGE 531 LINE 6

Census 3: 1880. 17TH. DIST., BRISTOL, SULLIVAN COUNTY, TENNESSEE PAGE 530A LINE 256

Elkanah married **Angelina**. Angelina was born in 1822 in Tennessee.

Noted events in her life were:

She appeared on the census in

1850. WASHINGTON COUNTY, TENNESSEE PAGE LINE 228

Census 1: 1860. 17TH. DISTRICT, SULLIVAN COUNTY, TENNESSEE PAGE 53 LINE 146

Census 2: 1870. SULLIVAN COUNTY, TENNESSEE PAGE 531 LINE 6

Children from this marriage were:

Source Citations

+430 M i. **James Polk Rader** was born on 26 Aug 1844 in Washington County, Tennessee.

James married **Mary Elizabeth**.

+431 F ii. **Dorcas L. Rader** was born in 1848 in Washington County, Tennessee.

+432 F iii. **Mary Jane K. Rader** was born in 1850 in Washington County, Tennessee.

+433 M iv. **Thomas W. Rader** was born in 1854 in Washington County, Tennessee.

+434 M v. **William H. "Will" Rader** was born in Oct 1857 in Washington County, Tennessee.

William married **Juniata** (b. Jun 1875).

+435 F vi. **Alice C. Rader** was born in 1860 in Washington Co, Tennessee.

+436 F vii. **Maggie Rader** was born in 1863.

76. Malinda Rader (*Peter ^{2}, Casper Sr ^{1}*) was born about 1817 in Blountville, Sullivan County, Tennessee.

Malinda married **James Vaughan Jr.**.

The child from this marriage was:

+437 M i. **Joseph Elkanah Vaughan** was born on 9 Feb 1836 in Wytheville, Wythe County, Virginia.

Joseph married **Mary E. Haun**.

Malinda next married **James Vaughn Jr.**.

The child from this marriage was:

+438 M i. **Joseph Elkanah Vaughan** was born on 9 Feb 1836 in Wythe County, Virginia.

Joseph married **Mary E. Haun**.

77. Calvin M. Rader (*Peter ^{2}, Casper Sr ^{1}*) was born on 9 Feb 1818 in Blountville, Sullivan County, Tennessee, died on 24 Apr 1890 in Blountville, Sullivan County, Tennessee at age 72, and was buried in Blountville Cemetery, Sullivan County, Tennessee.

Noted events in his life were:

He appeared on the census in 1850. DISTRICT 1, SULLIVAN COUNTY, TENNESSEE PAGE 28 LINE 247

He appeared on the census in 1850 in Sullivan Co., TN.

RADER CALVIN	34	M	W	TN	SULLIVAN	1-DIVN	897	17
RADER ELIZABETH	22	F	W	TN	SULLIVAN	1-DIVN	897	17
RADER ADELIA A	4	F	W	TN	SULLIVAN	1-DIVN	897	17
RADER LANDON H	2	M	W	TN	SULLIVAN	1-DIVN	897	17

Census 1: 1860. 4TH. DISTRICT, SULLIVAN COUNTY, TENNESSEE PAGE 73 LINE 490

Military: Apr 1865. CAPT. OWEN WHITES COMPANY, HOME GUARD, BRISTOL TENNESSEE CIVIL WAR CONFEDERATE

Census 2: 1870. 5TH. DISTRICT, SULLIVAN COUNTY, TENNESSEE PAGE 415 LINE 56

Census 3: 1880. 5TH. DISTRICT, SULLIVAN COUNTY, TENNESSEE PAGE 506D LINE 31

He appeared on the census in 1880 in Lewisburg, Greenbrier, West Virginia. 1880 United States Census

    Name Relation Marital Status Gender Race Age Birthplace Occupation Father's Birthplace Mother's Birthplace

    Jas. M. RADER Self S Male W 25 WV Farmer WV WV
    Calvin B. RADER Brother S Male W 20 WV Farmer WV WV

Source Information:
  Census Place Lewisburg, Greenbrier, West Virginia
  Family History Library Film 1255402
  NA Film Number T9-1402
  Page Number 366D

Calvin married **Elizabeth**. Elizabeth was born about 1820.

Children from this marriage were:

+439 F i. **Adelia A. Rader** was born in 1846 in Sullivan, Washington Co, TN.

+440 M ii. **Landon H. Rader** was born in 1848 in Sullivan, Washington Co, TN.

+441 M iii. **Joseph Rader** was born in 1850 in Sullivan, Washington Co, TN.

+442 F iv. **Margaret Rader** was born in 1852 in Sullivan, Washington Co, TN.

+443 M v. **Evaline V. Rader** was born in 1854 in Sullivan, Washington Co, TN.

+444 F vi. **Melvina Rader** was born in 1860 in Sullivan, Washington Co, TN.

Calvin next married **Elizabeth**. Elizabeth was born in 1828 in Tennessee.

Noted events in her life were:

She appeared on the census in 1850. SULLIVAN COUNTY, TENNESSEE PAGE 96 LINE 32

Census 1: 1860. 4TH. DISTRICT, SULLIVAN COUNTY, TENNESSEE PAGE 73 LINE 490

Children from this marriage were:

+445 F i. **Adelia A. Rader** was born in 1846.

    Adelia married **James D. Bowman**.

+446 M ii. **Landon H. Rader** was born in 1848.

+447 M iii. **Joseph "Jc" H. Rader** was born in 1850 in Tennessee.

    Joseph married **Ida**.

Joseph next married **Lillian** (b. 1857) in 1879.

+448 F iv. **Margaret E. Rader** was born in 1852 in Blountville, Sullivan County, Tennessee.

+449 F v. **Evaline V. Rader** was born in 1854 and died before 1917 in Blountville, Sullivan County, Tennessee.

+450 F vi. **Janet Melvina Rader** was born in 1860.

+451 F vii. **Susan Rader** was born in 1866.

+452 F viii. **Sarah C. Rader** was born in 1867.

Calvin next married **Lodemia Caroline Millard**, daughter of **Thomas Millard** and **Sarah Anna Bean**, on 7 Sep 1876 in Sullivan County, Tennessee. Lodemia was born on 9 May 1840 in Paperville, Tennessee, died on 4 Oct 1915 in Blountville, Sullivan County, Tennessee at age 75, and was buried in Blountville Cemetery, Sullivan County, Tennessee.

Noted events in her life were:

She appeared on the census in 1880. 5TH. DISTRICT, SULLIVAN COUNTY, TENNESSEE PAGE 506D LINE 31

Census 1: 1900. 5 DISTRICT, SULLIVAN COUNTY, TENNESSEE PAGE 51

Census 2: 1910. 5 DISTRICT, SULLIVAN COUNTY, TENNESSEE LINE 96 PAGE 6A

Children from this marriage were:

+453 F i. **Kate Mae Rader** was born in Aug 1877 in Blountville, Sullivan County, Tennessee.

Kate married **Southwell Bruce Cate** (b. Jun 1871).

+454 M ii. **Calvin Lynn Rader** was born in 1879 in Blountville, Sullivan County, Tennessee, died on 16 Jul 1892 in Blountville, Sullivan County, Tennessee at age 13, and was buried in Blountville Cemetery, Sullivan County, Tennessee.

78. Esq. Daniel Brown[19,22] (*Anna Marie 'Mary' Rader*[2], *Casper Sr*[1]) was born on 4 Apr 1803 in Sally Run, Wythe Co, Virginia,[19,22] died on 6 Sep 1856 in Wythe County, Virginia[19,22] at age 53, and was buried in St. Johns Lutheran Cemetery, Wythe County, Wytheville, Virginia.

General Notes: Alt Death: BET. 6 - 21 SEP 1856 Wythe County, VA[19,22]

Noted events in his life were:

He appeared on the census in 1830. WYTHE COUNTY, VIRGINIA CENSUS PAGE 313

Census 1: 1850. WYTHE COUNTY, VIRGINIA LINE 324 PAGE 48

Daniel married **Theresa Stanger** on 26 Dec 1822. Theresa was born on 27 Feb 1797, died on 9 Nov 1879 in Wythe County, Virginia at age 82, and was buried in St. Johns Lutheran Cemetery, Wythe County, Wytheville, Virginia. Another name for Theresa was Theresa Stranger.

Noted events in her life were:

Alt Birth: 27 Feb 1796.

Source Citations

She appeared on the census in 1850. WYTHE COUNTY, VIRGINIA LINE 324 PAGE 48

Alt Death: 7 May 1879, Wythe County, Virginia.

Children from this marriage were:

+455 M i. **Granville H. Brown** was born in 1825.

+456 F ii. **Jane Brown** was born in 1829.

+457 M iii. **James Wesley Brown** was born on an unknown date, died on 4 May 1846 in Wythe County, Virginia, and was buried in St. Johns Lutheran Cemetery, Wythe County, Wytheville, Virginia.

79. Sally 'Salome' Brown[19, 22, 56, 57, 58] (*Anna Marie 'Mary' Rader*[2], *Casper Sr*[1]) was born on 22 Oct 1806 in Sally Run, Wythe Co, VA,[22] died on 4 Dec 1891 in Wytheville, Wythe County, Virginia[22] at age 85, and was buried in St. Johns Lutheran Cemetery, Wythe County, Wytheville, Virginia. Another name for Sally was Salome Brown.

Noted events in her life were:

She has conflicting birth information of Alt. Birth and 22 Oct 1806.[19]

Alt Birth: 22 Oct 1807, Sally Run, Wythe Co, Virginia.

She appeared on the census in 1850. WYTHE COUNTY, VIRGINIA PAGE 243 LINE 278

Census 1: 1860. WYTHE COUNTY, VIRGINIA 68TH. DISTRICT PAGE 35

Census 2: 1870. WYTHE COUNTY, VIRGINIA BLACKLICK TOWNSHIP

Census 3: 1880. WYTHE COUNTY, VIRGINIA LINE 248 PAGE 29

Alt Death: 14 Dec 1891, Wythe County, Virginia.

Alt Death: 14 Dec 1891, Wytheville, Wythe County, Virginia.[22]

Sally married **Captain Rufus Repass**,[19, 22, 56, 57, 58, 59] son of **Unknown** and **Unknown**, on 23 Sep 1827 in Wythe County, Virginia.[22] Rufus was born on 8 May 1805 in Wythe County, Virginia,[22, 59] died on 31 Jul 1878 in Wytheville, Wythe County, Virginia[22, 59] at age 73, and was buried in St. Johns Lutheran Cemetery, Wythe County, Wytheville, Virginia. Other names for Rufus were Rufus Repass, and Rufus Repass.

Noted events in their marriage were:

Alt Marriage: 3 Sep 1827.[22]

Alt. Marriage: Alt. Marriage, 23 Sep 1827.[19]

General Notes: Rufus and Sally were living at Blacklick, Va in 1870. There is a Rufus Repass Road from the public road near the German Meeting house in the direction of the cove on lands of the church. Rufus surveyed from the German Meeting House to Reeder's Mill.

Noted events in his life were:

He appeared on the census in 1850. WYTHE COUNTY, VIRGINIA PAGE 243 LINE 278

Census 1: 1860. WYTHE COUNTY, VIRGINIA 68TH. DISTRICT PAGE 35

Census 2: 1870. WYTHE COUNTY, VIRGINIA BLACKLICK TOWNSHIP

Children from this marriage were:

+458 M i. **Rev. John Christopher Repass** was born on 4 Jan 1830 in Wythe County, Virginia.

Rev. married **Mary E.**.

+459 M ii. **John Christopher (Rev) Repass**[22, 56, 57, 58, 89] was born on 17 Aug 1828 in Wytheville, Wythe County, Virginia[22, 56, 57, 58] and died on 14 Jun 1903 in Rural Retreat, VA[22] at age 74.

John married **Annie (Anna) Cregar**[22, 56, 57, 58, 89, 90, 91] (b. 5 May 1823, d. 9 Dec 1906) on 3 Aug 1848 in Rural Retreat, VA.[22]

+460 F iii. **Elza Ann Repass** was born on 4 Jan 1830 in Wythe County, Virginia.

Elza married **Michael Cassell** (b. 26 Nov 1827) on 19 Sep 1850 in Wythe County, Virginia.

+461 F iv. **Elizabeth Mary Repass**[22] was born on 10 Sep 1831 in Wythe County, Virginia, died on 29 Mar 1911[22] at age 79, and was buried in St. Johns Lutheran Cemetery, Wythe County, Wytheville, Virginia.

Elizabeth married **Stephen Gose Perry**[22] (b. 1824, d. 1863).

+462 M v. **James Andrew Repass**[22] was born on 17 Apr 1834 in Wythe County, Virginia,[22] died on 4 Jan 1857 in Independant County, Roanoke, Virginia[22] at age 22, and was buried in St. Johns Lutheran Cemetery, Wythe County, Wytheville, Virginia.

+463 F vi. **Maria Thresa Repass**[22] was born on 30 Jun 1836 in Wythe County, Virginia[22] and died on 6 May 1898[22] at age 61.

Maria married **Stephen A Ruben Sharitz**[22] on 23 Aug 1856 in Surry Co, NC.[22]

+464 F vii. **Lydia Emaline Repass**[22] was born on 5 Mar 1841 in Wythe County, Virginia, died on 14 Sep 1900 at age 59, and was buried in St. Johns Lutheran Cemetery, Wythe County, Wytheville, Virginia.

Lydia married **Daniel Kegley**[22] on 24 May 1877 in Wythe County, Virginia.

+465 M viii. **Rev. Stephen Albion Repass** was born on 25 Nov 1838 in Wythe County, Virginia.

+466 M ix. **Stephen Albion Repass**.[22]

Stephen married **Frances Hancock**.[22]

+467 F x. **Sarah Henrietta Repass**.[22]

Sarah married **Thomas Perry**.[22]

Source Citations

+468 F xi. **Eleanor Brown Repass** was born on 17 Aug 1843 in Wythe County, Virginia, died on 20 Jun 1919 in Wythe County, Virginia at age 75, and was buried in St. Johns Lutheran Cemetery, Wythe County, Wytheville, Virginia.

Eleanor married **Jacob Foster Fisher** (d. 22 Mar 1924) on 9 Nov 1871 in Wythe County, Virginia.

+469 F xii. **Ellen Brown Repass**.[22]

Ellen married **Jacob Fischer**.[22]

+470 F xiii. **Sarah Henrieta Repass** was born on 17 Aug 1843.

+471 M xiv. **Granville Brown Repass**[22] was born on 27 Dec 1846, died on 2 Jun 1918 in Wythe County, Virginia at age 71, and was buried in St. Johns Lutheran Cemetery, Wythe County, Wytheville, Virginia.

Granville married **Rosa Bell Morehead**[22] (b. 26 Nov 1858, d. 7 Mar 1927) on 18 Nov 1883 in Virginia.

+472 F xv. **Eliza Repass**.[22]

Eliza married **Michael Cassell**.[22]

80. **Jesse Brown**[19, 22] (*Anna Marie 'Mary' Rader*[2], *Casper Sr*[1]) was born on 16 Jun 1808 in Wytheville, Wythe County, Virginia.[19, 22]

81. **Lydia Brown**[19, 22] (*Anna Marie 'Mary' Rader*[2], *Casper Sr*[1]) was born on 11 Jan 1809 in Sally Run, Wythe Co, Virginia,[22] died on 14 Jul 1897 in Wythe County, Virginia[22] at age 88, and was buried in St. Johns Lutheran Cemetery, Wythe County, Wytheville, Virginia.

Noted events in her life were:
She has conflicting birth information of Alt. Birth, 11 Jan 1809 and Wytheville, Wythe County, Virginia.[19]
She appeared on the census in 1850. WYTHE COUNTY, VIRGINIA LINE 653 PAGE 94
Census 1: 1860. WYTHE COUNTY, VIRGINIA 68TH. DISTRICT PAGE 44
Census 2: 1870. WYTHE COUNTY, VIRGINIA BLACK LICK DISTRICT
She has conflicting death information of Alt. Death, 14 Jul 1897 and Wytheville, Wythe County, Virginia.[19]

Lydia married **Jesse Repass**,[22, 59] son of **Unknown** and **Unknown**, on 24 Oct 1824 in Wythe County, Virginia. Jesse was born on 4 Aug 1802 in Wythe County, Virginia,[22, 59] died on 3 Nov 1849 in Wythe County, Virginia[22, 59] at age 47, and was buried in St. Johns Lutheran Cemetery, Wythe County, Wytheville, Virginia.

Noted events in their marriage were:
Alt Marriage: 24 Oct 1826, Wythe County, Virginia.
Noted events in his life were:
He appeared on the census in 1830. WYTHE COUNTY, VIRGINIA CENSUS PAGE 351

Census 1: 1850. WYTHE COUNTY, VIRGINIA LINE 653 PAGE 94

Children from this marriage were:

+473 F i. **Mary Elender Repass** was born on 20 Nov 1828 in Wythe County, Virginia, died on 10 Sep 1853 at age 24, and was buried in St. Johns Lutheran Cemetery, Wythe County, Wytheville, Virginia.

Mary married **John Repass** (b. 8 Jan 1821, d. 29 Oct 1904).

+474 F ii. **Elias Jane Repass** was born on 11 Sep 1829 in Wythe County, Virginia.

+475 M iii. **Joseph Washington Repass** was born on 18 Mar 1830 in Wythe County, Virginia and died in Listed As Missing In Civil War, Cane Hill, Arkansas.

+476 M iv. **James Augustus Repass** was born on 22 Jun 1831 in Wythe County, Virginia and died on 4 Jan 1857 in Roanoke, Virginia at age 25.

+477 M v. **George Flohr Repass** was born on 26 Jun 1832 in Wythe County, Virginia, died on 8 Jun 1882 in Wythe County, Virginia at age 49, and was buried in St. Johns Lutheran Cemetery, Wythe County, Wytheville, Virginia.

+478 M vi. **Newton Hurshel Repass** was born on 1 Jan 1835 in Wythe County, Virginia and was buried in St. Lukes Luthern Cemetery, Wytheville, Wythe County, Virginia.

Newton married **Margaret Agnes Brown** (b. 13 Feb 1843) on 14 Aug 1872 in Wythe County, Virginia.

+479 F vii. **Matildy Brown Repass** was born on 8 Jan 1837 in Wythe County, Virginia.

+480 F viii. **Sarah K. Repass** was born in 1839.

+481 F ix. **Mariah Repass** was born in 1841.

+482 F x. **Annie Repass** was born in 1843.

+483 F xi. **Eleanora Catherine Repass** was born in 1843.

+484 M xii. **Henry L. Repass** was born in 1846 and died in Ft. Morton, Indiana Civil War.

+485 F xiii. **Victoria Repass** was born in 1848.

82. Rosanna Brown[19,22] (*Anna Marie 'Mary' Rader*[2], *Casper Sr*[1]) was born on 4 Jun 1810 in Sally Run, Wythe Co, Virginia, died on 7 Oct 1901 in Wytheville, Wythe County, Virginia[19,22] at age 91, and was buried in St. Johns Lutheran Cemetery, Wythe County, Wytheville, Virginia. Another name for Rosanna was Rosannah Brown.

Noted events in her life were:

Alt Birth: 3 Jun 1810, Wytheville, Wythe County, Virginia.[19,22]

She appeared on the census in 1850. WYTHE COUNTY, VIRGINIA PAGE 314 LINE 1259

Census 1: 1860. WYTHE COUNTY, VIRGINIA 68TH. DISTRICT

Census 2: 1900. WYTHEVILLE TOWN, WYTHE COUNTY, VIRGINIA LINE 143 PAGE 192B

Alt Death: 17 Oct 1901, Wytheville, Wythe County, Virginia.[19,22]

Rosanna married **Stephen Repass**,[22] son of **Unknown** and **Unknown**, on 20 Oct 1829 in Wythe County, Virginia. Stephen was born on 2 Aug 1805,[22] died on 7 Aug 1876 in Wythe County, Virginia at age 71, and was buried in St. Johns Lutheran Cemetery, Wythe County, Wytheville, Virginia.

Noted events in their marriage were:
Alt Marriage: 20 Aug 1828, Wythe County, Virginia.
Noted events in his life were:
He appeared on the census in 1850. WYTHE COUNTY, VIRGINIA PAGE 314 LINE 1259
Census 1: 1860. WYTHE COUNTY, VIRGINIA 68TH. DISTRICT
He was employed on 1 Jan 1882. COUNTY SUPERINTENDANT OF SCHOOLS

Children from this marriage were:

+486 M i. **Imus A. Repass** was born in 1831 in Virginia.

Imus married **Jane** (b. 1830).

+487 F ii. **Barbara Repass** was born in 1833.

+488 F iii. **Mary Repass** was born in 1835.

+489 M iv. **William Gordon Repass** was born on 2 Jun 1838 in Wytheville, Wythe County, Virginia, died on 29 Nov 1895 in Wythe County, Virginia at age 57, and was buried in St. Johns Lutheran Cemetery, Wythe County, Wytheville, Virginia.

William married **Sarah Jane Fisher** (b. 22 Feb 1839, d. 5 Jul 1914) on 22 Sep 1859 in Wythe County, Virginia.

+490 M v. **Rufus B. Repass** was born in 1841 in Wythe County, Virginia and was buried in St. Johns Lutheran Cemetery, Wythe County, Wytheville, Virginia.

Rufus married **Margaret E. Fisher** (b. 1854).

+491 F vi. **Lucinda Katherine "Kate" Repass** was born in 1847 in Wythe County, Virginia, died in 1934 in Wythe County, Virginia at age 87, and was buried in St. Johns Lutheran Cemetery, Wythe County, Wytheville, Virginia.

Lucinda married **Joseph S. Fisher** (b. 1840, d. 1919).

+492 F vii. **Infant Repass** was born on an unknown date.

+493 F viii. **Margaret Repass** was born on an unknown date in Wythe County, Virginia.

Margaret married **Henry D. Derrick** (b. 10 Oct 1863).

+494 M ix. **James A. Repass** was born on an unknown date.

83. John A. Brown (*Anna Marie 'Mary' Rader*[2], *Casper Sr*[1]) was born in 1819 in Wythe County, Virginia, died in 1905 in Wythe County, Virginia at age 86, and was buried in St. Johns Lutheran Cemetery, Wythe County, Wytheville, Virginia.

Noted events in his life were:

He appeared on the census in 1850. WYTHE COUNTY, VIRGINIA 68TH. DISTRICT

Census 1: 1860. WYTHE COUNTY, VIRGINIA 68TH. DISTRICT PAGE 116

Census 2: 1870. WYTHE COUNTY, VIRGINIA 68TH. DISTRICT

John married **Sarah Tartar**. Sarah was born on 27 Nov 1820 in Wythe County, Virginia, died on 28 Feb 1900 in Wythe County, Virginia at age 79, and was buried in St. Johns Lutheran Cemetery, Wythe County, Wytheville, Virginia.

Noted events in her life were:

She appeared on the census in 1850. WYTHE COUNTY, VIRGINIA 68TH. DISTRICT

Census 1: 1860. WYTHE COUNTY, VIRGINIA 68TH. DISTRICT PAGE 116

Census 2: 1870. WYTHE COUNTY, VIRGINIA 68TH. DISTRICT

Children from this marriage were:

+495 M i. **Nicholas Brown** was born in 1840 in Wythe County, Virginia.

+496 F ii. **Josephine Brown** was born in 1842 in Wythe County, Virginia.

+497 M iii. **Robert A. Brown** was born in 1844 in Wythe County, Virginia.

+498 M iv. **Oregon Brown** was born in 1845 in Wythe County, Virginia.

+499 F v. **Maria Louisa Brown** was born in 1847 in Wythe County, Virginia.

+500 F vi. **Lavona Brown** was born in 1849 in Wythe County, Virginia.

+501 M vii. **William K. Brown** was born in Apr 1852 in Wythe County, Virginia, died on 17 Aug 1866 in Wythe County, Virginia at age 14, and was buried in St. Johns Lutheran Cemetery, Wythe County, Wytheville, Virginia.

+502 M viii. **Rev., Stephen F. Brown** was born on 26 Jan 1854 in Wythe County, Virginia.

Stephen married **Eugenia F. Brown** (b. 14 Oct 1857) on 30 Sep 1879 in Wythe County, Virginia.

+503 F ix. **Laura Brown** was born in 1857.

+504 M x. **James David Brown** was born in 1859 in Wythe County, Virginia.

+505 F xi. **Ida Sue Brown** was born in 1863 in Virginia.

84. Rev., James Andrew Brown[19,22] (*Anna Marie 'Mary' Rader*[2], *Casper Sr*[1]) was born on 22 Dec 1815 in Sally Run, Wythe Co, VA,[19,22] died on 4 Mar 1900 in Wythe County, Virginia[19,22] at age 84, and was buried in 1900 in St. John Cemetery, Wytheville, Wythe Co., VA.[19,22]

General Notes: For 41 years Mr. Brown has been engaged in labor with the people of his church. He resides on his estate of 200 acres, near Wytheville, which is his postoffice address.

Noted events in his life were:

Military: CAPTAIN WAR OF 1812

He was employed. LUTHERAN MINISTER

He was baptized on 17 May 1816. ST. JOHNS LUTHERN CHURCH, WYTHEVILLE, VIRGINIA
Alt Birth: 21 Dec 1816, Sally Run, Wythe Co, Virginia.
He graduated about 1843 in Pennsylvania Col, Gettysburg, PA.
He appeared on the census in 1850. WYTHE COUNTY, VIRGINIA PAGE 242 LINE 268
Census 1: 1860. WYTHE COUNTY, VIRGINIA 68TH. DISTRICT PAGE 34
Census 2: 1870. WYTHE COUNTY, VIRGINIA FORT CHISWELL TOWNSHIP

James married **Eleonora "Ellen" C. Herbst** on 9 Jul 1843 in Virginia. Eleonora was born on 1 Aug 1819 in Gettysburg, Adams County, Pennsylvania, died on 20 Jul 1879 in Sally Run, Wythe County, Virginiowa at age 59, and was buried in St. Johns Lutheran Cemetery, Wythe County, Wytheville, Virginia.

Noted events in her life were:
She appeared on the census in 1850. WYTHE COUNTY, VIRGINIA PAGE 242 LINE 268
Census 1: 1860. WYTHE COUNTY, VIRGINIA 68TH. DISTRICT PAGE 34
Census 2: 1870. WYTHE COUNTY, VIRGINIA FORT CHISWELL TOWNSHIP

James next married **Alice Virginia Sharitz**, daughter of **John P. Sharitz** and **Clementine R. Hudson**, on 19 Sep 1880 in Rosenbaum Chapel, Wythe County Virginia. Alice was born on 4 May 1856 in Wythe County, Virginia, died on 23 Nov 1931 in Wythe County, Virginia at age 75, and was buried in St. Johns Lutheran Cemetery, Wythe County, Wytheville, Virginia.

Noted events in her life were:
She appeared on the census in 1860. WYTHE COUNTY, VIRGINIA 68TH. DISTRICT PAGE 37
Census 2: 1880. WYTHE COUNTY, VIRGINIA PAGE 5 LINE 46
Census 3: 1900. WYTHEVILLE TOWN, WYTHE COUNTY, VIRGINIA LINE 191 PAGE 183A
Census 4: 1910. REFFERS FERRY PRECINCT, WYTHE COUNTY, VIRGINIA LINE 26 PAGE 2A
Census 5: 1920. WYTHEVILLE TOWN, WYTHE COUNTY, VIRGINIA LINE 78 PAGE 4B

Children from this marriage were:

+506 M i. **Scott Brown** was born on 13 Apr 1888 in Virginia.

+507 F ii. **Ruth Ella Brown** was born on 16 Sep 1889 in Sally Run, Wythe County, Virginiowa, died on 16 Apr 1957 in Wythe County, Virginia at age 67, and was buried in St. Johns Lutheran Cemetery, Wythe County, Wytheville, Virginia.

Ruth married **Estel Stephen Kegley** (b. 25 Jan 1886, d. 6 Feb 1939).

+508 M iii. **James Augustin Brown Sr.** was born on 17 Oct 1891 in Sally Run, Wythe County, Virginiowa, died on 28 Sep 1977 in Wythe County, Virginia at age 85, and was buried in St. Johns Lutheran Cemetery, Wythe County, Wytheville, Virginia.

James married **Enid Spence** (b. 1 Mar 1902, d. 2 Nov 1936).

James next married **Ethel Crabtree** (b. 4 Dec 1897, d. 27 Jan 1991).

+509 F iv. **Leah Ester Brown** was born on 10 Sep 1893 in Sally Run, Wythe County, Virginiowa and was buried in St. Johns Lutheran Cemetery, Wythe County, Wytheville, Virginia.

85. John Ahaz Brown[19, 22] (*Anna Marie 'Mary' Rader*[2], *Casper Sr*[1]) was born before 12 Apr 1818 in Wytheville, Wythe County, Virginia[19, 22] and died in Feb 1905 in Wytheville, Wythe County, Virginia.[19, 22]

86. Joseph Washington Brown[19, 22] (*Anna Marie 'Mary' Rader*[2], *Casper Sr*[1]) was born on 22 Mar 1820.[19, 22]

87. Dr. Joel Leedy[9] (*Catherine Rader*[2], *Casper Sr*[1]) was born on 9 Mar 1806 in Wythe County, Virginia, died on 2 Jul 1882 in Lee, Virginia at age 76, and was buried in Sugar Run, Lee County, Virginia.

Noted events in his life were:

He has conflicting birth information of Alt. Birth and 9 Mar 1806.

Joel married **Mary Magdalena "Polly" Kegley**, daughter of **Unknown** and **Unknown**, in 1828 in Black Lick District, Wythe County, Virginia. Mary was born on 20 Feb 1801 in Wytheville, Wythe County, Virginia, died on 26 May 1860 in Lee, Virginia at age 59, and was buried in Sugar Run, Lee County, Virginia.

Noted events in her life were:

Alt Birth: 28 Aug 1801, Wythe County, Virginia.

Alt Birth: 1803, Wythe County, Virginia.

Children from this marriage were:

+510 F i. **Mondana Nadine Leedy** was born on 5 Jul 1829 in Black Lick District, Wythe County, Virginia and died after 1874.

Mondana married **Dr. James Gasaway Carroll** (b. 1807, d. After 1874) on 24 Aug 1864 in Lee County, Virginia.

+511 M ii. **Rufus Leedy** was born in Nov 1830 in Black Lick District, Wythe County, Virginia and died after 1900 in Richmond District, Wise County, Virginia.

Rufus married **Sarah Rebecca Orr** (b. 1 Mar 1837, d. 11 May 1862) on 6 Mar 1858 in Lee Co., Virginia.

Rufus next married **Mary Elliott** (b. Abt 1843, d. Bef 1871) about 1865 in Lee County, Virginia.

Rufus next married **Elizabeth Burton** (b. Abt 1836, d. After 1872) on 27 Dec 1870 in Lee County, Virginia.

+512 F iii. **Almeda Leedy** was born on 1 Apr 1832 in Wythe County, Virginia and died on an unknown date.

+513 F iv. **Isabella Leedy** was born on 22 Nov 1833 in Black Lick District, Wythe County, Virginia and died in 1906 in Cisco, Eastland County, Texas at age 73.

Isabella married **John Clifton** (b. Mar 1834, d. 1913) on 23 Nov 1865 in Lee County, Virginia.

+514 M v. **Alfred Leedy** was born on 8 Jan 1835 in Black Lick District, Wythe County, Virginia and died after 1874 in White Sholes District, Lee County, Virginia.

Alfred married **Rebecca Catherine Debusk** (b. Jul 1841, d. 1874) on 1 Aug 1866 in Lee County, Virginia.

Alfred next married **Mary** about 1879.

+515 F vi. **Elizabeth Leedy** was born on 3 Sep 1836 in Washington County, Virginia and died on 19 Apr 1860 in Jonesville, Lee County, Virginia at age 23.

+516 M vii. **Joseph Leedy** was born on 5 Mar 1838 in Jonesville, Lee County, Virginia and died on 5 Mar 1912 in District 7, Hancock County, Tennessee at age 74.

Joseph married **Nancy Jane Elliott** (b. 17 Aug 1843, d. 25 Sep 1910) on 21 Nov 1860 in Jonesville, Lee County, Virginia.

+517 M viii. **Isaac Calloway Leedy** was born on 5 Jan 1839 in Jonesville, Lee County, Virginia and died on 1 Feb 1924 in Bluefield, Mercer County, Virginia at age 85.

Isaac married **Sarah Goins** (b. 28 Dec 1839, d. 16 Jun 1887) on 16 Jan 1869 in Lee Co., Virginia.

Isaac next married **Mary Hall** (b. Abt 1851, d. Bef 1922) on 16 Nov 1887 in Jonesville, Lee County, Virginia.

+518 F ix. **Selina Leedy** was born in 1842 in Jonesville, Lee County, Virginia and died in Apr 1886 in Jonesville, Lee County, Virginia at age 44.

Selina married **Charles C. Elliott** (b. Oct 1840, d. Unknown) on 5 Mar 1865 in Jonesville, Lee County, Virginia.

+519 M x. **Samuel Leedy** was born on 6 Aug 1846 in Jonesville, Lee County, Virginia and died on 17 Oct 1932 in Jessamine, Kentucky at age 86.

Samuel married **Lucy Ann "Annie" Stephens** (b. 24 Sep 1853, d. 14 Apr 1930) in 1873 in Lee, Virginia.

+520 F xi. **Ellen Leedy** was born in 1848 in Jonesville, Lee County, Virginia and died on 13 Sep 1853 in Jonesville, Lee County, Virginia at age 5.

+521 F xii. **Mary Leedy** was born in Aug 1849 in Lee County, Virginia.

Joel next married **Alvira Cress**, daughter of **Unknown** and **Unknown**, on 23 Oct 1866 in Lee Co., Virginia. Alvira was born in 1832 in Rockingham Co., Virginia and died on an unknown date.

Children from this marriage were:

+522 M i.   **Robert L. Leedy** was born about 1868 in Jonesville, Lee Co., Virginia and died on an unknown date.

+523 F ii. **Martha L. Leedy** was born in Jan 1870 in Jonesville, Lee Co., Virginia and died on an unknown date.

+524 F iii. **Alpha Leedy** was born in 1873 in Jonesville, Lee Co., Virginia and died on 1 Aug 1876 in Jonesville, Lee Co., Virginia at age 3.

Joel next married **Mary Magdalena "Polly" Kegley**, daughter of **Unknown** and **Unknown**, WFT Est 1820. Mary was born on 20 Feb 1801 in Wytheville, Wythe County, Virginia, died on 26 May 1860 in Lee, Virginia at age 59, and was buried in Sugar Run, Lee County, Virginia.

Noted events in her life were:

Alt Birth: 28 Aug 1801, Wythe County, Virginia.

Alt Birth: 1803, Wythe County, Virginia.

Joel next married **Elvira A. Crass** after 1860.

88. Rachel K. Leedy[9] (*Catherine Rader*[2], *Casper Sr*[1]) was born on 20 Jun 1807 in Wythe County, Virginia and died in 1861 in Stark, Elliott County, KY. at age 54.

Noted events in her life were:
She has conflicting birth information of Alt. Birth and 20 Jun 1807.
She appeared on the census in 1850. WYTHE COUNTY, VIRGINIA   PAGE 240B-241A LINE 242
Alt Death: 1861, Stark, Elliott Co., KY.

Rachel married **Abraham Kegley**, son of **Unknown** and **Unknown**, in 1828 in Wytheville, Wythe County, Virginia. Abraham was born on 4 Aug 1806 in Wytheville, Wythe County, Virginia and died after 1880 in Stark, Elliott, Kentucky.

Noted events in their marriage were:
Alt Marriage: Abt 1825.
General Notes: U.S. CENSUS RECORDS WYTHE CO VA LINE 242 1850 SHOWS THE FOLLOWING:
ABRAHAM KEGLEY AGE 43
RACHEL AGE 42

CHILDREN:

JOEL AGE 22, EPHRAMIN AGE 21, WILLIAM AGE 19, ALFIE (ALFRED) AGE 17, MARGARET AGE 15, AUSTIN AGE 13, NANCY AGE 11, JOHN AGE 9, GUSTAEN AGE 7, JAMES L AGE 1. ALSO SHOWS NANCY LEEDY AGE 22 (RACHEL'S SISTER)

ABRAHAM WAS BORN AUG 4 1806 AND BAPTIZED SEPT 7, 1806 AT ST JOHN LUTHERAN CHURCH IN WYTHEVILLE, VA. WRITTEN IN GERMAN. LIVED IN CARTER CO., KY.

ABRAHAM CAME TO CARTER CO, KY IN 1860 SURVEYED THE LANDS AND BOUGHT LAND AND RETURNED IN 1861 WITH HIS FAMILY.

Noted events in his life were:

Fact 1: Fact 1, Could Be Spelled Gockle.
He had a residence. LIVED IN CARTER COUNTY, KY.
Alt Birth: 2 Aug 1806, Wythe County, Virginia.
He was baptized on 7 Sep 1806. ST. JOHNS LUTHERAN CHURCH, WYTHEVILLE, VIRGINIA
He appeared on the census in 1850. WYTHE COUNTY, VIRGINIA PAGE 240B-241A LINE 242
Census 2: 1870. DISTRICT 5, ELLIOTT COUNTY, KENTUCKY LINE 87 PAGE 12
Census 3: 1880. ELLIOT COUNTY, KENTUCKY LINE 220

Children from this marriage were:

+525 M i. **Joel Kegley**^{9} was born in 1828 in Wythe County, Virginia and died on an unknown date.

+526 M ii. **Reverend Joel Kegley** was born on 31 Aug 1826 in Wythe County, Virginia and died on 5 Jun 1887 in Stark, Elliott, Kentucky at age 60.

Reverend married **Delilah Hounshell** (b. 2 Jul 1830, d. 29 Dec 1919) on 2 Feb 1851 in Wytheville, Wythe County, Virginia.

+527 M iii. **Ephriam Kegley**^{9} was born on 9 Jan 1829 in Black Lick District, Wythe County, Virginia, died on 4 Oct 1910 in Groseclose, Wythe County, Virginia at age 81, and was buried in Oct 1910 in Pleasant Hill Cemetery, Groseclose, Wythe County, Virginia.

Ephriam married **Polly Cline** (b. 8 Dec 1828, d. 7 Sep 1899) on 17 Oct 1850 in Wytheville, Wythe County, Virginia.

+528 F iv. **Nancy Jane Kegley** was born on 13 Jan 1832 and died on 3 Mar 1924 in Pike Co., KY at age 92.

Nancy married **Joseph Calhoun** (b. 26 Oct 1831, d. 17 Dec 1895) on 28 Nov 1849.

+529 M v. **William Kegley**^{9} was born on 1 Jan 1831 in Wythe County, Virginia and died about 1909 in Rowan County, Kentucky about age 78.

William married **Sofia M. Grubb** (b. 1835, d. Bef Nov 1862) on 11 Aug 1851 in Wytheville, Wythe County, Virginia.

William next married **Jane Cox** (b. 1831, d. Bef 1890) on 2 Nov 1862 in Carter County, Kentucky.

William next married **Elizabeth "Eliza" Mullins Wright** (b. Unknown, d. Unknown) on 18 Jul 1890 in Rowan Co., Kentucky.

William next married **Jane Grubbs** (b. 1830, d. WFT Est 1867-1925) about 1854.

William next married **Jane Cox Williams** (b. WFT Est 1824-1850, d. WFT Est 1877-1938) on 2 Nov 1862 in Carter County, Kentucky.

William next married **Elizabeth Mullins** (b. 1863) about 1878.

+530 M vi. **Alfred Kegley**[9] was born on 20 Feb 1833 in Wytheville, Wythe County, Virginia and died after 1900.

Alfred married **Savannah Cline** (b. Abt 1830) in 1858 in Virginia.

+531 F vii. **Margaret Kegley**[9] was born on 8 Sep 1835 in Black Lick District, Wythe County, Virginia and died on 21 Jan 1912 in Virginia at age 76.

Margaret married **Charles Francis "Frank" Grubb** (b. 31 Mar 1833, d. 24 Oct 1912) on 5 Apr 1852.

+532 F viii. **Nancy Kegley**[9] was born in 1839 in Wythe County, Virginia and died on an unknown date.

+533 M ix. **Austin Kegley Md**[9] was born on 12 May 1838 in Wythe County, Virginia and died before 1900 in Stark Ridge, Elliot, Kentucky.

Austin married **Nancy B. Frye** (b. 5 Feb 1837) on 5 Feb 1857 in Wythe County, Virginia.

Austin next married **Elizabeth "Betty" Mcmillian** (b. 1847, d. 1932) about 1882.

+534 M x. **John J. Kegley**[9] was born in 1842 in Wythe County, Virginia and died on an unknown date.

+535 F xi. **Nancy Mary Kegley** was born on 18 Dec 1840 in Black Lick District, Wythe County, Virginia and died on 12 May 1927 in Engadine, Mackinaac, Michigan at age 86.

Nancy married **Benjamin Franklin Elliott** (b. 4 Jan 1834, d. 1884) on 12 Aug 1858 in Carter County, Kentucky.

+536 M xii. **Gustavus Kegley**[9] was born in 1846 in Wythe County, Virginia and died on an unknown date.

+537 M xiii. **John Jacob Kegley** was born on 8 May 1844 in Wythe County, Virginia and died on 10 Feb 1904 in Stark Ridge, Elliot County, Kentucky at age 59.

John married **Della Elliott** (b. 1858, d. Unknown) about 1874 in Elliott, Kentucky.

John next married **Mary Elizabeth Wells** (b. Aug 1866, d. 10 Jan 1942) about 1889 in Elliott, Kentucky.

+538 M xiv. **Augustus Davis Kegley** was born on 3 Feb 1847 in Wytheville, Wythe County, Virginia and died on 15 Jul 1905 in Limestone, Carter, Kentucky at age 58.

Augustus married **Sela Jenny Collier** (b. May 1855, d. 19 Jan 1934) on 15 Jul 1881 in Soldier, Carter Co., Kentucky.

+539 M xv. **James Lafayette Kegley**[9] was born on 6 Aug 1849 in Wythe County, Virginia and died on 9 May 1926 in Engadine, Mackinaac, Michigan at age 76.

James married **Elizabeth Frances Bird** (b. 7 Aug 1847, d. After 1887) on 18 Sep 1873 in Black Lick District, Wythe County, Virginia.

+540 M xvi. **Samuel William Kegley**[9] was born on 8 Feb 1852 in Black Lick District, Wythe County, Virginia, died on 11 Nov 1904 in Elliot County, Kentucky at age 52, and was buried in Clay Cemetery, Elliott County, Kentucky.

Samuel married **Malissa Burton** (b. 8 Sep 1860, d. 5 Jul 1932) on 12 Jul 1877 in Elliott County, Kentucky.

89. Anna Mary Leedy[9] (*Catherine Rader*[2], *Casper Sr*[1]) was born on 26 Sep 1808 in Wythe County, Virginia and died on an unknown date. Another name for Anna was Mary "Polly" Leedy.

Noted events in her life were:

She appeared on the census in 1830. WYTHE COUNTY, VIRGINIA CENSUS PAGE 351

Census 1: 1850. WYTHE COUNTY, VIRGINIA LINE 705 PAGE 102

Anna married **James Repass** on 8 Sep 1825 in Wythe County, Virginia.

Anna next married **James "Rippas" Repass**, son of **Unknown** and **Unknown**, on 8 Sep 1825 in Wythe County, Virginia. James was born in 1801 in Wythe County, Virginia and died on an unknown date.

Noted events in his life were:

He appeared on the census in 1830. WYTHE COUNTY, VIRGINIA CENSUS PAGE 351

Census 1: 1850. WYTHE COUNTY, VIRGINIA LINE 705 PAGE 102

The child from this marriage was:

+541 M i. **Harvey Repass** was born on 28 Sep 1826 and died on 29 Jul 1890 at age 63.

Harvey married **Elizabeth Repass**.

90. Salome "Sally" Leedy[9] (*Catherine Rader*[2], *Casper Sr*[1]) was born on 4 Jun 1810 in Wythe County, Virginia and died on an unknown date. Another name for Salome was Sallie Leedy.

Salome married **Enoch Bales** on 10 Oct 1833 in Wythe County, Virginia. Enoch was born on an unknown date and died on an unknown date.

Source Citations

Salome next married **Enoch T. Bails** on 10 Oct 1833 in Wythe County, Virginia.

91. Josiah Leedy^9 (*Catherine Rader*^{2}, *Casper Sr*^{1}) was born on 5 Sep 1813 in Wythe County, Virginia, died on 24 Dec 1903 in Wytheville, Wythe County, Virginia at age 90, and was buried in East End Cemetery, Wytheville, Wythe County, Virginia. Other names for Josiah were Josiah "Siah" Leedy, and Josiah "Sish" Leedy.

> General Notes: JOSIAH WAS A BLACKSMITH. MEMBER OF ST JOHN'S LUTH CHURCH, THEN LEBANON CHURCH. SPOKE ONLY GERMAN IN YOUTH. PROBABLE THE ISAIAH (SIC) LEEDY, PVT., CAPT EARHART'S CO., BLACK LICK HOME GUARDS, CSA. ALL HIS CHILDREN BRON ON HIS FARM ON BLACK LICK NEAR REED CREEK, WYTHE CO., VA. THEIR 17 CHILDREN LIVED TOMATURTIY AND LEFT THEM 84 GRANCHILDREN AND 79 GR. GRAND CH. AN IMMEDIATE POSTERITY OF 180 SOULS. AT HIS 75TH BIRTHDAY PARTY 69 GRANDCH. WERE PRESENT. CHILDREN: ROSANNA, MARTIN, FRANCES, REBECCA, SOPHRONIA V., MARY, SARAH LOANNAS, JOHN ASA, RUFUS STEWART (OR STUART), WILLIAM HENRY, DAVID KEGLEY, AND OTHERS.

> Noted events in his life were:

> He has conflicting birth information of Alt. Birth and 5 Sep 1813.

> He appeared on the census in 1850. WYTHE COUNTY, VIRGINIA PAGE 303B LINE1101

> Census 1: 1860. WYTHE COUNTY, VIRGINIA 68TH. DISTRICT PAGE 70

> Census 2: 1870. WYTHE COUNTY, VIRGINIA BLACK LICK DISTRICT

> Josiah married **Sally Kegley**, daughter of **Unknown** and **Unknown**, on 8 Oct 1837 in Wytheville, Wythe County, Virginia. Sally was born on 4 Apr 1818 in Evansham {Wytheville}, Wythe, Virginia, died on 27 Nov 1894 in Wytheville, Wythe County, Virginia at age 76, and was buried in East End Cemetery, Wytheville, Wythe County, Virginia. Other names for Sally were Sally Kegley, and Sarah "Sally" Kegley.

> Noted events in her life were:

She has conflicting death information of Alt. Death and Also Known As Sally.
She has conflicting birth information of Alt. Birth and 4 Apr 1818.
Alt Birth: 4 Aug 1818, Black Lick District, Wythe County, Virginia.
She appeared on the census in 1850. WYTHE COUNTY, VIRGINIA PAGE 303B LINE1101
Census 1: 1860. WYTHE COUNTY, VIRGINIA 68TH. DISTRICT PAGE 70
Census 2: 1870. WYTHE COUNTY, VIRGINIA BLACK LICK DISTRICT

> Children from this marriage were:

+542 F i. **Rosannah Leedy** was born on 25 Aug 1838 in Wytheville, Wythe County, Virginia, died on 11 Sep 1894 in Wythe County, Virginia at age 56, and was buried in St. Paul's Rural Church, Wytheville, Virginia.

Rosannah married **Ephraim Catron** (b. 12 May 1827, d. 15 Feb 1895) on 16 Oct 1864 in Wytheville, Wythe County, Virginia.

+543 M ii. **Martin Leedy** was born in 1840 in Wythe County, Virginia and died in Oct 1861 in Civil War at age 21.

+544 M iii. **Marin Leedy** was born on 2 Feb 1840 in Wytheville, Wythe County, Virginia and died on 26 Dec 1861 in Mercer, West Virginia at age 21.

+545 F iv. **Frances Leedy** was born in 1843 in Wythe County, Virginia.

+546 F v. **Francis Leedy** was born on 7 May 1841 in Wytheville, Wythe County, Virginia and died on 22 Aug 1927 in Unknown at age 86.

Francis married **David Carr Sweeny** (b. 1838, d. 1900).

+547 F vi. **Rebecca Leedy** was born on 15 May 1842 in Wytheville, Wythe County, Virginia and died on 17 Jun 1921 in Unknown at age 79.

Rebecca married **Henry Milam Hicks** (b. Abt 1838, d. Unknown) about 1862 in Wythe County, Virginia.

+548 F vii. **Sophrona Leedy** was born in 1844 in Wythe County, Virginia.

+549 F viii. **Saphrona Leedy** was born on 27 May 1843 in Wytheville, Wythe County, Virginia and died on an unknown date in Unknown.

Saphrona married **W. M. Bales** (b. Abt 1842, d. Unknown).

+550 F ix. **Mary Leedy** was born on 20 Jun 1845 in Wythe County, Virginia and died on 30 Jul 1870 in Wytheville, Wythe County, Virginia at age 25.

Mary married **Simon Umberger** (b. 1849, d. 1930) on 7 Jan 1867 in Wythe County, Virginia.

+551 F x. **Sarah Loannas Leedy** was born on 29 Jun 1846 in Wytheville, Wythe County, Virginia, died on 10 Feb 1932 in Wytheville, Wythe County, Virginia at age 85, and was buried in Lebanon Lutheran Cemetery, Wythe County, Virginia.

Sarah married **Alexander Umberger** (b. 22 Mar 1845, d. 21 Jan 1940) before 1866.

+552 M xi. **John Albert Leedy** was born on 8 Sep 1847 in Black Lick, Wythe, Virginia, died on 7 Jul 1903 in Wytheville, Wythe County, Virginia at age 55, and was buried in Mt. Pleasant Cemetery, Wythe County, Virginia.

John married **Delilah Cline** (b. 4 Mar 1848, d. 15 Mar 1930) on 28 Aug 1866 in Wytheville, Wythe County, Virginia.

+553 M xii. **Rufus Stewart Leedy** was born on 11 Apr 1849 in Wythe County, Virginia and died on 5 Apr 1933 in Wytheville, Wythe County, Virginia at age 83.

Rufus married **Rhoda Jane Umberger** (b. 20 Feb 1853, d. 1 Mar 1887) on 29 Aug 1872 in Wytheville, Wythe County, Virginia.

Rufus next married **Rhoda J. Umbarger** (b. 1843).

+554 M xiii. **William Henry Leedy** was born on 19 Aug 1850 in Wytheville, Wythe County, Virginia and died on 26 Feb 1935 in Bluefield, West Virginia at age 84.

William married **Ellen Leonard** (b. Unknown, d. Unknown).

+555 M xiv. **David Kegley Leedy** was born on 14 Apr 1852 in Wytheville, Wythe County, Virginia, died on 3 Sep 1916 in Wytheville, Wythe County, Virginia at age 64, and was buried in East End Wytheville, Wythe County, Virginia.

David married **Caroline Virginia Wolford** (b. 22 Jul 1854, d. Between 1927 and 1940) on 15 May 1873 in Wytheville, Wythe County, Virginia.

David next married **Caroline Virginia** (b. 1854).

+556 F xv. **Margaret Missouri Leedy** was born on 22 Oct 1853 in Wytheville, Wythe County, Virginia, died on 29 Sep 1902 in Wytheville, Wythe County, Virginia at age 48, and was buried in St. Johns Lutheran, Wytheville, Virginia.

Margaret married **Lemuel Edley Kegley** (b. 17 Sep 1853, d. 10 Jul 1931) on 25 Jan 1872 in Wytheville, Wythe County, Virginia.

+557 F xvi. **Katherine "Kitty" Leedy** was born on 5 Feb 1854 in Wytheville, Wythe County, Virginia and died on 12 Mar 1958 in Wytheville, Wythe County, Virginia at age 104.

Katherine married **Elisha Bedsaul** (b. Unknown, d. Unknown) on an unknown date in Unknown.

+558 F xvii. **Mariah Callie Leedy** was born on 2 Nov 1855 in Wytheville, Wythe County, Virginia and died on 13 Jan 1937 in Wytheville, Wythe County, Virginia at age 81.

Mariah married **Robert C. Earhart** (b. 4 Aug 1854, d. 12 Aug 1927) on 18 Aug 1875 in Wythe County, Virginia.

+559 F xviii. **America Alice Leedy** was born on 17 Nov 1856 in Wytheville, Wythe County, Virginia, died on 10 May 1926 in Wythe County, Virginia at age 69, and was buried in St. James Cemetery, Greene County, Tennessee.

America married **Thomas Ebenezer Yonce** (b. 31 Oct 1849, d. 19 Sep 1900) in Jan 1876.

+560 M xix. **Montgomery Earhart Leedy Sr.** was born on 22 Aug 1859 in Wytheville, Wythe County, Virginia and died on 8 Feb 1924 in Virginia at age 64.

Montgomery married **Ida Hoyt Halt** (b. Unknown, d. Unknown) on 25 Dec 1884.

Montgomery next married **Edna H.** (b. 1870).

+561 F xx. **Katherine Leedy** was born in 1864.

+562 M xxi. **Joel Tarter Leedy** was born on 3 Feb 1862 in Wytheville, Wythe County, Virginia and died on 5 Jul 1943 in Wytheville, Wythe County, Virginia at age 81.

Joel married **Nancy Caroline King** (b. 10 Aug 1867, d. 6 Mar 1929) on 19 Jun 1884.

Joel next married **Lola Davison** (b. Unknown, d. Unknown) in 1929.

+563 F xxii. **Callie Leedy** was born on an unknown date.

92. Isaac Leedy[9] (*Catherine Rader*[2], *Casper Sr*[1]) was born about 1815 in Wythe County, Virginia and died on an unknown date.

Noted events in his life were:

Other: Died As A Child.

93. Malinda Leedy[9] (*Catherine Rader*[2], *Casper Sr*[1]) was born on 14 Apr 1818 in Wythe County, Virginia and died in Jun 1880 at age 62.

Noted events in her life were:

Alt Birth: 20 May 1818, Wythe County, Virginia.
She appeared on the census in 1850. WYTHE COUNTY, VIRGINIA   PAGE 242   LINE 258
Census 1: 1860. WYTHE COUNTY, VIRGINIA 68TH. DISTRICT
Census 2: 1870. WYTHE COUNTY, VIRGINIA FORT CHISWELL TOWNSHIP

  Malinda married **Abram Ebenezer Yonce** on 13 Sep 1838 in Wythe County, Virginia. Abram was born in 1815.

  Noted events in his life were:

  He appeared on the census in 1850. WYTHE COUNTY, VIRGINIA   PAGE 242   LINE 258

  Children from this marriage were:

+564 M   i.   **James Yonce** was born on 16 Oct 1840 in Wythe County, Virginia, died on 31 Jul 1912 in Wythe County, Virginia at age 71, and was buried in Mountain View Cemetery, Wythe County, Virginia.

  James married **Lucy M.** (b. 20 Apr 1835, d. 30 Aug 1902).

+565 F   ii.   **Katherine Yonce** was born in Jun 1843 in Wythe County, Virginia, died in 1908 in Wythe County, Virginia at age 65, and was buried in St. Johns Lutheran Cemetery, Wythe County, Wytheville, Virginia.

  Katherine married **James W. Morehead** (b. Jun 1826, d. 1903).

+566 F   iii. **Sarah Ellen Yonce** was born in 1846 in Wythe County, Virginia.

+567 M   iv.   **Thomas Ebenezer Yonce** was born on 31 Oct 1849 in Wythe County, Virginia, died on 19 Sep 1900 in Wythe County, Virginia at age 50, and was buried in East End Cemetery, Wytheville, Wythe County, Virginia.

  Thomas married **America Alice Leedy** (b. 17 Nov 1856, d. 10 May 1926) in Jan 1876.

  (Duplicate Line. See Person 559)

94. Rosina Leedy[9] (*Catherine Rader*[2], *Casper Sr*[1]) was born on 14 May 1820 in Wythe County, Virginia and died on an unknown date in Wythe County, Virginia.

Noted events in her life were:

Other: Died As A Child.

95. Samuel Leedy[9] (*Catherine Rader*[2], *Casper Sr*[1]) was born on 4 Mar 1822 in Wythe County, Virginia and died on 13 Mar 1890 in Stark, Elliot County, KY. at age 68.

Source Citations

General Notes: 1850 WYTHE CO, VA CENSUS 15 OCT 1850 658-658 SHOWS; SAMUEL AGE 27 FARMER, W: POLLY AGE 29 CHILDREN: ELIZABETH AGE 6, WILLIAM AGE 5, JANE AGE 4, BARBARA AGE 3, ELLEN AGE 1 AND FATHER JONATHAN LEEDY AGE 60

Noted events in his life were:

He has conflicting birth information of Alt. Birth and 4 Mar 1822.

He appeared on the census in 1840. WYTHE COUNTY, VIRGINIA PAGE 86

Census 1: 1850. WYTHE COUNTY, VIRGINIA PAGE 242 LINE #260

Census 4: 1880. MOCCASIN PRECINCT, ELLIOTT COUNTY, KENTUCKY LINE 211 PAGE 635D

Samuel married **Mary Polly Adeline Repass**, daughter of **Unknown** and **Unknown**, on 8 Dec 1842 in Wythe County, Virginia. Mary was born about 1821 in Wythe County, Virginia and died on an unknown date. Another name for Mary was Mary Pauline Adeline Repass.

Noted events in her life were:

She appeared on the census in 1850. WYTHE COUNTY, VIRGINIA PAGE 242 LINE #260

Children from this marriage were:

+568 F i. **Elizabeth Leedy** was born in 1844.

+569 F ii. **Eliza Louisa Leedy** was born on 11 Feb 1853 in Reed Creek, Wythe Co., Virginia and died on 19 May 1929 in Carter County, Kentucky at age 76.

Eliza married **Julian Dulaney "Lane" Lambert** (b. 14 Feb 1849, d. 20 Aug 1933).

+570 M iii. **William Leedy** was born in 1845.

+571 F iv. **Jane Leedy** was born in 1846.

+572 F v. **Barbara Leedy** was born in 1847.

+573 F vi. **Ellen Leedy** was born in 1849.

Samuel next married **Susan Pennington** on 25 Dec 1875. Susan was born on an unknown date and died on an unknown date.

Samuel next married **Susannah** about 1860. Susannah was born in 1843 in Kentucky.

Noted events in her life were:

She appeared on the census in 1880. MOCCASIN PRECINCT, ELLIOTT COUNTY, KENTUCKY LINE 211 PAGE 635D

Children from this marriage were:

+574 F i. **Manevey S. Leedy** was born in 1861 in Elliot County, Kentucky.

+575 M ii. **John A. Leedy** was born in 1868 in Elliot County, Kentucky.

+576 M iii. **Samuel T. Leedy** was born in 1877 in Elliot County, Kentucky.

+577 M iv. **Charles R. Leedy** was born in 1878 in Elliot County, Kentucky.

+578 M v. **Robert P. Leedy** was born in 1879 in Elliot County, Kentucky.

96. Rebecca Leedy[9] (*Catherine Rader*[2]*, Casper Sr*[1]) was born on 5 Aug 1824 in Wythe County, Virginia and died on an unknown date in Wythe County, Virginia.

General Notes: was engaged to James Brown, and several days before the wedding she became ill and died. She was buried wearing her wedding apparel.

97. Sophia Leedy[9] (*Catherine Rader*[2]*, Casper Sr*[1]) was born about 1826 in Wythe County, Virginia, died on 19 Mar 1908 in Wythe County, Virginia about age 82, and was buried in St. Johns Lutheran Cemetery, Wythe County, Wytheville, Virginia.

Noted events in her life were:

She appeared on the census in 1850. WYTHE COUNTY, VIRGINIA PAGE 249 LINE 350

Census 2: 1870. WYTHE COUNTY, VIRGINIA BLACK LICK DISTRICT

Census 3: 1880. WYTHE COUNTY, VIRGINIA LINE 113 PAGE 12

Sophia married **Steward Dabney Painter** on 24 May 1849 in Wythe County, Virginia. Steward was born on 15 May 1828 in Wythe County, Virginia, died on 6 Jun 1890 in Wythe County, Virginia at age 62, and was buried in St. Johns Lutheran Cemetery, Wythe County, Wytheville, Virginia.

Noted events in his life were:

He was employed. MILLER

He appeared on the census in 1850. WYTHE COUNTY, VIRGINIA PAGE 249 LINE 350

Census 2: 1870. WYTHE COUNTY, VIRGINIA BLACK LICK DISTRICT

Census 3: 1880. WYTHE COUNTY, VIRGINIA LINE 113 PAGE 12

Children from this marriage were:

+579 M i. **Marion Painter** was born in 1860 in Wythe County, Virginia.

+580 M ii. **Francis Marion Painter** was born on 18 Oct 1850 in Wythe County, Virginia.

+581 M iii. **Charles W. Painter** was born on 20 May 1852 in Wythe County, Virginia and died on 27 Sep 1860 in Wythe County, Virginia at age 8.

+582 F iv. **Lydia B. Painter** was born on 2 Feb 1855 and died on an unknown date.

+583 F v. **Cynthia Painter** was born in 1866 in Wythe County, Virginia.

+584 M vi. **John H. Painter** was born on 13 May 1857 in Wythe County, Virginia and died on 20 Oct 1860 in Wythe County, Virginia at age 3.

+585 F vii. **Sophia Malinda Painter** was born in 1868.

+586 M viii. **James W. Painter** was born on 9 Aug 1859 in Wythe County, Virginia and died on 27 Sep 1860 in Wythe County, Virginia at age 1.

+587 M ix. **Frederick Painter** was born on an unknown date in Pennsylvania.

Frederick married **Elizabeth Boggs**.

+588 F x. **Cynthia P. Painter** was born on 27 Nov 1860 in Wythe County, Virginia and died on an unknown date.

+589 M xi. **Jefferson Davis Painter** was born on 8 Jul 1861 in Wythe County, Virginia and died on 6 May 1944 in Wythe County, Virginia at age 82.

Jefferson married **Many** (b. 1871).

+590 F xii. **Alice V. Painter** was born on 30 Mar 1864 in Wythe County, Virginia and died on an unknown date.

+591 F xiii. **Malinda Sophia Painter** was born on 19 Nov 1869 in Wythe County, Virginia and died on 9 Oct 1956 in Virginia at age 86.

98. Nancy Leedy^9 (*Catherine Rader*^{2}, *Casper Sr*^{1}) was born on 2 Feb 1828 in Wythe County, Virginia and died on 24 Feb 1904 in Wytheville, Wythe County, Virginia at age 76.

Noted events in her life were:

Alt Birth: 2 Feb 1818, Wythe County, Virginia.
Alt Birth: 22 Jan 1828, Wythe County, Virginia.
She appeared on the census in 1850. WYTHE COUNTY, VIRGINIA LINE 242
Census 1: 1870. WYTHE COUNTY, VIRGINIA BLACK LICK DISTRICT
Census 3: 1900. WYTHEVILLE TOWN, WYTHE COUNTY, VIRGINIA LINE 299 PAGE 199B
Alt Death: 21 Feb 1904.
Alt Death: 21 Feb 1904, Wytheville, Wythe County, Virginia.
Nancy married. (b. 1871)

Her children were:

+592 M i. **Vinson Leedy** was born in 1857.

+593 F ii. **Emma** was born on an unknown date.

+594 F iii. **Emma Leedy** was born in 1867.

99. Catherine Leedy^9 (*Catherine Rader*^{2}, *Casper Sr*^{1}) was born on 4 Oct 1830 in Wythe County, Virginia, died on 7 Jun 1901 in Wythe County, Virginia at age 70, and was buried in Fairview Methodist Cemetery, Wythe County, Virginia. Another name for Catherine was Katherine Leedy.

Noted events in her life were:

She appeared on the census in 1860. WYTHE COUNTY, VIRGINIA 68TH. DISTRICT PAGE 33
Census 1: 1870. WYTHE COUNTY, VIRGINIA BLACK LICK DISTRICT

Census 2: 1880. WYTHE COUNTY, VIRGINIA LINE 279 PAGE 33
Census 3: 1900. WYTHEVILLE TOWN, WYTHE COUNTY, VIRGINIA LINE 167 PAGE 182A

Catherine married **Daniel M. Sharitz**, son of **Joseph Sharitz** and **Beatta Yonce**, on 17 Jul 1852 in Wythe County, Virginia. Daniel was born on 23 Oct 1829 in Wythe County, Virginia, died on 3 Jan 1900 in Wythe County, Virginia at age 70, and was buried in Fairview Methodist Cemetery, Wythe County, Virginia.

Noted events in his life were:

He appeared on the census in 1860. WYTHE COUNTY, VIRGINIA 68TH. DISTRICT PAGE 33
Census 1: 1870. WYTHE COUNTY, VIRGINIA BLACK LICK DISTRICT
Census 2: 1880. WYTHE COUNTY, VIRGINIA LINE 279 PAGE 33

Children from this marriage were:

+595 F i. **Nancy A. Sharitz** was born in 1852 in Wythe County, Virginia.

+596 F ii. **Cynthia J. Sharitz** was born in 1855 in Wythe County, Virginia.

+597 F iii. **Eleanora Tracy Sharitz** was born in 1857 in Wythe County, Virginia.

+598 M iv. **John Sharitz** was born in 1859 in Wythe County, Virginia.

+599 M v. **Harvey M. Sharitz** was born in 1859.

+600 F vi. **Susan Sharitz** was born in 1862.

+601 F vii. **Emily C. Sharitz** was born on 15 Oct 1866 in Wythe County, Virginia, died on 14 Nov 1897 in Wythe County, Virginia at age 31, and was buried in Fairview Methodist Cemetery, Wythe County, Virginia.

+602 M viii. **Thomas J. B. Sharitz** was born in Sep 1868 in Wythe County, Virginia.

Thomas married **Minnie A.** (b. Feb 1871).

+603 F ix. **Ollie V. Sharitz** was born in 1871.

100. Samuel Emerey Rader[5, 13, 18, 37, 38] (*Daniel*[2], *Casper Sr*[1]) was born on 20 Apr 1805 in Wytheville, Wythe County, Virginia,[17, 18, 32, 38] died on 22 Nov 1895 in Union, Fulton County, Arkansas[17, 18, 38] at age 90, and was buried in 1895 in Wesley's Chapel, Union, Fulton County, Arkansas.[17]

General Notes: Samuel's second wife was Elizabeth Franks. Elizabeth was the older sister of Lemuel Franks, who married Samuel Rader's daughter, Annie.

Fought In Bishop's Company, Second Alabama Mounted Volunteers in the Creek War 1836-1837. Received a pension for this service in 1893. his second wife, Elizabeth Franks Rader Received a pension for the service after his death. Her application for the pension as a widow was made on December 17, 1895. He was a Private. He was 5'9" tall, had blue eyes, black hair and a fair compelxion.

Samuel's great granddaughter, Inez Ladd Powell, said that Samuel had served as a riverboat worker at sometime. Realizing that the Raders lived in Desoto County, Mississippi, located on the Mississippi River, this story could be true. When Samuel lived in Fulton County, Arkansas, he was a farmer.

Noted events in his life were:

He was employed. FARMER

He was baptized on 1 Jun 1805 in Wytheville, Wythe County, Virginia. Samuel Rader was christened on June 1, 1805 at St. John's Luthern Church in Wytheville, Virginia.

He appeared on the census in 1850. SO. DIST., DESOTO COUNTY, MS. PG. 706 #577

Unknown2088: 24 Oct 1850, Southern Dist, Desoto Co, MS, Pg 706, #577.[38]

Census 1: 1860. UNION TOWNSHIP, IZARD COUNTY, ARK. PG. 86

He appeared on the census in 1860 in Union Tsp, Izard Co, AK, Pg. 86.

Resided: 1865, Desoto County, Mississippi. Samuel was living in Izard Co., KS, near Pineville in the late 1860's (letter from his sister Eleanor Elizabeth Rader Gann of Senatobia, MS to their brother James Daniel Rader of Texas dated July 186?)

2 of Sams sons were murdered in the time of the Civil war. Jayhawks heard them shooting turkey one morning up in the hills and slipped up on them and shot them both and left them laying. Samuel's great granddaughter, Inez Ladd Powell, said that Samuel had served as a riverboat worker at sometime. Realizing that the Raders lived in Desoto County, Mississippi, located on the Mississippi River, this story could be true. When Samuel lived in Fulton County, Arkansas, he was a farmer.

Census 2: 1870. UNION TOWNSHIP, IZARD COUNTY, ARK. LINE 18 PAGE 3

Census 3: 1880. UNION TOWNSHIP, FULTON COUNTY, ARKANSAS LINE 24 PAGE 23

Fact 12: 16 Jun 1880, Union, Fulton, Arkansas.[38] 1880 United States Census

Name Relation Marital Status Gender Race Age Birthplace Occupation Father's Birthplace Mother's Birthplace

Samuel RADER   Self   M   Male   W   75   VA   Farmer   VA   VA
Elizabeth RADER   Wife   M   Female   W   58   TN   Keeping House   NC   NC
Jerry D. RADER   Son   S   Male   W   20   AR   Work On Farm   VA   TN
Newton J. RADER   Son   S   Male   W   18   AR   Work On Farm   VA   TN
Mary A. FRANKS   GDau   S   Female   W   18   AR   At Home   AL   MS

Source Information:
 Census Place Union, Fulton, Arkansas
 Family History Library Film   1254045
 NA Film Number   T9-0045
 Page Number   31D
 Union Tsp, Fulton Co, AK, Ed 68, Pg.23, #24

Samuel married **Elizabeth Franks**,[18,38] daughter of **Jeremiah Franks** and **Morning Fisher**, on 11 Jul 1854 in DE Soto County, Mississippi.[17, 18, 38, 60, 61] Elizabeth was born in Dec 1821 in Tennessee, died on 29 Apr 1903 in Union Township, Izard County, Ark.[17, 18, 38] at age 81, and was buried in 1903 in Wesley's Chapel, Union, Fulton County, Ark..

Noted events in her life were:
Alt Birth: 1821, TN.[17]
Alt Birth: 1827, TN.[17, 18, 38]
She appeared on the census in 1860. UNION TOWNSHIP, IZARD COUNTY, ARK. PG. 86
Census 1: 1870. UNION TOWNSHIP, IZARD COUNTY, ARK. LINE 18 PAGE 3
Census 2: 1880. UNION TOWNSHIP, FULTON COUNTY, ARKANSAS LINE 24 PAGE 23
Census 3: 1900. CLEVELAND TOWNSHIP, FULTON COUNTY, ARKANSAS PAGE #254B LIVING W SON JERRY

Children from this marriage were:

+604 F i. **Malinda Rader** was born about 1858 in Mississippi.

+605 M ii. **Jeremiah Daniel Rader**[37] was born on 1 Apr 1860 in Calico Rock, Izard County, Arkansas,[17, 18, 38] died in 1924 in Lone Chimney Pawnee, Oklahoma[17, 18, 38] at age 64, and was buried in Ioof Cemetery, Meramac, Pawnee County, Oklahoma.

Jeremiah married **Tryphena Ellen Grills** (b. Oct 1860) in 1887 in Arkansas.[17, 60]

Jeremiah next married **Alice H. Price** (b. Abt 1859) on 13 Dec 1922 in Pawnee, Pawnee County, Okl.

+606 M iii. **Newton Jasper Rader**[18, 37, 38] was born on 6 Apr 1862 in Thorn Hill, Izard County, Arkansas[17, 18, 38] and died on 3 Apr 1938 in Taft, Kern County, California[17, 18, 38] at age 75.

Newton married **Mary Ellen Pearson** (b. 12 Jun 1863, d. 3 Aug 1948) on 13 Dec 1882 in Union, Fulton County, Arkansas.[60]

Newton next married **Mary** (b. 3 Jun 1863) in Arkansas.[17]

Newton next married **Mary E.**[18, 38] (b. Jan 1868, d. WFT Est 1903-1963) about 1883.[18, 38]

Samuel next married **Elizabeth Byram**[18, 38] on 27 Aug 1829 in Madison County, Alabama.[17, 18, 38, 62] Elizabeth was born on 26 Feb 1812 in Madison County, Alabama, died on 4 Nov 1852 in Desoto County, Mississippi at age 40, and was buried in Botetourt County, Virginia.

Marriage Notes: Marital status: Other
Noted events in their marriage were:
Alt Marriage: 27 Aug 1827, Madison County, Alabama.[17, 18, 38, 62] Marriage Notes: Marital status: Other
Alt Marriage: 27 Aug 1829, Alabama.[17, 18, 38, 62] Marriage Notes: Marital status: Other

Alt Marriage: 27 Aug 1829, Madison, AL.

Noted events in her life were:

She has conflicting birth information of Alabama.[62]

She has conflicting death information.[62]

She was employed. HOUSEWIFE

Alt Birth: 22 Jul 1807, Botetourt County, Virginia.[17, 18, 38]

Alt Birth: Abt 1810, Alabama.

Alt Birth: Abt 1811, Alabama.

Alt Birth: 1811, Tennessee.

She appeared on the census in 1850. SO. DIST., DESOTO COUNTY, MS. PG. 706 #577

Alt Death: Abt 1852, Desoto County, Mississippi.

Alt Death: 11 Jun 1874, Desoto County, Mississippi.[17, 18, 38]

Children from this marriage were:

+607 M i. **Samuel Rader Jr.** was born about 1830 in AL.

Samuel married **Elizabeth Franks**[18, 38] (b. Dec 1821, d. 29 Apr 1903) on 11 Jul 1854 in Mississippi.

+608 M ii. **William Franklin Rader**[5, 13, 18, 37, 38] was born on 9 Sep 1832 in Izard County, Arkansas,[17, 18, 38, 60] died on 13 Apr 1889 in Wideman, Izard, AR[17, 18, 38, 60] at age 56, and was buried on 16 Apr 1889 in Wideman, Izard, AR.

William married **Permelia Caldonia Bray** (b. 1839, d. 1917) on 4 Dec 1856 in Desoto County, Mississippi.[17]

+609 F iii. **Martha Elizabeth "Annie" Rader**[5, 13, 18, 37, 38] was born in 1836 in Madison County, Alabama.[17, 18, 38, 62]

Martha married **Lemuel Franks**[18, 38] (b. 1834, d. Abt 15 Aug 1873) on 19 Oct 1854 in DE Soto County, Mississippi.[18, 38, 62, 92]

+610 M iv. **George William Rader**[5, 13, 18, 37, 38] was born about 1834 in AL[17, 18, 38] and died WFT Est 1835-1924[17, 18, 38] about age 1.

George married **Hiley Sexton** (b. 1838).

+611 F v. **Maria M. Rader**[5, 13, 18, 37, 38] was born in 1838 in Madison County, Alabama[17, 18, 38] and died WFT Est 1839-1932[17, 18, 38] at age 1.

Maria married **William Jasper Langston** (b. 15 Aug 1836, d. 3 Mar 1910).

Maria next married **W. Wilson** on 27 Dec 1872 at Home Of Bridegroom.

Maria next married **William Jasper Langston** about 1855.

Maria next married **William Jasper Langston** (b. 1832, d. WFT Est 1877-1924) WFT Est 1851-1882.

+612 F vi. **Elmira Jane Rader**[5, 13] was born on 5 Aug 1834 in Alabama, died on 6 Apr 1924 in Izard County, Arkansas at age 89, and was buried in Trimble Old Campgrounds Cemetery, Izard County Ark..

Elmira married **William Jasper Langston** (b. 15 Aug 1836, d. 3 Mar 1910) on 30 Jan 1850 in DE Soto County, Mississippi.

Elmira next married **Samuel Turner** on 30 Jan 1850 in DE Soto County, Mississippi.

Elmira next married **William Jasper Langston** (b. 1832, d. WFT Est 1877-1924) WFT Est 1848-1880.

+613 M vii. **James A. Rader**[5, 13, 18, 37, 38] was born in 1845 in Desoto County, Mississippi.[17, 18, 38]

James married **Priscilla** (b. 1855).

James next married **Elsie**.

+614 F viii. **Sarah Adella Rader**[5, 13, 18, 37, 38] was born about 1842 in Alabama.[17, 18, 38]

Sarah married **Jeff Wilson**.

+615 M ix. **John H. Rader**[5, 13, 37, 93] was born about 1848 in Desoto County, Mississippi[18, 38] and died after 1920 in Sharp County, Arkansas.[17, 18, 38]

John married **Rebecca Jones** (b. 22 Dec 1852, d. 7 May 1941) in Sharp County, Arkansas.[17]

John next married **Rebecca** (b. 1856).

+616 F x. **Mary Rader**[5, 13, 18, 37, 38] was born on 8 Oct 1850 in Mississippi[18, 38] and died on 17 Nov 1904[18, 38] at age 54.

101. Malinda Rader[5, 13, 18] (*Daniel*[2], *Casper Sr*[1]) was born about 1807 in Wythe County, Virginia[17, 18] and died in Desoto County, Mississippi.[17, 18]

General Notes:

John was probably killed in the Civil War. Malinda was
living with her married daughter Eleanor Baker Wilson (wife of
Blake Wilson) in the late 1860's.
Noted events in her life were:
She appeared on the census in 1850. SO. DIST., DESOTO COUNTY, MS. PG. 706 #566
Malinda married **John Baker** on 15 Dec 1831 in AL. John died in 1844 in Desoto County, Mississippi. Another name for John was Jehu "John" Baker.

Noted events in their marriage were:

Alt Marriage: 15 Dec 1831, AL.

Children from this marriage were:

+617 M i. **John Franklin Becker**.

+618 M ii. **John D. Baker**[5, 13] was born about 1833 in Alabama.

+619 F iii. **Ellenor "Eller" A. Baker** was born about 1844 in Alabama.

Ellenor married **Blake Wilson**.

+620 F   iv.   **Sarah E. Baker**[5,13] was born about 1835 in Alabama.

+621 F   v.   **Ellen A. Baker**[5,13] was born about 1844 in Mississippi.

+622 F   vi.   **Eleanor 'Eller' Baker** was born in Desoto County, Mississippi.

Eleanor married **Blake Wilson** (b. WFT Est 1815-1843, d. WFT Est 1841-1925) WFT Est 1841-1881 in Desoto County, Mississippi.

102. George W. Rader[5,13,18] (*Daniel*[2], *Casper Sr*[1]) was born about 1809 in Wythe County, Virginia[17] and died in 1861 in Kaufman County, Texas[17,18] about age 52.

General Notes:

From: Kathey Hunt [mailto:kkhunt@mycvc.net]

Sent: Saturday, June 17, 2006 7:59 AM

To: jim@rader.org

Subject: RADERs in Kaufman TX

Concerning the info you sent the Kaufman Co TXGenWeb Project on the RADER family -

We have not been able to prove the cemetery was named for G W Rader - although he did own land in the area of the Rader cemetery, it is not situated on land he owned, but adjacent to it. We feel the cemetery must have been named for him, since he was the only Rader in this county, although there were Raders in Henderson Co, not far away.

There are no tombstones with the name RADER on them there, but we feel that GW & LArinda are probably buried there. SOme of their children & grandchildren are buried there.

There is an Original HeadRight named for him- #A419 - Rader, Geo. W .

He is on the 1860 Kaufman Co TX Census- Cedar Fork PO - HH# 501/501

with Sophia Ann - 17, Mary J 15, J H - 12 - living next to his daughter Josephine Ballard & husband.

George W Rader is not on the 1846 Poll Tax Lists of Texas, but in Henderson Co TX there is an Aaron C Rader listed, and a Davis Rader listed in Cass Co. The first Tax List he is listed on here is the 1849 Tax List & Voters List of Kaufman County.

If John H Rader was born in this area in Jan 1848, it would not have been in Kaufman County, as the county did not exist until late February 1848. In 1848, all of what became Kaufman County was situated in Henderson County and before 1846 was in the Nacogdoches Territory. Also, I noted that "LOCKHART, TEXAS" was also listed as John H Rader's birthplace - there is not a community called Lockhart in this county. Lockhart is in Caldwell Co TX, in south Texas. I do know from doing research on this family that there were many Raders in Caldwell Co.

Larinda Rader, wife of GW died in Kaufman County in Feb 1860 per the Mortality Schedule here.

58 Rader, Lorinda 41 f M NC Feb - Pneumonia 4 501/501 **Here are some Kaufman Co marriages of RADERs:**

Rader, Annie 25 Apr 1861 A. K. McDonald Bk 2   Rader, C. W. L. 21 Dec 1887 Trudie Stroud Bk 4   Rader, Josephine 18 Sep 1856 Anthony L. Ballard Bk 1

Kathey Hunt

Kaufman TX

4 M John H. Rader
    Born: Jan 1848 - Kaufman County, Lochart, Texas
    Spouse: Hannah Sykes (1856-   )
    Marr: 1885

Noted events in his life were:

Alt Birth: Bef 1807.[18]

Alt Birth: Abt 1809, Greene County, Tennessee.

He appeared on the census in 1850. KAUFMAN COUNTY, TEXAS   PGE 257 LINE #258

George married **Larinda Or Lucinda Larinda** about 1861 in ?. Larinda was born in 1818 in North Carolina and died in Feb 1860 in Kaufman County, Lochart, Texas at age 42. Another name for Larinda was Lucinda.

Noted events in her life were:

Alt Birth: 1819, North Carolina.

She appeared on the census in 1850. KAUFMAN COUNTY, TEXAS   PGE 257 LINE #258

Children from this marriage were:

+623 F   i.   **Josephine Rader** was born about 1841 in Madison County, Alabama.

+624 F   ii. **Sophelia Rader** was born about 1843 in Desoto County, Mississippi.

+625 F   iii. **Mary E. Rader** was born about 1845 in Desoto County, Mississippi.

+626 M   iv. **John H. Rader** was born in Jan 1848 in Kaufman County, Lochart, Texas.

John married **Hannah Sykes** (b. Mar 1856) in 1885.

103. Rebecca Rader[5,13,18] (*Daniel*[2], *Casper Sr*[1]) was born about 1811 in Wythe County, Virginia[17,18] and died about 1860 in Senatobia, Mississippi[17,18] about age 49.

Noted events in her life were:

Alt Birth: 1811, Tennessee.

She appeared on the census in 1850. THE SOUTHERN DIST., DESOTO COUNTY, MISSISSIPPI PAGE 362 LINE 698

Alt Death: Bef 1860, Desoto County, Mississippi.

Rebecca married **Alfred Bryam** on 5 May 1831 in Madison County, AL. Alfred was born in 1808 in Alabama.

Noted events in his life were:

Alt Birth: Abt 1843.

He appeared on the census in 1850. THE SOUTHERN DIST., DESOTO COUNTY, MISSISSIPPI PAGE 362 LINE 698

(Duplicate Line. See Person 18)

104. **James Daniel Rader**[5, 13] (*Daniel*[2], *Casper Sr*[1]) was born on 13 Nov 1813 in Tennessee, died on 20 Aug 1887 in Wilson County, Texas[17, 18] at age 73, and was buried in 1887 in Steele Branch Cemetery, Stockdale, Wilson County, Texas. Another name for James was James David Rader.

General Notes:
In the early 1850's he moved his family to Wilson Co., TX, in the Stackdale area, where he farmed and raised cattle. He was a Methodist.

Noted events in his life were:

Alt Birth: 13 Nov 1813, Wythe County, Virginia.[17, 18]

He appeared on the census in 1850. SO. DIST., DESOTO COUNTY, MS. PG. 706 #567

Alt Death: 27 Sep 1887, Wilson County, Texas ?.

He has conflicting death information of 27 Sep 1887 and Near Stockdale.

James married **Nancy Ann Caroline Montgomery** on 4 Oct 1842 in Desoto County, Mississippi. Nancy was born on 12 Nov 1823 in Fayette, Hardeman Co., TN, died on 23 Feb 1908 in Wilson Co, TX at age 84, and was buried in 1908 in Steele Branch Cemetery, Stockdale, Wilson County, Texas.

Noted events in her life were:

Alt Birth: 12 Nov 1823, Greene County, Tennessee.

She appeared on the census in 1850. SO. DIST., DESOTO COUNTY, MS. PG. 706 #567

She appeared on the census in 1900. 4 JUSTICE PRECINCT, WILSON COUNTY, TEXAS PAGE 170

Children from this marriage were:

+627 F   i.   **Nancy E. Rader**[5, 13] was born on 21 Sep 1843 in Desoto County, Mississippi and died on 5 Nov 1850 in Desoto County, Mississippi at age 7.

+628 M   ii. **Thomas G Rader**[5, 13] was born on 27 Sep 1845 in Desoto County, Mississippi and died on 11 Jun 1851 in Desoto County, Mississippi at age 5.

+629 M   iii. **William Carroll Rader**[5, 13] was born on 5 Dec 1848 in Desoto County, Mississippi, died on 23 May 1931 in Yokeum, Williamson Co, TX at age 82, and was buried in Farmer's Cem., On I35 Bet, Georgetown, Jarrell.

William married **Mary Ann Wiley** (b. 3 Jul 1856, d. 13 Aug 1908) on 11 Jul 1872 in Stockdale, Wilson County, Texas.[94]

+630 M iv. **Robert H. Rader**[5, 13] was born on 17 Dec 1849 in Desoto County, Mississippi and died on 16 Jun 1851 in Desoto County, Mississippi at age 1.

+631 M v. **James Scott Rader** was born on 10 Oct 1852 in Desoto County, Mississippi, died on 15 Nov 1936 in Atacosa Co, TX at age 84, and was buried in Christine Cem, TX.

James married **Camilla Fort Bird** (b. 7 May 1854, d. 14 Feb 1933) on 28 Oct 1876 in Wilson County, Texas.

James next married **Emaline** (b. 1853).

+632 F vi. **Mary S. Rader** was born on 2 Feb 1855 in Wilson Co, TX,[95] died on 21 Oct 1867 in Wilson County, Texas Buried Steele Branch, Cemetary[95] at age 12, and was buried on 21 Oct 1869 in Steele Branch, Stockdale, Wilson Co, TX.

+633 M vii. **John Henry Rader** was born on 28 Mar 1858 in Wilson Co, TX, died on 15 Sep 1864 in Wilson County, Texas at age 6, and was buried in Steele Branch, Stockdale, Wilson Co, TX.

+634 F viii. **Harriette Malinda 'Hattie' Rader** was born on 3 Aug 1861 in Wilson Co, TX, died on 12 Nov 1950 in Wilson County, Texas Buried Steele Branch, Cemetary at age 89, and was buried in Steele Branch Cemetery, Stockdale, Wilson County, Texas.

Harriette married **Robert B. May** (b. Aug 1857) on 18 Oct 1888 in Wilson County, Texas.

+635 F ix. **Jane Franklin 'Frankie' Rader** was born on 19 Nov 1863 in Wilson Co, TX, died on 24 May 1953 in Stockdale, Wilson County, Texas at age 89, and was buried in Steele Branch Cemetery, Stockdale, Wilson County, Texas.

Jane married **Oscar Franklin Montgomery** (b. 29 Jul 1857, d. 29 Jan 1928) on 10 Sep 1882 in Stockdale, Wilson County, Texas.

+636 F x. **Martha Caroline Rader** was born on 21 Aug 1866 in Wilson Co, TX, died on 9 Jan 1940 in Wilson County, Texas Buried Steele Branch, Cemetary at age 73, and was buried in Steele Branch Cemetery, Stockdale, Wilson County, Texas.

Martha married **Robert Volney 'Vol' Hawkins** (b. 3 Oct 1856, d. 7 Feb 1937) on 6 Apr 1884 in Wilson County, Texas.

105. Martha "Marie" Rader[5, 13, 18] (*Daniel^2, Casper Sr^1*) was born about 1815 in Wythe County, Virginia.[17] Another name for Martha was Mariah Rader.

Noted events in her life were:

Alt Birth: Bef 1807.[18]

Martha married **Wesley Whitsel**. Wesley was born about 1809 in ? and died before 1864 in Civil War.

The child from this marriage was:

+637 F i. **Julia Whitsel** was born on an unknown date.

Martha next married **Allen Rader**, son of **John Mcclung Rader Sr.** and **Elvira 'Elvia' Lemasters**. Allen was born about 1838 in Nicholas Co, WV and died in 1922 about age 84.

106. Mary Ann 'Jake' Rader[5, 13, 18] (*Daniel*[2], *Casper Sr*[1]) was born about 1816 in Tennessee[17, 18] and died in 1860[17, 18] about age 44.

107. Sarah C. Rader[5, 13, 18] (*Daniel*[2], *Casper Sr*[1]) was born about 1821 in Madison County, Alabama[17] and died about 1854 in Madison County, Alabama[17, 18] about age 33.

Noted events in her life were:

Alt Birth: Abt 1815.[18]

Alt Death: WFT Est 1839-1915, Desoto County, Mississippi Senatobia, Mississippi.

Sarah married **John D. Gann**, son of **Samuel Gann** and **Sarah C. Rader**, WFT Est 1835-1857. John was born about 1845 in Mississippi and died about 1863 in Civil War about age 18. The cause of his death was DIED IN CIVIL WAR.

Noted events in his life were:

Alt Birth: Abt 1821.

Children from this marriage were:

+638 F i. **Mary A. Gann** was born about 1846 in Mississippi.

+639 F ii. **Martha A. Gann** was born about 1851 in Mississippi and died WFT Est 1844-1946 about age -7.

+640 M iii. **John M. Gann** was born WFT Est 1839-1861 in Desoto County, Mississippi and died WFT Est 1859-1943 at age 20.

John married **Louise** (b. WFT Est 1839-1868, d. WFT Est 1859-1951) WFT Est 1859-1901.

+641 M iv. **William James Gann** was born about 1854 in Mississippi.

Sarah next married **Samuel Gann**. Samuel was born in 1822 in Alabama and died in 1861 in Desoto County, Mississippi at age 39.

Children from this marriage were:

+642 M i. **John D. Gann**[5, 13] was born about 1845 in Mississippi and died about 1863 in Civil War about age 18.

John married **Sarah C. Rader**[18] (b. Abt 1821, d. Abt 1854) WFT Est 1835-1857.

(Duplicate Line. See Person 107)

+643 F ii. **Mary A. Gann** was born about 1846 in Mississippi.

+644 F iii. **Martha A. Gann** was born about 1851 in Mississippi.

+645 M iv. **William James Gann** was born about 1854 in Mississippi.

108. Eliza Jane Rader[18] (*Daniel*[2], *Casper Sr*[1]) was born about 1825 in Madison County, Alabama[17,18] and died before 1860 in Desoto County, Mississippi.[17,18]

Noted events in her life were:

Fact 1: Fact 1, Had Three Sons And Three Daughters.

Alt Birth: Abt 1825, Madison County, Alabama.

Eliza married **Samuel Turner** on 31 Jan 1850. Another name for Samuel was Sam Turner.

Eliza next married **William Kader**. William was born in 1843 in PA.

General Notes: 1880 United States Census

```
William KADER    Self  M  Male    W  57  PA  Butcher        PA  PA
Elizabeth RADER  Wife  M  Female  W  54  PA  Keeping House  PA  PA
Elizabeth RADER  Dau   S  Female  W  18  PA  Helps - Home   PA  PA
William RADER    Son   S  Male    W  17  PA  At School      PA  PA
```

Source Information:
  Census Place Cedarville, Chester, Pennsylvania
  Family History Library Film   1255115
  NA Film Number   T9-1115
  Page Number   413C

Children from this marriage were:

+646 F i. **Elizabeth Rader** was born in 1862 in PA.

+647 M ii. **William Rader** was born in 1863 in PA.

109. Eleanor Elizabeth Rader[5,13,18] (*Daniel*[2], *Casper Sr*[1]) was born in 1828 in Madison County, Alabama[17,18] and died in Desoto County, Mississippi Senatobia, Mississippi.[17,18] Another name for Eleanor was Elizabeth Eleanor Rader.

General Notes: Alt Birth: Abt 1828 Wythe Co, VA[17]

Noted events in her life were:

Alt Death: Desoto County, Alabama.

Alt Birth: After 1807.

Eleanor married **William C. Gann** on 28 Sep 1847 in DE Soto County, Mississippi. William was born in 1826 in Tennessee.

Noted events in their marriage were:

Alt Marriage: 31 Jan 1848, Desoto County, Mississippi.

Noted events in his life were:

Fact 1: Fact 1, Remained In Mississippi Through 1880.

Children from this marriage were:

+648 M i. **George Denton Gann** was born on 1 Dec 1849 in Desoto County, Mississippi, died on 20 Mar 1853 in Harmony, Tate County, Mississippi at age 3, and was buried in Harmony Cemetery, Tate County, Mississippi.

+649 F ii. **Nancy Denton Gann** was born on 1 Dec 1849 in Desoto County, Mississippi and died in Sep 1850 in Desoto County, Mississippi.

Nancy married **Michael Sanders**.

+650 M iii. **George D. Gann** was born in Jun 1850 in Desoto County, Mississippi and died before 1860 in Desoto County, Mississippi.

+651 F iv. **Mary Louemma Gann** was born in 1853 in Desoto County, Mississippi.

+652 F v. **Martha Ann Gann** was born on 3 Nov 1854 in Desoto County, Mississippi, died on 29 Nov 1931 in Mt. Pleasant, Deport County, Texas at age 77, and was buried in Highlands Cemetery, Deport County, Texas.

Martha married **William Eudy** on 22 Sep 1875 in Tate County, Mississippi.

+653 F vi. **Matilda Jane Gann** was born in 1855 in Mississippi.

+654 F vii. **Maria Lavania Gann** was born on 3 Sep 1859 in Desoto County, Mississippi, died on 10 Dec 1936 in Truslow, Tate County, Mississippi at age 77, and was buried in Truslow, Tate County, Mississippi.

Maria married **John Porter Floy** (b. WFT Est 1839-1859, d. WFT Est 1873-1945) WFT Est 1870-1903.

Maria next married **Joseph Porter Floyd** (b. 25 Dec 1855, d. 11 May 1936) on 3 Feb 1875 in Tate County, Mississippi.

+655 F viii. **Nancy Denton Gann** was born in 1859 in Mississippi.

+656 F ix. **Willie Ella Gann** was born about 1860 in Mississippi.

+657 M x. **John Smith Gann** was born in Jan 1864 in Desoto County, Mississippi, died in 1944 in Tate County, Mississippi at age 80, and was buried in Mt. Zion, Tate County, Mississippi.

John married **Emma E. Irby**.

+658 F xi. **Diana Mire Gann** was born on 14 Jul 1867 in Desoto County, Mississippi, died on 28 Aug 1936 at age 69, and was buried in Longtown Cemetery.

Diana married **James F. Green** on 23 Dec 1885.

+659 F xii. **Sarah Virginia Gann** was born on 22 Mar 1868 in Desoto County, Mississippi, died on 14 Apr 1869 in Tate County, Mississippi at age 1, and was buried in Harmony Cemetery, Tate County, Mississippi.

Sarah married **John W. Whitesell** (b. WFT Est 1836-1872, d. WFT Est 1863-1950) WFT Est 1863-1907.

110. Nancy C. Rader (*Daniel^2, Casper Sr^1*) was born in 1830 in Desoto County, Mississippi and died WFT Est 1844-1924 at age 14.

Nancy married **William R. Robinson** WFT Est 1844-1877. William was born WFT Est 1813-1833 and died WFT Est 1847-1919 at age 34.

Source Citations

1 (7353 Terre Haute
   Indianna 47802
   812-299-1500
   MrSwervinMerv@aol.com).
2 Pedigree Resource File CD 35 (Salt Lake City, UT: Intellectual Reserve, Inc., 2001).
3 margie Etter, GEDCOM file imported on 26 Oct 1998.
4 Kathy Frye Genealogy Report Nov 2000.
5 Pedigree Resource File CD 44 (Salt Lake City, UT: Intellectual Reserve, Inc., 2002).
6 Pedigree Resource File CD 16 (Salt Lake City, UT: Intellectual Reserve, Inc., 2000).
7 Pedigree Resource File CD 97 (Salt Lake City, UT: Intellectual Reserve, Inc., 2004).
8 Pedigree Resource File CD 66 (Salt Lake City, UT: Intellectual Reserve, Inc., 2003).
9 Pedigree Resource File CD 96 (Salt Lake City, UT: Intellectual Reserve, Inc., 2004).
10 margie Etter, *GEDCOM file imported on 26 Oct 1998.*.
11 margie ETTER, GEDCOM file imported on 26 Oct 1998. (Imported GEDCOM file).
12 GEDCOM file imported on 28 Oct 1998.
13 h6912 Nibroc@prodigy.
14 GEDCOM file imported on 28 Oct 1998. (Imported GEDCOM file).
15 *GEDCOM file imported on 28 Oct 1998.*.
16 Casper.FTW.
17 Brøderbund Software, Inc., *World Family Tree Vol. 10, Ed. 1* (Release date: May 6, 1997).
18 Brøderbund Software, Inc., World Family Tree Vol. 4, Ed. 1 (Release date: August 23, 1996), Tree #1246.
19 Sallie Brown.FTW.
20 Statler Family Website.
21 Tombstone.
22 Repass Family Tree.FTW.
23 Penn's East Side Applications survey A-40-149 (over the blue mountains on Swatara Creek and Trout Creek).
24 *Cumberland County Deed book Vol 1, book P, page 156-157.*
25 *Pennsylvania Archives, Volume Info: Fifth Series*, Volume VI, page 222 Captain James Bell had 3 Classes of Militia the 5th, 6th and 7th. Casper Retter was in the 6th class with; Peter Miller, David Page, Phillip Gillan, David Valker, Stofel Miars and Henry Umberger.
26 Ibid, Vol VI; pg 224 Cap Jas. Bell's 1 st Company, 6th Class. Casper Readers served with Peter Miller, David Hoge, Phillip Gillin, David Walker, Stofel Miers and Hen'y Humbarger.
27 *Rev. J. C. Stoever Jr's Pa. Marriages & Baptisms (1730-1779)*, pg. 13 Bethel Marriages ROEDER, Caspar to Regina GERHARDT.
28 Family Files of Ralph Cansler.
29 *St John's Lutheran Church cemetery Inscriptions.*
30 *Nancy O. Rader bible 'Conrad Rader died May 14, 1845 aged 79 years.*
31 *Fincastle & Mont Marriage book.*
32 *kegley.*
33 Janet Lynn Skelton, *Skelton GEDCOM* (Janet Lynn Skelton
   624 Windsor Drive
   Conyers, GA 30094).

34	Brøderbund Software, Inc., *World Family Tree Vol. 7, Ed. 1, The Submitter for Volume 7, Tree 2060 ANGELA H SHEPHERD, ROUTE 4 BOX 332-0, MARTINS BRANCH, CHARLESTON, WV 25312* (Release date: October 17, 1996).
35	Margaret Elizabeth Morrett Riley (3 page essay written in 1917).
36	*Customer pedigree..*
37	(ancestry file # 81820, submitter Billy Joe Williams, 331 W. Aspen Dr. Mustang, OK 73064, williamsx4@email.msn.com).
38	Brøderbund Software, Inc., *World Family Tree Vol. 4, Ed. 1, The Submitter for Volume 4, Tree 3573 MARY A BLAYLOCK 4871 PIONEER DRIVE HILLSBORO, MO 63050-3535* (Release date: August 23, 1996), Tree #1246.
39	*Nancy O Rader bible 'Elizabeth Rader died May 6, 1848 aged 75 yr 10m 25.*
40	*Lyman Henry Davis III.*
41	*Nancy F. Byrd, 922 South Coleman Str, Tooele, UT 84074 (1995).*
42	Federal Census.
43	Pedigree Resource File CD 52 (Salt Lake City, UT: Intellectual Reserve, Inc., 2002).
44	*east TN mar.*
45	Brøderbund Software, Inc., *World Family Tree Vol. 4, Ed. 1, The Submitter for Volume 4, Tree 3573 MARY A BLAYLOCK 4871 PIONEER DRIVE HILLSBORO, MO 63050-3535* (Release date: August 23, 1996).
46	*Cem Book.*
47	*Mary C. McKamey: 738 W Cnty Rd 11505Cloverdale, IN 46120.*
48	*bible of George Alexander Rader.*
49	Greene County Deed book, Book 9 pages 438 and 439.
50	*Mrs W. R. Mosby III, 634 Knollwood Circle, Conyers, GA 30208.*
51	*Karen L. Woody, Rt1 Box 187E, Bluefield, WV 24701 (304) 325-3562.*
52	Historic Greene Co, TN, page 317.
53	Greene Co TN Marriages, G.F. Burgner, p 79.
54	*Greene County Marriage # 3200.*
55	janet skelton.FTW.
56	Repass.ged.
57	Repass Family History.FTW.
58	Copy of Copy of 783554.ged.FTW.
59	Jacob Rippas.FTW.
60	*Patricia Frances Rader.*
61	*Marriage Certificate, State of Mississippi.*
62	Broderbund Software, Inc., *World Family Tree Vol. 4, Ed. 1* (Release date: August 23, 1996), Tree #1246Date of Import: Nov 15, 1998.
63	*Phyllis Hembree, PO Box 643, Twain Harte, CA 95383.*
64	*Mary Blaylock, 30 Edwards Circle, Union, MO 63084-2044.*
65	Greene County Deed book, Book 13 page 7.
66	Ibid, book 18 page 167.
67	Ibid, Book 19 page 67.
68	WFT Volume 7, Tree # 2032.
69	Family Files of Ralph Cansler, Page 132.
70	Ibid, Page 215.
71	*Matson's Bible.*
72	Mills7.FTW.
73	US CENSUS 1900 CLAY CO.IN CASS TWPS.
74	Edgar Smith fcounts@msn.com.

75	(Sinking Springs Churchbook), p63.
76	*Family reunion info 1936.*
77	*Bible of Lemuel Crosby and Nancy Hawkins Crosby.*
78	Jackie Robinson, *Geocities web site* (Rt 2 Box 2738Rogersville, TN 37857).
79	*Greene co marr book pg 181.*
80	Federal Archives, 1850, Greene County, Tennessee Federal Census.
81	Family Files of Ralph Cansler, Page 198.
82	Ibid, Martha Jane Cobble death certificate registered 3/19/1925.
83	Ibid, Martha Jane Cobble's death certificate registered 3/19/1925.
84	*Byron Sistler's 'Early East Tennessee Marriages'.*
85	Greene Co TN Marriages, G.F. Burgner, p 216.
86	*Fonce Harold Rader.*
87	A.L. Kingman, *New Historical Atlas of Fulton Co. Indiana, illustrated, Kingman Bro's* (A.L. Kingmam, 1883)), pg 39-40.
88	*IGI.*
89	Holbrook and Baumgardner.FTW.
90	Repass Family to 1568.FTW.
91	Cregar-2.FTW.
92	*De Soto County, Mississippi marriage records.*
93	*WFT vol 10*, submitter 2331 WFT vol 10.
94	*Karon Mac Smith, Box 190 Rt 1, Nixon, TX 78140-9501.*
95	Brøderbund Family Archive #164, Ed. 1, Mortality Index: United States, Texas Mort Sch, WILSON CO., TX 1870, Date of Import: Jul 21, 1997, Internal Ref. #1.164.1.7721.34.
96	*LDS AF95-105709.*
97	*Whaley Cemetery Book.*
98	*Obituary* (Greybull Standard, Greybull, Wyoming.), 18 Feb 1921, Obituary.
99	Ibid.
100	karen (Kragdoll5@aol.com).
101	H. H. Hardesty, *Presidents, Soldiers, Statesmen* (Vol II copyright 1898).
102	*death certificate.*
103	Carolyn S. Gregg, *Salem Lutheran Church Cemetery* (http://ftp.rootsweb.com/pub/usgenweb/tn/greene/cemeteries/salemluth.txt).
104	*hartman bible.*
105	*bible.*
106	*Hartman family Bible.*
107	Franklin Co, TN, *Minute Book 6, Page 527-8 Chancery Court.*
108	*Greene Co., TN Marriage records.*
109	*Emma Hinote.*
110	US CENUS 1900 CLAY CO. CASS TWPS.IN.
111	US CENUS 1900 CLAY CO CASS TWPS INDIANNA.
112	RUBY BELL DAUGHTER.
113	*Norman K. Toole, Author's Addr: Norman L. Toole6647 HardingTaylor, MI 48180,1829103364.1666@compuserve.com(313) 381-8844* (17Apr1997).
114	INDIANA VITAL RECORDS B-H-2 P-22.
115	*1910 census.*
116	1261878.ged.
117	Pamela Forslund Cousins July, 2000.
118	Papers of Nova Estelle (Gardenhire) Sullivan, Obituary.
119	Ann Tabor 2001.
120	Donna Fitzgerald letter 31 Mar 2000.

Source Citations

121 *SSN 409-66-8478.*
122 *Diane Mueller, 530 Silver Pine Trail, Roswell, GA 30076 (No. Fulton).*
123 Bent Creek Cemetery Headstone Listing.
124 William H. Craft Personal Family Archives.
125 State Archive, Leonard Cemetery, Leonard, Fannin County, Texas Records (US GenWeb for Fannin CountyTex).
126 1910 U.S. Federal Census (Narional Archive).
127 William H. Craft, Jr. Personal Family Archives (Unknown).
128 *Methodist Providence circuit records Greene Co Pioneer vol 10.*
129 Family Files of Ralph Cansler, IDA CANSLER CERTIFICATE OF DEATH.
130 Ibid, James A. Cansler Application For Annuity To Railroad Retirement Board, R.R.B.No. A22303.
131 Ibid, Ida Cansler death certificate 2-3010.
132 Ibid, James Alexander Cansler CERTIFICATE OF DEATH.
133 Ibid, "Application For Annuity To Railroad Retirement Board R.R.B. No. A22303... James A. Cansler... Date Signed August 10, 1936."
134 Ibid, Death No. 56-10450.
135 Ibid, James A. Cansler Application For Annuity, R.R.B. No. A22303.
136 Ibid, James A. Cansler Application For Annuity To Railroad Retirement Board, R.R.B. No. A22303.
137 *Mildred J. Rader, po box 846, Bath ME 04530 (207-433-3955).*
138 *russell leo rader.FTW.*
139 *SSN death record 563-10-4544.*
140 *Laura Sharon Jackson.*
141 *Marriage Certificate, State of Arkansas.*
142 Ibid.

Name Index

"CLARA"
    Clarinda (WFT Est 1837-WFT Est 1880) 198
(   )
    Eliza Jane (Abt 1844-   ) 229
    Sarah 223
(No surname)
    Angelina (1822-   ) 143, 299
    Anna (1839-   ) 245
    Augusta (1835-   ) 245
    Elizabeth (1836-   ) 222
    Elizabeth (Abt 1820-   ) 143, 301
    Emaline (1853-   ) 331
    Loisa P (1838-   ) 189
    Margaret (1785-   ) 187
    Mattie (1858-   ) 261
    Priscilla (1855-   ) 327
    Rachiel (1804-   ) 141, 292
    Rebecca (1856-   ) 327
    Sarah J. (1827-   ) 201
A.
    Minnie (1871-   ) 323
ACREA
    Mary Catherine (1850-1923) 198
ADKINS
    Delona Delaney (1831-1915) 239
    Eliza 239
    Luke G. 240
ALTOM
    Betty (Abt 1833-   ) 223
    Elizabeth (Abt 1826-   ) 223
    Ervin (Abt 1820-   ) 223
    George (Abt 1843-   ) 224
    James (Abt 1794-   ) 119, 223
    James (Abt 1841-   ) 224
    Jesse (Abt 1832-   ) 223
    John (Abt 1820-   ) 223
    Joseph (Abt 1818-After 1885) 223
    Martha Ann (Abt 1837-   ) 223
    Riley (Abt 1815-1855) 223
    Susan (Abt 1840-   ) 224
ALVERY
    Tiney 48, 122
ANDES
    Elizabeth (1775-1846) 176
    George (1772-   ) 216
    Lydia (1813-1880) 104, 216
ANN
    Mary (1828-1914) 141, 276
ANN: 265
ARMBRISTER
    Barbara (Abt 1775-1845) 48, 133
ARMPRISTER
    George 133, 154
BABCOCK
    James L. 282
BAILS
    Enoch T. 152, 316
BAKER
    Eleanor 'Eller' 328
    Ellen A. (Abt 1844-   ) 328
    Ellenor "Eller" A. (Abt 1844-   ) 327
    John (-1844) 154, 327
    John D. (Abt 1833-   ) 327
    Sarah E. (Abt 1835-   ) 328
BALES
    Enoch 152, 315
    W. M. (Abt 1842-   ) 317
BALL
    Aaron Miller (1827-   ) 141, 295
    William Dyer (1791-1870) 295
BARBARA: 133, 154
BARLOW
    John 254
BARNES
    Emma Prisilla (1859-1927) 205
BASINGER
    Elizabeth Betsy (1816-   ) 200
    George 199
    George William (1832-1865) 199
    Hamilton (1827-   ) 199
    Isaac (1824-   ) 200
    Jacob 199
    Jacob Dreher 230
    John 200
    Levina (1830-1886) 200
    Margaret Ann (1834-1856) 199
    Mary E. (1840-1857) 200
    Michael (1824-   ) 200
    Michael Jr. (1806-1855) 104, 199
    Phillip 199
    Sally 199
    Samuel (1848-   ) 200
    William (1826-   ) 199
BAUGHARD
    Andrew (1828-   ) 217
    Valentine 'Von' (1842-   ) 217
BAYSINGER
    Peggy (Abt 1805-   ) 119, 230
BEAN
    Sarah Anna (1809-1915) 302
BECKER
    John Franklin 327
BEDSAUL
    Elisha 318

BELFORD
    Clara (1860-1948) 198
BELL
    Elizabeth D. (1837-   ) 227
BEYERS
    (   ) 175
BIBLE
    Louisa "Eliza" J. (1823-1856) 226
    Phillip M. (K.) (Abt 1845-   ) 250
    William Harrison (1843-1925) 250
BIDDLE
    Sarah (1806-1871) 292
BIRD
    Camilla Fort (1854-1933) 331
    Elizabeth Frances (1847-After 1887) 315
BOGGS
    Elizabeth 322
BORDEN
    Henry C. (1848-1890) 218
    Susan A. (1831-1915) 173
BOWER
    Christian Jr. (1768-1830) 176
BOWERS
    Caroline J. (1832-   ) 177
    Catherine D. (Abt 1847-   ) 177
    Christian (Abt 1820-   ) 177
    Elizabeth (1832-   ) 177
    Henry (1818-1901) 177
    John A. (Abt 1837-   ) 177
    Jonas (1796-1838) 103, 176
    Lewis (1826-1911) 177
    Martha (1834-   ) 177
    Mary Ann 'Pollyan' (1831-1895) 190
    Samuel (1824-   ) 177
    William (1816-1909) 176
BOWLING
    James Edward (1824-1904) 174
BOWMAN
    James D. 301
BRADFORD
    Sarah Angeline (1844-1917) 217
BRAY
    Permelia Caldonia (1839-1917) 326
BRIDEWELL
    Francis Asberry (1825-   ) 194
BRITTON
    Jane P. (1827-Abt 1855) 189
    Rebecca Amelia (1834-Abt 1855) 189
BROWN
    Anny (1805-Abt 1833) 104, 194, 202
    Christopher A. 'Stophel' Jr (1774-1850) .. 49, 145
    Daniel (Esq.) (1803-1856) 150, 302
    Eugenia F. (1857-   ) 308

    Granville H. (1825-   ) 303
    Ida Sue (1863-   ) 308
    James Andrew (Rev.,) (1815-1900) 150, 308
    James Augustin Sr. (1891-1977) 309
    James David (1859-   ) 308
    James Wesley (-1846) 303
    Jane (1829-   ) 303
    Jennie E. (1860-1946) 276
    Jesse (1808-   ) 150, 305
    John A. (1819-1905) 150, 307
    John Ahaz (Bef 1818-1905) 151, 310
    Joseph Washington (1820-   ) 151, 310
    Josephine (1842-   ) 308
    Josephus (1855-   ) 258
    Laura (1857-   ) 308
    Lavona (1849-   ) 308
    Leah Ester (1893-   ) 310
    Lydia (1809-1897) 150, 305
    Margaret Agnes (1843-   ) 306
    Maria Louisa (1847-   ) 308
    Michael (-1785) 145
    Nicholas (1840-   ) 308
    Oregon (1845-   ) 308
    Robert A. (1844-   ) 308
    Rosanna (1810-1901) 150, 306
    Ruth Ella (1889-1957) 309
    Sally 'Salome' (1806-1891) 150, 303
    Sarah 282
    Scott (1888-   ) 309
    Stephen F. (Rev.,) (1854-   ) 308
    William K. (1852-1866) 308
BRYAM
    Alfred (1808-   ) 93, 155, 168, 330
BULLEN
    J. W. 261
BULLENTON
    Joseph 236
BULLINGTON
    David (1852-1924) 237
BURROUGHS
    John 197
BURTON
    Elizabeth (Abt 1836-After 1872) 311
    Malissa (1860-1932) 315
BYRAM
    Elizabeth (1812-1852) 154, 325
    Hannah M. (1832-   ) 168
    Julia F. (1841-   ) 168
    Martha A. (1846-   ) 168
    Susan E. (1849-   ) 168
    Susan S. (1839-   ) 168
CALHOUN
    Joseph (1831-1895) 313

CAMPBELL
    (_____) 190
    George W. (1840-   ) 190

CARRIETT
    Oscar J. (WFT Est 1825-WFT Est 1834) 297

CARROLL
    Dr. James Gasaway (1807-After 1874) 310

CARTER
    Lot 282

CASH
    Catherine 230

CASSELL
    Michael 305
    Michael (1827-   ) 304

CATE
    Southwell Bruce (1871-   ) 302

CATRON
    Catharine (Ketron) (Abt 1823-1896) 130, 174, 249
    Ephraim (1827-1895) 317
    Jemima (1818-   ) 177
    Valentine (-Abt 1832) 249

CHAMPLIN
    Alexander 199

CLICK
    Jennie (1869-1917) 262

CLIFFORD
    Patrick (Abt 1823-   ) 252
    Thomas (1830-   ) 252

CLIFTON
    John (1834-1913) 311

CLINE
    Delilah (1848-1930) 317
    Polly (1828-1899) 313
    Savannah (Abt 1830-   ) 314

COBBLE
    Anna (1831-After 1880) 189
    Anna (1842-Bef 1860) 253
    Barbara (1822-1910) 177
    Elizabeth 'Bets' (1835-   ) 252
    Frederick W. 217
    Frederick Washington (1826-1908) 217
    Jacob 'Jake' (1798-Bef 1860) 130, 252
    James (1836-1916) 252
    John (1831-   ) 252
    Joseph Washington (1849-1937) 218
    Martha Jane (1838-1925) 253
    Polly Ann (1833-   ) 252
    Sarah Elizabeth (1825-1891) 177
    Tennessee (1846-   ) 253
    Unknown (Between 1825-   ) 252

COLE
    Clara E. (1874-   ) 198

COLLETT
    James C. (1829-1911) 174

COLLIER
    Sela Jenny (1855-1934) 315

COLYER
    William (1818-1893) 120, 237

COX
    Jane (1831-Bef 1890) 314

CRABTREE
    Ethel (1897-1991) 310

CRASS
    Elvira A. 152, 312

CREGAN
    John 122, 238

CREGAR
    Annie (Anna) (1823-1906) 304

CRESS
    Alvira (1832-   ) 152, 311
    Margaret Rebecca (-Bef 1813) 48, 138

CROSBY
    Sarah 'Sally' (1839-1916) 228

CROSIER
    Nancy Isabelle (1824-1910) 222

CUPP
    Jeremiah 140, 265

CUSHMAN
    Unk 282

DALGARN
    Elisha 198
    Sarah Jennie 198

DARLINA
    (1840-   ) 197

DAVIS
    Elizabeth (1789-1849) 49, 154
    Nancy J. (1840-   ) 190
    Sarah Ann (1840-1921) 197
    Sudie 262

DAVISON
    Lola 318

DAWSON
    Delila (1839-1904) 141, 292
    James Esq. (1809-1877) 292

DAY
    James A. Riley (1842-1916) 250

DEBUSK
    Rebecca Catherine (1841-1874) 311

DENMAN
    Mary Elizabeth (1846-   ) 257

DERRICK
    Henry D. (1863-   ) 307

DODSON
    Christina P. (Abt 1824-   ) 172

DORCAS

Tarkis (Dorcas) (1783-1868) 48, 143
DRAKE
    Edward M. (1818-1877) 227
    Estel M (1824-1909) 227
    Estell M. (Abt 1818-1877) 227
E.
    Mary 304
    Mary (1868-WFT Est 1903) 325
    Teresa (1837-1901) 234
EARHART
    Robert C. (1854-1927) 318
EAST
    Helen Wallace (1847-1870) 198
EGMAN
    Phebe J. 276
ELIZABETH
    (1828-   ) 143, 301
    Mary 300
ELKINS
    Andrew (1824-   ) 240
ELLIOTT
    Benjamin Franklin (1834-1884) 314
    Charles C. (1840-   ) 311
    Della (1858-   ) 314
    Mary (Abt 1843-Bef 1871) 310
    Nancy Jane (1843-1910) 311
ELSIE: 327
EMMA
    (1849-   ) 263
EMMA: 322
ENYART
    Clark (1854-   ) 282
ETTER
    Amanda C. 'Mandy' (1842-   ) 258
    Andrew (1844-   ) 258
    Catherine (Abt 1772-Abt 1847) 47, 102
    Daniel (1750-1803) 102, 116
    Eliza Emmeline (1850-   ) 258
    Elizabeth (1841-   ) 229
    Fredrick Washington (1805-1856) 119, 228
    George W. (1839-   ) 229
    James Goodan (1830-   ) 228
    Jefferson (1837-   ) 257
    John (1778-1855) 228, 257
    John (1847-   ) 258
    Joseph (1857-   ) 258
    Martha Ann (1832-   ) 257
    Martin Luther (1831-1916) 229
    Mary (1776-1848) 48, 116, 243
    Mary (Abt 1839-   ) 229
    Mary Jane (1834-   ) 257
    Samuel (1834-   ) 229
    Valentine (1833-   ) 229
    William (1806-1860) 131, 257
    William Laughner (1852-1857) 258
EUDY
    William 334
FARMER
    Jane 245
FENTRES
    Joseph 140
FEREE
    Emma J. 276
FISCHER
    Jacob 305
FISHBACK
    Harriett E. (1832-   ) 164
    Jacob T (1765-   ) 93, 162
FISHER
    Absolom (1808-1887) 93, 166
    Andrew Clark (1850-1850) 168
    Augustus (1835-1835) 167
    David (1777-1855) 166
    Elizabeth (1840-1921) 168
    Frances Ann (1843-1862) 168
    Isaac Melville (1853-1857) 168
    Jacob Foster (-1924) 305
    James R. (1847-1862) 168
    Joseph S. (1840-1919) 307
    Louisa (1836-1890) 141, 286
    Margaret E. (1854-   ) 307
    Morning (1793-   ) 324
    Nancy Ory (1843-1862) 168
    Sarah Jane (1839-1914) 307
    Thomas Wilson (1837-1921) 168
FLOY
    John Porter (WFT Est 1839-WFT Est 1873) 334
FLOYD
    Joseph Porter (1855-1936) 334
FORE
    Catharine "Katie" (Abt 1775-After 1830) 173
FORTRESS
    Joseph 140, 263
FRANKS
    Elizabeth (1821-1903) 154, 324, 326
    Jeremiah (Abt 1791-Bef 1870) 324
    Lemuel (1834-Abt 1873) 326
FRITTS
    Jesse 198
FRY
    Leanna 239
FRYE
    Nancy B. (1837-   ) 314
GAIL
    Susannah (-1794) 121
GAMMON

Elizabeth (1824-1892) 104, 218
Ruben J. (1851-1930) 218
GANN
 Diana Mire (1867-1936) 334
 George D. (1850-Bef 1860) 334
 George Denton (1849-1853) 334
 John D. (Abt 1845-Abt 1863) 155, 332
 John M. (WFT Est 1839-WFT Est 1859) 332
 John Smith (1864-1944) 334
 Maria Lavania (1859-1936) 334
 Martha A. (Abt 1851-) 333
 Martha A. (Abt 1851-WFT Est 1844) 332
 Martha Ann (1854-1931) 334
 Mary A. (Abt 1846-) 332, 333
 Mary Louemma (1853-) 334
 Matilda Jane (1855-) 334
 Nancy Denton (1849-1850) 334
 Nancy Denton (1859-) 334
 Samuel (1822-1861) 155, 332
 Sarah Virginia (1868-1869) 334
 William C. (1826-) 155, 333
 William James (Abt 1854-) 332, 333
 Willie Ella (Abt 1860-) 334
GARRIOTT
 Oliver (-1871) 142, 297
GERHARD
 Regina 46
GERHARDT
 John Conrad (Abt 1720-) 46
 Regina 'Rachel' (1746-1816) 46
GOINS
 Sarah (1839-1887) 311
GOSLIN: 200
GRABLE
 Mary C. (1835-1919) 194
GREEN
 James F. 334
GRILLS
 Tryphena Ellen (1860-) 325
GRUBB
 Charles Francis "Frank" (1833-1912) 314
 Sofia M. (1835-Bef 1862) 314
GRUBBS
 Jane (1830-WFT Est 1867) 314
GUTHRIE
 Andrew "Andy" (1846-1916) 236
 Andrew (1801-1867) 120, 235
 Andy Andrew (1846-1916) 236
 Emaline (1838-) 236
 Emeline (Abt 1838-) 236
 Isabel (1851-) 237
 James 235
 James C. (1834-1862) 236

 John A. (1841-1923) 236
 Joseph (1846-1919) 236
 Laney J. (1845-) 236
 Lewis W. (1834-1914) 236
 Linda A. (1852-1928) 237
 Malinda A. (1852-1928) 237
 Mary A. (1836-) 236
 Nancy (1852-) 237
 William (1835-) 236
H.
 Edna (1870-) 318
HAGER
 Eliza (Abt 1837-1914) 240
 Elizabeth (WFT Est 1814-WFT Est 1831) ... 239
 Henderson (1824-) 239
 James "Black Jim" Jr. (1791-1859) 122, 238
 John (1832-) 239
 Joseph (Abt 1818-) 239
 Lavina Melvina (1824-After 1900) 239
 Malvina 239
 Mary Elizabeth (1830-) 239
 Rebecca (Abt 1836-) 240
 Russell Sr. (1829-1917) 239
 Sarah (Abt 1833-) 240
 Silas (1828-1906) 240
 William P. (1823-1865) 239
HALL
 Elbert (Abt 1848-) 253
 Mary (Abt 1851-Bef 1922) 311
HALT
 Ida Hoyt 318
HANCOCK
 Frances 304
HARMON
 Candace (1849-) 254
 James Taylor (1847-1917) 254
 Wes 217
HARRIETT
 (1868-) 205
HARRISON
 Mary Jane Earnest (1858-1894) 190
HARTMAN
 Marshall Jr (1820-1887) 189
HAUFF
 Barbara (1803-1883) 104, 187
 Joseph (1781-1852) 187
HAUN
 Christopher A. (1825-1861) 252
 Eli 255
 Hannah Elizabeth (1846-1889) 261
 John 261
 Mary E. 300
 Seymore (1825-1879) 250

Unknown 252
HAWKINS
    Robert Volney 'Vol' (1856-1937) 331
HEBARGER
    Amanda J. (1858-   ) 258
HEDRICK
    Elizabeth Woods Been (1771-1860) 48, 129, 224
HELVEY OR ALVERY
    Christina 'Diney' (1770-1815) 48, 121
HELVY
    Christina 48, 122
HELWIG
    Henry Sr. (1744-1792) 121
HENDERSON
    Laura R (1861-1932) 190
    Rachael Rhoda (1861-   ) 219
HERBST
    Eleonora "Ellen" C. (1819-1879) 150, 309
HICKEY
    Hugh A 257
HICKS
    Henry Milam (Abt 1838-   ) 317
HILL
    Charles W 277
    Mary M 277
    Permelia Ann (1852-   ) 239
HINE
    Nancy "Jennie" Jane (1855-1931) 276
HINES
    Isabella E. (1854-1939) 166
HOFFMAN
    Charles 245
HOOD
    Eunice Emaline (1851-   ) 189
HOUNSHELL
    Delilah (1830-1919) 313
HOUSLEY
    Hattie May (1869-1915) 292
HUDSON
    Clementine R. (1834-   ) 309
    Jesse (1840-1888) 234
    Leander M. (1809-1879) 120, 230
    Minerva (1835-1917) 233
HULL
    Elizabeth C 176
HUNTER
    Cynthia Adaline (1823-1901) 222
IDA: 301
IRBY
    Emma E 334
ISLEY
    Nancy Susong (1837-   ) 252
JACKSON
    Aquilla 174, 175
    Lollie Laura (1847-1909) 250
    Sarah M. 'Sallie' (1841-1907) 228
JANE
    (1830-   ) 307
    Permilia (1839-   ) 143, 298
JENKINS
    Catherine (Abt 1846-   ) 238
    David 265
    David C 140, 265
    David Clarkson (1822-1892) 140, 265
    Jackson (Abt 1844-   ) 238
    Jane (Abt 1848-   ) 238
    Mary (Abt 1841-   ) 237
    Mary E. (1839-   ) 194
    William (1815-   ) 120, 237
JOHNSON
    James A. (1830-   ) 165
    Mary Elizabeth (1852-1912) 198
JONES
    Rebecca (1852-1941) 327
    Unk 282
JR.
    James Vaughn 143, 300
JUNIATA
    (1875-   ) 300
KADER
    William (1843-   ) 155, 333
KEESLING
    Mary 223
    Susanna 223
KEGLEY
    Abraham (1806-After 1880) 152, 312
    Alfred (1833-After 1900) 314
    Augustus Davis (1847-1905) 315
    Austin Md (1838-Bef 1900) 314
    Daniel 304
    Ephriam (1829-1910) 313
    Estel Stephen (1886-1939) 309
    Gustavus (1846-   ) 314
    James Lafayette (1849-1926) 315
    Joel (1828-   ) 313
    John J. (1842-   ) 314
    John Jacob (1844-1904) 314
    Lemuel Edley (1853-1931) 318
    Margaret (1835-1912) 314
    Mary Magdalena "Polly" (1801-1860) .. 152, 310, 312
    Nancy (1839-   ) 314
    Nancy Jane (1832-1924) 313
    Nancy Mary (1840-1927) 314
    Reverend Joel (1826-1887) 313
    Sally (1818-1894) 153, 316

Samuel William (1852-1904) 315
William (1831-Abt 1909) 313
KETRON
    Catherine (1822-1896) 174
KING
    Isabella 235
    Nancy Caroline (1867-1929) 318
KINSER
    Delilah (1812-   ) 120, 234
    George (1791-Abt 1865) 218
    Lillie (1813-   ) 104, 218
KIRK
    Joseph Jr. (1819-1884) 174
KIRKPATRICK
    Melvina 227
KIRPATRICK
    Melvina A. (1834-1911) 227
L.
    Nancy (1816-   ) 93, 164
LADY
    Mary A. 'Polly' (1815-1895) 131, 256
    William (1829-   ) 256
LAMBERT
    Julian Dulaney "Lane" (1849-1933) 320
LANE
    Isaac 256
    Joseph O. (1849-1910) 257
LANGSTON
    William Jasper 326
    William Jasper (1832-WFT Est 1877) ... 326, 327
    William Jasper (1836-1910) 326, 327
LARINDA
    Larinda Or Lucinda (1818-1860) 155, 329
LATHAM
    Gracia 199
LAUCHNER
    John (1790-1849) 103, 173, 251
LAUGHNER
    Catharine 174
    Catherine (1823-1896) 130, 174, 251
    Christian (1769-Between 1830) 173
    Daniel (1819-1846) 174
    Eliza J. (Between 1822-1903) 174
    Louisa (1825-   ) 175
    Margaret (1822-1891) 174
    Mary Ann (Abt 1830-Abt 1899) 174
    Valentine 'Val' (1829-1871) 174
    William (1832-1909) 175
LEADY
    Jonathan (1779-1852) 49, 151
LEEDY
    Alfred (1835-After 1874) 311
    Almeda (1832-   ) 311

Alpha (1873-1876) 312
America Alice (1856-1926) 318, 319
Anna Mary (1808-   ) 152, 315
Barbara (1847-   ) 320
Callie 318
Catherine (1830-1901) 153, 322
Charles R. (1878-   ) 321
David Kegley (1852-1916) 318
Eliza Louisa (1853-1929) 320
Elizabeth (1836-1860) 311
Elizabeth (1844-   ) 320
Ellen (1848-1853) 311
Ellen (1849-   ) 320
Emma (1867-   ) 322
Frances (1843-   ) 317
Francis (1841-1927) 317
Isaac (Abt 1815-   ) 153, 319
Isaac Calloway (1839-1924) 311
Isabella (1833-1906) 311
Jane (1846-   ) 320
Joel (Dr.) (1806-1882) 152, 310
Joel Tarter (1862-1943) 318
John A. (1868-   ) 320
John Albert (1847-1903) 317
Joseph (1838-1912) 311
Josiah (1813-1903) 152, 316
Katherine "Kitty" (1854-1958) 318
Katherine (1864-   ) 318
Malinda (1818-1880) 153, 319
Manevey S. (1861-   ) 320
Margaret Missouri (1853-1902) 318
Mariah Callie (1855-1937) 318
Marin (1840-1861) 317
Martha L. (1870-   ) 312
Martin (1840-1861) 317
Mary (1845-1870) 317
Mary (1849-   ) 311
Mondana Nadine (1829-After 1874) 310
Montgomery Earhart Sr. (1859-1924) 318
Nancy (1828-1904) 153, 322
Rachel K. (1807-1861) 152, 312
Rebecca (1824-   ) 153, 321
Rebecca (1842-1921) 317
Robert L. (Abt 1868-   ) 312
Robert P. (1879-   ) 321
Rosannah (1838-1894) 316
Rosina (1820-   ) 153, 319
Rufus (1830-After 1900) 310
Rufus Stewart (1849-1933) 317
Salome "Sally" (1810-   ) 152, 315
Samuel (1822-1890) 153, 319
Samuel (1846-1932) 311
Samuel T. (1877-   ) 320

Saphrona (1843-   )..........................317
   Sarah Loannas (1846-1932)............................317
   Selina (1842-1886) 311
   Sophia (Abt 1826-1908)........................ 153, 321
   Sophrona (1844-   )..........................317
   Vinson (1857-   ).............................322
   William (1845-   ).............................320
   William Henry (1850-1935)............................317
LEMASTERS
   Elvira 'Elvia' (1804-1882) 332
LEONARD
   Ellen..318
LILLIAN
   (1857-   )....................................302
LISTER
   Nancy (1829-   ).............................200
LONAS
   Adam (1821-1905).....................................253
LONG
   Lourena (1835-1915)..................................229
LOUISE
   (WFT Est 1839-WFT Est 1859) 332
LUCAS
   Andrew J. (1831-   )..........................257
LYNCH
   William 256
M.
   Francis (1854-   ).................... 141, 286
   Lucy (1835-1902).....................................319
   Mary (1852-   )...............................258
MACE
   Anna Mary (1816-1883)....................104, 195, 203
   Elizabeth (1820-   )..........................172
   Henry................................... 195, 203
   Ruhama (1823-   ).............................172
   Ruma (1818-   )...............................172
MANY
   (1871-   )....................................322
MARTHA
   (Abt 1765-   )................................240
MARY
   (1863-   )....................................325
MARY:..311
MASONER
   Margaret D. (1845-1889)..............................253
MATHEWS
   Nancy (1808-1894) 104, 200
MATTHEWS
   Levi H. (1856-   )............................277
MAY
   Robert B. (1857-   ).........................331
MCCOLLUM
   Robert...245

MCMILLIAN
   Elizabeth "Betty" (1847-1932).........................314
MCNEELY
   Martha Ellen (1832-1896) 239
MCNEW
   Jacob (1837-   )..............................256
MELTON
   Martha A. 'Mattie' (1863-1928) 261
MEYERS
   Emily Jane (1841-1880) 190
MICHAELS
   Phobe (1779-1861).............................. 228, 257
MILES
   Arenas "Anna" Matilda (1825-1907) 222
MILLARD
   Lodemia Caroline (1840-1915)................ 143, 302
   Thomas (1806-1876)...................................302
MILLER
   Catherine (1829-1900) 174
MILLIRON
   Mary Ann (1840-1933)............................... 48, 133
MINTON
   Amanda Ella (1869-1943) 201
MISSEMER
   Eve..249
MONICAL
   Moses H. (1836-   )..........................245
MONTGOMERY
   Nancy Ann Caroline (1823-1908) 155, 330
   Oscar Franklin (1857-1928) 331
MOORE
   Eliza Jane (1824-1901)...............................227
   Ellendine (1840-1900)................................236
   Rhoda N. (1843-   )...........................236
   Sarah Ann 236
   Sarah Ann (1842-1920)................................236
MOREHEAD
   James W. (1826-1903).................................319
   Rosa Bell (1858-1927)................................305
MORELOCK
   Henry (1850-1928) 205
MORRETT
   William Michael (1860-1936)..........................276
MULLINS
   Elizabeth (1863-   )..........................314
MURBARGAR
   Elizabeth (1842-1884)................................197
   John 'Pap' III (1838-1918) 198
MURDEN
   Julien (1818-   ).................... 140, 262
MYERS
   Elizabeth Ann (1831-1856)............................227
   Hyla Ann (1838-   )...........................177

James Wesley (1829-   )..........................254
John Tivis (1830-1902) 254
NANCY
(1832-   )...........................240
NEAS
Narcissa (1844-1885) 205
NELSON
Joseph H. (1850-1916)..........................276
NORRIS
Lizzie 282
ORR
Sarah Rebecca (1837-1862)...................310
ORY
Calvin... 92
Elizabeth (1772-1848)........................47, 92
OTTINGER
Benjamin (1845-1897)...........................205
Elizabeth (1831-1874) 172
Elizabeth (1832-1908)............................175
Henry..172
Henry (1829-WFT Est 1890)..................172
John D. (1820-1900) 172
Lewis Barney (1836-1901)......................173
Margaret (1839-   ) 173
Mary Ann (1836-1913)............................173
PAINTER
Alice V. (1864-   ) 322
Charles W. (1852-1860) 321
Cynthia (1866-   ) 321
Cynthia P. (1860-   ) 322
Francis Marion (1850-   )..................321
Frederick 322
James W. (1859-1860) 322
Jefferson Davis (1861-1944)...................322
John H. (1857-1860) 321
Lydia B. (1855-   ) 321
Malinda Sophia (1869-1956)..................322
Marion (1860-   )..........................321
Sophia Malinda (1868-   )................322
Steward Dabney (1828-1890) 153, 321
PALMER
Harriet 140, 263
PARSONS
Sarah (1826-   )...........................239
PATTON
Valentine 119, 229
PAULEY
Rachel (1821-   )..........................239
PAYNE
Sarah Parsons Or (Abt 1829-   )..........239
PEARSON
John (1836-   )............................264
Mary Ellen (1863-1948) 325

William N.................................... 140, 264
PENNINGTON
Susan.. 153, 320
PERRY
Stephen Gose (1824-1863).............................304
Thomas 304
PETERS
Jane (Abt 1810-   )..........................199
Rachael Fernsler (1776-1833) 166
PETERSON
Sarah (1815-   ).............................222
PHILLIPS
Melissa Jemima (1848-1918)..........................261
PICKARD
Margaret..223
PITTMAN
Morgan J...218
PITTS
Harriet (Abt 1867-   ).........................205
PORTER
John (Abt 1815-   )..........................200
POWERS
Jonathan W. II (1829-1905)...........................233
PRICE
Alice H. (Abt 1859-   )......................325
William L (1856-   )..........................240
PROPTS
Catherine.. 47, 105
RADER
Adelia A. (1846-   )..........................301
Adolphus L. (1847-   ).......................298
Albert W. (1877-   )..........................299
Albert Wilber (1858-1914) 276
Alexander (Abt 1829-   )....................245
Alice C. (1860-   )...........................300
Allen (Abt 1838-1922) 155, 332
Almedia (1865-   )..........................286
Andrew (1828-1856) 189
Andrew (1828-1900) 141, 282
Andrew G. (1823-1863)................................222
Andrew Jackson 'Big Andy' (1852-1917).......218
Andrew Jackson G. (1853-1891).....................257
Andrew Thomas Jackson (1846-1922)...........198
Andrew W. S (1812-1889)..................... 104, 205
Anna Marie 'Mary' (1778-1849)............... 49, 144
Arlena 'Orlena' (1840-   ).......................256
Austin (1849-   )............................263
Barbara (1832-1898)........................ 141, 293
Barbara Emmeline (1836-1887) 217
Caleb Stradley (1850-1853)............................275
Calvin Lynn (1879-1892)..............................302
Calvin M. (1818-1890) 143, 300
Caroline (1841-   )..........................217

Caroline (1844-)	234
Carroll Drake (1855-)	261
Casper (1829-1834)	133, 262
Casper (1838-1863)	190
Casper J Jr. (1851-1888)	198
Casper J. Jr. (1801-1883)	104, 191
Casper Jr. (1774-1830)	48, 131
Casper Sr (1732-After 1812)	15
Catherine "Caty" (Abt 1797-)	119, 222
Catherine (1781-1844)	49, 151
Catherine (1822-)	140, 264
Catherine (1838-)	164
Catherine (1838-1933)	197
Catherine (Abt 1789-)	93, 162
Catherine M. (1816-Bef 1859)	104, 218
Charles Holiday (1847-1853)	275
Charles W. (1866-)	299
Christina Bethany (1826-1904)	141, 277
Clara Luella (1864-1914)	276
Conrad (1766-1845)	47, 91
Conrad (Abt 1790-)	93, 164
Cordelia M. (1879-)	299
Daniel (1808-1854)	104, 200
Daniel (1829-1864)	172
Daniel (Abt 1782-1827)	49, 153
Daniel C. (1860-)	277
David Andrew "Cap" Capt. (1830-1908)	141, 286
David Powell (1844-1918)	205
Dawson R. (1849-1929)	261
Dorcas L. (1848-)	300
Dulsena Candace (1858-1860)	199
E. Leona (1873-)	299
Elbert J. (1831-)	245
Eleanor Elizabeth (1828-)	155, 333
Eleanor S. (1850-)	298
Eliza (1812-)	143, 297
Eliza (1836-)	234
Eliza Jane (1826-1827)	227
Eliza Jane (1833-1852)	141, 294
Eliza Jane (Abt 1825-Bef 1860)	155, 333
Elizabeth (1799-1871)	119, 130, 224, 243
Elizabeth (1812-WFT Est 1813)	143, 297
Elizabeth (1844-)	263
Elizabeth (1852-)	198
Elizabeth (1862-)	333
Elizabeth (Bef 1818-Bef 1856)	172
Elizabeth 'Betsey' (1795-1866)	103, 175
Elizabeth 'Eliza' (1808-1893)	130, 250, 253
Elizabeth J. (WFT Est 1819-WFT Est 1824)	189
Elizabeth Jane (1831-1915)	194
Elizabeth Laura Jane 'Eliza' (1849-1932)	250
Elizabeth Louise (1855-1909)	257
Elkanah D. (1817-)	143, 299
Elmira Jane (1834-1924)	326
Emaline (1820-)	120, 237
Emaline (1824-)	172
Emiline Jane (1846-1899)	250
Estella Edith (1878-1878)	293
Eunice F. (1866-)	277
Evaline V. (1854-)	301
Evaline V. (1854-Bef 1917)	302
Florence E. (1851-)	261
Francis J. (1819-)	140, 263
Frank D. (1869-1927)	292
George Alexander (1844-1908)	217
George H. (1845-1910)	261
George W. (1831-1870)	173
George W. (Abt 1809-1861)	154, 328
George Washington (1829-1881)	194
George William (Abt 1834-WFT Est 1835)	326
Granville (1847-1928)	205
Granville (1868-)	299
Grover C. (1888-)	296
H. Florence (1874-)	299
Hanna G. (1826-)	172
Hanna J. (Abt 1823-)	140, 265
Hannah (1827-)	172
Harriette Malinda 'Hattie' (1861-1950)	331
Heinrich 'Henry' Sr (1768-1851)	47, 93
Henrietta (1818-)	140, 262
Henry (-1826)	133, 262
Henry (1833-1865)	194
Henry C. (1836-)	141, 295
Henry J (1835-)	201
Henry L. (1829-1864)	189
Henry Thomas Jr. (1810-1860)	104, 201
Indiana (1847-)	298
Isaac Newton (1855-1926)	198
Isaac Newton (1866-1903)	262
Isabella (1845-)	201
Isabella 'Ibbie' (1813-1884)	120, 235
Issabella (1819-1879)	105, 219
Jacob (Abt 1772-1822)	48, 122, 224
Jacob (Abt 1809-Bef 1822)	131, 255
Jacob Harrison (1849-1852)	275
Jacob W. (Abt 1843-)	245
James (1801-)	93, 164
James (1819-After 1871)	172
James (Abt 1834-)	245
James A. (1839-)	164
James A. (1845-)	327
James C. (1834-)	234
James C. (1870-)	299
James Daniel (1813-1887)	155, 330
James G. (1863-1863)	292

James H. (Abt 1825-) 222
James J. (1814-) 143, 297
James M. (1816-) 172
James Polk (1837-1863) 256
James Polk (1844-) 300
James Scott (1852-1936) 331
Jane Franklin 'Frankie' (1863-1953) 331
Janet Melvina (1860-) 302
Jeremiah Daniel (1860-1924) 325
Jesse (1804-1890) 130, 174, 246, 255
Jesse (1822-) 172
Jesse (1829-1900) 227
Jesse H. (1837-) 164
Jessie (1816-) 119, 230
Johannes Pieter Richard (1820-1820) 105, 220
John (1793-1839) 103, 168
John (1822-1900) 189
John (Abt 1769-1840) 47, 105, 243
John (Abt 1800-Bef 1822) 130, 243
John Anderson (1827-1901) 222
John Asberry (Dr.) (1835-1894) 250
John H. (1848-) 329
John H. (Abt 1848-After 1920) 327
John Henry (1858-1864) 331
John Jr. (1795-After 1860) 119, 220
John Mcclung Sr. (1802-1879) 332
John Nelson (1843-1889) 198
John T. (1846-1904) 261
John W. (1850-) 276
John Wesley Sr. (1826-1889) 172
Joseph 189
Joseph "Jc" H. (1850-) 301
Joseph (1850-) 301
Joseph (Abt 1801-) 130, 244
Joseph James (1831-1918) 190
Joseph M (1842-) 201
Josephine (Abt 1841-) 329
Judith Ora (1811-1887) 93, 166
Julia Ann (1838-1898) 142, 296
Kate Mae (1877-) 302
Landon C. (1871-) 299
Landon H. (1848-) 301
Lavina Elizabeth (1857-1936) 218
Lawson G. (1843-) 256
Lemuel (1832-1899) 227
Lewis (1847-) 234
Lewis Franklin (1837-1914) 228
Louis Franklin (1847-1933) 201
Louisa C. (1854-) 257
Lourinda E. (1850-1923) 256
Louvina (1824-1909) 227
Lovinia (1818-1877) 227
Lucinda (1819-1893) 120, 237

Lydia Angeline 'Ann' (1850-1919) 218
Madison (Doctor) (1842-1913) 190
Maggie (1863-) 300
Malinda (Abt 1807-) 154, 327
Malinda (Abt 1817-) 143, 300
Malinda (Abt 1858-) 325
Malinda J. (1843-) 164
Malinda Jane (1839-1862) 198
Margaret (1842-) 298
Margaret (1846-1870) 190
Margaret (1849-) 235
Margaret (1852-) 301
Margaret E. (1852-) 302
Margaret J. (1838-) 201
Maria M. (1838-WFT Est 1839) 326
Mariah (1817-1895) 171
Martha "Marie" (Abt 1815-) 155, 331
Martha (1836-) 298
Martha A. (1845-) 263
Martha Ann 'Matt' (1848-1934) 198
Martha Caroline (1866-1940) 331
Martha Conmella (1848-Bef 1860) 218
Martha Elizabeth "Annie" (1836-) 326
Martha J. (1839-1919) 250
Martha V. (1862-) 277
Martin (1831-1853) 190
Martin George (1811-Bef 1850) 131, 255
Mary (1806-Bef 1847) 119, 230
Mary (1820-1899) 140, 263
Mary (1836-) 197
Mary (1850-1904) 327
Mary (Abt 1794-1848) 103, 173, 251
Mary (Abt 1836-) 245
Mary Ann (1800-) 121, 238
Mary Ann (1837-1900) 173
Mary Ann (1842-) 217
Mary Ann (Abt 1830-Bef 1891) 250
Mary Ann 'Jake' (Abt 1816-1860) 155, 332
Mary E. (Abt 1845-) 329
Mary Elizabeth (1850-Bef 1900) 205
Mary Jane K. (1850-) 300
Mary Jane 'Mollie' (Abt 1851-1906) 261
Mary M. 172
Mary S. (1834-) 222
Mary S. (1855-1867) 331
Mary T. (1845-) 256
Melissa A. (Abt 1863-Bef 1877) 261
Melvina (1835-) 256
Melvina (1839-) 234
Melvina (1860-) 301
Molly (1846-1917) 217
Nancy C. (1830-WFT Est 1844) 155, 335
Nancy C. (1847-1929) 250

Nancy E. (1843-1850) 330
Nancy Elizabeth (1836-1913) 217, 256
Nancy O. (1805-1885) 93, 164
Newton Jasper (1862-1938) 325
Nicholas Marion (1855-1935) 198
Penelope Ann (Abt 1841-   ) 245
Peter (1780-1858) 48, 142
Peter R. (1819-1877) 131, 258
Philip (1835-1915) 197
Philip Jr. (1824-1899) 140, 265
Phillip Sr. (1782-1853) 48, 134
Powell (Abt 1844-   ) 205
Rachel (Abt 1803-1855) 104, 199
Rebecca (1834-   ) 164
Rebecca (Abt 1811-Abt 1860) . 93, 155, 168, 329
Rebecca Jane (Abt 1838-   ) 245
Reuben M. (1822-1887) 222
Robert H. (1849-1851) 331
Rosella E. (1857-   ) 277
S. Cornelius (1835-1863) 227
Samuel (1802-   ) 122, 240
Samuel (1824-1899) 172
Samuel (1832-   ) 227
Samuel (Abt 1810-Bef 1850) 120, 234
Samuel Emerey (1805-1895) 154, 323
Samuel Jr. (Abt 1830-   ) 326
Sarah Adella (Abt 1842-   ) 327
Sarah Alice (1862-   ) 261
Sarah C. (1867-   ) 302
Sarah C. (Abt 1821-Abt 1854) 155, 332
Sarah Elizabeth (1854-1939) 276
Sarah J. (1854-   ) 205
Sarah Jane (1835-1859) 217
Sarah Jane (1839-   ) 256
Sarah Melvina (Abt 1843-Abt 1860) 228
Sarah 'Sallie' (1824-1902) 189
Sarah 'Sally' (1806-Bef 1860) 130, 251
Sarah 'Sally' A. (1801-1886) 119, 228
Schuyler Colfax (1856-1934) 276
Sophelia (Abt 1843-   ) 329
Sophia (1808-1868) 120, 230
Susan "Susannah" (1800-   ) 122, 238
Susan (1866-   ) 302
Susannah (Abt 1812-1892) 131, 257
Synthia (1812-   ) 140, 262
Tennessee (Abt 1845-   ) 245
Thomas G (1845-1851) 330
Thomas J. (1855-   ) 276
Thomas W. (1854-   ) 300
Ulysses Grant (1864-1939) 262
Valentine Sevier (1822-1902) 226
William (1799-1877) 119, 130, 224, 240
William (1822-   ) 222
William (1826-1895) 140, 276
William (1836-   ) 173
William (1863-   ) 333
William (Abt 1770-1802) 48, 120
William (Abt 1805-   ) 119, 229
William A. (1842-1928) 234
William 'Bill' (1841-1916) 198
William Carroll (1848-1931) 330
William Franklin (1832-1889) 326
William H. "Will" (1857-   ) 300
William J. (1847-   ) 263
William M. 'Bill' (1838-1897) 217, 256
William Minnis (1851-1935) 254
William Nelson (1852-1918) 276
William W. (1798-1880) 104, 177
REAT
   Georgia (1853-   ) 298
REIN
   Mary Magdalen (1750-1821) 102, 116
REISS
   Sally Ann (1836-1897) 199
REPASS
   Annie (1843-   ) 306
   Barbara (1833-   ) 307
   Eleanor Brown (1843-1919) 305
   Eleanora Catherine (1843-   ) 306
   Elias Jane (1829-   ) 306
   Eliza 305
   Elizabeth 315
   Elizabeth Mary (1831-1911) 304
   Ellen Brown 305
   Elza Ann (1830-   ) 304
   George Flohr (1832-1882) 306
   Granville Brown (1846-1918) 305
   Harvey (1826-1890) 315
   Henry L. (1846-   ) 306
   Imus A. (1831-   ) 307
   Infant 307
   James 152, 315
   James "Rippas" (1801-   ) 152, 315
   James A. 307
   James Andrew (1834-1857) 304
   James Augustus (1831-1857) 306
   Jesse (1802-1849) 150, 305
   John (1821-1904) 306
   John Christopher (Rev) (1828-1903) 304
   Joseph Washington (1830-   ) 306
   Lucinda Katherine "Kate" (1847-1934) 307
   Lydia Emaline (1841-1900) 304
   Margaret (1875-   ) 307
   Maria Thresa (1836-1898) 304
   Mariah (1841-   ) 306
   Mary (1835-   ) 307

Mary Elender (1828-1853) 306
Mary Polly Adeline (Abt 1821-   ) .. 153, 320
Matildy Brown (1837-   ) 306
Newton Hurshel (1835-   ) 306
Rev. John Christopher (1830-   ) 304
Rev. Stephen Albion (1838-   ) 304
Rufus (Captain) (1805-1878) 150, 303
Rufus B. (1841-   ) 307
Sarah Henrieta (1843-   ) 305
Sarah Henrietta 304
Sarah K. (1839-   ) 306
Stephen (1805-1876) 150, 307
Stephen Albion 304
Victoria (1848-   ) 306
William Gordon (1838-1895) 307
RHEA
 Kezia S. (1824-1903) 131, 262
RHEA RAY?
 Kegish S. 'Kissiar' (Abt 1824-1903) 131, 260
ROBINSON
 William R. (WFT Est 1813-WFT Est 1847) 155, 335
ROLLER
 Barbara (-1848) 216
RUDY
 A. M. 141, 294
SANDERS
 Michael 334
SANDERSON
 Rhoda Ann (1865-   ) 198
SARAH
 (1850-   ) 142, 296
SCOTT
 Hannah (1795-1871) 103, 170
SEAGLE
 Elizabeth (1824-   ) 165
 George Augustus (1850-   ) 166
 Henry Lee (1837-1853) 166
 Isabella Foster (1841-   ) 166
 Jacob C (1829-1833) 165
 James (1801-1883) 93, 164
 James Brown (1847-1912) 166
 John Sanders (1844-1864) 166
 Judith Angelina 'Judie' (1832-1883) 165
 Maria Wax (1827-1884) 165
 Mary Jane (1835-   ) 165
SEXTON
 Hiley (1838-   ) 326
SHARITZ
 Alice Virginia (1856-1931) 151, 309
 Cynthia J. (1855-   ) 323
 Daniel M. (1829-1900) 153, 323
 Eleanora Tracy (1857-   ) 323

Emily C. (1866-1897) 323
Harvey M. (1859-   ) 323
John (1859-   ) 323
John P. (1826-   ) 309
Joseph (1803-1879) 323
Nancy A. (1852-   ) 323
Ollie V. (1871-   ) 323
Stephen A Ruben 304
Susan (1862-   ) 323
Thomas J. B. (1868-   ) 323
SHAW
 Mary E. 205
 Susan N (1848-1894) 205
SHEETS
 Catherine (-1852) 48, 141
SHEPPARD: 142, 297
SIDDON
 Catherine Elizabeth (1796-1826) 48, 139
SIMMERMAN
 Alex 168
SIPES
 George 224
SMILEY
 Ethelinda M. (1796-Bef 1860) 119, 222
SMITH
 Alfred H. (1847-   ) 219
 Arthur (1849-   ) 220
 Candesa (1846-   ) 220
 Ezekiel 111 (1821-1900) 200
 George A. (1842-   ) 219
 Henry 177
 Isaac (1823-   ) 105, 220
 James W. (1857-   ) 219
 John F. Washington (1813-1896) 105, 219
 Margaret E. (1839-   ) 219
 Martha A. (1837-   ) 219
 Mckindrie (1845-   ) 219
 William C. (1840-   ) 219
SOLOMON
 Thomas A. 236
SPENCE
 Enid (1902-1936) 310
SPRAKER
 Jonas 165
SPRANKER
 Louisa Lenora (1848-1920) 168
STAFFORD
 Mary Elizabeth (1856-1895) 189
STANGER
 Theresa (1797-1879) 150, 302
STANSBURY
 Mary C. (1850-   ) 245
STARK

Harriett (1842-1902)..234
STEIN
    Susannah (1832-1908)................................190
STEPHENS
    Lucy Ann "Annie" (1853-1930).....................311
STEVENS
    Aleba (1854-   ).................................282
    Austin..282
    Hezekiah M..282
    Ida (1859-   ).....................................282
    Jabes O. (Rev.)...282
    Jacob Esq. (1824-Abt 1886)................141, 278
    James B...282
    Lucinda (1845-   ).............................282
    Mary...282
    Nellie..282
    Rilla..282
    Schuyler..282
STOWERS
    William (1812-1902)...............................122, 238
STRADLEY
    Caleb...273
    Margaret (1827-1907)...........................140, 273
STRAND:..257
STROUD
    James Sutre (1834-1916)............................257
SUMMITT
    Jacob Eusebius (1815-1873)......................172
SUSAN
    (1833-   )...199
SUSANNAH
    (1843-   ).....................................153, 320
SWATZELL
    Elizabeth "Lizzy" (1825-   )..................199
SWEENY
    David Carr (1838-1900)...............................317
SYKES
    Hannah (1856-   )..............................329
T.
    Elizabeth T. (1810-   )....................143, 298
TARTAR
    Sarah (1820-1900).................................150, 308
TAYLOR
    James Anderson (1837-1901).....................217
TEETER
    Mary Alice (1856-1913)................................276
TENNESSEE
    Tennessee (Abt 1805-   ).............130, 245
THOMAS
    George..223
THOMPSON
    Francis...239
    Francis "Frank" (1812-Bef 1900)................239

TULLEY
    Martha (1850-1913).....................................253
TURLEY
    John Sr. (Abt 1750-   )..........................240
    Nathan (1797-   )..............................122, 240
TURNER
    Samuel..155, 327, 333
UMBARGER
    Rhoda J. (1843-   )...............................317
UMBERGER
    Alexander (1845-1940)................................317
    Rhoda Jane (1853-1887)............................317
    Simon (1849-1930)......................................317
UNKNOWN:..218
VANCE
    Marion B. (1830-1897).................................250
VANNATTER
    Allen (1827-   )......................................240
    Bejamin...239, 240
    Benjamin Franklin (1828-After 1900)...........239
VAUGHAN
    James Jr..143, 300
    Joseph Elkanah (1836-   )....................300
VIRGINIA
    Caroline (1854-   )................................318
WALKER
    Susan (1877-1952).....................................236
WALLACE
    Thomas...223
WAMPLER
    Andrew (1831-   )..................................177
    John A..177
WARD
    Martha Ann (1855-   )...........................236
WELLS
    Mary Elizabeth (1866-1942)........................314
WELSH
    Betty E. (1855-   )..................................166
WHITESELL
    John W. (WFT Est 1836-WFT Est 1863).....335
WHITMAN
    Clarke S..165
WHITSEL
    Julia...332
    Wesley (Abt 1809-Bef 1864)................155, 331
WIDNER
    Margaret (1790-1863).................................295
WILEY
    Mary Ann (1856-1908).................................331
WILHOIT
    Minnie..282
WILKINSON
    Lydia..264

WILLHITE
　　Citha P. 229
WILLIAMS
　　Jane Cox (WFT Est 1824-WFT Est 1877) 314
WILLOUGHBY
　　Anna (1835-1921) 254
　　Bedford (Abt 1843-　　) 254
　　Eliza J. 'Hannah' (1854-1938) 130, 250, 254
　　Elizabeth (1830-1908) 254
　　Elizabeth (Abt 1810-1875) 130, 249
　　Granville (1841-1863) 254
　　John Bedford (1843-1865) 254
　　John M. (1805-1869) 131, 250, 253
　　Mary (1832-　　) 254
　　Nancy (1847-1928) 254
　　Sarah 'Sadie' Jane (1849-1938) 254
　　William (Abt 1837-　　) 254
　　William R. (1838-1884) 254

　　Winnie (1845-1845) 254
WILSON
　　Blake 327
　　Blake (WFT Est 1815-WFT Est 1841) 328
　　Jeff 327
　　W. 326
WOLFORD
　　Caroline Virginia (1854-Between 1927) 318
WRIGHT
　　Elizabeth "Eliza" Mullins 314
YONCE
　　Abram Ebenezer (1815-　　) 153, 319
　　Beatta (1803-1845) 323
　　James (1840-1912) 319
　　Katherine (1843-1908) 319
　　Sarah Ellen (1846-　　) 319
　　Thomas Ebenezer (1849-1900) 318, 319

www.ingramcontent.com/pod-product-compliance
Lightning Source LLC
Chambersburg PA
CBHW080421230426
43662CB00015B/2174